Learning, Creating, and Using Knowledge

This fully revised and updated edition of *Learning, Creating, and Using Knowledge* recognizes that the future of economic well being in today's knowledge and information society rests upon the effectiveness of schools and corporations to empower their people to be more effective learners and knowledge creators. Novak's pioneering theory of education presented in the first edition remains viable and useful. This new edition updates his theory for meaningful learning and autonomous knowledge building along with tools to make it operational— that is, concept maps, created with the use of CmapTools and the Vee diagram.

The theory is easy to put into practice, since it includes resources to facilitate the process, especially concept maps, now optimized by CmapTools software. CmapTools software is highly intuitive and easy to use. People who have until now been reluctant to use the new technologies in their professional lives will find this book particularly helpful. *Learning, Creating, and Using Knowledge* is essential reading for educators at all levels and corporate managers who seek to enhance worker productivity.

Changes in the Second Edition

- Uses concept maps extensively to illustrate key ideas from learning theory, theory of knowledge, and instructional theory
- Includes new examples of how the theory applies in school and corporate settings
- Gives more emphasis to the importance of applying educational ideas in corporations
- Discusses ideas on metacognition and other strategies for enhancing learning
- Looks at learner misconceptions, including suggestions for remediating misconceptions

Joseph D. Novak, Professor Emeritus, Cornell University, Education and Biology, is Senior Research Scientist, Florida Institute for Human & Machine Cognition.

Learning, Creating, and Using Knowledge

Concept Maps as Facilitative Tools in Schools and Corporations

Second Edition

Joseph D. Novak

Routledge
Taylor & Francis Group

NEW YORK AND LONDON

First published 1998
by Lawrence Erlbaum Associates, Inc.

This edition published 2010
by Routledge
270 Madison Avenue, New York, NY 10016

Simultaneously published in the UK
by Routledge
2 Park Square, Milton Park, Abingdon, Oxon OX14 4RN

Routledge is an imprint of the Taylor & Francis Group,
an informa business

Typeset in Minion by RefineCatch Limited, Bungay, Suffolk
Printed and bound in the United States of America on acid-free
paper by
Edwards Brothers, Inc.

Library of Congress Cataloging-in-Publication Data
Novak, Joseph Donald
    Learning, creating, and using knowledge : concept maps as
    facilitative tools in schools and corporations / Joseph D.
    Novak.
        p. cm.
    Includes bibliographical references.
    1. Learning, Psychology of.   2. Cognitive maps (Psychology)
    3. Instructional systems—Design.   4. Constructivism
    (Education)   I. Title.
    LB1060.N677 2010
    370.15′23—dc22   2009044207

ISBN10: 0–415–99184–6 (hbk)
ISBN10: 0–415–99185–4 (pbk)
ISBN10: 0–203–86200–7 (ebk)

ISBN13: 978–0–415–99184–1 (hbk)
ISBN13: 978–0–415–99185–8 (pbk)
ISBN13: 978–0–203–86200–1 (ebk)

For Joan

In Memory Of
David P. Ausubel
1928–2008

Contents

Foreword

The Carnegie Corporation-Institute for Advanced Study Commission on Mathematics and Science Education has just (June 2009) issued a new report[1] urging the United States to seize the opportunity to close the gap between our students' current levels of achievement and the levels needed to meet future demands of a rapidly changing world. To this end, the commission calls for national standards in mathematics and science education, improved mathematics and science teaching and nothing less than the redesign of schools and school systems to provide excellent and equitable education to all students.

Learning, Creating, and Using Knowledge lays out one possible approach to that redesign. As Joseph Novak makes clear in this second edition today's "education crisis" is a real and frustratingly recurrent theme in American education. This book, he notes, "is for anyone who believes education can be significantly improved and who is frustrated with the parade of educational 'innovations' of the past half century that seem to have accomplished so little."

What is so frustrating for Novak and many of us is that we have the theories and tools to improve education and some of those theories and tools have been around for a good fifty years. Indeed, Novak laid out one possible theory and tool set more than 30 years ago in *A Theory of Education*.[2] Ralph Tyler, writing the Foreword, noted that "[m]any instructors . . . have wished for a comprehensive theory of learning and education that would furnish a consistent basis for explaining their successful efforts and guide their daily work." Novak had done so back then; that's what so frustrating now. In *A Theory of Education*, he likened education reform to Brownian motion, constantly changing but going nowhere. In *Learning, Creating, and Using Knowledge* he notes: "I asserted then, and I would assert even more forcefully now, that this characterization is likely to persist unless educators in every educational setting, businesses as well as schools, seek to base change on a comprehensive theory of education."

---

1 http://www.opportunityequation.org/
2 Novak, J.D. (1977). *A theory of education.* Ithaca, NY: Cornell University Press.

Learning, Creating, and Using Knowledge is about a theory and a set of tools for significantly improving U.S. education (and business). Fundamental to this theory is the proposition that "**the central purpose of education is to empower learners to take charge of their own meaning making.** Meaning making involves thinking, feeling, and acting, and all three of these aspects must be integrated for significant new learning, and especially in new knowledge creation."

What is key to Novak's theory is that students *engage in* and *exert effort* in their learning; they must relate new information to existing ideas. To this end, the content of education must be conceptually rich and challenging. Engaged and effortful learning occurs when students, confronted with challenging-but-within-reach-material *choose* to cognitively reorganize that material by modifying their prior knowledge to accommodate the new knowledge.

If meaning making and knowledge organization are the conceptual underpinnings of Novak's theory, the key tool for bringing this about on the one hand and evaluating learning on the other is the concept map. A concept map is a (hierarchical) network comprised of concept-terms (nodes) and directed lines linking pairs of nodes; the linking lines are labeled with explanations of the relationship between node pairs. Concept maps provide a window into students' minds—they reflect students' knowledge structures. As an instructional tool, concept maps encourage students to explicitly organize and make public their (current version of) knowledge. Concept maps encourage them to engage content and put effort into deeply thinking about the content. These maps also provide an invaluable evaluation tool. They enable teachers and students to track learning, to find gaps in knowledge, and to work on closing those gaps.

These ideas are captured in Novak's six principles for teaching and learning: (1) Students should be motivated to learn—that is, they must *choose to learn*—otherwise no learning will occur. (2) Teachers should understand and engage the students' prior knowledge, both accurate and inaccurate conceptualizations. (3) Teachers should *organize* the conceptual knowledge they want to teach. (4) Teachers should organize the educational context to facilitate learning. (5) Teachers must be knowledgeable and sensitive to students' knowledge and feelings. And (6) teachers should continually assess students' learning for the purpose of guiding teaching and learning and motivating students.

You are about to embark on an adventure, one that will likely change the way you see education—that is, *reorganize your knowledge and feelings*. As Novak admits, sometime it will be challenging—but hang in there. The journey is well worth it!

Richard J. Shavelson
Stanford University

Preface

This fully revised and updated Second Edition recognizes that the future of economic well-being in today's knowledge and information society rests upon the effectiveness of schools and corporations to empower their people to be more effective learners and knowledge creators. The theory of education presented in the first edition remains viable and useful. This new edition updates my theory for meaningful learning and autonomous knowledge building along with tools to make it operational, that is concept maps, created with the use of CmapTools and the Vee diagram. The theory is easy to put into practice, since it includes resources to facilitate the process, especially concept maps, now optimized by CmapTools software. CmapTools software is highly intuitive and easy to use. People who have until now been reluctant to use the new technologies in their professional lives will find this book particularly helpful.

Changes in the Second Edition

Concept maps are used extensively to illustrate key ideas from learning theory, theory of knowledge, and instructional theory. Additional examples of how the theory applies in school and corporate settings have been added and more emphasis is given to the importance of applying educational ideas in the corporate setting. This edition includes discussion of ideas on metacognition and other strategies for enhancing learning. Reflecting the continuing interest in learner misconceptions, I discuss my work in this area and suggestions for remediating misconceptions.

History

In the decade since the first edition of this book was published, there has emerged a broad consensus among educators and psychologists that human learning involves building on prior knowledge and that this requires active construction of new meanings. This is gratifying, since this idea was a primary pillar in the arguments I presented in *A Theory of Education* (1977), in the first edition of this book (1998), and in a previous book, *Learning How to Learn* (1984), which has subsequently been published in eight other languages. There has also been an explosive growth in the power of computers and the World Wide Web, as well as in other technologies that now permit the move toward what we call a New Model for Education, discussed in the last chapter of this book.

It has been my good fortune to work with the Institute for Human and Machine Cognition (IHMC) since 1987, and to serve part-time as a Senior Research Associate for the past decade. When Kenneth Ford sought in 1987 to direct a different kind of research organization that would focus on the use of computers to facilitate human capacities, not replace them, he saw concept mapping as one vehicle to do this. Under the leadership of Alberto Cañas, the Institute has developed outstanding software for making concept maps and facilitating collaboration in building concept maps and what we call *knowledge models*. This work has been funded in part by NASA, the Department of Navy, the National Security Agency, and other governmental and private organizations, all of which employ concept maps in some of their work. The software is available at no cost at: <http://cmap.ihmc.us>. All of the concept maps I prepared for this book used this software, and they can be accessed via the latter web site, selecting IHMC-Internal, JDN LCUK. To gain a better understanding of the ideas presented in the book, I suggest that the reader download the CmapTools software and move these concept maps to your own computer (under My Cmaps), and see how you can modify them to capture better the meanings expressed in these maps as you read the text.

My education as a scientist convinced me that the development and refinement of theories to guide research and derivative practices was the primary reason for the successes we have seen in sciences and technology. It was my conviction that we needed to build a comprehensive theory of education if we are to substantively improve educational research and educational practices. My first effort, *A Theory of Education* (1977), was helpful to me and my students and colleagues, serving as a textbook, along with *Learning How to Learn* (1984), for a course I taught at Cornell University for 20 years, Theory and Methods of Education. I learned much from my students, visiting professors, and other colleagues regarding strengths and weaknesses of the theory, including more recent colleagues and collaborators at the Florida Institute for Human and Machine Cognition. The expanded theory of education presented in the first edition of this book has been even more useful to our programs.

The work I did as a consultant to Procter and Gamble from 1993 to 1998 and work with other corporations and governmental agencies convinced me that the ideas and tools we developed in our educational research programs were equally valuable in the corporate world. Some of the better writings in the field of business have been supportive of this thesis and are cited in the first edition and this new edition of this book. I was somewhat surprised to find that relatively few new ideas appeared in the business literature in the past decade, except the realization that accelerating globalization is further changing the way the world does business.

Since my retirement from Cornell University in 1995, I have had the opportunity to work with corporations, the IHMC, and other organizations to apply what we have learned to improve knowledge retrieval and knowledge archiving as well as educational practices. One reason I chose to retire early was to have time to work with Procter and Gamble, and this association has been most rewarding. I was surprised to see how well the ideas and tools we developed in our education programs were valid and useful in the corporate world. Although we had done some work with corporations earlier, such as with Kodak and Corning, there appeared to be significant resistance to new ideas. For one thing, my background was science education and biology, not business. I had a credibility problem, and this was evident in my early association with Procter and Gamble. In fact, from my first meeting in June, 1993 with Larry Huston, who became Vice President for Innovation, until our first meeting with R&D staff in December, 1993, more than six months had elapsed. When introducing me to large groups of senior staff members in various meetings that followed, Huston often commented that they found the useful ideas we were to hear about came not from the business world, but from a professor of science education! Over the years, Huston has been very supportive of our work, and I owe a debt to his leadership at Procter and Gamble. Under the current Chairman and CEO, A.G. Lafley, Procter and Gamble continues to be a leader in new ideas for business, and I quote in several places the good ideas in his recent book with Ram Charan (2008).

My work with Alberto Cañas, Associate Director of IHMC and a native of Costa Rica, and other colleagues in the Latin world, has been most rewarding. The work we have done together over the years, including work to produce the current version of CmapTools and the implementation of an extensive program to improve education in Panama, has been personally and professionally gratifying. With the primary initiative of Cañas, we have held three international conferences on research using concept mapping tools and ideas. (see: http://cmc.ihmc.us)

The work and ideas I have been presenting have been especially well received in Latin countries in South America and Europe, as well as in other countries. Thanks to efforts by Ricardo Chrobak and his colleagues, I was pleased to receive my first Honorary Doctoral degree from the University of Comahue in Argentina in 1998. Fermin Gonzales and colleagues helped to arrange for a second Honorary Doctorate from the University of Navarra in Spain in 2002, and Giuseppe Valitutti and colleagues made possible a third Honorary Doctorate from the University of Urbino in 2006 on the occasion of the 500th anniversary of the University.

Over the years, I have been fortunate to have many excellent graduate students, visiting professors, and other close collaborations (over 350). They have been my mentors, and I continue to learn from them. Many of them are now leaders in their profession in many different countries. These associations have been and continue to be most rewarding.

As we move to into what Fareed Zakaria (2009) calls *The Post American World*, we shall face many new challenges, not only in the USA but throughout the world. It is pretty much agreed that vastly improved education is the key to avoid worldwide disaster. I am pleased that I chose to be an educator, rather than another botanist, in the 1950's, though at the time my botany professor advised against this. I hope this book will make some contribution to the improvement of education and the creation and use of knowledge both in schools and in corporations throughout the world. This may be what President Barack Obama (2006) called the *Audacity of Hope*, but I believe there are reasons to believe such improvement is possible.

References

Novak, J.D. (1977). *A theory of education.* Ithaca, NY: Cornell University Press.

Novak, J.D., & Gowin, D.B. (1984). *Learning how to learn.* New York: Cambridge University Press.

Obama, B. (2006). *The audacity of hope: Thoughts on reclaiming the American dream.* New York: Crown.

Zahkaria, F. (2009). *The post-American world.* New York: Norton (paperback).

Acknowledgments

For over five decades, I have been blessed with many excellent graduate students, including the team that helped to develop the concept mapping tool in the early 1970s. I have also enjoyed the stimulation, support and insights from many visiting professors from all parts of the world. These people have been my mentors and we have learned together. The Department of Education and the Department of Biological Sciences in the College of Agriculture and Life Sciences at Cornell University have been a hospitable home for my work for 31 years. Professor Alan McAdams of the Johnson Graduate School of Management has been especially helpful in assisting me to understand business issues and problems, especially through a course we co-taught in the Johnson Graduate School of Management at Cornell University. My colleagues at Procter and Gamble, Larry Huston and Larry Hughes and others, have also been excellent mentors.

Since 1987, I have worked with colleagues at the University of West Florida and the Florida Institute for Human and Machine Cognition (IHMC). This has been crucial to advancing our work in helping people learn, as well as more recent efforts to capture and archive expert knowledge and to encourage collaborative learning. The IHMC has developed some outstanding software for concept mapping under the leadership of Alberto Cañas, and this software is available at no cost to school and corporate clients at: http://cmap.ihmc.us. Dr. Cañas and his wife Carmen have also been a constant source of ideas, constructive criticism, and warm personal relationships. Advances in the World Wide Web and CmapTools have made possible what Dr. Cañas and I call a New Model for Education. My three children, two grandchildren, and my wife, Joan, have been a source of energy, ideas, and inspiration. Much of the credit for the ideas in this book belongs to these mentors, but the shortcomings are my own. I extend my warm and grateful thanks to all of these good folks. I also wish to thank Professor Shavelson for taking time from his busy schedule to read and write a Foreword to this book.

Chapter 1

An Overview of the Book

Introduction

This book is for anyone who cares deeply about education. It is for anyone who believes education can be significantly improved and who is frustrated with the parade of educational "innovations" of the past half century that seem to have accomplished so little. During the 1970s, standardized test scores were steadily declining, while school budgets were increasing. From 1955 to 1985, per-pupil expenditures rose 300 percent *after* adjustment for inflation, and the growth in school budgets continues. For five decades Americans have pumped money into schooling. In 1984, Goodlad wrote in his report on American schools, "There is even a growing mood that some schools are now beginning to improve rather than continuing to get worse . . . The change in mood may stem from little more than the belief that conditions in our schools have bottomed out. The only way to go now is up" (p. xv). Public school per pupil expenditures increased from $5879 in 1985 to $9928 (in constant dollars) in 2007.[1] Now, 25 years later, there is little evidence that schools are getting better.

The connection between educational attainment and economic development in the world is well documented (Lutz, et al., 2008). But in the USA, the evidence now is that little progress has been made in school improvement. Almost daily we read in our papers reports on new studies that indicate American children lag behind those in most industrialized nations. Our national illiteracy rate and school dropout rates are also among the highest for all developed nations. School dropout rates are depressing, exceeding 50 percent in the 50 largest cities in the USA, with only about 70 percent finishing high school in four years nationwide (Fields, 2008). Such poor school performance has very negative consequences for the cities and for the US economy. Even teacher dropout rates are high, with 30 percent leaving within five years (Truesdale, 2008). Why? Why has progress been so slow, even in the

---

1 See: http://nces.ed.gov/

exceptional schools? I shall argue that education cannot be improved by doing more of the same things. We need to move to new educational practices that are guided by sound theory and make better use of new technologies.

On the corporate side, we have been doing better. The gross domestic product (GDP) for the United States continues to be the highest in the world, and although our growth comparative with other countries has declined, we remain the envy of most nations. However, as international trade continues to increase and we approach what Friedman (2005) calls "The Flat World" brought on by increased globalization of trade, the United States faces some important challenges, as do all other countries. To sustain and propel the explosive economic growth in India and China, the leadership is moving rapidly to improve the quality of education and to increase school enrollments, especially in higher education. As Friedman notes, "In the 2004 Intel Science Fair, China came home with thirty-five awards, more than any other country in Asia, including one of the top three global awards" (p. 266). The question growing in leadership circles in the USA is whether we can maintain our economic status without enormously improving education. In the first edition of this book I highlighted the increasing importance of knowledge assets for corporate growth as, for example Nonaka and Takeuchi's (1995) views on the *Knowledge-Creating Company*. Today every corporate leader talks about the importance of knowledge and knowledge creation. This is a concern I shall visit frequently. In reviewing a number of recent books dealing with issues in the field of business, I was surprised to see how little new thinking has emerged in the past decade. Most of the authors cited in 1998 are still some of the popular authors, but few present new ideas. In addition to Friedman (2005), Tapscott & Williams' (2007) *Wikinomics* and Lafley and Charan's (2008) *Game Changer* present new ideas which I will discuss at some length. What these three books all stress is the enormous increase in globalization and the power of the Internet to transform the way business is done.

Have you wondered why so many people you encounter seem unable to think out the simplest of problems? Indeed, have you wondered why you may have failed to see the solution to a problem which, retrospectively, appeared so simple? Contrast this with observations we all have made where very young children have seen solutions before we have. Why is it that finding and executing solutions to common problems appears to be so uncommon? In short, why do people have so much difficulty in organizing, using, and creating knowledge? This is a question for which I will propose answers. It's a difficult question, and the answers I give are not always simple. And, to understand the solutions I propose will require learning more about the nature of learning and the nature of knowledge and knowledge creation than you may want to know at this point in your life. But, stay with the book; in the end, I believe you will say, as so many have over past decades, "This makes sense. Why aren't we doing more of the things proposed?" My hope is that, after you study this book, you will help to change the way we educate, use, and create knowledge in school, governmental, and corporate settings.

It is a cliché to say that we are today in a crisis. There have been so many crises in the past and yet somehow the world goes on. But, great empires have fallen; the cultural and economic power of the orient gave way to the dominance of the West; and maybe we shall see history repeat itself. As Prestowitz (1988) argued, the United States is "trading places" with Japan. In a decade, the United States moved from the largest creditor nation in the world to the largest debtor nation—and the debt increases continue! The economic consequences of stupidity are enormously negative. Perhaps more than at any time in the history of capitalism, the well-being of American citizens, and all who depend upon us, is at stake. We need to learn how to educate ourselves better, both as individuals and as organizations. American companies need to become "knowledge-creating" companies as Nonaka and Takeuchi (1995) advise.

In his book, *Post-Capitalist Society*, one of America's economic gurus, Peter Drucker (1993, p. 198) advises that we need radically different schools from those we see today. These schools must have the following specifications:

- The school we need has to provide universal literacy of a high order—well beyond what "literacy" means today.
- It has to imbue students on all levels and of all ages with motivation to learn and with the discipline of continuing learning.
- It has to be an open system, accessible both to highly educated people—to people who for whatever reason did not gain access to advanced education in their early years.
- It has to impart knowledge both as substance and as process—what the Germans differentiate as *Wissen* and *Können*.
- Finally, schooling can no longer be a monopoly of the schools. Education in the post-capitalist society has to permeate the entire society. Employing organizations of all kinds—businesses, government agencies, nonprofits—must become institutions of learning and teaching as well. Schools, increasingly, must work in partnership with employers and employing organizations.

You may want to amend or add to Drucker's specifications, but it is difficult to deny the value of any of those listed. How can society move to achieve these revolutionary schools? There are no easy answers. A basic assumption of this book is that we must look to new partnerships and exchange of ideas between schools and business, and we must build educational change into both on the basis of a comprehensive *theory of education*. This book attempts to provide such a theory and framework.

There continues today unprecedented movement toward "globalization" of the world's economies. This process accelerated rapidly in the 1990s and is likely to continue to increase as new technologies continue to facilitate global communications and global commerce. While I see little evidence that schools, especially universities, are leaping to address the new educational challenges, it is likely that corporate America, and corporations throughout the world, will move to employ the most powerful ideas and tools available to enhance their effectiveness. Continued globalization of the economy will *require* this—the alternative being increasing corporate bankruptcy. The US and European countries will face many challenges as the economies of India, China, and Brazil as well as other countries improve. We may be entering into what Zakaria (2009) called the Post-American World. The next decade or two should be an exciting time for everyone, and especially for educators who seek to grasp the challenges we face. It is my hope this book will contribute to better education of all the peoples of the world.

Synopsis of the Book

A graphic summary of the book is presented in Figure 1.1. This is an example of a concept map, many of which will be shown in the following chapters. Concept maps are a knowledge representation tool, and this map represents a general overview of this book. Concept maps should be read from the top to the bottom, proceeding from the "higher order" more general concepts at the top to the "lower order" more specific concepts at the bottom. Concept maps also have "crosslinks" that show relationships between ideas in different

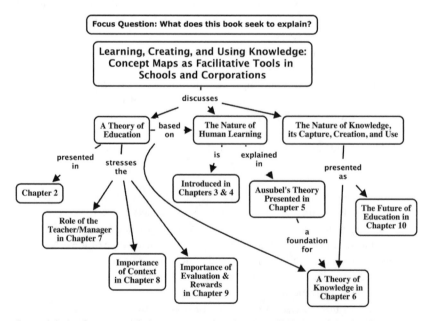

Figure 1.1 An Overview of ideas presented in the second edition of this book.

segments of the map. Figure 1.1 shows that three major concepts or ideas will be presented in this book: (1) the nature of knowledge, its capture, creation and use; (2) the nature of human learning; and (3) a theory of education that will tie together aspects of the latter two ideas and explain how these interrelate. Review the map before you proceed to read the synopsis of the book. Figure 1.1 was prepared using CmapTools software developed by the Florida Institute for Human and Machine Cognition (IHMC), and this software is available for anyone to use at: http://cmap.ihmc.us. This software has features that open up new possibilities of capturing and archiving knowledge and for educating in any setting. Some of these new possibilities will be discussed in later chapters. The software also provides a place to enter a *focus question*, that is, a question that helps to define what the ideas shown in the concept map should help to answer. This issue will be discussed in other chapters.

Chapter 2 discusses the need for a Theory of Education to help us deal with the many questions, issues, and problems faced in educating people, educating them in a manner that will empower them to become powerful, confident, and committed knowledge creators and knowledge users. There are five *elements* in my theory of education, each of which interacts with all the others, and all must be considered simultaneously to create a powerful educational event. The five elements presented are: (1) learner; (2) teacher; (3) knowledge; (4) context; and (5) evaluation. Each of these and their interactions are discussed in Chapter 2.

Chapter 2 also stresses the crucial role that *meaningful* learning, as distinct from *rote* learning, plays in successful education. In fact, the idea of meaningful learning is the very foundation for the theory of education presented. While the *learner must choose* to learn meaningfully, the teacher (live or vicarious) can do much to encourage and facilitate meaningful learning.

Theory can improve practice directly by providing an explanatory framework to guide practice, and indirectly, by helping to improve research in education. If we are going to make the quantum leap forward in education necessitated by evolving social and business demands, educational research and practice must be dramatically improved.

Chapter 3 defines meaningful learning and the fundamental elements that knowledge is made from—facts, concepts, propositions, and principles. The nature of human memory and the role of the major memory systems are discussed. Our early work in the development of the concept map tool to represent knowledge and applications in school and corporate settings are described briefly. Finally, the role of meaningful learning for the empowerment of individuals and organizations is sketched out.

Chapter 4 develops further how humans construct new meanings and the role that concepts and propositions play in the process. Humans construct, over time, complex concept and propositional frameworks as they develop, idiosyncratically, their knowledge structures, or, as psychologists refer to them, their *cognitive structures*. The monumental works of Jean Piaget and his ideas on cognitive development are presented briefly, along with brief discussion of emerging newer ideas.

Chapter 5 presents, in detail, David Ausubel's assimilation theory of meaningful learning, along with numerous examples and some modifications that derive from our studies and recent work in cognitive sciences. Ausubel (1962; 1963) was one of the pioneers who helped to move psychology away from *behavioral* models of learning based largely on animal studies in the 1930s through the 1970s, to *cognitive* models that focus on how humans construct new meanings and use knowledge in creative problem solving. The nature of creativity and intelligence as seen through assimilation theory is discussed. For readers new to the field of learning psychology, this chapter may prove to be a challenge. However, to acquire a deep understanding of how humans create and use knowledge, careful study of Chapter 5 can prove rewarding. In spite of many newer theories advanced to explain human learning, I still see Ausubel's theory, with some modifications and additions, as the most comprehensive and most powerful. Where recent advances in cognitive psychology add to Ausubel's ideas, these will be presented as well.

Understanding meaningful learning is the foundation needed to understand the nature of knowledge and knowledge creation. Chapter 6 presents a theory of knowledge that builds on the theory of learning presented in Chapter 5. The Vee heuristic is presented as a tool to help illustrate the structure of knowledge and the 12 elements involved in knowledge creation. Each of the 12 elements are defined, and examples are given to show how the Vee can be used to represent the knowledge creation process, or the structure of knowledge in any specific domain of knowledge.

Different forms of knowledge, such as *tacit* contrasted with *explicit* knowledge are discussed. Methods for capturing tacit knowledge are presented, and various approaches for capturing and using knowledge are discussed. Both academic and business examples are used to illustrate the principles and methods involved. Special attention is given to capturing and using knowledge from consumers. A fundamental principle of meaningful learning is that new learning must build on specific relevant knowledge the learner already has. Thus, understanding what knowledge individuals possess, be they school learners or consumers, is crucial to moving them to new levels of understanding and competence.

Chapter 7 focuses on the third element involved in educating and empowering people—the teacher or manager. I take the position that management, if it is to be effective, is essentially teaching. Therefore, the issues and ideas discussed apply equally to teaching and management. For example, I believe both require emotional sensitivity, commitment, honesty, and caring. Of course, there are teachers and managers who have been judged successful who do not evidence these characteristics consistently. There are always exceptions when we are dealing with the complex feelings, thoughts, and actions of people. This chapter seeks to put forward ideas that evidence suggests will be most effective most of the time with most people. The ideas presented are consistent with and build upon the theory of learning and theory of knowledge presented in earlier chapters.

All educative events take place in some space, time, social, and cultural milieu. Chapter 8 deals with issues related to the context for effective teaching or management. Once again, emphasis on the emotional experience is stressed. The effective teacher or manager can do much to help develop a context that will maximize the effectiveness of the learner or employee. Gender, race, and other social and cultural factors may present a challenge to the teacher or manager, but conscious, deliberate efforts to ameliorate deleterious influences can pay off in developing more effective learners and employees. Moreover, there are costs associated with ignoring or dealing ineffectively with contextual issues influencing learning and performance. In the school setting, these include high dropout rates, failure to learn, and ego destruction that can lead to individual disempowerment and a lifetime of failure. The societal costs for this are enormous. In business or government, failure to develop strong positive environments for workers reduces productivity, leads to high turnover rates that are costly, and failure to capture and utilize optimally the energy, talents, and creativity of workers. Furthermore, practices that discriminate on the basis of gender or race are illegal in the United States and other countries, and recently very large corporations have paid very large penalties for such discrimination. In worst cases, corporations go bankrupt, and governmental institutions fail at a high cost to everyone affected.

Chapter 9 deals with the last, and in some ways most crucial, element involved in educating or managing. The methods we use to evaluate and reward learning and performance can enhance or undermine all of our best efforts in dealing with the other four elements of educating. In school settings, the widespread use of multiple-choice type tests, most of which have limited validity at best, tends to encourage rote learning and learning patterns that can stifle rather than enhance creativity. In business settings, similar problems can occur in selection or promotion of workers. Ineffective assessment of consumer knowledge, interests, and desires can lead to failures in developing the kind of products or services that go beyond consumer demands and lead to corporate growth and greater societal contributions. Alternative forms of evaluations are discussed and their merits presented.

The last chapter (10) of the book looks to the future. What are the chances for enhanced educating and managing? Given my thesis that significant advances in education are unlikely unless teacher education and school practices are guided by a comprehensive theory of education, and given the snail's pace at which this is occurring, it is difficult to be optimistic about substantive improvements in schools in the near term. We see "new" programs introduced into schools, such as new reading programs, but the empirical evidence is that these programs do not improve learning. For example a new reading program introduced in 10 urban districts involving 6350 students showed no improvement (Zehr, 2009). In Miami, a $100 million dollar program in 39 schools that paid for longer school days and a longer school year showed a net loss in student performance (McGrory, 2009). But most of these "new programs" are essentially more of the same, and lack a focus on the facilitation of meaningful learning. Why should one expect improvement? There are other factors that are operating now that could alter the normally slow advances in school educational practices. Globalization of the economy is placing an accelerating demand on businesses to be more creative to remain competitive. Enhancing the creativity of our workforce can best be accomplished by education that confers a capacity for and commitment to high levels of meaningful learning for everyone. This must include minority groups, who are rapidly becoming majority groups in large cities and soon in the whole of the USA. Unfortunately, these groups too often receive the most boring, rote-learning dominated programs.

Other factors operating that could influence the rate of change are "privatization" of public schools. However, the evidence to date is that "for profit" corporations do no better than the public schools in effecting student achievement, even when assessed by relatively simplistic evaluation measures. Increasing use of technology, in combination with privatization, also has had limited success at best. So where is the new innovation to come from that can and must lead to the very substantive improvements that are needed in schools? My hope lies in the willingness of some schools and some corporations and governmental agencies to try employing new ideas, including the ideas presented in this book. Competitive pressures in business will, in the next decade or so, drive businesses to adopt radically new ways and new ideas for creating, sharing, and using knowledge. I believe we shall also see adoption of the kind of theory and methods discussed in this book in education and management in corporations. Subsequently, either by example, such as with Silesky's school discussed below, or a new genre of privatization, or both, education in schools and tertiary institutions will be driven toward truly significant advances.

I believe that schooling as we know it now ranks a two or three on a scale of ten, where ten represents the best we can do by applying fully the ideas and tools we have now. I predict we shall see improvements to a level of seven or eight within the next decade or two in the more innovative programs. Considering that almost no progress has been made in the past 40 years, I recognize how optimistic my prediction is. My hope is that this book will make some small contribution to achieving this goal.

A Sample Case that Illustrates the Possible

In June, 2002, Alberto Cañas and I gave an invited lecture to faculty, students, and visitors at the University of Costa Rica. One of the persons in the audience was a principal of a local school that served students from fourth grade through high school. These students are multicultural, multi-race, and range from brilliant to students who are significantly compromised in learning. Some students chose the school because they were interested in using different learning methods. Otto Silesky's school, Instituto de Educación Integral, is a private school, but it also receives some public support. Silesky had a staff who was willing to try new things, and they had the freedom to proceed. A major innovation introduced was *that all teachers in all subject areas and all grades* agreed to use concept maps and CmapTools in their instruction and assessment, as well as to make changes in their instructional strategies. They discussed at length the difference between rote memorization and truly meaningful learning, and how moving to more meaningful learning would require change in teaching practices. At the same time, they introduced laptops for students to use in the classroom, making it easy for students to build concept maps while in the classroom, and collaborate while doing so. Needless to say, this was not an easy transition for teachers or students, since their instructional methods had been relatively traditional, that is, information was presented by teachers and textbooks, and students were expected to memorize this information.

It is not easy to shift from programs that center on memorizing information and tests that mostly required verbatim recall of information to instruction that centers on understanding the subject matter, and finding applications to real-world examples to serve as the principal form of assessment. In fact, the first year of the program (2003) was difficult, and this was reflected in the fact that performance on standard National High School Graduation Exams *decreased* from 65 percent passing the exams in the previous year (2002) to 55 percent passing in 2003. This is not surprising given all the changes that both teachers and students had to master in going from old practices to new practices that emphasized meaningful learning. However, both students and teachers reported many positive things that were happening in their classrooms during 2003. Silesky and his staff persisted with their efforts and in subsequent years, the percentage passing these exams increased to 92 percent in 2004, 93 percent in 2005, 97 percent in 2006, and 100 percent in 2007 and 2008. The data are summarized in Figure 1.2. The results were so remarkable that staff from the University of Costa Rica came to visit to learn more about the instruction being used. What they found were students and teachers who were highly enthusiastic about the new methods they were using to learn. Another positive outcome was that Silesky's school experienced an immense increase in the percentage succeeding for those graduates who took the University admission exams, from 0 percent passing entrance exams in 2004 to 75 percent passing in 2005, 76 percent passing in 2006, and 75 percent passing in 2007. In fact, many students who may not have planned on college studies were not only succeeding in university work, but they were also spreading the word on the newer methods of learning they had acquired in high school.

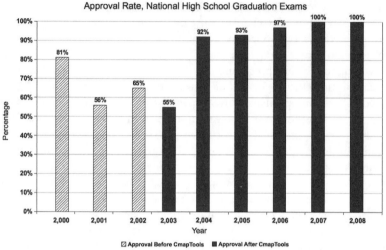

Figure 1.2 Approval rate on National Graduation Exams for students in Silesky's high school. Drawn by Carvajal based on data in Silesky, 2008. Reproduced with permission from R. Carvajal.

Admittedly, this is but a single case, and at this time of writing I am not aware of any other school that has made the changes that were made in Silesky's school. But then, we only needed to land a human being on the moon one time to prove that it can be done! I present this case because it demonstrates a clear case of the promise that exists for highly significant improvement in education. Not only did students improve markedly in performance on National exams, but also Silesky reported that the most significant thing to him was the very positive effect the new program had on student's self-confidence and their pleasure in learning. When we consider that graduation rates in US schools vary with an average of 70 percent graduating on time, but only some 30 percent graduating from inner-city schools, the results in Silesky's school are impressive. I shall present some other studies that support the validity of ideas in this book and point to the promise I believe is possible in the transformation of education in schools, corporations and other organizations.

There is another message here, and an answer to a question I am frequently asked when I lecture to an audience of educators. Will our students do well on high stakes State achievement tests if we change to the kinds of methods and learning tools you are suggesting? The answer is not simple, since so much depends on where the teachers and students are when we begin the transition, and how willing we are to persist in quality efforts to achieve meaningful learning. It was not until the second year that the staff and students saw payoff when National exams were the criterion of success, but they did succeed, even by this criterion which is not a full measure of what the students really achieved. In Chapter 7 (Figure 7.8), I will show that when the evaluation criteria require novel problem solving, positive effects of greater efforts to achieve meaningful learning result in weeks. There are many issues regarding the kinds of assessment used in schools and corporations, and I discuss some of these in Chapter 9. Other studies have also shown positive effects from use of concept mapping and other meaningful learning strategies, and many of these can be found in Proceedings of the three International Conferences on Concept Mapping (see: http://cmc.ihmc.us).

Chapter 2

The Need for a Theory of Education

My thesis in this book is the same as it was in the first edition and in my earlier book, *A Theory of Education* (Novak, 1977a): Education, in any setting, is an enormously complex human endeavor; there are more ways to make changes that will be harmful or of little value than ways to make constructive improvements in education. A comprehensive *theory* of education is needed to give vision and guidance for new practices and research leading to steady improvement of education. The ideas in this book should apply to all educational settings, including schools, universities, corporations, technology-mediated education, and non-formal education, such as museums or hobbies.

Theories are ideas that *explain why* some set of phenomena in the universe behave as they do. The sciences have been enormously successful in devising theories, and though even the best theories evolve and change over time, these still make possible a steady advance in knowledge about how the natural world works and in prediction and control over an ever-widening range of events or phenomena. The theory of education presented in this book will explain why educational experiences we judge as effective are effective, and why those experiences we judge as ineffective are ineffective. For example, the theory of learning I will present explains why learning by *rote* is ineffective for long-term retention and application of knowledge and why *meaningful* learning is effective and necessary for creative thinking. As with all theories, there are no simple, direct answers (consider, for example, the theory of evolution), and yet I hope to explain, on a theoretical basis, what is in the ballpark of being "better" and what appears to be outside of this ballpark. The theory of education presented will be a composite of a theory of learning, a theory of knowledge, and a theory of teaching and management, each of which complements and supports the others.

Educating is more than science; it is also an art. It requires personal judgments, feelings, and values. Increasingly, of course, we are coming to recognize that the latter are also involved in science. Keller (1983) chose to title her biography of Nobel Laureate biologist Barbara McClintock, *A Feeling for the Organism*, expressing not only the careful research done by her but also her commitment and sensitivity to understanding plants. Issues of sensitivities and values are becoming increasingly important in the sciences also, especially with the growing application of scientific ideas and tools for manipulating plant and animal (including human) genes. Throughout this book I shall make reference to issues that concern both the science of educating and the art of educating.

I will claim that *the central purpose of education is to empower learners to take charge of their own meaning making.* Meaning making involves thinking, feeling, and acting, and all three of these aspects must be integrated for significant new learning, and especially in new knowledge creation. In some ways, this is not a new idea. In the monograph published by the Educational Policies Commission (EPC), this statement was published in 1961:

> The purpose which runs through and strengthens all other educational purposes—the common thread of education—is the development of the ability to think. This is the central purpose to which the schools must be oriented . . . the development of every student's rational powers must be recognized as centrally important. (p. xiv)

One of the shortcomings of the EPC report is that it failed to recognize the central role that meaningful learning and acquisition of powerful conceptual frameworks in basic disciplines play in the ability to engage in rational thought. It also failed to recognize that students need explicit guidance in learning about learning and in the use of tools and strategies to facilitate meaningful learning. This guidance in learning and the use of tools to facilitate learning and understanding is becoming especially important in the corporate world. Learning and integrating new knowledge in collaborative settings is especially important in the highly competitive global markets in which corporations are operating. These will be some of the issues focused upon in this book.

Successful education must focus upon more than the learner's thinking. Feelings and actions are also important. We must deal with all three forms of learning. These are acquisition of knowledge (*cognitive* learning), change in emotions or feelings (*affective* learning) and gain in physical or motor actions or performance (*psychomotor* learning) that enhance a person's capacity to make sense out of their experiences. A positive educational experience will enhance a person's capacity for thinking, feeling, and/or acting in subsequent experiences. A maleducative or miseducative experience will diminish this capacity. Humans engage in thinking, feeling, and acting, and these combine to form the *meaning* of experience (Figure 2.1). Recent research indicates that emotions are involved in an important way as we organize and retain experiences (Niedenthal, 2007). This book will focus on how to enhance the meaning of experience for any person.

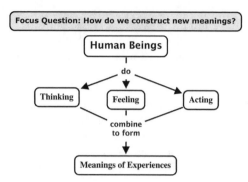

Figure 2.1 The meanings we construct from our experiences are a composite of our thinking, feeling, and acting during the experience.

The Five Elements of Education

In 1973, Joseph Schwab proposed that education involved what he called "four *commonplaces*." His "commonplaces" were learner, teacher, subject matter, and social matrix. Each commonplace was necessary to consider and could not be "reduced" into one of the others (analogous to finding the lowest common denominator in fractions). Schwab's commonplaces, and many of his other ideas, have proven to be of value to educators. They provide a kind of "check list" to assure that we are covering all the key checkpoints necessary to understand or to design an effective educational intervention.

Our studies in schools and other settings, notably corporate settings, however, have shown that much of what happens in teaching and/or learning depends upon the forms of appraisal used. Therefore, I wish to propose *evaluation* as a fifth *element* in education. I prefer the term *elements* to commonplaces because it connotes the idea that each is a building block for myriads of combinations that form educational events, much as the 100 or so elements of chemistry form an infinite variety of molecules.

My five elements are: (1) learner; (2) teacher; (3) knowledge; (4) context; and (5) evaluation. I add the last element because so much of what happens to people in life is based upon evaluation. For better or worse, the evaluations we are subjected to determine whether or not we can drive an automobile, graduate with "honors" or enter a university or graduate program or succeed in a corporate or other work setting. Unfortunately, so much of the "testing" that is done is really poor at evaluating human competencies, and I will deal with this issue throughout the book. Nevertheless, I see evaluation as an additional key element in education. Figure 2.2 shows a concept map with these elements. Concept maps, a knowledge representation tool that was developed in 1972 in our research program (Novak & Musonda, 1991), will be used extensively in this book. Strategies for developing and using concept maps have been

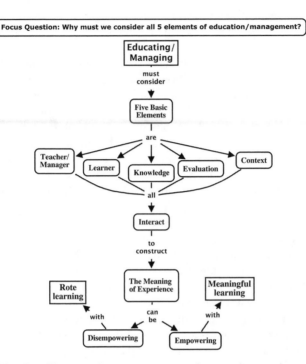

Figure 2.2 The Five Elements that comprise any educational event: learner, teacher, knowledge, evaluation, and context. All elements are present in an educative event and combine to construct or reconstruct the meaning of experience.

described in numerous publications and in *Learning How to Learn* (Novak & Gowin, 1984). As we shall see, concept maps and Vee diagrams (see Chapter 6) can also be powerful tools to aid learning as well as tools for evaluation.

Two additional factors operate in education: money and time. These are factors that influence any human enterprise and are not uniquely relevant to education. In general, we can improve any endeavor if we have more money and/or more time to pursue that endeavor. Moreover, the past few decades have illustrated that simply spending more money on education may not lead to significant improvement in student achievement (Hanushek, 1981;1989; 1996). Lengthening the school day and/or the school year might lead to improvement in achievement; while I favor a 12-month school calendar, evidence for this is equivocal. It would certainly increase the cost of education. My thesis is that more money and time are not the primary needs for improvement of education. The debate on whether or not expenditures are related to student achievement is one that has gone on and will continue (cf. Hanushek, 1981; 1989; 1996; Hanuchek, et al., 2008); Hedges, et al., 1994; Wainer, 1993). What is needed are promising new ideas and determination to apply these ideas and to set standards. A viable theory of education can help to generate and identify promising ideas and strategies to improve education in any setting. It can also help to set and reach functional high standards. Whatever money or time or resources are made available can then be used much more efficiently. Resnick and Nolan (1995) observe that, "Countries known for their outstanding students have several practices in common; clear, consistent demanding standards head the list" (p. 6). However, as Howe (1995) points out, setting academic standards without dealing with poverty and limited resources in poor districts will not solve our educational problems. But money alone is not the solution. Wainer (1993) cites data from the National Heritage Foundation that show the ten states with the highest per pupil expenditure rank 31st to 49th on SAT (Scholastic Aptitude Test) scores, whereas the ten states with lowest per pupil expenditure rank 2nd to 22nd in SAT rank.

I am not alone in recognizing the need for theory. Brown (1994), in her presidential address to the American Educational Research Association, points out that the advances in learning theory of the past century are not being applied in schools, a position with which I agree. Shuell (1993) calls for an integrated theory of teaching and learning to improve education, but I contend this is not enough. More recently, Villarini-Jusino (2007) argues that we need theories in education that are comprehensive, open, complex, and scientific in nature. We need a theory that integrates all five elements of the educative process leading to honest, authentic, and productive achievement, and this is the goal of this book. In spite of these early calls, there has been little progress evident in most educational literature in recent years that we are moving toward more theory-based educational research and practice.

In the corporate world, similar problems prevail. While corporations recognize that continued change in the ways in which manufacturing and marketing are done to meet the competition requires continued education of employees, they tend to look for short-term solutions that *train* employees in new methods or techniques. What they seldom do is to *educate* employees to understand the ideas that underlie the new methods or techniques. This training usually takes the form of memorizing new rules, procedures, or rationales, without the requisite *conceptual* understanding necessary for employees to take command of their work—and to contribute their own creative ideas. The result in a rapidly changing market environment can at times be ineffective at best and disastrous in worst cases.

Theory of Education for Human Beings

Human beings do three things: they *think, feel,* and *act.* A theory of education for human beings must consider each of these and help to explain how to improve the ways in which humans think, feel, and act. Throughout this book I will consider each of these forms of human experience and how they relate to education.

In schooling, work, or any educational setting where we have a teacher, even if it is a textbook or a computer program serving as a proxy for a teacher, we must recognize that the learner's world and the teacher's world are never the same. Thus, we must recognize that the interplay between learner and teacher involves two different sets of interacting elements. Figure 2.3 shows this relationship. I shall argue throughout this book that businesses need to look at customers and employees in a manner similar to the way teachers should look at their students. I also emphasize that there needs to be *negotiation of meanings* between the teacher and the learner, and the same can be said for businesses dealing with employees or with customers. The interactions suggested in Figure 2.3 apply both to school and business settings.

One emerging potential of technology-mediated education is that faulty ideas or biases that may be introduced by the teacher might be reduced. In earlier work using audiotape as an instructional vehicle, we found that carefully designed lessons could be highly effective without teacher intervention (Novak, 1972; Novak & Musonda, 1991). One disadvantage of technologically-mediated instruction is that machines do not express emotions, the caring, warmth, and excitement that an effective human teacher can share. We must recognize that teaching and learning are interactive events and involve the thoughts, feelings, and actions of both teacher and learner. This is illustrated in Figure 2.3.

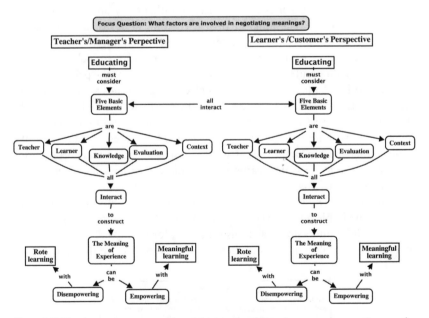

Figure 2.3 Teacher or manager and each learner has his or her own perspectives on the five elements operating in an educative event. The challenge is to negotiate a shared perspective on each element. In the business world, we should also see the consumer as the teacher in this model.

Also shown in Figure 2.3 is a fundamental idea in my theory of education. Any educational event is a shared *action* to seek to exchange *meanings* and *feelings between* the learner and the teacher. This exchange or negotiation will be emotionally positive and intellectually constructive when learners gain in their understandings of a segment of knowledge or experience; conversely, it will be negative or destructive when understanding is obfuscated or feelings of inadequacy emerge. And since learner and mentor share thoughts, feelings, and actions, the teacher will also experience positive feelings and a sense of power over knowledge when the educative event is successful. When learner and teacher are successful in negotiating and sharing the meaning in a unit of knowledge, *meaningful learning* occurs. In its simplest form, my theory of education states: Meaningful learning underlies the constructive integration of thinking, feeling, and acting leading to human empowerment for commitment and responsibility. I show this in Figure 2.4 to give emphasis to this idea. This book will set forth the key concepts, principles and philosophy underlying this theory. It is a book for learners, for teachers, and for managers. Kouzes and Posner (2006) argue at length that the best business leaders are teachers, as they describe them. When education is most effective, managers become teachers, teachers are also learners, and learners are also teachers. This can be especially true where learners are engaged in "cooperative learning activities," and I will discuss this idea again in later sections. Fundamental to constructive interaction between teachers and learners is authenticity and honesty, since this is fundamental to building the trust needed for both teacher and learner to share meanings and develop new, more powerful meanings.

In the business world, leaders such as Procter and Gamble's Chairman, A. G. Lafley (Lafley and Charan, 2008), see the consumer as the primary source of new learning. Lafley goes so far as to place the consumer as "boss" and all real business innovation must be "consumer centric." He identifies eight elements that he sees as essential to success in business and these match reasonably well with ideas I will discuss as essential for success in education. We shall see that the consumer should also be seen as a teacher and corporations must structure to be better learners. I will discuss Lafley's ideas more fully in later sections of this book.

Meaningful learning is the key concept in my theory of education, a concept that is both simple and universally known, but also extraordinarily complex and never fully understood, as is also the case, for example, for the concepts of energy or evolution in the sciences or renaissance in the humanities.

A Theory of Education
Meaningful learning underlies the constructive integration
of thinking, feeling, and acting leading to empowerment
for commitment and responsibility.

J. Novak

Figure 2.4 Briefly stated, this is my theory of education.

Throughout this book I will try to add clarity to the idea of *meaningful* learning, and also distinguish this from *memorization* or *rote* learning, so prevalent in much of schooling and business training. So many of the "games" people play in school or work settings are inherently fraudulent and do not lead to enhancement of learner or teacher. In addition, I will seek to show how meaningful learning contrasts with rote learning in terms of the neurobiology of brain functioning, albeit the relationships between learning phenomena and brain structures remain an area of intense research (see Gazzaniga, 1989; 1995; 2008).

Rote learning may be useful on occasions, such as when we memorize a poem, the score for a piece of music, or multiplication tables. But the real value of rote learning comes when we also move to understand the *meaning* of what we have memorized and it is meaning that confers power to our learning. The person who simply plays the notes he or she has memorized is, at best, a technician, whereas the artist understands and interprets the meaning of the music intended by the composer. The good teacher helps to move the learner beyond rote learning by negotiating meanings with the learner.

For almost a century, most of the "scientific" research on learning was done with animals in laboratory settings. The idea was that as "basic knowledge" about learning processes were elucidated through studies with animals, this knowledge could later be applied to improving education of human beings. One of the prominent psychologists who had his early training in this "scientific" behavioral psychology later observed, "What was important was the promissory note that, once we understood simple conditioning [in animals], we would understand complex behavior [of humans]. The promissory note turned out to be a rubber check. At least, by 1966, nobody has been able to cash it in" (Mandler, 1967, p. 6). Nevertheless, the dogmas generated by behavioral psychologists remain very much in vogue and continue to guide practice in schools and corporations. For example, Glasser (1994) observes this problem in corporations:

> To review briefly, boss-managers, like almost all human beings, believe in and manage according to the traditional theory of human behavior; stimulus-response (S-R) psychology. They follow it mostly because it supports their common-sense belief that people can be made, through reward or punishment, to do what the manager wants them to do whether they like it or not. And, to some extent, they follow it because no one has ever offered them another theory. They have nothing to turn to if they suspect, as I am sure many do, that what they believe may be wrong. Therefore, it is not that they believe in S-R theory so absolutely that they cannot change. It is more that, for almost all people, stimulus-response theory is all there is. (p. 48)

Glasser suggests a new kind of control theory that is predicated on the need to help people construct new meanings and see value in a new idea, thing, or procedure. He asserts, "*You cannot make anyone do what he or she does not want to do. You can only teach him a better way and encourage him to try it. If it works, there is a good chance he will continue*" (p. 50, italics in original).

One reason I prefer the word "act" to "behave" is that it implies a conscious, deliberate, and emotion-laden event, not the kind of passive event we associate with a trained rat or bird. Very little human activity is *behavior* in the animal sense. Most of it is deliberate action, and at least in the mind of the actor, the action makes sense. In *Wikinomics*, Tapscott and Williams (2007) claim that we are seeing the rise of a new kind of labor force. ". . . a generation of young people are entering the workforce with a radically different philosophy of work. As eighty million young people in the United States alone enter the workforce they will bring high-technology adoption, creativity, social connectivity, fun, and diversity to the companies they work for, and increasingly to the companies they found" (p. 240). This digital generation will demand that the work they do makes sense, and that it is fun. We need educational practices that better integrate human thoughts, feelings and actions.

Improving Educational Research and Evaluation

Agriculture and medicine are two areas in which we have seen dramatic advances in the last few decades. We spend far more on research in these fields than on research in education, and much of what has been spent on educational research has yielded little of value. Most research in education is *method driven* rather than *theory driven*. That is, researchers have often compared two or more methods of instruction, usually with little or no theoretical justification for the design of the instruction, or they have used a variety of tests or "scales" as methods for assessing achievement, often with little or no theory behind the choice of these instruments. Most of this research has led to the conclusion that "no significant differences were found between methods or groups," or conflicting results are reported comparing one study to another. Many of the tests used produce not facts, but poor artifacts about human performance.[1] The net result has been that teachers and the public are skeptical at best regarding educational research "findings" and most of the research that has been done has had little or no lasting effect on the improvement of education.

A major limitation of educational research has been the weak or inappropriate evaluation tools employed. Almost all educational research utilizes some form of questionnaire or multiple-choice or true–false test for evaluation of attitudes, knowledge or aptitude. And yet we know that most of the test results have near zero correlation with real-life performance and at

---

1 For dozens of examples of this kind of research, see Gage, 1963; Richardson, 2001; Saha and Dwarkin, 2009.

best they measure only about 10 percent of the range of human abilities.[2] Unfortunately, many people's lives and futures are determined by this kind of evaluation, not only in the United States, but even more so in developing countries. Sternberg (1996), a distinguished professor of psychology at Yale University, observed: "As an elementary school student, I failed miserably on the IQ tests I had to take. I was incredibly test anxious. Just the sight of the school psychologist coming into the classroom to give a group IQ test sent me into a wild panic attack" (p. 17). With strong parental support and a wise fourth-grade teacher, Sternberg did go on to succeed in school and later achieved worldwide recognition for his outstanding work.

As an alternative to typical "testing," concept mapping is proving to be a powerful tool for evaluation and this, together with other new evaluation methods that are beginning to emerge, shows promise for both educational research and practice. It is impossible to improve practice based on research when the evaluation tools used in the research have limited validity at best, and in some cases are *negatively* correlated with valuable human performance such as creativity.

Education is an enormously complex set of events. Comparing my research experiences in botany as a graduate student with my experience over the past four decades as a researcher in education, I would say educational research is an order of magnitude more complex and difficult than most research done in botany. Moreover, botany and other sciences have relatively well-defined theoretical foundations, and also well-defined theory-based methodologies for gathering data, to say nothing about comparatively sophisticated instrumentation. In spite of the morass that educational research has represented (see, for example, Kaestle, 1993), I now feel highly optimistic about future improvement in educational research and subsequent improvement in educational practice. My optimism is based in part on an increasingly powerful theoretical foundation for education and a slow but steady movement toward its application, driven by new global economic pressures.

There is a great need for strengthening the linkages between researchers and practitioners. We already know much that could be extremely useful for the improvement of teaching and learning. There are many skilled and creative teachers in schools, universities and corporations. Slowly but surely, managers in private and public organizations are learning to be teachers of the kind I seek to encourage with this book. An important challenge is to find better ways to increase the flow of information between researchers and practitioners, and the flow must be in both directions. Federal, state, and local budgeting to encourage this exchange and broaden the context of educational research are needed. New initiatives along the lines of the highly successful Federal Hatch

---

2 For a critique of typical educational testing, see Hoffman (1962); Keddie (1973); Gould (1981); and Ziliak & McClosky, 2008).

Act (passed in 1865) and the Extension system that has been so successful for our advances in agriculture could yield enormous advances in education. What has been needed is a vision or, more specifically, a comprehensive *theory of education* to guide the changes needed. The foundations for theory/research-based improvement of education are being laid. We need to seek better institutional structures to advance and build upon these foundations. There are no easy solutions to the political problems that will need to be solved to effect this advance. With the growing importance of education in every phase of our lives, including our economic well-being, I am confident that solutions will be found

With the accelerating "globalization" of business and the growing importance of creating and using knowledge to remain competitive, we have seen in the past decade significant growth in corporate interest in educating—that is educating that empowers people to be more creative as well as more content. I see a future where new partnerships will be formed between businesses and educational institutions, where a new kind of sharing and seeking solutions will take place. The first few decades of the twenty-first century are likely to be revolutionary in many respects, and most importantly in how we learn better to educate people for whatever the needs may be.

Chapter 3

Meaningful Learning for Empowerment

Meaningful learning results when the *learner chooses* to relate new information to ideas the learner already knows. Its quality is also dependent upon the conceptual richness of the new material to be learned and the quantity and quality of the organization of the relevant knowledge held by the learner. Rote learning occurs when the *learner memorizes* new information without relating it to prior knowledge or when learning material that has no relationship to prior knowledge. As will be discussed in the next chapter, creativity is seen as resulting from very high levels of meaningful learning. There is a continuum in learning from "pure" rote to highly meaningful, and Figure 3.1 represents this continuum. Meaningful learning has three requirements:

1. Relevant prior knowledge: That is, the learner must know some information that relates to the new information to be learned in some non-trivial way;
2. Meaningful material: That is, the knowledge to be learned must be relevant to other knowledge and must contain significant concepts and propositions;
3. The *learner must choose* to learn meaningfully: That is, the learner must consciously and deliberately choose to relate new knowledge to relevant knowledge the learner already knows in some non-trivial way.

This raises the question: What are non-trivial relationships? For example, if a learner knows that Ohio, California, and New York are states, it is comparatively trivial to learn that Michigan is also a state, unless one goes further and recognizes that states are relatively large geographic units and there are only 50 in the United States, including Alaska and Hawaii. The learner needs to seek to build an *organized* knowledge structure that moves toward recognition of the differences between towns, cities, states, and countries.

When knowledge structures are well organized, "higher order" concepts that are more inclusive and more general *subsume* "lower order" concepts that are more specific and less general. Figure 3.2 illustrates these relationships for the study of history, where the superordinate concept is HISTORY, and two

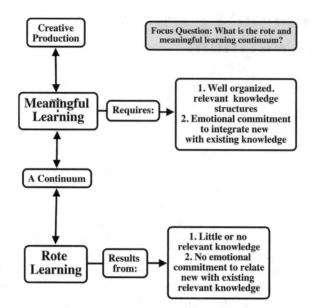

Figure 3.1 The rote–meaningful learning continuum. High levels of meaningful learning require: (1) well-organized, relevant concepts and propositions held by the learner; (2) materials that are rich in concepts and meanings; (3) learner's desire to integrate new knowledge with prior knowledge. Creativity is viewed as very high levels of meaningful learning.

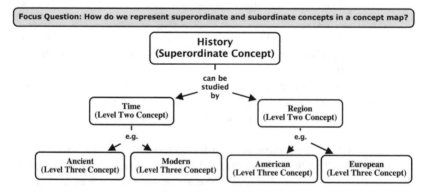

Figure 3.2 A concept map dealing with the superordinate concept HISTORY and showing second- and third-level subordinate concepts.

levels of subordinate concepts are shown. The hierarchical organization is, of course, dependent upon the context we are dealing with, and a remarkable characteristic of our minds is that we may use the same concepts in many different contexts and many different hierarchies. For example, for the study of geography, the concept *European* might hold a more subordinate position on a concept map dealing with geography of the world, and it would also have a somewhat different meaning in this context.

Facts, Concepts, Propositions, and Principles: Components of Knowledge

The universe consists of *objects* and *events*. Objects are composed of atoms and molecules whereas events involve objects and exchanges of energy. For example, this page and the words on it are objects composed of carbon, cellulose, and other substances. Energy was required to produce this page.

Concepts. Your reading of this page is an event that requires mental activity, and this requires energy in the form of biochemical changes in your brain cells. Human beings are unique among animals in their ability to *perceive regularities in objects and events* and to code these regularities symbolically using language (Gazzaniga, 2008). While other animals code experience in sets of neurons that Tsien (2007) calls "neural cliques," only humans use what we call language to represent experiences we have stored. These symbols for regularities in events or objects are usually words (about one million in the English language), but may also be signs such as $+$, $-$, Σ, Δ, etc. The symbols represent *concepts*, which I will define as *perceived regularities or patterns in events or objects, or records of events or objects, designated by a symbol* (Figure 3.3). For example, there are various shapes and kinds of things we call a chair, but once a child acquires the *concept chair*, that child will label correctly almost anything with a seat, back, and legs as a chair (see Macnamara, 1982; Bloom, 2000).[1]

Facts and Artifacts: No one has ever seen an atom disintegrating, but we can observe regularities in *records of events* (such as counts of a geiger counter) that *we interpret* to mean atomic decay or disintegration. Similarly, no one has ever seen a dinosaur, but we have bones, footprints, and other records whose regularities allow us to construct the concept of a dinosaur. Much of what humans know is constructed from records of events or objects rather than direct observations. We shall use the term *fact* to indicate a *valid record*. It is a fact that water boils at 212° Fahrenheit, but if our thermometer reads only 200°F in boiling water, we may be some thousands of feet above sea level, or we

> **Concept**
> **A perceived regularity or pattern**
> **in events or objects, or records**
> **of events or objects, designated by a label.**
> **J. Novak**

Figure 3.3 My definition for *Concept.*

---

1 For a more sophisticated, esoteric discussion on acquisition of language see Pinker (2007).

may have a faulty thermometer. In the sciences, and especially in the social sciences, it is not always easy to see regularities in events or objects since often times our records are faulty or our measuring instruments are limited or faulty. This is a huge problem in the study of education. Facts are not always easily distinguished from *artifacts*. The pottery fragments studied by anthropologists are human constructions (not naturally occurring objects) and these records of human activity are artifacts. Their meanings must be interpreted, and interpretations may vary widely.

Propositions. When two or more concepts are related by the use of what we will call linking words, propositions are formed. These become the fundamental units of meaning stored in our cognitive structure. The richness of the meaning will depend on the precision and clarity of the component concepts, as well as the specificity of the linking words, and this will depend on the quality of learning that has taken place in forming the concepts, and in turn the meanings of the propositions. We often find confusion between propositions and prepositions, the latter being a grammatical term for words such as "to," "on," "beside," etc. Prepositions may make up linking words, but they are not fundamental units of knowledge, as are propositions. Statements such as: "all men are created equal" and "do unto others as you would have them do unto you" are familiar examples of propositions. Figure 3.4 shows key ideas regarding propositions.

Principles are relationships between concepts. Principles tell us *how* events or objects work or how they are structured. In physics, for example, we have the

Figure 3.4 A concept map showing the meaning of proposition.

principle: force equals mass times acceleration (F = ma). This principle involves the concepts force, mass, and acceleration. In education we know that learning is in part a function of study time, but the relationship is complex and we cannot write a mathematical formula to express this principle. This book attempts to present a number of principles regarding education and management, principles that I believe are valid even though they derive largely from records that have limited accuracy and validity.

Human Memory Systems

The early pioneering studies of memory go back to the work of Ebbinghaus (1885) who studied his own capacity to remember. He invented "nonsense" syllables, short three-letter words that had no language meaning, to avoid interference from memory of prior knowledge. Nonsense syllables have been used widely in psychological studies, but we now recognize such studies as of little value in understanding human learning. Bartlett's (1932) pioneering work focused on studies with meaningful material and would have been more influential in psychology if behavioral psychology had not crowded out cognitive learning studies for some 75 years. The human brain is a complex organ. It contains at least 300 trillion cells, and each of the cells that functions in storage of information has some thousands of axons and dendrites that permit these cells to store and pass along information. Part of the brain, the lower or limbic region, records information about our feelings, positive or negative. Brain cells are also connected to the skin, heart, lungs and other organs of our body, as well as to the many muscles of our body that produce our movements or actions. In some wonderful way, the brain serves to integrate our thinking, feeling, and acting. The challenge of education and management is to help us most constructively to achieve this integration in a wide variety of contexts. Recent research indicates that "congruence between the recipient's bodily expression of emotion and the sender's emotional tone of language, for instance, facilitates comprehension of the communication, whereas incongruence can impair comprehension" (Niedenthal, 2007). Recent research also indicates that the way our brain codes memories involves a large population of neurons acting in concert to form a memory of an experience (Tsien, 2007). Research by Tsien and his colleagues indicates that memories are formed in the hippocampus region of the brain, and signals produced in the process can be categorized to produce a "codebook of the mind." Grove (2008) also reports that their research indicates that the hippocampus plays a role in organizing information in memory. The hippocampus also functions in the retrieval of memories and imagining new events (Miller, 2007). The amygdula region of the brain functions in organizing and storing feelings associated with experience. While many questions remain, we can expect great progress in the next decade in our understanding of memory processes in the brain.

Our knowledge storage system consists of at least three parts: (1) sensory or perceptual (PM) memory; (2) short-term or working memory (STM); and (3) long-term or "permanent" memory (LTM). Each of these memory systems depends upon the others, and what is stored in LTM strongly influences what will be perceived, how it will be processed in STM and finally how it will be stored in LTM. Our brain also stores memories of feelings, perhaps primarily in the amygdula region of the brain. And our brain and spinal chord stores memories of actions or physical movements. Study Figure 3.5 and notice that the arrows show interaction between all of our memory systems.

Many of our human limitations derive from our perceptual limitations. Most of us cannot hear sounds below 80 hertz or above 20,000 hertz, nor can we see light in the ultraviolet or infrared range. No amount of learning can overcome these inherited biological limits on our sensory organs. Nevertheless, there remains an enormous range of events we can respond to within our limitations, and instruments we have developed permit us to extend greatly the sights, sounds, and feelings we can record and respond to. While it is true that instruments yet to be developed may give us wonderful new powers to observe regularities in as yet unobserved events or objects, there is perhaps even greater promise in learning how to use the information we now can

Key Memory Systems of the Brain

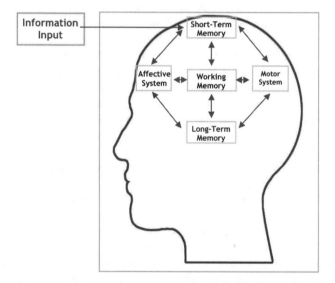

Figure 3.5 A representation of the memory systems involved in human learning. Note that each system interacts with the others, both limiting and facilitating the acquisition of information. Note that this diagram does not represent the actual structure of the brain. That can be seen at many Google sites using "structure of the brain".

gather by learning to improve our use of our working memory and the quality of the organization of knowledge stored in our long-term memory.

In 1956, George Miller published an article entitled "The magical number seven, plus or minus two." In this article Miller presented data to show that our short-term or working memory system can only operate on about seven "chunks" of information at a time. In a later article, Simon (1974) asked, "How big is a chunk?" Simon's answer was basically, the size of a "chunk" depends on the knowledge you have in long-term memory. This has been confirmed by numerous studies including our own work. For example, people who recognize numbers as symbols can remember six to eight numbers after a short (five to ten second) exposure to a list. The learning time must be long enough to perceive the material through sensory memory, but not long enough to "rehearse" or repeat the information, until it is set into long-term memory. The same is true for letters, but often letters can be "chunked" as words or word-like units, and hence nine or ten "chunks" might be recalled after a short exposure. In our work we find that the letters Q C V M E P Y T O are often chunked by people as Q, C, V, Me, Pyto, and all ten letters can be recalled. Familiar words may contain several letters but each word is a psychological "chunk," and five to nine words may be recalled after a short exposure. Very familiar strings of words can also be processed as single "chunks." For example each of the following statements could be a chunk: Jack and Jill went up the hill; to be or not to be, that is the question; pi is equal to the circumference divided by the diameter; profit is equal to the price minus the costs. If all of these statements are already well known by you, you could easily recall all four after a quick reading, since they would represent only four "chunks" in your short-term or working memory. Most people would not have stored in their long-term memory easily recallable meanings for all of these statements, and hence most would have difficulty recalling all four statements after a single quick reading. Certainly every reader has had the experience of listening to a lecture where all of the words used by the speaker were familiar, but when presented rapidly, especially when long sentences are used, the *meanings* of the sentences cannot be processed in working memory and the lecture is incomprehensible.

To return to the idea that meaningful learning requires *relevant* prior knowledge, we can see that for any learner, the quantity and quality of the relevant knowledge he or she has will vary from topic to topic. Therefore, even with intense willingness to learn meaningfully, any learner has limitations on the *degree* of meaningfulness that can occur in a given learning task. Refer again to Figure 3.1. Highly meaningful learning that includes novel problem solving and creativity is only possible in domains of knowledge where the learner has considerable, well-organized prior knowledge. Thoughtful practice or rehearsal also contribute. The dependence of meaningful learning on the adequacy of our prior relevant knowledge is both a blessing and a curse. The more we learn and organize knowledge in a given domain, the *easier* it is to acquire and use new knowledge in that domain. The curse is that when we try to learn new knowledge in a domain where we know little, and/or what we know is poorly organized, meaningful learning is difficult, usually time-consuming and tiring. Too often we may escape the challenge by resorting to rote learning, even though we know that what we learn will soon be forgotten and it will not be of value in future learning. Such fraudulent learning may allow us to pass school exams, but contributes little or nothing to future learning or acting (Edmondson and Novak, 1993).

Human beings are not only remarkable in their acquisition, storage, and use of knowledge; they also manifest complex patterns of feelings or emotions. Feelings, or what psychologists call *affect*, are always a concomitant of any learning experience and can enhance or impair learning. We know relatively little about the memory systems humans have for feelings, although we do know that the amygdula region of the brain is heavily involved, as are also the endocrine or hormone systems of the body. The involuntary or autonomic nervous system is also involved in some complex, but not well-understood manner. There is a complex interplay between our knowledge or thinking systems of the brain and those systems involved with emotion or feelings. Much remains to be learned about those systems of our body that produce and store emotional experiences, and this is currently a very active area of research. I believe we will see some breakthroughs in this in the next 10 years.

Human beings act. They consciously and deliberately move. I prefer the term act to behave, because the latter is so commonly used to describe animal movements, many of which are controlled genetically or by the environment, and not consciously by a thinking brain. Except for the patellar or knee-jerk reflex and a few other movements, most human movement is under control of our minds. Herrigel (1973) spoke well of this control in his book, *Zen in the Art of Archery*. We know that the lower brain regions and the spinal cord are involved in learning and storing information that controls our muscles, but as with feelings, our knowledge of the nature of this memory system is poor. Nevertheless, the complex interaction that takes place between stored information about knowledge, feelings and actions is very important in education. This interaction needs to be considered. Figure 3.6 illustrates these interacting systems. Recall also that learning is one element in education that interacts with the other four elements: teacher, knowledge, context and evaluation (see Figure 2.2).

An example of a learner seeking to integrate a new experience occurred when my granddaughter bought a new lock for her school locker. My six-year-old grandson also wanted one of these combination locks. We tried to suggest an easy-to-use keyed lock instead, but he insisted on getting one like his sister's. These locks have a combination such as: right 10, left 36, right 22. Joseph began trying to open his lock and continued try after try. Then he asked me to try, and I opened it quickly. Knowing that it was possible to open the lock, Joseph proceeded to try and try again. I noticed that he was not always

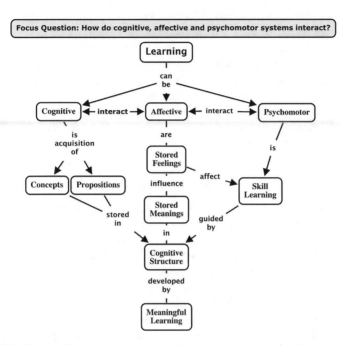

Figure 3.6 Humans have three distinct but interacting systems for learning, each of which has its own forms of information storage. Meaningful learning underlies development of cognitive structure that strongly influences our affective and psychomotor learning.

getting the number exactly on the mark before turning to the next number and pointed out this requirement for successful action (i.e., opening the lock). He persisted to try and try again, but still his lock would not open, and he came back to me for help. I asked him to show me and explain what he was doing, and I noticed he was not turning the lock one full rotation before turning to the second number. This was a key piece of knowledge that was missing from the lock code attached to the lock, but one I recalled from previous experience with this type of lock. Once he got this information— wow! the lock opened on the next try. Joseph was so excited, he kept on closing and opening the lock, showing his sister, parents, and grandmother how easily he could open the lock. In short, he had achieved successful integration (with a bit of help from his mentor—me) of thinking, feeling, and acting—and the result for Joseph was euphoria!

Any human experience that results in strongly negative feelings can contribute to a breakdown of the normal interplay between how we think, feel, and act. If such experience is repeated over and over, or is extraordinarily emotionally intense, we may observe actions that signal deviation from acceptable norms or in extreme cases, psychotic actions and what we label as "mental illness." Most mental illness is notoriously difficult to "cure," partly because so little is known about the ways in which our thinking, feeling, acting systems store information and influence one another. The best "cure" is prevention, and an important source of illness is maleducation. For example, in one of our studies, we found that every bulimic or anorexic subject we interviewed used primarily rote-mode learning strategies and had a sense of *disempowerment* over their learning (Hangen, 1989). One of my objectives in building a theory of education is to help to improve education not only to empower humans, but also hopefully to reduce maladaptive practices and, in the extreme, psychotic actions.

Concept Maps and Knowledge Organization

During the early 1970s our research program struggled with the problem of making records of what children know about a domain of knowledge before and after instruction. We tried every conceivable form of paper-and-pencil test and found that these poorly represented the children's knowledge. Interviewing children on how or why they selected their answers showed that many chose the right answer for the wrong reasons and most knew either more or less about the subject than the test question answers indicated. We moved to the use almost exclusively of interviews patterned after the work of Jean Piaget (Pines, et al., 1978), but then we were faced with numerous audiotapes or typed transcripts of these tapes. It was exceedingly difficult to analyze these records and find patterns or regularities that could help us understand how and why children were learning or failing to learn the new subject matter. Working from Ausubel's (1963; 1968) theory of meaningful learning, we decided to examine interview transcripts for concept words and propositions given by the students, for these would indicate prior knowledge and post-instruction knowledge. After trying several ways to organize the concept words and propositions, our research group came up with the idea of *concept mapping*. At first we tried to strip away all text except for concept labels, and to show how these are related in a hierarchical structure, but without linking words. Figure 3.7 is an example from an early study by Moreira (1977). While the relationships may be obvious to one who understands these concepts, there is an obvious lack of clarity for most people. We soon insisted on inclusion of linking words to express the propositional meanings in the clearest possible manner. However, Moreira did find that her concept maps significantly improved a student's ability to critique novels.

We soon found that concept maps could help students who were doing poorly in reading and in school in general. When one sixth-grade boy we worked with who was in a remedial reading program began making concept maps he soon moved to leading his class in understanding their readings using his concept maps. His self-image soared and his teachers praised his achievement. Figure 3.8 shows the first concept map made by this student.

We found that concept maps were a good way to help a teacher organize

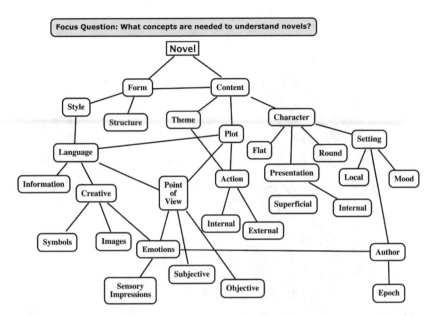

Figure 3.7 An example of an early concept map made without linking words. We soon insisted on the use of linking words to express concisely the relationship between the concepts and the propositional meanings expressed in the map. Reproduced with permission, Moreira, 1977, p. 100.

knowledge for instruction, and a good way for students to find the key concepts and principles in lectures, readings or other instructional material (cf. Novak, 1991). Moreover, as students gained skill and experience in constructing concept maps, they began to report that they were "learning how to learn." They were becoming better at *meaningful* learning and found they could reduce or eliminate the need for rote learning. Concept maps were helping to *empower* them as learners. They also help to empower the teacher, for they are useful as a tool for teachers to negotiate meanings about knowledge with students, and also to design better instruction.

More recently, we have begun to use concept maps in a variety of corporate settings. For example, Figure 3.9 shows a concept map of the structure of a New York company illustrating internal communication problems. With maps such as this, teams can identify problems and move toward more creative solutions. In essentially every company we have worked with, we find the same problems prevail as described by Crosby (1992): management of organizations don't understand the organization (pp. 5–6). Every organization I have worked with has found profit in trying to develop a concept map of the organization that is structured to show what the organization is all about. How can one engage in creative management when he or she doesn't comprehend the nature and purpose of the organization? I shall return to this issue in later chapters.

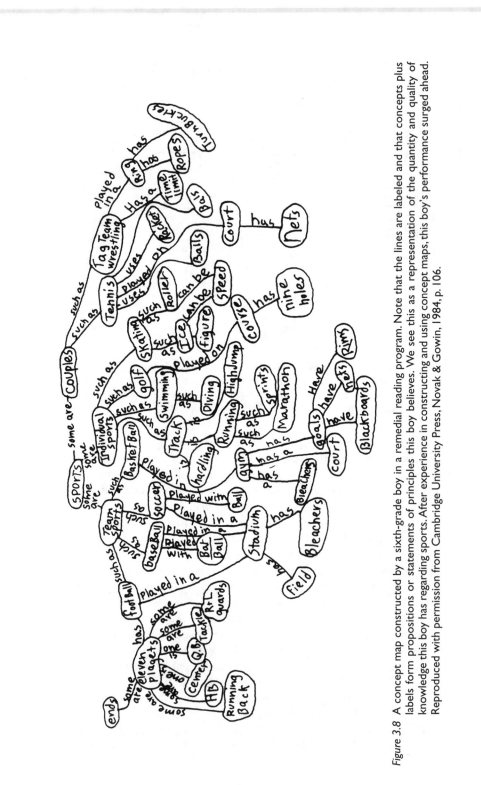

Figure 3.8 A concept map constructed by a sixth-grade boy in a remedial reading program. Note that the lines are labeled and that concepts plus labels form propositions or statements of principles this boy believes. We see this as a representation of the quantity and quality of knowledge this boy has regarding sports. After experience in constructing and using concept maps, this boy's performance surged ahead. Reproduced with permission from Cambridge University Press, Novak & Gowin, 1984, p. 106.

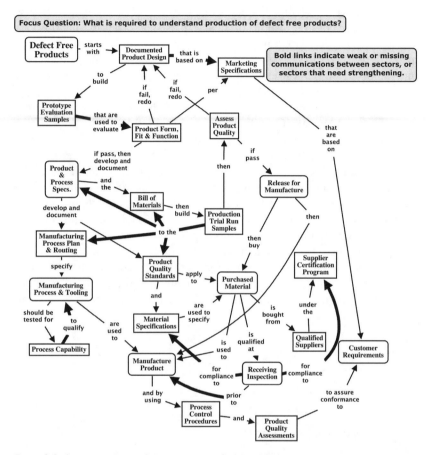

Focus Question: What is required to understand production of defect free products?

Figure 3.9 A concept map of the structure of a New York company illustrating internal communication problems dealing with product quality. Bold lines indicate where improvements are needed.

Our research, and more recent studies by many others in countries all over the world, has shown that young children learn quickly how to make good concept maps, whereas secondary school or university students often have difficulty, partly as a result of years of habit with rote learning (Novak & Wandersee, 1990). We have also found that to benefit from concept maps presented in text or lectures, learners needed to construct their own maps and learn this method of organizing their own knowledge. Our work and other studies led to the publication of *Learning How to Learn* (Novak & Gowin, 1984), now translated into Spanish, Italian, Chinese, Thai, and Japanese, Portuguese, Arabic, and Finnish. Concept maps will play a key role as a tool to represent knowledge held by a learner, and also the structure of knowledge in any subject matter domain. Begin to build your skill by starting now to make your own concept maps for this book or for other subjects you are learning. Appendix I provides suggestions on how to make good concept maps. A variety of computer software is now available to assist in construction of concept maps. Figure 3.10 shows a concept map for key ideas about concept maps. For more information on how to construct good concept maps see *Learning How to Learn* (Novak and Gowin, 1984).

Since the publication of the first edition of this book, The Florida Institute for Human and Machine Cognition in Pensacola, Florida has developed some exceptional software, CmapTools, for producing concept maps. Designed explicitly for construction of concept maps, this software is very user-friendly, and most children can learn to use this software in an hour or two. This software also has a unique patented feature that allows easy attachment of any digital resource to individual concepts linking words, and these resources become part of the stored file for the concept map and can be retrieved by simply clicking on an icon on a concept and selecting the desired resource. Figure 3.11 shows a concept map about the Kuna Indians that children in Panama created as part of a project designed to bring new teaching and learning strategies, including the use of computers and the Internet, to every fourth-, fifth-, and sixth-grade classroom. The inserts on the concept map

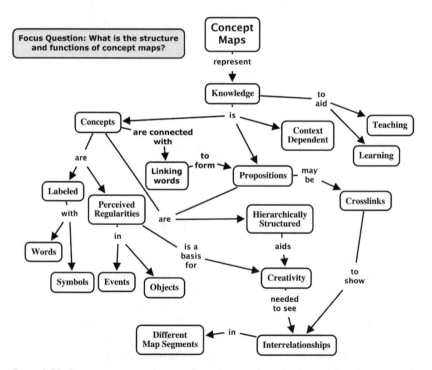

Figure 3.10 A concept map showing key ideas and principles exhibited in a good concept map.

Figure 3.11 A concept map about the Kuna Indians showing some resources attached that can be accessed by clicking on icons. Made using CmapTools by fifth-grade children in Panama.

show some resources that can be accessed by clicking on icons on the map. More will be said about this and other projects using CmapTools in later sections. The reader is invited to download this free software at: http://cmap.ihmc.us and try using it to build concept maps.

Meaningful Learning is Empowering

Knowledge that we have learned meaningfully, that we have constructed from a union of our actions, feelings, and thought, is knowledge we control. The nature of consciousness is itself an area of inquiry (Hofstadter, 2007), but I will not explore this subject. Think of any domain of knowledge where you can relate what you know to how that knowledge operates to make sense out of experience in that domain and you have an example of knowledge you have learned meaningfully. This is knowledge you control and with which you feel a sense of ownership and power. Then think of a domain of knowledge that you learned mostly by rote. By contrast, this will be knowledge that you have largely forgotten, or for which you see little relationship to experience and over which you feel little sense of power or control. Unfortunately, so much of school learning for most people has been essentially by rote, and this *disempowerment* has made most of us fearful of learning in one or more fields like, science, history, mathematics, music, or athletics. The goal of this book is to provide a theory that can guide us to develop educational experiences that are meaningful, that facilitate meaningful learning and reduce the need for rote learning. *Education should lead to a constructive change in a person's ability to cope with experience;* this will be the objective this book will address. Too many students at the school and tertiary level are swimming in a sea of meaninglessness when they should be helped to grasp the meanings of what they are studying and experience the satisfaction and motivation that come with this.

Paulo Freire, in his work with illiterate adult peasants in Latin countries, developed a pedagogical strategy beginning instruction in language with a few words that had important meaning in the day-to-day lives of the people. These *generative* words, as he called them, could then be used as language building blocks and gradually the people gained control over reading and writing their own language. The acquisition of literacy led to both increased self-confidence and increased political power. Freire's work to *empower* the peasants led to his imprisonment in Brazil and later exile. Freire's teachings and writings (see, for example, *The Politics of Education*, 1985) have gained worldwide recognition not only for their power in helping adults acquire literacy, but for their general value for empowerment of people.

Most education, Freire asserts, assumes the person is an "empty vessel" to be filled with information (Figure 3.12). The reality is much more complex as shown in Figure 3.5. This "banking" concept of education proceeds by rote memorization of material that has little or no relevance nor meaning for the learner. It leads to *domestication* (Freire's term), which makes the learner always

Figure 3.12 Much teaching proceeds as if our mind were an empty vessel that needs to be filled with information.

dependent on the master for new learning or decision making. By contrast, working with "generative words" that have significance and meaning in the life of the learner leads to the learner's control over the acquisition and use of new knowledge. This *empowers* the learner to become autonomous and in charge of his or her destiny. Needless to say, education for empowerment is often a risky business. It also tends to threaten the status quo. Too often in schools and other organizations, people and/or ideas that are innovative are threatening, resulting in a coalescence of forces to quiet or remove the threat.

Organizational Learning

At the present time, most education takes place in some organizational setting. In schools, churches, corporations, and other groups, many of the constraints on effective learning are imposed by the structure and functioning of the organization. Organizations are an important aspect of the *context* of education, as well as exerting influence on what is learned, how it is learned, and how it is evaluated. Senge (1990), focusing on business organizations, observes that organizations do not know how to learn, and others have shown similar limitations in organizational learning that, in turn, constrain the learning of individuals operating in these organizations. The theory, ideas, and tools put forward in this book will address applications to organizations as well as to individuals.

A major problem faced by organizations is how to deal with information, especially information acquired by staff in the course of their years of experience in the organization. While this is a problem in school settings, it is especially critical in corporate settings where knowledge has become more important than the traditional resources of land, labor, and capital. As Nonaka and Takeuchi (1995) observe:

> Knowledge is created only by individuals. An organization cannot create knowledge on its own without individuals. It is, therefore, very important for the organization to support and stimulate the knowledge-creating activities of individuals or to provide the appropriate contexts for them. Organizational knowledge creation should be understood as a process that "organizationally" amplifies the knowledge created by individuals and crystallizes it at the group level through dialogue, discussion, experience sharing, or observation. (p. 239)

While the knowledge created by an organization is an important asset, Nonaka and Toyama (2007) point out the importance of "knowledge to create knowledge, such as the organizational capability to innovate. Although current views on knowledge assets tend to focus on the former because they are easier to measure and deal with, it is the latter that need more attention because they are the source of new knowledge to be created, and therefore a source of future value of the firm" (p. 25). In Ichijo and Nonaka (2007, eds.) the importance of knowledge creation is stressed repeatedly. This book will deal extensively with understanding the nature of knowledge and knowledge creation.

In recent years some of my colleagues and I have put a good deal of time into working with corporations to help them become more effective at capturing, storing, sharing, and creating new knowledge. This work will be discussed throughout the book, showing how the ideas that empower learners are also the ideas that are need to empower organizations.

Chapter 4

The Construction of New Meanings

The Meaning of *Meaning*

From infancy onward, healthy human experience is a constant search for meaning. The one- or two-year-old child begins to recognize that older people use sounds to represent things or events and soon the powerful hereditary potential begins to be expressed as "mama," "dada," "doggie," and so on. Human beings have the innate capacity to do something no other animal species is capable of doing, albeit there is some debate on this (Gazzaniga, 2008). They can recognize and use language labels (or sign language) to represent regularities in events or objects. It is this incredible ability that distinguishes *Homo sapiens* from all other species of animals. The marvels of change in living things over the eons of time have somehow led in the last 50 millennia to an animal species that has this unique language capability. *Humanness* implies this capacity, and it also implies a capacity to discern these regularities with *feelings*. Humans think, feel, and act. Every experience they have involves thinking, feeling, and acting. This is as self-evident as the sun rising in the east and setting in the west. What is not obvious is why and how humans construct their *meanings* for events or objects.

The *meaning* of an event or object we observe depends upon what we already know about that kind of event or object. School, work, joy, and fear are labels for regularities in experience, but their meanings may be radically different depending on a person's experience. Meaning to a person is always a function of how he or she has experienced the combination of thinking, feeling, and acting throughout a lifetime of experiences. How humans *choose* to act depends on how they think *and* feel about an object or event to which they relate. School, work, joy, and fear involve experiences that can lead to radically different meanings for children growing up in radically different environments. It is evident that the *context* of experience has an important impact on the *meaning* of an experience. Here we see the important interaction of the learner and the context of the learning.

From birth onward, each human being creates his or her own meanings. Each of us has had a unique sequence of experiences, hence each of us has constructed our own idiosyncratic meanings. However, there is sufficient commonality in our meanings that we can use common language labels to share, compare, and modify meanings. Of course, the more disparate the sequences of experiences of individuals, the more difficulty they experience in sharing meanings. This is the root source of racial, ethnic, cultural, religious, geographic, and other barriers we experience in societies. This will be discussed further in Chapter 8.

Some of the key concepts associated with the acquisition of meanings will be presented, and I shall move to discussion of Ausubel's (1963; 1968) theory of meaningful learning. A few of the key concepts in his theory are shown in Figure 4.1.

Building Blocks of Meaningful Learning

Concept Learning and Representational Learning

We have defined concept as: a perceived regularity or pattern in events or objects, or records of events or objects, designated by a label. One of the issues in the psychology of concept learning has been which comes first, the perception of the regularity or the acquisition of the label? Piaget in his numerous writings argued that the perception of the regularity must come first, and this

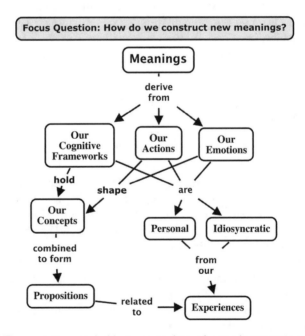

Figure 4.1 The meanings we hold are a product of our idiosyncratic sequence of experiences and hence vary, at least to some degree, among all people.

was dependent upon the "cognitive developmental stage" of the learner. Vygotsky (1962), on the other hand, held that the availability of a label for a concept can be helpful in acquisition of the concept. For example, if we suggest to a child that dogs, cats, and lions are all *carnivores*, the child may inquire further as to what other animals are or are not carnivores, thus accelerating acquisition of the concept carnivore. Learning the definition of a word is essentially *representational* learning. On the other hand learning what the word means, the regularity or pattern that a word or symbol stands for, is *concept* learning. While many people may know the word carnivore, they may never acquire a deeper meaning or *conceptual* understanding of this concept label. Language development is highly correlated with brain growth between the ages of 0 and 7 years (Sakal, 2005), but later development is primarily a function of the quality of education experienced.

Macnamara (1982) sees in his studies of how children acquire "names for things" that either the perception of a regularity or the name (word) for a regularity may come first, but facility in proper use of the word requires that both the word label and its associated meaning be integrated. Since meaning is always context-dependent, the *meanings* of a concept label will always have some idiosyncratic elements, for no two people experience an identical sequence of events (contexts) in which a given concept label is applied. Whorf (1956) was one of the first and most prominent researchers to recognize that the cultural context in which a person lives shapes the meaning of that person's concepts.

Representational Learning

As noted above, this is a form of meaningful learning where the learner recognizes a word, sign, or symbol as a label for a specific object or event or category of events or objects. Proper nouns are learned through representational learning (e.g., *Fido* is our dog) Representational learning may precede concept learning, where a label is learned before the *generic* attributes or regularities in events or objects are recognized (Ausubel, 1968). Once a child learns that all *dogs* have certain common characteristics, he or she has acquired the *concept dog*. Similarly, children may recognize similarities between dogs, cats, lions, and tigers long before they learn the word *carnivore* to label or represent this group of flesh-eating animals. Thus *concept* learning may occur before *representational* learning.

In learning foreign languages, we may learn synonyms for English words through representational learning but the subtle connotative meanings for the foreign language words may be acquired much later. Learning the vocabulary used in a new field of study frequently involves much representational learning, but the full *conceptual* meaning of technical vocabulary may take years, and for some students little more than representational meaning may be achieved. When definitions for vocabulary words are learned by rote, representational learning does not automatically advance to conceptual learning. However, representational learning may provide language labels that may serve to facilitate concept learning (Vygotsky, 1962).

Unfortunately, much school learning that should be *concept* learning is little more than representational learning for many students. They learn definitions for concepts, but they do not acquire the true *meanings* for the concepts. For example, many biology students learn that a cell "is the basic unit of structure of living things," but they really cannot explain what that definition means in ways that make sense to them. They have not acquired the *concept cell*. All of us have done this at times, and often tests do not require us to have more than definitions for labels for concepts, and certainly not a deep meaning of the concepts *per se*. We will look further at this issue in Chapter 9.

Young children are very competent at learning new concepts. I recall when two of my children were under three, they both referred to a thing adults call umbrellas as *underbrellas*. I'm not sure if it was because it was easier for them to pronounce this word that they chose to use it or if it was because the word *made sense* as a concept label. After all, people do walk and stand under umbrellas.

It is important for teachers and administrators to remember that they live in a culture in some ways significantly different from their students or subordinates. Therefore, the same word can have significantly different meanings for each person. This is why we emphasize the constant need to *negotiate meanings* between teacher and learner (refer to Figure 2.3). The problem is confounded further in that almost every word in the English language (or any language) serves as a label for two or more concepts. For example, we may use the word "red" to refer to a color, high temperature (as in red hot), a political position, and numerous other regularities in events or objects. Many times a student will fail to understand a teacher because the teacher is using one or more words that are being identified by a student as labels for concepts other than those the teacher intends to convey. Technical vocabulary frequently contains many words that are applied to common concepts, sometimes totally unrelated to the technical concept meanings.

Situativity

The fact that what we learn is influenced by the context in which the learning takes place has been much more actively researched in the past twenty years. This context-dependency for learning, and for the application of what we learn, has been referred to as *situativity*, and there is now quite a literature on this subject. Greeno (1998) has published an excellent review of various issues associated with situativity. As he points out:

> All teaching and learning are situated; the question is what their situated character is. At the same time, by focusing attention on the practices of

learning, knowing, and reasoning in which students participate, many educators have become committed to developing learning environments in which students learn how to participate in practices of reasoning and understanding that go beyond learning computational procedures or acquiring cognitive structures. (p. 19)

The challenge is how to optimize the learning environments to effect the highest levels of meaningful learning, and there are no easy answers. In fact, this is essentially what this whole book is about. Helping us deal with this complexity is, I believe, one of the reasons a comprehensive theory of education is needed.

One reason we are enthusiastic about concept mapping as an instructional and evaluation tool is that concept maps can be enormously useful to teachers, managers, administrators, and learners to move toward sharing the same *concept meanings* for the words or symbols presented. They can also be helpful to move the learner from mere representational meaning to richer conceptual meaning. Concept maps show not a simple definition of a concept but rather an integrated set of propositions that show how the meaning of that concept is related to other concepts in the particular domain of knowledge. Even with relatively sophisticated learners, concept maps can help to share meanings of concepts and to facilitate creation of new knowledge. We found this to be the case with a research group studying plant root growth at Cornell University. Figure 4.2 shows an example of a "global map" created by the group to facilitate their discussions and research. Even with highly educated specialists in a knowledge domain, it is common for individuals to find it difficult to share meanings about concepts used in that domain. Concept maps are proving helpful in research settings both for academic and corporate groups.

Propositional Learning

Propositions are two or more words combined to form a statement about an event, object, or idea. Propositions can be valid (e.g., the sky appears blue), invalid (e.g., Paris is the capital of England) or nonsensical (e.g., the door looked). *Propositions are the principal units that make up meaning.* We can liken a concept to an atom and a proposition to a molecule. There are only 100 or so elements in the universe, but there are an infinite variety of molecules that make up an infinite variety of substances. In an analogous way, there are about one million words in the English language, but they can be combined to form an infinite variety of propositions. Poets, novelists, and other writers will never exhaust the possibilities for creating new works.

The meaning we acquire for a given concept is formed from the composite of propositions we know that contain that concept. The richness of meaning we have for a concept increases exponentially with the number of valid propositions we learn that relate that concept to other concepts. This is one reason

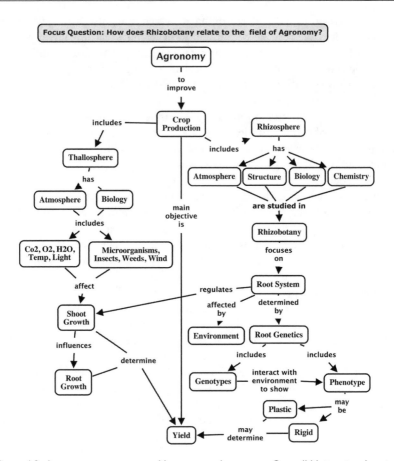

Figure 4.2 A concept map prepared by a research group at Cornell University showing key concepts and principles guiding the research program in agronomy and plant root studies.

why we represent learning on a continuum (see Figure 3.1), where rote learning may be no more than verbatim memorization of a concept definition, whereas meaningful learning can involve relating new concepts through valid propositions for a person's lifetime. Refer to Figure 4.2 and consider how the propositions shown here may enrich your meaning for the concept "root." Concept maps are a tool for representing some of the concept-propositional or meaning frameworks a person has for a given concept or set of concepts. If a person could draw all possible concept maps in which a given concept is related to other concepts, for all possible contexts, we would have a total representation of the *meaning* the concept has for that person. This is obviously impossible. As a matter of fact, none of us knows the full potential meaning for concepts we have, since a new context or a new related proposition could yield meanings we had never thought about before. In addition, the feelings we experienced when we were learning a given concept place an affective valence on the concept and this can be considered a part of the idiosyncratic nature of concept meanings. Virtually everyone who prepares a concept map for some domain of knowledge they possess discovers that they "knew" propositions they had never thought about before, and also that some of their concepts have much more ambiguous meanings than they recognized before. In fact, the latter experience is very common. For both teachers and learners, the construction of concept maps can be very revealing of knowledge frameworks they possess. Figure 4.3 shows a concept map presenting some of the ideas discussed above.

Concept Formation and Concept Assimilation

Concept learning occurs in two ways: *concept formation,* and *concept assimilation.* By age 30 months, most children have recognized and accurately learned to label some 200–300 regularities or patterns with word labels (see Macnamara, 1982.) In the young child, this recognition of regularities and use of language labels to designate these regularities is a kind of learning Ausubel calls *concept formation.* The child is *discovering* through trial and error the language labels older persons use to label the regularities the child recognizes in the surroundings. This is an incredible *learning* feat that only humans can

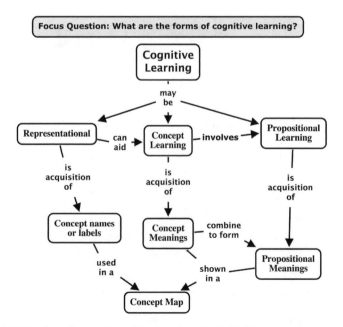

Figure 4.3 The three forms of cognitive learning, all of which interact.

perform, and all non brain-damaged children do it successfully by age three! The child is constructing meanings for words, but simultaneously constructing concepts. There is, in my view, no difference in the process the child uses to learn names for things or events than that which adults use to construct new concepts. Both are fundamentally meaningful learning processes. It is part of the genetic capacity of every normal human being to construct their own idiosyncratic concept meanings from regularities observed in events or objects. Older learners and more sophisticated learners (such as researchers) also construct concepts from records of events or objects. And concept meanings grow as concept labels are linked to one another to form propositions or statements about events and/or objects. These ideas are shown in Figure 4.4.

Ausubel (1968, pp. 524–525) distinguishes between *primary concepts* and *secondary concepts*. Primary concepts are formed by young children by directly observing objects or events and recognizing regularity in these in the hypothesis testing phase of concept formation, and subsequent incorporation of concepts into cognitive structure. Dog, mom, growing, and eating are examples of primary concepts formed by young children. As the child builds cognitive structure he or she can acquire secondary concepts by the process of *concept assimilation*. Here concepts and propositions in the child's cognitive structure are used to acquire new concept meanings, including concepts that have no visible exemplars such as molecule, love, and history. New concepts

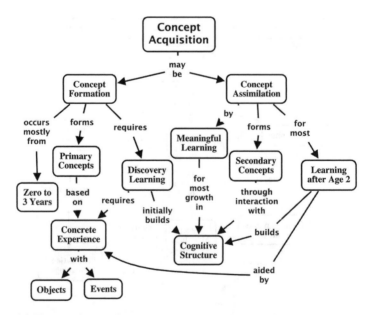

Figure 4.4 The two forms of concept acquisition and their relationship to experience and cognitive structure.

are acquired by using spoken or written words and propositions that already have meaning for the learner. By school age almost all concept learning is concept assimilation.

Concept meanings grow as concept labels are linked to one another to form propositions. New concepts can be acquired by *concept formation* or by *concept assimilation* where the *meanings* for new concept labels are acquired when these labels are associated with propositions containing already known concepts. When we use a dictionary to acquire the meaning of an unfamiliar concept label (word), we are engaged in at least the first stage of concept assimilation. Unfortunately, sometimes the synonyms or definition given are not familiar and we cannot begin to grasp the meaning of the new concept (word) from the dictionary. Even if the synonyms or definitions are familiar, however, we have only the first beginning of developing a full, functional meaning for the concept. Some concepts, such as evolution, bureaucracy, or capitalism, may undergo growth and changes in meaning over our lifetime. Concept assimilation for most significant concepts is a process of meaning building that is never finished. After age three, however, it is the process by which most new concept learning occurs (see Figure 4.5). Schooling, when it is effective, can markedly accelerate concept assimilation.

When my grandson was five years old, he asked me at lunchtime one day, "Grandpa, what's annoy?" Joseph has a sister who is six years older, so you can

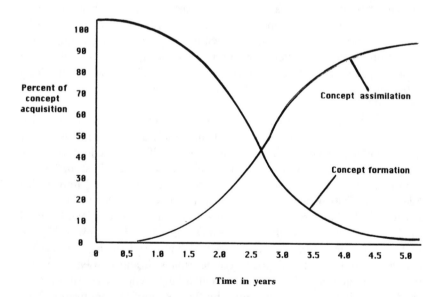

Figure 4.5 Early concept learning by infants is totally by the process of *concept formation*, where the child builds through discovery of primary concepts that permit later learning by *concept assimilation*. By school age, almost all concept learning is by concept assimilation.

easily imagine a context where he heard the word "annoy." Trying to use concepts and propositions I thought might have meaning for Joseph, I explained that something that bothers you or something unpleasant being done to you is annoying, along with several other examples. Before I finished, it seemed evident that Joseph was no longer paying attention to me, and I thought my attempt to help him assimilate the meaning of "annoy" probably failed. The next day we were boating, and Joseph fell asleep with his life-jacket on. When we got to the shore, I laid him down on a hammock to let him continue sleeping. After 15 minutes or so, he got up and walked over to me tugging on the life-jacket and said, "Grandpa, take this thing off. It's annoying me." Not only had he assimilated the meaning of "annoy," he even got the verb tense correct! And from that day on, Joseph evidenced that the meaning for this concept had been assimilated and was a thoroughly functional part of his cognitive structure.

More recently, Brown and others have recognized the constraints that the context of learning places on concept development, describing what they call *situated cognition* (Brown, Collins & Duguid, 1989; Greeno, 1998). They argue that "knowledge is situated, being in part a product of activity, context, and culture in which it is developed and used" (p. 32). My children's development of the concept of *underbrella* was a clear case of situated cognition. The word made sense in terms of the context in which they used it. In widely differing cultures or contexts, the same word may have substantially different meanings or connotations, sometimes leading to embarrassment of either speaker or listener. Using English synonyms for foreign words (or vice versa) can be equally embarrassing at times. Even within English-speaking cultures, the same words may have different meanings. I recall my first experience in an Australian shop when the clerk asked, "Are you right?" She was not inquiring about my health. She meant what American clerks mean when they say, "May I help you?"

Young children can be enormously persistent in pursuing meanings for concepts and propositions. My wife, Joan, recalls an experience with our granddaughter, Rachel, when she was two-and-a-half years old. Joan said, "We are going to the grocery store to get some groceries." Rachel asked, "Why?" Joan replied, "Because we need to get some more food to eat." And Rachel asked, "Why?" Joan replied, "We need to eat to stay healthy and to grow." Rachel asked, "Can't we grow without eating?" Joan replied, "No, we need food to grow." Rachel asked, "If we keep eating, will we keep growing?" Joan replied, "To some extent." Rachel asked, "Why?". And so the conversation continued on and on, until Joan became exhausted and refused to answer more "why?" questions. Now to some extent asking "Why?" is a great way for a child to get an adult's attention, and this, too, is significant motivation. Any reader that has been around two- or three-year-olds recently probably has had a similar experience. But asking "Why?" is also a great way for a child to acquire meanings for new concepts and propositions. So most parents and grandparents have developed a pretty high level of tolerance for the persistent Why? questions from their young children.

Development of Cognitive Frameworks

At the time of birth, the billions of neurons of the human brain have already been formed. Growth of associated glial cells and formation of myelin around neurons will result in continuing growth in brain size and weight, with most growth occurring between birth and age two, and almost no brain growth occurring after age seven. Learning and associated cognitive development begins at birth and continues until senescence or death. There have been speculations on the influence of listening to classical music or other environmental influences on a child's cognitive development prior to birth, but no valid evidence exists to support such speculations. Soon after birth, however, cognitive development begins and by age fifteen months, most children begin to use language to express their ideas. Again, I refer to Macnamara (1982) and Bloom (2000) who have provided a careful description of research on language acquisition.

Piaget's Developmental Theory

The best known studies on cognitive development are those done by the Swiss scientist, Jean Piaget. Piaget's Ph.D degree dealt with the phylogeny of mollusks (snail and clam types), but after working with Binet on developing "intelligence tests," Piaget turned most of his energy to the study of cognitive development in children. Piaget's theory deals with the development of cognitive *operational* capacities, which are generic in character and are presumed to apply in a wide variety of subject matter. Piaget (1926) proposed that children undergo four major developmental stages. The first he called the *sensory-motor* stage (ages zero to two years) during which time most of the child's development is primarily physical. During the sensory-motor stage, according to Piaget, the child comes to recognize, among other things, that objects do not disappear when they are moved out of sight. This cognitive capacity to recognize the permanence of objects is a key characteristic of the end of this Piagetian stage.

During the age period two to seven, children move through what Piaget called the *preoperational stage.* This stage is characterized by the child's egocentric view of objects and events in the world and their inability to *decenter*, that is to see an object or an event from a perspective other than their own. For example, when a liquid is poured from a short, wide container into a tall, narrow container, the child will frequently say that the tall container contains *more* liquid. The child fails to *decenter* from the height dimension and thus erroneously concludes that the tall container holds more liquid.

Piaget's third developmental stage occurs between the ages of seven to eleven. In this *concrete operations* stage, the child can decenter and recognize, for example, that the taller vessel is also narrower and that no liquid was lost in the transfer from the short, wide container. However, these cognitive operations require concrete, visible props and the child cannot reason *hypothetically* to recognize that *any* form of a container will not alter the amount of substance when it is transferred from one container to another.

The final cognitive developmental stage Piaget describes is the *formal operational* stage, roughly from age eleven or twelve onward. In this stage the child (or adult) can make inferences or predictions in hypothetical cases as well as for concrete events or objects observed. For example, a child could predict that a given amount of liquid or sand poured into cylinders of varying diameters will be higher or lower in a ratio inversely proportional to the diameter of the cylinder. Formal operational subjects can "control variables" and predict that a pendulum bob on a long string will move back and forth more slowly than a bob on a short string and that the weight of the bob makes no difference.

Piaget's developmental theory has had enormous popularity in educational circles, especially after the early 1960s when his work was "rediscovered" (Ripple & Rockcastle, 1964). Hundreds of researchers came forth with studies that showed, in general, that older subjects were more successful at various tasks than younger subjects. Explicit curricular recommendations were made suggesting inclusion or exclusion of specific instructional events based on the cognitive operational capacity presumably required for understanding the events (see, for example, Shayer & Adey, 1981).

My own studies, and my interpretation of other studies, led to a lack of enthusiasm for Piaget's developmental stage theory at best. For example, consider the data shown in Figures 4.6. This figure makes it very difficult to argue that cognitive development as indicated by Piagetian tasks follows the scheme proposed by Piaget. If most 12-year-olds (seventh grade) are in the "concrete operational stage" and most 17-year-olds (12th grade) should be formal operational, why do we get the results shown in Figure 4.6? It has appeared to me much more valid and more parsimonious[1] to interpret these kinds of data through Ausubel's assimilation theory of learning and development (Novak, 1977b). Considering cognitive development more broadly, my view is that Vygotsky's (1962; 1986) ideas are much more powerful for educators than those of Piaget. Although Piaget and Vygotsky were born in the same year (1896), Vygotsky died in 1934 and Piaget continued to be active in research and writing until his death in 1980. Many of Vygotsky's writings were available only in Russian and inaccessible to most scholars in the West. More recently, new applications of his work have appeared (Moll, 1990). His emphasis on the special role that school learning can play, in contrast to Piaget, was evidenced in our own research.

---

1 For a discussion of parsimony, see pp. 108–9.

Figure 4.6 Percentage of seventh-grade students and twelfth-grade students performing correctly on eight different Piagetian conservation tasks. Notice that there is essentially no difference in performance between seventh-grade and senior high school students on the various Piagetian "conservation concept tasks." From Nordland, et al., 1974. Reproduced with permission from Science Education, Wiley.

Our hypothesis is the notion that although learning is directly related to the course of child development, the two are never accomplished in equal measure or in parallel. Development in children never follows school learning the way a shadow follows the objects that cast it. In actuality there are highly complex dynamic relations between developmental learning and processes that cannot be encompassed by an unchanging hypothetical formulation. (Vygotsky, in Kozulin, 1990, p. 91)

It is this complex interplay between developing cognitive structure and school learning that has been the focus of our research programs for the past five decades. Since the publication of Ausubel's (1963) *The Psychology of Meaningful Verbal Learning,* which placed emphasis on the role of concept and propositional learning in schools, we have found more power and parsimony in his ideas than in those of Piaget and his followers. While other learning theorists, such as Anderson (1983; 1990; 2000) and Sternberg (1986; 2008) may be more popular currently, I still find greater power and relevance in Ausubel's (1963; 1968) ideas for understanding educational issues and applications. Wittrock (1974), a former student of Ausubel's, has put forth a "generative theory" of learning, but this builds heavily on Ausubel's ideas, with some changes in terminology. Arguments for the relevance and power of Ausubelian ideas will be developed throughout this book.

Many teachers and other school people leaped to embrace Piagetian developmental stages as a way to explain why so many students fail to learn and retain usable ideas taught in school. The inadequacy of the student's developmental readiness, both in individual cases and in groups, has been a convenient scapegoat for what in many cases could be better explained as inadequate prior preparation or inappropriate instruction. Numerous researchers are now showing the power of children's thinking in language development (Macnamara, 1982), philosophy (Matthews, 1980, 1984), science (Chi, 1983) and many other areas (Donaldson, 1978; Carey, 1985; Novak & Musonda, 1991; Gelman, 1999). Based on the collective body of evidence, it seems reasonable to conclude that by age three years, all normal children can think hypothetically and deductively ("formal operationally," in Piaget's terms) *in domains where they have acquired adequate conceptual/propositional frameworks.* Obviously, older children and adults in general possess much richer and more varied knowledge structures than most young children, so there are *cognitive developmental* differences between young children and older children or adults. Nevertheless, the educative potential of even young children is probably enormously greater than we observe under current educational practices. Bloom (1968; 1976; 1981) has been a strong proponent of the idea that students of all ages can learn much more than traditional school practices achieve. His efforts to help students learn for *mastery* of subject matter at any grade level place central importance on instructional strategies to improve school learning. I will return to issues of instructional design in later chapters.

Flavell (1985), who has done much to help bring clarity and understanding of Piaget's monumental work to English readers, provided a cogent statement on the status of Piaget's work:

> It can be argued, with Piaget, that the cognitive systems of infants are indeed fundamentally and qualitatively different from those of older humans. Although Piaget also believed that the cognitive systems of early-childhood, middle-childhood, and adolescent-adult thinkers are likewise qualitatively different from one another, there is growing doubt in the field that these differences, too, are that radical and stage-like. Older minds may appear to be more qualitatively different from younger ones than they really are. One reason for this is that older minds have accumulated much more organized knowledge, or expertise, in many more knowledge domains than younger ones have, and we now know a number of specific ways that the possession of expertise in a domain [of knowledge] can dramatically improve the quality of one's cognitive functioning within that domain. We would hesitate to say that older minds truly

are qualitatively different from younger ones—constitute distinct and different cognitive systems—if disparities in domain-specific expertise were largely responsible for the appearance of qualitative difference. For one thing, the older mind might look almost as immature as the younger one when operating in domains in which it, too, is an utter novice. More generally, both child and adult minds can vary considerably over domains and occasions in the quality of their cognitive performance. At present, therefore, it is difficult to identify really clear-cut, stage-like "cognitive metamorphoses" during the childhood and adolescent years. It is far easier, instead, to defend and document the existence of very important and substantial "developmental trends" during these years. (Flavell, 1985, p. 114)

It should be recognized that although Piaget may have been "on the wrong track" with his idea of cognitive developmental stages, his monumental studies over six decades have done much to advance our understanding of how children's minds develop and the necessity for each child to construct her or his own conceptual meanings from experience. We owe much to Piaget for his continuing research efforts to understand how students construct meanings, at a time when such research was shunned or ridiculed in much of North America. Partly for this reason, his work was too long ignored in North America. Application of Piaget's ideas to education laid some of the ground-work for what became in the 1970s a revolutionary change in the study of education, and the rise of what we now call *constructivism*, to be discussed later.

Throughout this book, I will deal with some of the cognitive developmental principles and trends and show how they relate to education and to knowledge creation. Human development involves physical, emotional and cognitive changes, and these in turn are influenced importantly by how we construct new meanings. Therefore, I shall move next to an extensive discussion of Ausubel's learning theory, for I believe this remains the most powerful, most comprehensive theory available to understand better ways for educating.

Chapter 5

Ausubel's [1] Assimilation Learning Theory

When Ausubel's work came to my attention in the early 1960s, the emphasis on the role of concepts in meaningful learning appealed to me; but it took more than three years and six seminars in which Ausubel's work was emphasized before I began to feel comfortable interpreting his theory to others. His work began to make real sense after a five-day conference [2] on concept learning in 1965 at which I had extensive opportunity to talk privately with him. A sabbatical leave during 1965–1966 at Harvard University offered opportunities to study and analyse the work of Jerome Bruner and others. These experiences, and particularly the new interpretations that my students and I were seeing in our research data, led to a growing conviction that Ausubel's learning theory, especially as presented in his 1968 book, was a powerful model of learning to guide education.

David Ausubel first introduced his theory of Meaningful Learning in 1962 under the title, "A Subsumption Theory of Meaningful Verbal Learning and Retention." In 1963, he published *The Psychology of Meaningful Verbal Learning*, elaborating on the ideas presented earlier. Finally in 1968, a more comprehensive view of his ideas was published in *Educational Psychology: A Cognitive View* (Ausubel, 1968). These two books were the primary source of ideas on learning that guided our work in the 1960s and 1970s.

It should be remembered that the late 1930s to the early 1960s when Ausubel was formulating his ideas was also the heyday of behavioral psychology. Not only in the field of psychology in general, but also in educational psychology, behaviorism was the overwhelmingly dominant paradigm, and, along with it, positivistic epistemology was also strongly in control. Positivism and other epistemologies dealing with the nature of knowledge and the nature

---

1 Some of the ideas expressed in this chapter represent my views on Ausubel's theory. The description in this and subsequent chapters more closely follows that in a description of Ausubel's (Ausubel, et al., 1978) assimilation theory of cognitive learning to be found in the second edition of his *Educational Psychology: A Cognitive View.*

2 A report of this conference was published in Herbert J. Klausmeier and Chester W. Harris, *Analysis of Concept Learning* (New York: Academic Press, 1966).

of knowledge creation will be discussed at length in Chapter 6. The key idea in positivistic views is that there is "one true answer" to questions, and these answers will be self-evident if we simply observe and record events carefully. Current ideas see that the nature of questions we ask, the kinds of records we make and especially the ways we interpret these records are dependent upon a whole set of contextual and conceptual factors. The views that Ausubel put forward in the early 1960s were strongly in discord with the prevailing behaviorist ideas and Ausubel experienced considerable difficulty in finding publication outlets in respectable journals of psychology or educational psychology. Recall also that Kuhn's book, *The Structure of Scientific Revolutions*, was published in 1962, and the movement toward newer epistemologies was only in its infancy at the time Ausubel's work emerged.

The prevailing behaviorist dominance not only created a hostile climate for many of Ausubel's ideas, but also helped to prevent wide acceptance of Piagetian ideas, which had been put forth since the 1920s in Geneva, Switzerland. In fact, it could be said that Piaget was not discovered in this country until the mid 1960s (Ripple & Rockcastle, 1964).

Not surprisingly, Ausubel's ideas on learning made slow progress in the 1960s, even though there was a relatively immediate recognition of the importance of his work in some circles and the beginning of a substantial worldwide acceptance of his ideas outside of North America. Remember also behavioral psychology did not succeed in dominating the thinking in most European and Eastern countries.

Our research group first became familiar with Ausubel's work in 1964 when we began careful study of his *Psychology of Meaningful Verbal Learning*. The theory put forward explained many of the difficulties we found in interpreting data we were gathering on student problem solving. Working initially with an information processing model of learning (Novak, 1958), we assumed that problem solving was a function of two independent traits: knowledge stored in the mind, and information processing capability. What we found suggested in Ausubel's theory was that these two processes are confounded in the process of new learning, where integration of new and old knowledge is a function of both the quantity and the quality of cognitive structure organization. This interpretation closely followed the pattern of our research results. Further elaboration of this movement away from information processing models and toward Ausubel's assimilation theory has been presented elsewhere (Novak 1977a).

After moving in 1967 from Purdue University to Cornell University, our research group there proceeded not only in the study of problems associated with science learning but also in the design of new instructional approaches based on assimilation theory. These included the development of an audio-tutorial elementary science program that served as a foundation for many of our research studies with elementary school students. It was from this research dealing with a 12-year longitudinal study of science concept learning that the technique of concept mapping was developed by our research group in 1972 (Novak & Musonda, 1991). Since 1974, much of our research and many of our innovative practices in teaching have involved the utilization of concept mapping in the form that we developed it. There are a number of graphic representations that are called concept maps, but they are not based on Ausubelian psychology and do not have explicit concept-link-concept propositional structure, forming explicit propositions (see Jonassen, et al. 1993; Cañas & Novak, 2008; Novak and Cañas, 2006a).

One strength of Ausubel's theory is that it allows integration of many observations on learning into a single, coherent theory. This coherence is a prime source of difficulty in grasping his theory; each part makes most sense when associations with other parts are understood. But how can one initially grasp the meaning of these associations? It is partly because of this difficulty that we have found a variety of diagrams and concept maps to be valuable. Figure 5.1 shows a concept map of the key concepts and principles (propositions) in Ausubel's theory as I now view his theory, together with some key ideas from epistemology. It is apparent from this figure that his theory is not simple at first glance. However, as one begins to work through the figure, it can be seen that each part of the figure makes sense, and the key problem centers around understanding the "six basic principles" shown in the center-right of

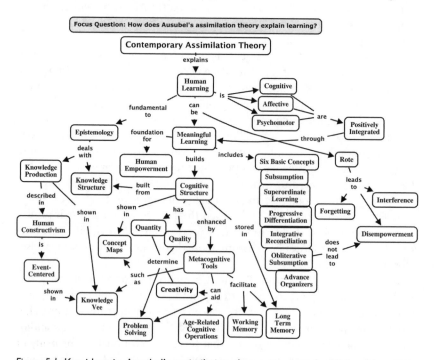

Figure 5.1 Key ideas in Ausubel's assimilation theory integrated with key ideas from epistemology. These ideas will be elaborated further.

this figure. These principles will be discussed below. The reader might be helped by making a copy of this figure as a kind of "road map" as she or he proceeds through this chapter.

Ausubel's theory addresses primarily *cognitive* learning or the acquisition and use of knowledge. *Affective* learning, or that information that is stored in our lower brain centers, results from *internal* signals and interacts with and plays a role in cognitive learning. Ausubel's theory relates to affective learning and we have adopted and extended some of his ideas in our work. Throughout this book I will emphasize the interplay between thinking (cognition) feeling (affect) and acting (motor or psychomotor). Although Ausubel's first doctoral degree was in medicine, and he studied and practiced psychiatry until his retirement in 1994, his theory of learning centers on *cognitive* learning, but it also has important implications for affective and motor learning.

David Ausubel died in 2008, and this book is in part a tribute to his great contributions. He was a rather quiet person, soft-spoken and often reticent in a group. Nevertheless, my wife and I found him to be a very engaging personality and we were often struck by the wide range of subjects on which he was very knowledgeable. Our last meeting with Ausubel and his wife Gloria was in 1989 when we toured upstate New York wineries together. Figure 5.2 shows a photo taken during our tour. Out of appreciation of his friendship and intellectual guidance, I honor his memory.

Figure 5.2 David Ausubel and his wife Gloria on a tour of Upstate New York wineries in 1989. Photo by Novak with permission of Ausubel.

Meaningful Learning; Rote Learning

The central idea in Ausubel's theory is what he describes as *meaningful learning*. To Ausubel, meaningful learning is a process in which new information is related to an existing relevant aspect of an individual's knowledge structure. However, the *learner must choose* to do this. The learner must actively seek a way to integrate the new information with existing relevant information in her or his cognitive structure. The teacher can encourage this choice by using tools such as concept maps. Although we do not know explicitly the biological mechanisms of memory (or the storage of knowledge), we do know that information is stored in different regions of the brain and that many brain cells (perhaps tens of thousands) are involved in the storage of a knowledge unit or proposition. Some of the recent findings on memory mechanisms were cited in Chapter 3. New learning results in further changes in brain cells, but some cells affected during meaningful learning are the same cells that already store information similar to the new information being acquired. In other words, the neural cells or cell assemblies active in storage during meaningful learning are undergoing further modifications and are probably forming synapses or some functional association with new neurons. With continued learning of new information relevant to information already stored, the nature and extent of neural associations also increase. Ausubel contrasts meaningful learning with *rote learning*, where the learner makes no effort to integrate new knowledge with existing relevant knowledge in cognitive structure. These ideas are shown in Figure 5.3.

Although they do not cite Ausubel's earlier work, Marton and Säljö describe what they call *deep learning* in a way similar to Ausubel's meaningful learning, and *surface learning* as similar to Ausubel's rote learning (Marton and Säljö, 1976a; 1976b).

Throughout this book, I use concept maps to represent the meaning structures that form the conceptual/propositional framework of knowledge that I am presenting. It is into our idiosyncratic knowledge frameworks that new knowledge must be *assimilated*. In fact, Ausubel's learning theory is often referred to as his *assimilation theory* of learning. To illustrate the process of

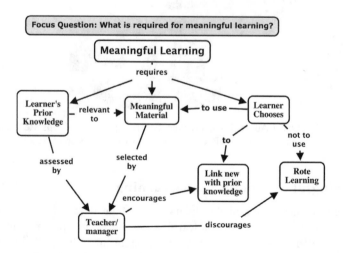

Figure 5.3 The three requirements for meaningful learning.

assimilation using concept maps, consider the knowledge structure of Denny shown in Figure 5.4. Denny was a six-year-old student who drew this concept map to show the meanings he had for the words listed on the left. This was the first concept map Denny had made after some thirty minutes of previous instruction in concept mapping. The list of words was provided on the paper. Incidentally, providing children with a list of concepts that should be familiar to them is a good way to help children begin to learn to do concept mapping.

Notice that Denny's map shows valid meanings for all the concept labels (words) except *vapor*. All of the words on the list are words discussed in Denny's class and the teacher thought these would be familiar to the students. Denny either overlooked the word vapor, did not recognize it, or did not know its *meaning* with enough clarity to "link" it into his concept map. Assuming the latter was the case, Denny could learn the concept of vapor *meaningfully*. First Denny would need to know what *regularity* or *pattern* is represented by the label vapor. He could learn this by *discovery* learning where he gradually came to recognize that water can appear in a variety of forms including an invisible form that makes air humid. This form is sometimes called *vapor*. Discovery learning would involve concept formation (see Figure 4.5) and could be highly meaningful to Denny, but it would take considerable time, even if school experiences were provided to help Denny observe vapor in various contexts. Most school learning proceeds otherwise, usually as *reception* learning where meanings of the new concepts (words) are given verbally and

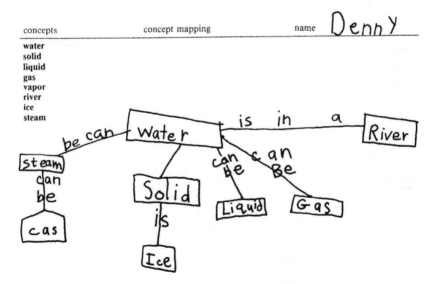

Figure 5.4 A concept map prepared by Denny, a six-year-old student, using the words provided on the left. Denny's class had 30 minutes of prior instruction in concept mapping. From Novak & Gowin, 1984, p. 106. Reproduced with permission, Cambridge University Press.

may result in concept assimilation (see Figure 4.5). For example, a teacher or book could define "vapor: water in the form of an invisible gas." *If* Denny *chose* to learn the concept meaningfully, he would need to relate the meaning of vapor to concepts and propositions he already knows in a substantive, non-arbitrary, non-verbatim manner. This might be illustrated as in Figure 5.5.

Too often children in school choose to learn by *rote*, and in this case the definition of vapor would be learned verbatim and not assimilated substantively and non-arbitrarily into his existing knowledge framework. This is illustrated in Figure 5.6.

Illustrated also in Figure 5.6 is a useful relationship that can exist between rote and meaningful learning. A learner can begin learning a new concept by memorizing a definition of the concept, this being representational learning. However, meaningful learning requires further effort; the learner must choose to relate the concepts and proposition(s) of the definition in some substantive way to what relevant knowledge already exists in the learner's cognitive structure. As all of us know from our own experience, this may take more effort, at least initially. As we build up knowledge frameworks in a given domain, learning the definitions *and* the meanings for concepts becomes easier and easier to do. Moreover, concepts learned meaningfully are retained much longer, some for a lifetime. The three basic requirements for meaningful learning were shown in Figure 5.3. This figure also shows the interplay between three elements essential in any educative event: the learner, teacher, and knowledge or subject matter.

Figure 5.5 Denny's concept map showing a way in which the concept "vapor" might have been incorporated following meaningful learning of this concept.

Figure 5.6 Denny's concept map showing the definition of vapor as learned by rote. The propositions in this definition are *not* related to, nor incorporated into, his prior conceptual framework, and would likely be soon forgotten.

Reception and Discovery Approaches to Learning

An important contribution in Ausubel's writings has been the distinction he emphasized between the rote–meaningful *learning* continuum and the reception–discovery continuum for *instruction*.

After the Russian launch of *Sputnik* in 1957, there was a national outcry that American education was weak and that we were falling behind the Russians. One of the condemnations of school learning was that too much school instruction, and too much of our testing, emphasized nothing more than rote learning. The alternative that became widely promulgated, especially in science and mathematics, was to move *instruction* toward greater emphasis on teaching strategies centered on *discovery learning*, now more commonly called *inquiry* learning. The result was the development of programs where students were provided activities where the answers were not given, and where manipulation of materials or equipment could lead to *discovery* of concepts. Since it is patently obvious that children in school settings could not *discover* the concepts and principles constructed by geniuses in various fields over the past few centuries, it was not surprising that the emphasis on learning by discovery soon led to disenchantment with this approach by teachers and the public. Even under the best of circumstances, and with considerable guidance, only the more able students were demonstrating significant achievement (see, for example, Shulman & Keislar, 1966; Mayer, 2004; Kirschner, et al., 2006).

Instruction emphasizing discovery learning began to disappear in schools, albeit most schools and teachers never embraced this approach.

In spite of a lack of evidence to support extensive use of inquiry learning in classrooms, the programs funded by the US National Science Foundation have been almost exclusively those that utilize inquiry learning approaches. Moreover, the two major organizations dealing with science and mathematics, the National Academy of Science (NAS) and the American Association for the Advancement of Science (AAAS), both place almost exclusive emphasis on the use of inquiry in science and mathematics classrooms in their guidelines for school instruction. AAAS published *Benchmarks for Science Literacy* in 1993 and the NRC published *National Science Education Standards* in 1996; both of these publications asserted that to improve science and mathematics education, schools must move to much greater emphasis on discovery or inquiry learning.

What was needed in the 1960s and 1990s, and what I believe is needed today, is not more emphasis on inquiry learning, but rather more emphasis on *meaningful* learning. Figure 5.7 illustrates the orthogonal relationship between the rote–meaningful *learning* continuum and the reception–discovery continuum for *instruction*. Any instructional strategy can lead to meaningful *or* rote learning. What Ausubel presented in his 1963, *The Psychology of*

Figure 5.7 The rote–meaningful *learning* continuum is distinct from the reception–discovery continuum for *instruction*. Both reception and discovery instruction can lead to rote learning *or* meaningful learning. School learning needs to help students move toward high levels of meaningful learning, especially in reception instruction that is the most common.

Meaningful Verbal Learning, was a psychology of learning that defended the role of reception or expository teaching in schools as necessary and efficient and pointed toward instruction and learning approaches that could move school learning from predominantly rote learning toward predominantly meaningful learning. Not surprisingly, his ideas were never embraced by AAAS or NRC primarily because most of the leadership in these organizations viewed his ideas as reactionary or irrelevant, or they simply did not understand them. Current preoccupation with setting test standards for students and teachers probably is moving much school learning increasingly toward rote learning, with negative consequences for acquisition of organized knowledge that can function to facilitate new learning and creative problem solving. The fundamental problem in all education is that learners are too often "swimming in a sea of meaninglessness," engaged primarily in rote learning. I shall return to this problem later. This book is an effort to offer a comprehensive alternative program, such as the program in Otto Silesky's school cited earlier.

In the corporate setting, as well as in schools, learning is too often by rote. This is especially the case when underlying reasons for rules, practices, and procedures are not explained to workers. Too often, corporate "training programs" are training almost in the way rats are trained to run a maze. Most of the learning encouraged is rote learning, and evaluation practices often encourage rote, not meaningful learning. In the simpler work environments before the "globalization effects" set in, rote learning in training programs was sufficient and generally more economical. With the rapid changes occurring in almost all work environments and the growing complexity of most jobs, "training" programs can lead to costly mistakes; what is required are "education" programs that provide for and foster meaningful learning. The military services, for example, are finding they need a different kind of recruit, one who knows how to think and how to learn *meaningfully*. Many high school graduates who apply fail to meet their criteria for recruitment.

Subsumption and Obliterative Subsumption

In the course of meaningful learning, new information is linked with concepts in cognitive structure. Usually this linkage occurs when more specific, less inclusive concepts are linked to more general existing concepts in cognitive structure. In order to place emphasis on this linking phenomenon, Ausubel has introduced the terms "subsuming concept" or "*subsumer*." The justification for adding these terms lies in the primary role that subsumers play in the acquisition of new information. A subsuming concept is not a kind of mental fly-paper to which information is stuck; the role of a subsuming concept in meaningful learning is an interactive one, facilitating movement of relevant information through the perceptual barriers and providing a base for linkage between newly perceived information and previously acquired knowledge.

Furthermore, in the course of this linkage, the subsuming concept becomes slightly modified, and the stored information is also altered somewhat. It is this interactive process between newly learned material and existing concepts (subsumers) which is at the core of Ausubel's *assimilation* theory of learning.

In my example with Denny, the concept vapor was subsumed under the concept gas and in turn under the concept water. This subsumption process would change in small ways Denny's meaning for the concept gas and the concept water. Moreover, other concepts in Denny's cognitive framework may also have had their meanings altered somewhat, perhaps in recognition that *steam* and *vapor* are both gases. If at a later date Denny obliteratively subsumes vapor as a concept (that is, he can no longer give a good description of the regularity represented by this label), his concept of water and steam would still be modified and probably enhanced as compared with the meanings Denny had before learning about "vapor." When you consider the fact that at least tens of thousands of neurons are involved in subsumption of a new concept, there are almost unlimited neurological possibilities for varying degrees of subsumption or obliterative subsumption in the course of meaning-ful learning and later when knowledge is retrieved.

Forgetting Contrasted with Obliterative Subsumption

Most information we learn cannot be recalled at some time in the future. Although the debate continues as to whether the biological mechanisms accounting for forgetting result in physical destruction of stored memory traces or whether forgetting is purely a psychological phenomenon, for purposes of education the fact that information becomes irretrievable some time after learning is of primary concern. Most careful research on retention has been done in laboratories where subjects are given nonsense syllables or word pairs to memorize and are then tested for later rote recall of information. Some studies have used poetry, story passages, and ordinary school materials for analysis of retention. These studies show that substantial forgetting occurs in a matter of hours for nonsense syllables; for poetry and story passages, much is lost in a matter of days; and for science, history, or other classroom information, retention drops to a fraction of original learning in a matter of weeks. Some information, however, is retained for months or years, especially information that has been rehearsed extensively. Forgetting has both an everyday meaning (i.e., a failure to recall something) and a specific tech-nical meaning (i.e., the kind of failure to recall after *rote* learning). Figure 5.8 shows the differences between forgetting and obliterative subsumption.

In Ausubel's theory, variation in amount of recall depends primarily on the degree of meaningfulness associated with the learning process. Informa-tion learned by rote (nonsense syllables and meaningless word pairs) cannot be anchored to major elements in cognitive structure and hence form a

Figure 5.8 Failure to recall is a different process following meaningful learning of information than that following rote learning. There remains a residual enhancement of cognitive structure and no interference with future related learning after obliterative subsumption.

minimum linkage with it. Unless materials learned by rote are restudied repeatedly to achieve *overlearning* (continued study after error-free recall has been achieved), they cannot be recalled several hours or several days after learning. Information that is learned meaningfully (associated with subsumers in cognitive structure) can usually be recalled for weeks or months after acquisition. The process of subsumption results in some modification of the stored information, however. As a result, recalled information may appear in a form slightly different from that originally learned. In time, recalled information may take on more general attributes of the subsuming concept(s) into which it was assimilated, and after obliterative subsumption has occurred, the *specific* messages learned are no longer retrievable. Nevertheless, there remain enhanced ideas in cognitive structure that can facilitate future learning. For example, we found that students who took algebra in ninth grade did substantially better with later studies on vectors in a physics class, even though much of their specific knowledge from algebra was obliteratively subsumed (Gubrud and Novak, 1973).

Rote learning has one important advantage over meaningful learning; I have already noted that sometimes it is useful to recall knowledge learned in *precisely* the same form as the original message. Phone numbers, for example, cannot be approximate. However, this process is all too frequently required in school testing. When recall of *verbatim* definitions of concepts or principles is required, meaningful learners can be at a disadvantage. This phenomenon underlies what Hoffman (1962) described as *The Tyranny of Testing*. Too many of the tests now used widely to assess student achievement, and in turn teacher performance, require predominantly rote recall of information. With meaningful learning, new knowledge is assimilated into existing cognitive structure, and if this contains misconceptions, the new learning will be distorted. Even when misconceptions are not present, some modification in meaning will occur during the subsumption process and using this knowledge later may result in somewhat idiosyncratic ideas that may not match exactly what the test-maker wanted, even though the ideas are correct. Evaluation problems will be discussed further in Chapter 9.

Meaningful learning has four important advantages over rote learning. First, knowledge acquired meaningfully is retained longer—much longer in many instances. Second, subsumed information results in increased differentiation of subsumers, thus adding to the capacity for easier subsequent learning of related materials. Third, information that is not recalled after obliterative subsumption has occurred has still left a residual effect on the subsuming concept, and in fact, the whole related framework of concepts. While we do not yet know the details of this process, we do know that complex neural networks are formed. Thus there is facilitation of new related learning even after loss of recall of a specific subordinate element has occurred. Fourth, and perhaps most important, information learned meaningfully can be applied in a wide variety of *new* problems or contexts; the transferability of knowledge is high. It is this power of transferability that is necessary for creative thinking.

The differences in recall of information after rote or meaningful learning is very important. Laboratory studies have shown that information learned by rote *inhibits* subsequent learning of additional similar information (Suppes & Ginsberg, 1963). Even information learned by rote that is forgotten inhibits learning of similar new information. The reverse effect operates after meaningful learning. While it is true that restudy or relearning of the *same* information is facilitated by prior retention in both rote and meaningful learning, the "savings" (as psychologists refer to this facilitation) in rote learning are only for relearning of precisely the same material, whereas meaningful learning will result in savings for relearning and facilitation (rather than inhibition) of learning new, similar (relevant to the same subsumer(s)) information.

Many students experience the feeling of being "snowed under" by the new material of a course. Usually this feeling becomes most intense six to eight weeks into a course. Some studies (see Hagerman, 1966)[3] indicate that most information learned by rote in schools is lost within six to eight weeks. As a

---

3 One might expect that studies of retention of school-taught information would be extensive. Unfortunately, this is not the case, except in more generic form where a variety of studies show school-taught information has little impact on cognitive structure building and remediation of misconceptions. (Cf., Helm & Novak, 1983; Novak, 1987; and Novak & Abrams, 1994.)

result, students recognize that they have forgotten much of the information presented earlier *and* that their earlier learning is now lost and is *interfering* with new learning. They must force themselves either into review and meaningfully restudy earlier materials, cram for hours to overlearn earlier material, or give up hope of passing the course. The same phenomenon may occur at the beginning of a course when materials are highly related to similar previous courses, and prior learning was rote in character. Rote learners must "cram" for final exams, whereas meaningful learners often mostly do a review of key ideas and meanings of key concepts.

Figure 5.9 illustrates the problem that derives from rote vs. meaningful learning. Because rote learning takes relatively little effort on the part of a learner initially, it is relatively efficient: that is, a learner can repeat *verbatim* some of the key concept definitions and propositions presented in the instruction. However, because the latter are stored *arbitrarily* and *non-substantively* in cognitive structure, they soon cannot be recalled *and* confer interference with new, related learning and recall of related information. During interviews on almost any topic, persons who have been learning by rote may recall bits of information but relate these in very inappropriate ways. For example, in a video developed at Harvard University, 21 out of 23 graduates and faculty members knew that the earth's orbit was not a perfect circle (actually, they thought it was much more elliptical than is the case), but they erroneously

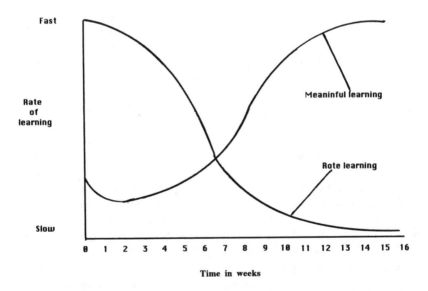

Figure 5.9 Early in a learning program, rote learning of information can be faster than meaningful learning of the information. However, as *forgetting* occurs, interference with new related learning occurs, and learning speed is relatively slower than that for meaningful learning where recall is stronger and *no* interference, but rather learning facilitation, occurs.

believed that the seasons on the earth (at least in the Boston area) were caused by the earth's proximity to the sun (Private Universe Project, 1989; see also Figure 7.4). Even in our best universities students arrive with misconceptions, and because many engage primarily in rote learning, these misconceptions do not get remediated. One must never under estimate the tenacity to which learners will hold on to old, faulty ideas in both school and corporate settings.

Progressive Differentiation

As meaningful learning proceeds, development and elaboration of subsuming concepts necessarily occurs. The refinement of concept meanings in cognitive structure giving more precision and specificity to these concepts is called *progressive differentiation* of cognitive structure. Addition of new, concepts through meaningful learning, or restructuring existing segments of cognitive structure, also produce progressive differentiation of the learner's cognitive structure. This was well illustrated in a study by Martin, et al. (1995).

In Ausubel's view, concept development proceeds best when the most general, most inclusive concepts are introduced first and then these concepts are progressively differentiated in terms of detail and specificity. For example, to introduce the concept of culture, we might begin by explaining that all the knowledge, skills, values, and habits passed on from parents to children constitute the culture of the human race. We could subsequently discuss Samoan or American Indian or urban American cultures, describing the methods and agencies by which the general cultural elements are transmitted. One of the great things about this Internet Age is that we can just go to the Web and find out about any culture and pump much more meaning into any concept.

Determination of what in a body of knowledge are the most general, most inclusive concepts and what are subordinate concepts is not easy. In a later chapter, I shall argue that good curriculum design requires an analysis first of the concepts in a field of knowledge and second consideration of some rela-tionships among these concepts that can serve to illustrate which concepts are most general and superordinate and which are most specific and subordinate. One reason school instruction and instruction in corporate training programs has been so ineffective is that curriculum planners rarely sort out the concepts they hope to teach and even more rarely do they try to search for possible hierarchical relationships among these concepts. As stated before, my premise is that concepts are primarily what we think with, that concept and prop-ositional learning is the principal function of educating. Therefore, we must sort out from the mass of knowledge those major superordinate and sub-ordinate concepts we wish to teach. Attitudes and skills are necessary and supportive elements for concept learning, but for most education these are associated or concomitant learning and do not constitute the primary structure of school curriculum. Even in trade schools, in the study of auto mechanics, for example, learning concepts in the field is at least as important as learning skills. Moreover, all skills require a cognitive framework to control the actions, and skills can be acquired better when this cognitive framework is made explicit. Many of the professions require skill learning as well as concept and propositional learning. In nursing, for example, Smith (1992) has shown that improving the quality of knowledge learned also led to improved performance of nursing skills. Some psychologist refer to knowledge required to perform certain skills as *procedural knowledge*. I will discuss this form of knowledge more fully in the next chapter, but it should be noted that procedural knowledge also comprises concepts and propositions.

To illustrate the idea of progressive differentiation I will refer again to the concept map made by Denny. If Denny could assimilate the *meaning* of the definition given for vapor (i.e., vapor is water in the form of an invisible gas), he would subsume several concepts under existing concepts he already has (see Figure 5.4). He might also recognize that water can be small droplets that can float in air, as in fog or clouds. He would recognize that these small droplets are droplets of liquid water that float in air. The conscious process Denny would need to engage in during meaningful learning may lead him to wonder: how is vapor different from fog? Why do the small droplets float in air? Is there also vapor in fog or clouds? What *is* a gas? To get answers to these questions, Denny would need to differentiate his knowledge further (hence the *progressive* nature of differentiation). Answers to these questions would also lead to new linkages between concepts he already holds and perhaps new discriminations, as for example, what is a gas and what is not a gas. These new meaningful learning experiences would result in integrative reconciliation (see Figure 5.10).

Integrative Reconciliation and Qualitative Improvement of Conceptual Hierarchies

Subsumption and progressive differentiation lead to more than quantitative addition of knowledge to a conceptual framework. There are also *qualitative* changes in that *each* of the concepts in the relevant structure are modified in meaning to some extent. It is evident that as we subsume concepts into a mapped hierarchy, the meanings of all the concepts are modified at least slightly because there are meaningful connections vertically and horizontally across the structure. Neurologically, at least some new synapses would be forming between the neurons storing the new concept and neurons storing all previously learned, related concepts. Thus we see that both quantitative and qualitative changes in knowledge result from *meaningful* learning. The same effects do not arise from rote learning, as illustrated in Figure 5.6.

Another form of cognitive differentiation arises when new *interrelationships* are seen between concepts in cognitive structure, relationships we can concepts   concept mapping   name Denny

water
solid
liquid
gas
vapor
river
ice
steam

Figure 5.10 Denny's hypothetical map showing further progressive differentiation and integrative reconciliation of concepts and propositions relevant to water.

represent as "crosslinks" on a concept map. These crosslinkages represent what Ausubel and others (1978) described as *integrative reconciliations*. They could arise from answers to the questions suggested on the previous page. Included in the category of integrative reconciliation of concepts would be understanding when a given concept is similar to but also different from another concept, such as how a vapor is like fog (it drifts about) and different from air (made of water molecules, not oxygen, nitrogen and other molecules). When integrative reconciliation occurs, there is simultaneously some improvement or progressive differentiation of cognitive structure. Figure 5.10 illustrates possible integrative reconciliations in Denny's concept map. In the course of seeking to make integrative reconciliations (resulting from answers to why and/or how questions) a learner often acquires one or more new concepts and integratively reconciles the meanings of the new and old concepts. There is *integration* because new concepts and/or relationships are substantively incorporated into the cognitive structure and there is *reconciliation* when meanings of similarities and/or differences are incorporated into cognitive structure. When meaningful learning is pursued by a learner in any subject matter over a span of time, subsumption, progressive differentiation and integrative reconciliation all occur simultaneously, at least to some degree.

To illustrate new concept learning, subsumption, progressive differentiation and integrative reconciliation, I refer to concept maps prepared from interviews with Paul in grade two and ten years later in grade twelve (Novak & Musonda, 1991). In grade two, Paul understood that some substances were made of "tiny chunks" and these substances could break into tiny chunks, as when sugar is put into water. He also recognized that these tiny chucks would not be seen (see Figure 5.11). After ten years of schooling, Paul had acquired the concept of *molecule*, and recognized that all substances were made of molecules, separated by space (a new concept) (see Figure 5.12). His initial concept of "tiny chunk" now had a new and more explicit meaning and he has also differentiated between atoms and molecules as "tiny chunks" of matter. He had acquired the concept *energy* and had integratively reconciled this concept with atom and molecule to understand why things dissolve, sublime, vaporize or melt. Concept maps made from interviews in grades seven and ten would show intermediate stages of concept development, differentiation reconciliation. What has been conspicuous in our 12-year study of concept learning in science is the remarkable degree to which new learning builds on prior knowledge, including prior misconceptions (faulty propositions), and also the limited extent of cognitive development for those students who have not been learning science meaningfully (Novak & Musonda, 1991).

Piaget's developmental theory presents the concepts of assimilation,

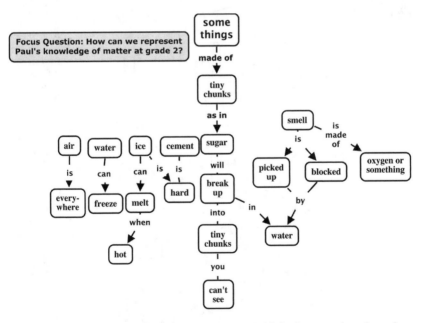

Figure 5.11 A concept map drawn from an interview with Paul, a second-grade student. From Novak and Musonda, 1991, p. 38. Copyright American Educational Research Association. Reproduced with permission.

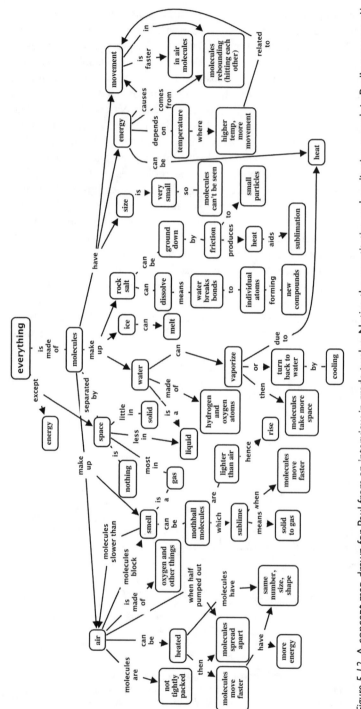

Figure 5.12 A concept map drawn for Paul from an interview in grade twelve. Notice the quantitative and qualitative growth in Paul's conceptual/ propositional knowledge about forms of matter. There are some misconceptions evident, such as the idea that space between molecules is greater in liquids than in solids. The reverse is true for water and some other substances. From Novak and Musonda, 1991, p. 39. Copyright American Educational Research Association. Reproduced with permission.

accommodation and equilibration. To Piaget, *assimilation* occurs when new learning fits into a cognitive *operational* structure and requires no change in that structure. *Accommodation* occurs when new learning requires some modification of an operational structure, leading to a new *equilibration* of the structure. Piaget's cognitive structures are *not* subject matter-specific conceptual/propositional frameworks such as I have been illustrating with Denny's and Paul's concept maps. Instead, they are general or generic *cognitive capacities* that presumably apply in any subject matter and that progress from sensory motor (ages zero to two) to preoperational, concrete operational and finally formal operational thinking (age eleven onwards). Thus there are some similarities between Ausubel's ideas of subsumption, progressive differentiation and integrative reconciliation and Piaget's ideas of assimilation, accommodation and equilibration—in both cases these take place over time—but there is also one crucial difference. Piaget's cognitive developmental periods refer to general reasoning capacity, whereas my version[4] of Ausubel's assimilation theory holds that reasoning capacity is *primarily* a function of the adequacy of the *relevant* conceptual framework a person has in a *specific* domain of knowledge. This is not to deny that older learners, in general, have better qualitative and quantitative knowledge frameworks for most domains of knowledge as compared with younger learners. However, as Chi (1983), Nussbaum and Novak (1976), Carey (1985), Papalia (1972), (Gelman, 1999), and others have demonstrated, young children can acquire large and complex knowledge frameworks in limited areas and their reasoning capacities in these areas may exceed that of many adults. It is the children in many homes who program the digital machines for their parents. Refer again to the quotation from Flavell (pp. 54–55).

There are, of course, generic *strategies* regarding learning, and older learners may acquire more powerful learning strategies than younger learners possess. In fact, the principal purpose of our work in helping students "learn how to learn" is to empower learners not only through helping them develop their conceptual frameworks but also through aiding them to gain more competence in acquiring and using strategies to gain qualitatively and quantitatively richer conceptual frameworks, and enhanced self-esteem. This idea will be discussed further in later chapters. Also discussed later (Chapter 8) are genetic or hereditary factors in learning.

Superordinate Learning

Occasionally in the history of any discipline, or in the life-span of an individual, new concepts are constructed that pull together and integrate large

---

4 Ausubel and I vary somewhat in our views on cognitive *reasoning* capacity, with my view being much more optimistic regarding young learners, perhaps because I have done much more research with young children.

domains of knowledge which were not recognized as intimately related previously. This was the case when Newton conceived of his law of gravitation that explained not only why objects fall toward the earth, as cannon balls do, but also why planets follow their orbits around the sun. Newton's concept of *universal gravitation* brought together domains of knowledge that most people saw as totally unrelated. Similarly, Einstein's concept of *relativity* led to his ideas on the reversibility of mass and energy and his now famous proposition, "energy is equal to mass times the square of the speed of light" ($e = mc^2$). Before Einstein, whoever thought that mass and energy could be so related?

In a similar manner, once in a while during the course of a lifetime, a learner may experience the acquisition of a new broad, general concept that then subsumes in powerful new ways the meanings of previously learned concepts and adds new and rich meanings to these concepts. This occurred for me when I began to understand more comprehensively the meaning of *meaningful learning*. Most of my graduate students have reported similar experiences, leading them to such remarks as, "Meaningful learning is truly the bottom line, isn't it? It ties together everything we know about learning and schooling!" As you study and grasp the ideas in this book, you may experience similar superordinate learning. It is easy to memorize verbatim the theory of education stated in Chapter 2: "Meaningful learning underlies the constructive integration of thinking, feeling, and acting leading to human empowerment for commitment and responsibility." It may take months or years for you to grasp the superordinate meaning of this idea or the concept of meaningful learning. I believe that my understanding of the meaning of the concept *meaningful learning* continues to grow with each new research project and with every class I teach.

One of the research projects we have done in the field of chemistry demonstrated the power of learning a superordinate concept for facilitation of other learning in chemistry. Cullen (1983) designed a study guide for freshman chemistry that sought to help students understand the meaning of *entropy* as a major superordinate concept which helps a student understand most of chemistry. Briefly stated, *entropy* is the degree of disorder in any system and energy is required to lower entropy (or disorder) in a system. Chemical reactions usually proceed in a direction that increases entropy, unless energy is supplied to "push" the reaction in the direction of less entropy. Now most of us can memorize the last two sentences rather easily, but what do they mean in terms of all the reactions students usually memorize when they study chemistry? To acquire the *meaning* of the concept entropy and to have this concept "rise" to the level of a superordinate concept in our conceptual framework takes time—and carefully guided instruction. This is what Cullen sought to do, although as a graduate teaching assistant in the course, he was limited in the degree of intervention permitted. His specially prepared laboratory study guide, some audio-tutorial lessons (Postlethwait, et al., 1972) available to "experimental" students in the library, and his own emphasis on entropy in "experimental" laboratory sections he supervised were the extent of intervention permitted. The lecture portion of the course, common to all students, also placed considerable emphasis on the entropy concept.

Cullen (1983) found that most of the students in the "experimental" sections performed no better than students in the "control" sections on regular course examinations. There was a significantly higher performance for one experimental section on a test for routine problem solving. Also, experimental students did not use the entropy concept to explain answers to problems more frequently than "control" students. These data are consistent with many of our research findings that most college (and secondary school) students resist moving toward meaningful learning strategies and may show little or no achievement gains on standard course exams. However, when Cullen looked at *individual* students who gave the best answers to complex, *novel* problems, *all 12* of these (out of 81) used the entropy concept as a major organizing idea. Eleven of these 12 were students in the experimental section. For them, substantial superordinate learning of the concept of entropy had occurred. For most of the others, superordinate learning of the concept of entropy had not occurred; they demonstrated no unusual proficiency in understanding chemistry. We have found in our work with both secondary school students and university students that the majority would prefer to get by with memorizing information rather than working to build conceptual understanding. Years of school experience with evaluation practices that require little more than rote recall may be at least partly to blame. Perkins (1992) also identifies other factors that discourage what he calls *complex cognition*:

> Complex cognition has more intrinsic interest and promises more payoff outside of school and later in life. But consider the cost to learners: complex cognition demands much more effort. It creates greater risk of failure. It introduces the discomforts of disorientation, as learners struggle to get their heads around difficult ideas. Peer status for complex cognition is certainly mixed; who wants to be known as a "brain?" And very commonly, so far as grades and teacher approval go, complex cognition buys students no more than the simpler path of getting the facts straight and the algorithms right. No wonder, then, that students perfectly reasonably do not automatically gravitate toward complex cognition. (pp. 59–60)

After 12 or 16 years of this kind of schooling, it is difficult for individuals to change the patterns of acting when they enter the real world. Waitley (1995) identifies eleven "action reminders" that may help some to achieve this transition in the business world, such as, "Invest in developing your knowledge and skills. The only real security in life is inside us. (p. 34).

It is always difficult to conduct research on learning in school settings, especially when the study one would like to do is not in line with the prevailing dogma. One of my colleagues in Venezuela did find it possible to conduct a study to test some of Ausubel's ideas, and also to use the concept mapping tool with a sample of students. As a science supervisor in Maracay, Bascones succeeded in enlisting a group of high school physics teachers to apply Ausubelian ideas that focused on meaningful learning, and who also had their students engage in concept mapping (Bascones & Novak, 1985). A comparable group of teachers agreed to participate in the study, using traditional materials and methods. Both groups of teachers agreed to administer unit tests that emphasized problem solving which required transfer of knowledge to new situations at the end of each of the eight study units. Raven's (1935) intelligence test was also administered to all students. Table 5.1 shows the results from this study. It can be seen that there was a highly significant difference ($F = 480.49$) between methods of instruction. While there was a significant difference in performance on the various problems in the tests, as might be expected, it is interesting to note that there were no significant differences among ability groups, indicating in part that the methods were equally effective across ability groups, but there were very significant differences among groups in problem solving scores, favoring the groups that did concept mapping and where meaningful learning was stressed. Figure 5.13 shows the results as bar graphs. It is important to note that though both groups showed improvement in test scores earlier in the semester (as they learned how to "do physics"), these gains dropped off for the students in traditional instruction but continued with students in the Ausubelian approach doing concept mapping. This is what might be expected if greater meaningful learning were occurring. We were at first surprised to see a drop in gains for the Ausubelian group in the Unit 4 problems, but then we realized that instruction had shifted

Table 5.1 Statistics showing highly significant differences in student performance on problem solving tests favoring groups using concept mapping and Ausubelian instruction. Reproduced from Bascones and Novak, 1985, p. 258, with permission from Taylor and Francis

Source	df	Mean square	F	Probability
Method	1	6836.19	480.49	0.00
Ability Group‡	2	36.97	2.60	0.08
Method × Ability	3	15.11	1.06	0.35
Error	70	14.23		
Problems	7	147.08	112.65	0.00
Problems × Method	7	16.26	12.40	0.00
Problems × Ability	14	2.74	2.10	0.01
Problems × Method × Ability	14	1.56	1.19	0.27

‡ Based on Raven test scores.

Figure 5.13 Excel graph from study with high school physics students showing performance on problem solving test for eight study units by method of instruction and ability group. Reproduced from Bascones and Novak, 1985, p. 258, with permission from Taylor and Francis.

from kinematics and dynamics to electricity and magnetism, and new major concepts (subsumers) had to be acquired. So again we see confirmation of basic Ausubelian principles, and the fact that switching to meaningful learning takes time.

Advance Organizers

Ausubel is perhaps best known for his idea of an *advance organizer*. In order to help learners bridge the gap between knowledge they already possess and new knowledge to be learned, Ausubel suggested that a small segment of instruction should be offered *prior* to the larger instructional unit that is *more general* and *more abstract* than the material in the larger unit. This prior instruction can serve as an advance organizer, helping the learner relate new knowledge to knowledge the learner already has. Advance organizers are easily the most researched idea from Ausubel's work, but this is only a very limited part of his assimilation theory of learning; advance organizers are primarily an instructional strategy. In the epigraph to his book, *Educational Psychology: A Cognitive View*, Ausubel (1968) made this statement:

> If I had to reduce all of educational psychology to just one principle, I would say this: the most important single factor influencing learning is what the learner already knows. Ascertain this and teach him accordingly.

What a growing body of cognitive research studies have shown in the last four decades is that for the most part, this Ausubelian principle is valid, especially if we consider ascertaining explicit cognitive frameworks relevant to the new concepts we seek to teach. We have found the use of concept maps to be powerful tools to "ascertain what the learner already knows," including faulty knowledge structures or misconceptions, and also to organize the subject matter of new material to be taught, as I will illustrate later. However, our research and the research of others is showing that *metacognitive* knowledge, including knowledge about how to learn *meaningfully*, is also crucially important.

To be effective, advance organizers must meet two requirements: (1) the learner's specific existing relevant conceptual and propositional knowledge must be identified; and (2) appropriate organization and sequencing of new knowledge to be learned must be planned in such a way as to optimize the learner's ability to relate the new knowledge to the concepts and propositions already held. This is no easy task, partly because of the range of variation in and adequacy of various learners' relevant concepts and propositions. However, we and others have found that for any given population of learners, there is often a common set of concepts and propositions that can serve to "anchor" the learning of new concepts and propositions. Carefully planned advance organizers can do much to facilitate this "anchorage." Skillful teachers have devised examples, analogies, stories, or demonstrations that serve as effective advance organizers, even if they never heard of this concept.

Concept maps and Vee diagrams (see Chapter 6) can serve as powerful advance organizers, and they can assist in the design of instruction that builds on learners' existing knowledge structures. If students are asked to build the best concept map or Vee diagram for a given topic or activity, they will reveal both their valid and their invalid ideas relevant to this topic or activity. The process of creating concept maps and/or Vees alerts the learner to the fact he or she does have *some* relevant knowledge for the new topic, thus adding to motivation to learn meaningfully. Maps and Vees can aid in planning the instruction in such a way as to build upon existing valid ideas, and reduce the chances for reinforcing existing invalid ideas. In general, encouraging collaborative group work also enhances learning.

Scaffolding Learning

Among the ideas that Vygotsky (1962) put forth is that language can be a powerful tool to facilitate cognitive development. In more recent years, other authors have built on Vygotsky's ideas and introduce the term "scaffolding" to describe cognitive assistance that may be offered to help learners acquire new ideas (Wood, et al., 1976; Hogan & Pressley, 1997). Ausubel's idea of advance organizer was also intended as a tool that would function in cognitive scaffolding. In any case, there is wide consensus today that helping learners acquire new ideas is a good thing. Concept maps and Vee diagrams can be

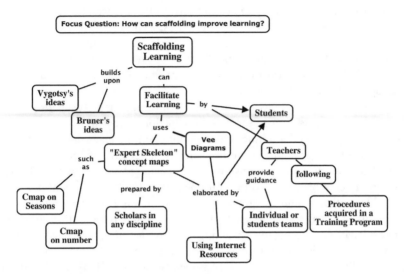

Figure 5.14 Scaffolding can facilitate meaningful learning, and concept maps and Vee diagrams can serve as scaffolds for learning.

effective scaffolding tools. Figure 5.14 illustrates the idea of scaffolding as a concept map.

Assimilation, Learning, and Constructivism

There is today much discussion about *constructivism* in educational circles. Descriptions of constructivism are almost as numerous as individuals who seek to describe this. What is most commonly described is the fact that each learner must construct his or her own concepts or knowledge. Often there are no precise definitions of concept or knowledge. Many of the discussions fail to clarify how *individuals* construct knowledge (the psychology of learning) versus how scholars in disciplines construct new knowledge (the epistemology of knowledge). I shall deal with constructivism extensively in the next chapter and show how assimilation theory explains both how individuals construct their knowledge and how knowledge is constructed by scholars in a discipline.

There are, of course, numerous other "theories of learning" that have been published since 1968. For example, Anderson's (1990) *Adaptive Character of Thought,* Sternberg's (1986) *The Triarchic Mind,* and Gardner's (1983) *Frames of Mind,* are widely cited in the literature. From my perspective, none of these nor other theoretical works possess at once the simplicity of Ausubel's assimilation theory nor the power to *explain why* learning succeeds or fails in any educational context, personal, school, university, or corporate. Trained in the sciences early in my career, I am an adamant proponent of theories that at once have simplicity, but *explain* complexity. In the sciences, this is known as *elegance*. Moreover, if one looks at publications, such as The American Psychological Association's "Learner-Centered Psychological Principles" (Marshall & McCombs, 1995), it is evident that all of these are not only consistent with Ausubel's theory, but also their principles can be *explained* and understood through his theory.

In the four-and-a-half decades during which we have used Ausubel's assimilation theory to guide our research and instructional innovations, we have not obtained any results that refute or cast doubt upon the major ideas described above. Most of our studies have been highly supportive of these ideas and have led to some modifications and we hope improvements in the theory. For example, in his earlier works (Ausubel, 1963; 1968), his ideas of progressive differentiation and integrative reconciliation were concepts referred to primarily in instructional design. Our research group has found these important explanatory concepts for explaining cognitive *learning*, as well as concepts that can be applied in instructional design. This was reflected in the 1978 second edition of Ausubel's book (Ausubel, Novak, and Hanesian, 1978). In the next chapter, I will argue that concepts from assimilation theory are also powerful explanatory ideas for understanding the process by which humans construct new knowledge. Partly for this reason, I see the idea of meaningful learning as the bedrock on which creative knowledge construction rests and the key concept in my theory of education.

Creativity

There are numerous definitions and descriptions of creativity. My view is that creativity is simply successful integrative reconciliation and/or superordinate learning—and the emotional desire to do this. As such, it ranges on a scale from relatively modest "creative insights," when relatively common integrative reconciliations are formed by a person, to those extraordinary integrative reconciliations and/or superordinate concept constructions that lead to Nobel or Pulitzer prizes. Everyone of us has some creative capacity (i.e., we make our own unique integrative reconciliations), but only a small fraction of the population appears to have the capacity and emotional drive to make the creative leaps that advance science, music, literature, or other fields of human endeavor. Koshland (2007), the former Editor of *Science*, divides creative discovery into three categories: *charge, challenge* and *chance*. *Charge* discoveries solve problems that are quite obvious, and Koshland quotes Nobel Laureate Szent-Gyorgyi as saying these discoveries occur when someone "sees what everyone else has seen, and thinks what no one else has thought." Einstein's theory of relativity would be an example here. *Challenge* discoveries occur from the accumulation of facts or concepts, and the discoverer perceives a new concept or theory that pulls these together onto one coherent whole. Darwin's (1873) theory of evolution would be an example of this. *Chance* discoveries occur when people have what Louis Pasteur called "the prepared mind." The discovery of penicillin and x-rays are two examples. In one way or another, I see all three of these forms of creativity as evidence of some high level of meaningful learning. Figure 5.15 illustrates the keys factors I see operating in creativity.

According to my view, the creative performance of everyone can be enhanced by improving the capacity and desire of people to learn meaningfully. It is retarded or inhibited by inordinate emphasis and reward for learning by rote. Since the latter has been so common in most school learning, it is not surprising that the biographies of geniuses often refer pejoratively to their experiences in schools. Schooling can be changed to encourage, reward and enhance meaningful learning *and* creativity. I will return to this idea in later chapters.

Sternberg (1988) proposed a "three-facet" model of creativity, suggesting that the creative person has a "blend" of these three facets and some combinations may be more "synergistic" than others. The three facets he identifies are: (1) intellectual or "intelligence;" (2) stylistic, such as legislative (rule-oriented), self-government (varying degrees of drive and tolerance); and (3) a personality facet, such as tolerance for ambiguity, willingness to grow, moderate risk-taking, and work for recognition. These are all traits that most people exhibit from time to time, and hence one must assume that the creative person has more of and a better "blend" of these traits.

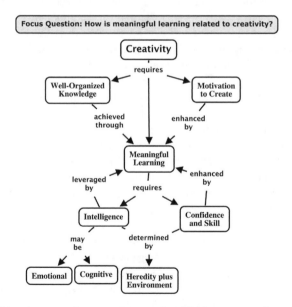

Figure 5.15 Necessary requirements for creative thinking, as seen through my theoretical framework. Ausubel's principles of meaningful learning also operate to effect creativity.

In a thoughtful book, Sternberg (1996b) distinguishes between "successful intelligence" and "inert intelligence" (see below). Successful intelligence is required for creative production. Sternberg states:

> I define creativity not only as the ability to come up with new ideas. I believe it is a process that requires the balance and application of the three essential aspects of intelligence—creative, analytical, and practical—the same aspects that, when used in combination and balance, make for successful intelligence. (p. 191)

Another book on creativity is Gardner's (1993) *Creating Minds*. Gardner studied the biographies of recognized geniuses and identified four separate components in the study of genius: (1) organizing themes, such as the relation between the child and the adult creator; (2) organizing frameworks, such as a life course perspective of creative work; (3) issues for empirical investigation, including individual, domain-specific, and field-related issues; and (4) emerging themes, such as the creative person's cognitive and affective support at the time of breakthrough.

We see in both Sternberg's and Gardner's *descriptions* of creative performance the richness and complexity of factors that have been associated with creativity. However, I do not believe these and similar descriptions *explain* creativity. To me, it is much more parsimonious and much more powerful to view creativity as a manifestation in individuals who seek high levels of meaningful learning. Each of the many "facets" or "components" of creativity described by Sternberg and Gardner can be viewed as the consequence of determined pursuit by the individual constantly to seek high levels of concept and propositional integration into well-structured cognitive frameworks. The intrinsic affective rewards that come from such cognitive development and differentiation drive the individual to seek out settings and supportive individuals that catalyze further the growing complexity and integration of his or her cognitive frameworks. It is the empowerment that comes from successful integration of thinking, feeling, and acting through meaningful learning that underlies and drives the creative process. To understand creativity requires that one understand in a profound way the meaning of meaningful learning.

Gardner (1993) emphasizes in his description of creativity that the creative individual produces products (things or ideas) that are, in time, recognized by society as creative products. He also stresses that often creative individuals encounter resistance to, or even ridicule of, their ideas or products, but in time, their ideas or products prevail. Sternberg (1996a), in a similar way, emphasizes that creativity combines creative, analytical, and practical intelligence that leads to sustained action eventually recognized as creative. Sometimes it may be difficult to distinguish between foolish and creative products, but both Gardner and Steinberg argue that, in time, the creative product will be recognized. In a similar vein, Higgins (1995), in his book *Innovate or Evaporate*, defines creativity as "the process of generating something new that has value," and an "innovation" is a creation that has significant value (p. 9). In most of the contemporary writing on creativity we see in current literature this emphasis on the need for recognized value as one criterion for judging an act as a creative act. Unfortunately for some creative people, this judgment may not come until after they are dead. Lafley and Charan (2008) stress the importance of creativity to drive innovation, and I shall discuss their ideas further in Chapter 8.

Intelligence

When I was an undergraduate student, one of my psychology professors defined intelligence as "the trait that intelligence tests measure." I remember at the time being very unhappy with this definition, for I was not convinced that intelligence tests, or any tests similar to these such as the one I took for college admission, had a great deal to do with "real intelligence." My experience somewhat mirrored that of Sternberg's.

Sternberg (1996a) describes what he calls "successful intelligence:" "Successful intelligence is, in part, what is sometimes called business sense. IQ doesn't measure this business sense at all. Indeed, many people with high IQ's seem not to be aware either that they have customers or that these customers are important" (p. 39). By contrast,

> Inert intelligence is what you show when you take an IQ test, or the widely used Scholastic Assessment Test (SAT), or the American College Test, or any of a large number of similar tests used for college and graduate-school admissions. Many people do well on these tests, thereby showing impressive academic prowess, at least according to those who believe in the tests. But the intelligence measured is inert—it doesn't lead to goal directed movement or action. As a result, these people's most impressive accomplishments may well be their test scores, or their grades in school. Those who can recall facts, who may even be able to reason with those facts, don't necessarily know how to use them to make a difference, either to themselves or to anyone else. (p. 11)

I find myself strongly in agreement with Sternberg's claims, and I believe his book has much of value to persons seeking a better way to conceptualize intelligence and creativity. And yet there is blind acceptance of measures of inert intelligence in both schools and business. As Sternberg observes:

> Yet many businesses—deceived into believing that inert intelligence makes a difference in job performance—use test in much the same manner as do colleges. The goal is to find people who will perform well in particular jobs. The military uses tests as well. The testing game itself is

big business, and tests are used to sort out those who are given better jobs and access routes to better jobs from those who are not. But it sorts them on IQ-type measures rather than on successful intelligence, which is what will truly determine who succeeds. (p. 39)

Over the years, our research work has supported the position taken by Sternberg, but very few scholars working in education or psychology have voiced the kind of concerns he has expressed, to say nothing about the vehemence with which he makes his assertions. Early in my career I thought things would change and the limited value of IQ and other similar measures would be recognized. What I underestimated was the depth of entrenchment of the "mental measurements" proponents and their enormous ability to prevail over the years. While there are a growing number of scholars such as Sternberg (1996a), who regard IQ tests, "Scholastic Aptitude" tests and similar tests as measures of at best "inert intelligence," what I refer to as measurement zealots remain dominant in the field of psychological and educational testing, both in school and in corporate settings. In part, this derives from an unwarranted reverence for precise numbers, as in an IQ of 121 or SAT scores of 760 and 540. The people who design and administer these tests are not quacks or charlatans; they really believe in the validity and reliability of their tests. The reliability of the tests is relatively good; that is, these tests tend to produce similar scores for the same individual on repeated testing. It is the validity issue that is the problem. When one correlates IQ, SAT, or similar test scores with measures of real-world job performance, the correlations are usually near zero! What IQ tests measure may be useful for creative thinking, but it is not the same aptitude as creativity (Getzelz and Jackson, 1962; Guilford and Christensen, 1973). This problem will be discussed further in Chapter 9.

More recently, there is a growing concern with the use of tests for selecting graduate students. Georgi (1996) reported that at Harvard University, Graduate Record Exam (GRE) scores in physics showed no correlation with graduate course grades. Moreover, Georgi observed that some of his most brilliant women students did very poorly on the physics GRE test. In general, women scored 100 points lower (out of a possible 990) than men, thus leading to serious gender bias against women in selection for graduate study in physics. At Cornell University our dean of the graduate school did an informal study of correlation of GRE scores with professors' rating of Ph.D students. He found a correlation of 0.02, about as close to zero as you can get. I have not been able to find similar data for business schools, but I'm sure such data will be reported in the future, if it is not "out there" now. Kuncel and Hezlett (2007) argue for the predictive value of standardized tests for success in various endeavors. While it is true that they show positive, significant correlations between standardized tests and subsequent performance, most of the correlations in their study are 0.4 or less. When we square these correlation coefficients to obtain the actual variance in scores predicted by the test, we see that they account for some 16 percent of variance in other performance indicators, leaving one to wonder what accounts for the other 86+ percent of variance?

There continues to be a debate about the value of taking Advance Placement (AP) courses in high school. These are courses designed by the College Board, a group of secondary and tertiary people who design the courses and the achievement exams. The idea is to offer a freshman college-level course to be taken in high school that can provide credit for advance standing in college, and thus accelerate graduation. There is considerable debate on the equivalency of the high school AP with freshman college courses. Nevertheless, with rising tuition and a desire to shorten college tenure, enrollment in AP courses has been increasing, with over 15 percent of public high school students taking at least one course in 2007 and scoring a grade of 3 (usually the minimum score on a scale of 1–5 required for college credit), an increase of some 25 percent in the last four years (Cech, 2008). However, there was a decline in the average AP test score, as might be expected with higher student participation rates.

One factor that is associated with performance in mathematics by females is the extent of gender discrimination in the culture. Countries where females enjoy a more equal status show no difference in math or reading performance (Guiso, et al., 2008). In another recent study, Hyde and colleagues (2008) found that in the US, girls now score as well as boys from grade 2 through grade 11. However, they also report that assessments used in the No Child Left Behind program fail to test for complex problem solving of the kind needed for success in science and mathematics careers. Summarizing recent research on gender and success in science and math careers, Ceci and Williams (2007) observe that while aptitude indicators are about the same for men and women, the fact that only women have babies and they usually take on a disproportionate share of work in child rearing accounts for much of the difference in research productivity and accomplishment.

Emotional Intelligence

The idea that intelligence is not a unitary, one-dimensional thing has been around for many years. Guilford (1959) suggested that intelligence can be factored into 120 separate components, and more recently we have the 7 different intelligences suggested by Gardner (1983). A somewhat novel idea has been put forward by Goleman (1995) in his book, *Emotional Intelligence*. There is no simple definition for emotional intelligence. Instead, Goleman describes characteristics such as social poise, cheerfulness, sympathy, sensitivity to other's feelings, empathy, outgoing attitude, confidence, low anxiety, and similar traits as typical of emotionally intelligent people. He presents numerous examples of successes by people high in emotional intelligence and failures by people low in emotional intelligence. In general, the data he gives shows little or no correlation between characteristics of emotional intelligence and

IQ or similar measures of cognitive ability. While there are some tests that claim to measure emotional intelligence (see Queendom.com), I will leave it to the reader to decide on their validity.

Both the biological foundations and the psychological implications of emotions have been studied with increasing intensity in the past two decades. We know much more about how and why emotional responses are generated and expressed. We have learned in the past decade that our brains contain "mirror neurons" that send signals to other regions of our brain which imitate the actions and feelings being observed, suggesting in part why we are sensitive to other people's thoughts, feelings and actions, providing also a basis for empathy (Gazzola, Aziz-Zadeh, & Keysers, 2006). There is also a growing body of literature on how to develop positive emotional intelligence in children, and actions that have deleterious effects on development. Unfortunately, bad parenting can lead to poor emotional intelligence and more bad parenting as these children become parents. The cycle is not easy to break, but there are educational approaches that have had positive results. Goleman's work and the work of many others interested in emotional intelligence needs more attention in schools and corporations. I would expect to see growing awareness and concern with these ideas in the next few decades.

So what is "the bottom line" on intelligence? That depends, in part, on the game you're playing. If you want to predict SAT scores or grade point averages, IQ scores will have reasonable reliability and validity. Unfortunately, they are also likely to predict your chances of admission to "better" colleges and universities because admission policies often emphasize performance on such tests. If you want to predict the number of patents a person will achieve, grade point averages or "achievement" test scores have almost no predictive value; and in some cases, these would severely penalize the most productive, most creative individuals (Novak, 1977a, pp. 254–263).

So how should we define intelligence and how should we measure intellectual achievement? As with most complex, desirable things, there are no easy answers. We need to assess both the quantity and the quality of knowledge a person has in those domains of knowledge that are pertinent to the field of work. Of course, it's not easy to define what is pertinent. Many creative achievements have come about precisely because the creator brought to bear some knowledge outside of the usual domain and saw new ways to connect it with domain knowledge well-known by most persons competent in the field. These are the kind of connections I refer to as major "integrative reconciliations" in that the creative person sees how to make the "right" connections between concepts in two domains of knowledge that were previously regarded as unrelated, or in some cases even contradictory. There may still remain the task of demonstrating to skeptics the power and validity of the new connection(s), but in due course, the dogged persistence of the creative person and his or her adherents is recognized and sometimes rewarded. This kind of intelligence is obviously precious to society at large and to corporations in their quest for competitive advantage. Attention to criteria that indicate emotional intelligence also need to be given more time and effort. Too few of the recruitment criteria used by corporations at the present time recognize that they may be doing a great job of selecting for "inert intelligence," but a poor or counterproductive job of selecting for "successful intelligence." The latter, from my perspective, is the person who has a history of seeking high levels of meaningful learning and a tenacity to persevere until his or her hunches begin to gain acceptance. Measurement and evaluation issues will be discussed further in Chapter 9.

It should be evident from the text and figures I have presented that I seek to facilitate *your* subsumption, progressive differentiation, and integrative reconciliation of concepts regarding human learning. This process will be aided if you construct *your own* concept maps representing your understanding of learning, both for smaller subsets of concepts, and ones for the large groups of concepts. Try to build your own composite maps—and also add illustrative examples from your own experiences. Then refer for comparisons to Figure 5.1 that shows a composite map for the key ideas of Ausubel's assimilation theory that I have constructed. As you gain in your understanding of assimilation theory, it should be possible for you to gain in your capacity to engage in high levels of meaningful learning. This, I will predict, will permit you to be more creative in those domains you choose to pursue.

Chapter 6

The Nature of Knowledge and How Humans Create Knowledge

The Nature and Sources of Knowledge

That humans learn is self-evident. It is also self-evident that humans organize and communicate knowledge to one another. What is not obvious is the *origin* of knowledge. Where does knowledge come from? This has been a question pondered by some of the best minds for centuries. Most of the great philosophers throughout history have spoken and written on this question.

It is not my purpose to review the long history of philosophical ideas about the nature of knowledge and knowing, but it is necessary to deal with some of the ideas that have been dominant in the past 300 years because they continue to influence teaching, learning, schools, businesses, and society today. First, however, I will try to make clear the philosophical ideas that now guide our work and my answer to the question: where does knowledge come from? The branch of philosophy that deals with the structure and origins of knowledge is called *epistemology*, and I shall try to make clear my epistemological ideas.

Knowledge comprises concepts and propositions, including concepts and propositions that deal with learning strategies and methods of conducting inquiries and also including the affective dimension of experience associated with those concepts and propositions. Meaningful learning underlies the constructive integration of thinking, feeling, and acting that occurs in human learning and in new knowledge construction. This interplay is unique to human beings and hence I choose to label it *human constructivism* (Novak, 1993). Human constructivism is a label I see as appropriate both for the way in which humans *learn* their usable knowledge and also for the way in which they *construct* new knowledge. The nature and process of *meaningful* learning underlies both human learning and human knowledge creation.

I will discuss below some older ideas about the nature of knowledge and origins of knowledge and reasons why I believe these ideas are in error, less powerful, and/or less relevant to education and knowledge creation. In this, I seek to present a view of epistemology that I believe has power for improving both learning and knowledge creation. Whether or not this view has power for the advancement of the field of philosophy dealing with epistemology is for others to decide. It will be seen that ideas of human constructivism are complementary to or congruent with emerging ideas on epistemology being advanced by contemporary philosophers and historians interested in the process of knowledge production.

Gowin's Epistemological Vee

My colleague, D. Bob Gowin (now retired from Cornell University), has been interested in the study of philosophy and epistemology as it applies to education, beginning with his Masters degree work six decades ago. His interests and expertise in philosophy have been valuable to our research program in science education, especially in research studies that have focused on science laboratory learning. In general, most students experience considerable anxiety and confusion in science laboratory work, especially when this work involves experimental or quasi-experimental studies. College students also find the reading of research reports frustrating or confusing, and sometimes completely opaque.

To aid students in understanding research reports, Gowin (1970) devised five questions, the answers to which could provide the student with a better understanding of the research. These five questions were:

1. What are the *telling questions*? These are questions that "tell" what the inquiry seeks to find out.
2. What are the *key concepts*? These are the dozen or so disciplinary concepts that are needed to understand the inquiry.
3. What *methods of inquiry* (procedural commitments) are used? These are the data gathering or data interpreting methods used.
4. What are the major *knowledge claims*? These are the answers *claimed* by the researcher as valid answers to the telling questions.
5. What are the *value claims*? These are claims, explicit or implied, about the worth or value of the inquiry and the answers found in the inquiry.

Gowin and I found the use of these questions to be helpful to students not only in the analysis of research reports but also in laboratory work, for the design of research, and as a tool for discussions on the meaning and value of research studies. However, many students found it difficult to relate key concepts to the telling questions and/or the events or objects being investigated. In pondering the problems experienced, Gowin came up with the idea of the *Knowledge Vee* heuristic in early 1977. Figure 6.1 shows the general form of the Vee.

We have found it is relatively easy to teach people to construct Vee diagrams once they are familiar with concept mapping, and the ideas that underlie concept maps. Appendix 2 shows a set of procedures we have found to be effective. The ideas presented in this chapter will aid in understanding both the concept map tool and the Knowledge Vee tool.

THE KNOWLEDGE VEE

CONCEPTUAL/THEORETICAL
(Thinking)

METHODOLOGICAL
(Doing)

WORLD VIEW:
The general belief and
knowledge system
motivating and guiding
the inquiry.

FOCUS QUESTIONS:
Questions that serve
to focus the inquiry
about events and/or
objects studied.

VALUE CLAIMS:
Statements based on
knowledge claims that
declare the worth or
value of the inquiry.

**PHILOSOPHY/
EPISTEMOLOGY:**
The beliefs about the nature
of knowledge and knowing
guiding the inquiry.

THEORY:
The general principles guiding the inquiry that explain
why events or objects exhibit
what is observed.

KNOWLEDGE CLAIMS:
Statements that answer the
focus question(s) and are
reasonable interpretations
of the records and trans-
formed records (or data)
obtained.

PRINCIPLES:
Statements of relationships
between concepts that explain
how events or objects can be
expected to appear or behave.

TRANSFORMATIONS:
Tables, graphs, concept
maps, statistics, or other
forms of organization of
records made.

CONSTRUCTS:
Ideas showing specific relationships between concepts,
without direct origin in events
or objects

RECORDS:
The observations made
and recorded from the
events/objects studied.

CONCEPTS:
Perceived regularity in events
or objects (or records of events
or objects) designated by a label.

EVENTS AND/OR OBJECTS:
Description of the event(s)
and/or object(s) to be
studied in order to answer
the focus question.

Figure 6.1 The Knowledge Vee showing a description of the 12 elements involved in the
construction of knowledge and value claims.

The beauty of the Vee heuristic is its comprehensiveness and also simplicity.
It serves to illustrate that there are a dozen or so "epistemic elements" that are
involved in constructing or examining a piece of knowledge, and yet it places
these elements into a simple structure that helps to illustrate how each of these
elements function. Although a variety of shapes for an epistemological heuristic could have been used, Gowin chose the Vee shape because it "points" to
events or objects, that segment of the universe we are trying to understand. It
also serves to distinguish the fact that both *thinking* (conceptual/theoretical)
elements and *doing* (methodological) elements are involved in knowledge

construction. Each element on the Vee interacts with every other element as our minds, hearts, and bodies work to construct new knowledge, or rather knowledge *claims*. However, those elements shown on the left side are "in our head and heart" and help to guide the actions on the right side that produce the knowledge and value claims. The Vee heuristic is a heuristic based on a *constructivist* view of knowledge wherein we recognize that the way a piece of universe we choose to study appears to look or behave depends upon other elements of the Vee. If we choose different questions, use different concepts, principles or theories, make different records or transform records differently, we can legitimately arrive at different knowledge claims about the same events or objects. In short, how we "see" events or objects in the world depends on how we personally construct our vision of these events or objects.

For example, early chemists saw burning as the loss of phlogiston, whereas the new chemical theory and principles we now follow see "burning" as the oxidation of carbon, hydrogen or other elements. "Modern" ideas explain why wood disappears (except for a small amount of ash) when it burns and why iron and mercury become *heavier* when they are "burned." The theory of phlogiston could not explain the latter two events and was contradicted by the weight records for iron and mercury before and after "burning." No chemist or physicist claims to know exactly how atoms and molecules behave when substances are burned, but our current theories and principles certainly have far more explanatory and predictive power than earlier theories. The "radical constructivist" (see Von Glasersfeld, 1984) holds that we will never know the "absolutely right" theories or principles, but we can make progress toward constructing principles and theories that have greater explanatory power. There is no apology by the constructivist for the fact that we can make only *claims* about how we believe some piece of the universe looks or behaves. Truth or absolute certainty is not the goal of the constructivist thinker. It has been the goal of positivist/empiricist philosophy for hundreds of years, and positivistic views abound in textbooks, lectures, and schooling in general. I will return to this issue later in this chapter.

In the business world, leaders also recognize the changing, evolving nature of knowledge. Ichijo and Nonaka (2007) observe:

> The central proposition of constructivism is that knowledge is constructed by the learner in order to maintain an equilibrium with his or her context, rather than passively absorbed from the preexisting body of knowledge. Business situations are again a case in point: the preexisting bodies of knowledge on international expansion, for example, while providing ideas, have no meaning for the manager who has not yet experienced the feedback of applying them in a variety of contexts. And the experienced manager is aware how tentative the knowledge remains when moving into new ventures. (p. 217)

The financial meltdown that occurred in the USA and the world in 2008 was in part a result of failure to recognize the enormous changes that had occurred in the ways in which homes and businesses were financed and the kind of bundling and leveraging of financial assets that had occurred. At this writing, it is difficult to see how this extraordinary change in business and finance will change the ways we look at the business world.

One of the difficulties constructivists experience in discussion with some religious people or followers of sects is that the latter see their beliefs as "absolute truths," not subject to debate or qualification. They seize upon the fact that the views of constructivists are tentative and often being modified as evidence that these views are false. For example, in the case of the age of the universe, climate change, or the origin and evolution of life, the ideas of science are often rejected as "only theories" and therefore dubious at best and false when vehemently opposed. Of course, these same people drive autos, fly airplanes, and watch weather forecasts even though these things are based on the very same science they see as "only theories". With the absolute zealots, there can be no "consensus view" other than theirs. Figure 6.2 shows some of the distinctions between constructivist and positivist or empirical epistemologies. It should also be noted that with the religious zealots or cultists, the ideas on the left side of the Vee in Figure 6.1 are not tentative and evolving, but rather constant and absolute and theories do not exist!

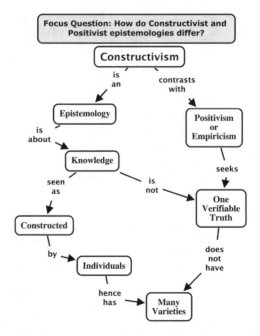

Figure 6.2 Some of the key concepts of constructivism contrasted with positivism/empiricism.

Elements of the Knowledge Vee

There are 12 "epistemic elements" shown on the Vee in Figure 6.1. Each of these elements functions in the construction of meanings and also in the construction of knowledge, although we are often not conscious of their roles nor do we consider how each element is operating for a given learning experience. It is possible to begin the discussion with any element on the Vee, but for convenience, I will begin at the top with the focus question(s).

Often new learning begins with a question. It may be a simple question such as, "what is that thing called?" Or it may be a more complex question such as, "how does that event take place?" For example, Rachel, my 3¾-year-old granddaughter, while weeding flowers with my wife, asked, "Is this a weed?", pointing to a small grass seedling. Soon she was skillful at discriminating young flowers from young weeds. At least in this context, she now understood the distinction between the concept *weed* and *flower*. As the weeding progressed, Rachel asked, "Do flowers eat dirt?" My wife explained that flowers do use some of the dirt to grow, but mostly they used water, air, and energy from the sun. Rachel then asked, "When the flowers get big, will there be less dirt?", to which my wife responded, "Yes, but only a very tiny bit less." What is evident in Rachel's questions was that she was not operating in a conceptual or theoretical vacuum; she had some concepts, principles and theories about what plants are and how they grow, acquired over the last two or three years of her short life. I will use this example to illustrate the knowledge elements of the Vee and how they interrelate. Figure 6.3 shows the concepts and relationships for the left side of the Vee, and Figure 6.4 shows a concept map representing ideas on the right side of the Vee.

World View. First we see that Rachel had a curiosity about flowers and how they grow. It was evident that her *World View* indicated a concern for flowers and a belief that there are reasons *why* things are the way they appear to be. Our world view is that constellation of beliefs and values that shapes the way we see events and objects in the world, and also what we choose to care about and learn about. Our world view is shaped by our values and the emotional commitments we have regarding happenings in our universe. It is shaped over our lifetime of experiences and influenced by our culture, religion, family and personal relationships.

Rachel's manifest philosophy was a rationalist/constructivist view that happenings in the universe should make sense, that there are reasons for how and why plants grow, and that these reasons are understandable. Philosophy and world view are not easily distinguished, in part because they are interdependent. However, we have found it useful to make a distinction, with world view representing the more global, value-laden ideas a person holds about the universe. In terms of the Vee, it is perhaps best to think of *philosophy* in terms of our epistemological beliefs, i.e., where do we believe knowledge comes from; how can we use knowledge?

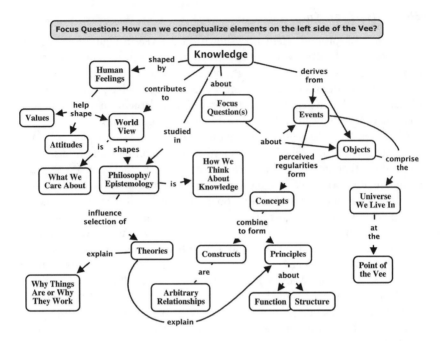

Figure 6.3 A concept map representing the ideas involved in the elements on the "left side" of the Knowledge Vee.

Matthews (1980; 1984) has done an analysis of interviews where young children (six to eight years old) raised some of the same questions and issues, and presented similar arguments, as those recorded in the writings of some of the greatest Western philosophers. Even very young children have already established philosophical ideas about how people behave and how the world works. In this respect, Matthews (1980, Chapter 4) rejects outright Piaget's claim that philosophical reasoning does not develop until teenage. In recent years, Matthews' view has become the more popular view.

Our world view motivates us to act, to construct questions, and to find answers. We have chosen to place "focus question(s)" at the top center of the Vee since these, in many ways, are what drive the inquiry that leads eventually to new knowledge. Rachel's question, "When flowers get big, will there be less dirt there (in the garden)?", was her focus question.

Theory. Moving "down" the left side of the Vee, we see that Rachel is manifesting and trying to refine some theories about plants and nutrients. She recognizes that plants like animals, need to "eat" to grow. This is also reflective of her emerging theory of conservation of substance or matter: The stuff in the large plant must come from somewhere, and if some dirt is used to grow, there

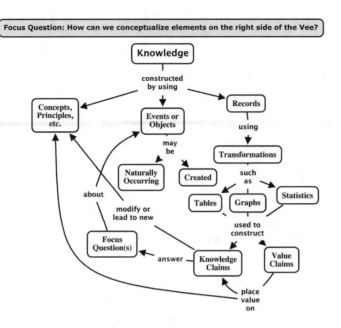

Figure 6.4 A concept map representing the ideas involved on the "right side" of the Knowledge Vee.

should be less dirt in the flower garden when plants get big. Theories we define as *explanations* for why and how things appear the way they do. Rachel was developing her theories for how living things grow (particularly plants) and where the stuff comes from that they need to grow. This curiosity may have been stimulated by Rachel's mother, who is a nutritionist, but the ideas were expressly Rachel's. She had a theory about dirt and correctly hypothesized that if plants use dirt to grow, there should be less dirt in the ground when the plants get big. Rachel is not unique in this regard. Any 3–4-year-old could develop such a theory and use it for abstract reasoning *if* they had a sequence of learning experiences similar to those of Rachel.

Principles. These describe *how* things work or how they appear to be structured. Rachel manifested several operating principles: (1) weeds look different from flowers (i.e., weeds were grass-like in our garden of marigolds and zinnias); (2) plants use dirt to grow; (3) when dirt goes into plants, the soil has fewer nutrients. The learning experience with her grandmother helped Rachel to consolidate and refine the meanings of these principles (propositions). The experience also helped Rachel to differentiate and integrate her concept meanings for plants, dirt, flowers, weeds, growing, and maybe also water, air, and energy. Rachel was engaged in meaningful learning.

Constructs. These are ideas that represent regularities not directly observable in events or objects. Often they represent two or more concepts that are connected in some arbitrary way. For example, if Rachel were to suggest that her grandmother's flowers were growing in *healthy air* or *healthy dirt*, she would be using constructs. Rachel had concepts of healthy and some concept of air and dirt which she could combine to suggest the conditions under which the flowers were growing. Halpern (1989, p. 46) defines *hypothetical constructs* as concepts having no external reality, giving learning and memory as examples. This could also be said of atoms, love, and photosynthesis, but it seems much more coherent to label these as concepts, representing specific regularities in events or objects, albeit they may be observed indirectly. Constructs such as IQ are arbitrary relationships between concepts—there is no necessary reason to divide mental age by chronological age, as is commonly done. Arbitrary constructs are more common in the social sciences. Constructs differ from principles because they do not *explain how* some aspect of the universe functions or is structured.

Concept. We have defined as a perceived regularity or pattern in events or objects, or records of events or objects, designated by a label. Clearly Rachel had established meanings for the concept labels noted above, and was refining these meanings; that is, she was becoming more discriminating as regards the regularities represented by each of the concept labels. Rachel did not work from records to build her concepts, as Van Helmont (seventeenth-century Flemish chemist) did with his willow tree experiment, but she will undoubtedly do so in the future in other experiences that relate to the concepts cited.

Events and Objects. Events are things that happen, such as growing, eating, running, wars, and so on. Objects are some unit of "stuff" or matter, such as plant, dirt, or weed. Everything in the universe is either an event or object, and all events involve objects; even changes in forms of energy involve objects in some way. Thus, at the bottom point of the Vee we anchor our experience to some piece of the universe. All meanings humans construct are anchored in events or objects they have experienced, or metaphors drawn from events or objects. Our concepts help us to perceive regularities in the events or objects we observe, and in some cases we construct new labels to designate new regularities. But without a functioning framework of relevant concepts and principles, it is more difficult to construct new knowledge. *This is one reason children's acquisition of language from birth to three years old is such an incredible learning accomplishment.*

It is very important to help learners become clear and specific about the events or objects they are trying to understand. We find repeatedly in science laboratory work that many students have at best only a fuzzy idea of the objects or events they are trying to understand, and for which they are trying to seek out the regularities. The same can be said for elements of events in sports, dance, music, or literature. Literature can be especially troublesome to learners because most good literature relies upon metaphor to structure the story. Similarly, mathematics is difficult for most of us because the concepts and principles of mathematics are usually not specified and/or not related to real-world events or objects for which we already have relevant knowledge. One reason why US students underperform in comparison with students from Hong Kong or Japan is that teachers in these countries use significantly more analogies to relate math concepts to real-world events (Richland, et al., 2007). A recent paper by Wiggins and McTighe (2008) emphasizes the need for putting priority on understanding in mathematics instruction. They argue that one of the reasons students see mathematics as boring is that they do not see relevance between what they study and the real world they live in.

Rachel's questions signaled clearly what events and objects she was trying to understand. Rachel was engaged in a relatively high level of meaningful learning. We could follow through with examples of how elements on the right side of the Vee could function in the construction of knowledge and value claims, but the limited context of Rachel's learning did not include making records or transforming records. Examples of this will come later in her life.

Experiments. Emerging in the seventeenth century, Galileo and others we now call scientists (they saw themselves as natural philosophers) developed the *experiment*. Experiments are events created by researchers and the conventional experiment requires that we observe both "experimental" events and control events. The requirement includes that all elements we are observing should be identical, except the *one experimental* variable. Differences in records we obtain from the events permit us to test "hypotheses" regarding the influence of the experimental variable on the event being studied. How we record and transform the records is determined, in part, by the hypotheses we seek to test. Hypotheses could also be called "anticipated knowledge claims." In the twentieth century, new statistical tools were developed that permit experiments to be done with multiple variables or experimental conditions, thus also permitting construction of hypotheses about how two or more variables interact to produce the records we obtain.

The success of experimental procedures in the natural or "hard" sciences as ways of producing useful knowledge has led to widespread efforts to apply this methodology to the social or "soft" sciences, including education and business. The two major difficulties in the social sciences is that we can seldom truly "control" events that involve people, and secondly, our methods of making records have serious problems of validity and reliability (see below and Chapter 9). A recent report by the US Department of Education (2007) criticized most evaluation studies for new programs for being rarely done as randomized experimental studies. However, a number of researchers pointed out in a report by Mervis (2007a) that classrooms are not like laboratories and good research can and should be done using other research models.

Nevertheless, used with sufficient caution and guided by theory and principles that have reasonable validity, some experiments can prove useful for knowledge creation in the business and the social sciences as well.

Records. These are literally the records we gather about events or objects observed. They can be simple descriptions of observations, such as the number of each kind of object observed, or they may be meter readings, computer print-outs, or other records made by complex instruments. In the latter cases, there is always the issue of reliability and validity of the records. Faulty equipment or the improper selection of equipment can produce faulty records. *Fact* is a label I will use for accurate, valid records, and many records gathered in research are not *facts*, especially in educational research where the data-gathering instruments (tests, for example) are often not highly reliable and highly valid record-making tools. Unfortunately, it is not always easy to know when our records are truly facts, acceptable but containing some error, or biased and distorted. Learners need to be helped in ways to make validity checks and reliability checks on their data. In work settings, workers often know better than their managers the limitations on records gathered. Corporations that respect and use this knowledge enhance their productivity.

Many advances in the sciences have come from invention of new ways to make records of events. The telescope and the oscilloscope are two examples. Telescopes have led to enormous advances in astronomy, and oscilloscopes have advanced our understanding of electricity and electromagnetic waves. Much of what we call "technological advances" results from modifying instruments developed for "basic research" to practical uses. Oscilloscopes laid the groundwork for television, and concept maps are central to our programs to help learners to learn and to create knowledge. Some research groups become so successful creating events or in refining record-making tools that they lead the world in new knowledge creation in their specialty. For example, this was true for the research group in Darmstaat, Germany, who have become so skillful in creating new elements that they are credited with creating chemical elements, 107, 108, 109, and the discovery of other new elements continues (Clery, 1994; http://en.wikipedia.org/wiki/Discoveries_of_the_chemical_elements).

The records we *choose* to make depend upon the question(s) we hope to answer, and all of the elements on the left side of the Vee. Usually we focus our attention on the principles guiding our inquiry, since these describe regularities or relationships we may find in the objects or events we are studying. We need to be sure that we are gathering records that are consistent with our principles and may allow us to confirm or deny the validity of the principles guiding our inquiry.

Artifacts. These are the records of human activity. The implements, pottery, and jewelry studied by archaeologists are products that are used to reconstruct the life of prehistoric people. Artifacts do not occur naturally in the universe but depend on human thinking and activity. Since humans have an infinite capacity to "change their minds," artifacts as records can give different messages from different people, or from different times. There are regularities in artifacts and reliable predictions can be made using this kind of record. Much that we deal with in education, and all of the social sciences, is basically *artifactual* records, such as test scores, interview data, and opinions or feelings about things. Although it is always a slippery business to interpret records of events or objects, it is especially difficult to interpret artifactual records. This is one of the reasons the social sciences are less "advanced" than the natural sciences. It is also a reason why viable theory may be even more powerful in the social sciences as a tool for guiding action. Theory helps us make judgments as to whether or not the artifactual records we used and the claims we constructed have a reasonable chance of being valid.

Record Transformations. Usually we do not try to construct knowledge claims from "raw data," or records as they are gathered from our observations. It is common to do some kind of transformation of the new data. Simple groupings, tables, charts, and graphs are some of the common record transformations we use. Data is a term usually used for any records or transformed records. Although Rachel did not record in writing her observations of flowers, she was making "mental records" of her observations and using previous "records" she had observed.

Record transformations we make should be guided by our concepts, principles, and theories. The transformations are also determined by the focus question(s) we hope to answer. Principles help us to organize our data to show patterns or relationships anticipated by applying our principles. For example, there is a principle of economics that holds that interest rates are dependent upon the money supply in an economy. Thus applying this principle, we would have gathered records on money supply (as reported from federal sources) each week or month for some period of time, and also records on the interest rates for each week or month. We could place these records into a table showing dates in one column, money supply in another column and interest rates in a third. However, a better view of the relationship would be a graph showing money supply on one axis and interest rates on the other axis. A nice line graph showing steady increase in interest rates with a regular decline in money supply would "confirm" or support our economic principle. Alas, if this did not occur in our record transformation, we might question the validity of the principle. More commonly, we begin to recognize that something else must be happening, and we may reach into our store of economic principles to see if any other principles can explain our graph. We may find the principle that consumer buying is related to interest rates, and now we must go back and gather more records, records on consumer spending over the time interval we are studying. Then we construct new transformations of our records. Of course, it is always possible that our principles may be faulty, and economics is a good example of a field where there is considerable dispute among experts as to which principles are valid or which are most important. For one thing, we are dealing with events (e.g., consumer willingness to buy or to borrow money) that are *choices* people make. The records of interest rates are therefore artifacts, not facts.

Statistical record transformations are very common in many fields, especially in educational research. Unfortunately, statistical transformations will not improve biased or invalid records, and these are all too common in the social sciences. Statistics will not make facts out of records that are artifact. Statistical tests and their interpretation are also subject to sets of concepts and principles, and too often these are not known or ignored by the researcher. For a good critique of statistics in education, especially the common use of factor analysis and similar tools, see Gould (1981).

Knowledge Claims. These are the answers to the focus questions that we *claim* our records and record transformations lead us to. Or we may simply make a knowledge claim from our observations of events without the precision that may come from good records and record transformations. Rachel's conjecture that there would be less dirt in the garden when the plants got large would be an example of this. The commonly used term, *hypothesis*, is an *anticipated knowledge claim*. However, hypotheses are not necessarily statements we are trying to prove or falsify. From a constructivist perspective, hypotheses have only limited value. Gathering different records or using different record transformations could lead to very different answers to the same questions about the same events. Moreover, we can never be certain about the validity and/or reliability of our records, and at least to some degree, deficiencies in our records could lead to faulty knowledge claims. The latter points are well illustrated in the field of medicine where the value of a given drug, e.g., estrogens, and their benefits have changed often in the past 20 years. As we noted earlier, applying different concepts, principles, or theories, and/or changes in the samples we study could change entirely the knowledge claims that emerge in any inquiry. Constructing knowledge claims is indeed a slippery business. There are so many ways to go wrong, so many ways to be in error. This is especially true in any field where principles and theories are either lacking or of dubious validity. This has been the case in much educational research (as well as research in other social sciences), so there is good reason why teachers and the general public are skeptical about so-called educational research *findings*. Moreover, with poor or non-existent theory, questionable principles and limited record-making tools so common in educational research, it is no wonder that research findings are often contradictory. The most common finding when alternative teaching or learning strategies are compared is: "There were no statistically significant differences between groups (or methods)." Kaestle (1993) has commented on "the awful reputation of educational research." He notes a lack of influence of research on practitioners, the disarray of the educational community, and the politicization of the field. He fails to note the theoretical poverty of the field.

Value Claims. These are about the *value* or *worth* of the inquiry for achieving the goal(s) that motivated the study. For example, some of our studies were designed to ascertain whether or not concept maps and Vee diagrams could be helpful to students, both in terms of knowledge achievement and in terms of gains in self-confidence and/or interest in the field of study. Our data generally support the knowledge claim that concept maps and Vee diagrams help learners to learn and to gain in confidence and interest (see, for example, Novak, Gowin, & Johansen, 1983). Therefore we make the *value* claim that these are *useful* tools that *should* be used by teachers and learners. Value claims are always linked to knowledge claims, but they are not the same thing. We have found it helpful to students and teachers to make deliberate efforts to identify and record value claims for every inquiry. This also helps both students and teachers to recognize that knowledge construction is a very value-laden endeavor! If Rachel had exclaimed that it was wonderful that beautiful flowers could grow from air, water, and dirt, she would have stated a value claim about flowers. I believe most of us would agree with such a value claim.

Concept maps are proving useful in the business world. In my work with Procter and Gamble in the 1990s, we found that research teams could identify the conceptual knowledge most pertinent to a given problem faced by a team, and this accelerated progress toward solutions. We also found that concept maps could lead to new marketing strategies, better ways to deal with regulatory agencies, and other applications. Unfortunately, the proprietary nature of this work does not permit publication of the work and the results. Now that CmapTools and training support are available (see: www.perigeantechnologies.com), we may see an acceleration in the application of concept mapping and ideas in this book to business problems.

Our world view and our philosophy will in many ways influence the fields we choose to study and the kinds of questions we seek to answer. There is a strong relationship between the value claims we seek to construct and our philosophy and world view. An important component of my world view is that I believe human beings have the power to reduce the degree of human suffering in the world, and that improved education, based on theory, is an important endeavor to reduce human suffering. That is why I have chosen education as a field of work, and why I have been striving to develop a theory and related principles to guide our research and practice. I may not live long enough to see convincing evidence that theory-based improvement in education can reduce human suffering, but some of our more recent work, and the work of others, makes me optimistic. An example, our current work in Panama, will be discussed later.

There is an important difference between schools or universities and the business world. Today every large business faces fierce competitive pressures, not only from other businesses in this country, but also from businesses located all over the world. The "globalization" of business, as so many writers are pointing out, means that survival of the business *requires* rapid, effective, and efficient new learning and new knowledge creation. As Friedman (2005, p.45) points out, globalization has been going on for centuries, but currently globalization is leading to the "flat earth" and this "process is happening at warp speed." Now any product or service can be produced or provided almost anywhere. We shall explore later some of the implications of the "flattening" process. Nonaka and Takeuchi's (1995) assertion that all businesses must become "knowledge creating organizations" suggests to me that some of the ideas and tools I am presenting in this chapter may find more rapid acceptance and application in the business world than in the academic world. They do not have the luxury of continually increasing taxpayers' support to sustain their ineffective approaches.

There are other epistemic elements that could be discussed; however, this is not a book on epistemology. Nevertheless, I regard an understanding of epistemology as essential to understanding the nature of the knowledge we seek to teach or to learn. It is essential for teachers, learners, and managers to acquire *metaknowledge*, that is, knowledge about knowledge. Of course, one could argue that teachers have taught and learners have learned and managers have managed for centuries without understanding the nature of knowledge and the processes involved in knowledge construction. The point is, if we want to improve the educative process by a quantum leap, teachers, learners, and managers need to learn more, not only about how humans learn but also about how they create knowledge. This was the central goal in our book, *Learning How to Learn* (Novak & Gowin, 1984), published in nine languages and still being read widely.

We have found the Vee heuristic to be helpful to students in our research group to design their own research projects, and also to serve as a vehicle for dialogue between individuals. On a single page, it is possible to present the key elements that are guiding the inquiry, the objects and/or events to be studied, the focus questions to be pursued, and the elements that will be used to construct knowledge and value claims. Figure 6.5 shows an example of a Vee constructed by one of my former Ph.D students for her thesis work in nutrition education. She has gone on to achieve a worldwide leadership position in the field, partly as a result of the power of her theory-driven research program.

The Interrelationship of Learning and Knowledge Creation

Throughout the last chapter and in this chapter, I have tried to show how I see meaningful learning and knowledge construction as highly related. In fact, in my view all knowledge construction is only an extension of the human capacity to construct new meanings (new concepts and concept relationships in

Conceptual (Thinking) Side

WORLD VIEW:
    The quality of life can be improved; i.e., life is open-ended.

PHILOSOPHY:
• Knowledge evolves within an individual (Piaget) and among individuals (Toulmin).

THEORY:
• Meaningful learning (Ausubel, et al., 1978; Novak, 1977).
• Ecology of human development (Bronfenbrenner, 1979).

PRINCIPLES:
• Meanings are constructed through cognitive assimilation, integration, and differentiation of concepts (Ausubel, et al., 1978).
• Meaning construction occurs via the process of social interaction (Bronfenbrenner, 1979).
• Children acquire most of their meanings from a person with whom an interpersonal relationship has been established, e.g., family (Bronfenbrenner, 1979).

CONCEPTS:
    meaning, learning, meaningful learning, cognitive structure, concepts, concept mapping, interviews, social interaction, assimilation, integration, differentiation, interpersonal relationships, family, parent, food and nutrition.

FOCUS QUESTION:
What concepts about food and nutrition do children share with parents?

Methodological (Doing) Side

VALUE CLAIM:
• Before designing curricula, educators should be aware of the conceptual frameworks that children have about food and nutrition.
• One goal of nutrition education should be to encourage parents to recognize the effect that they have as educators of their children about food and nutrition

KNOWLEDGE CLAIMS:
• Young children will have rich but unique individual conceptual structures re: food and nutrition.
• In their conceptual structures, children's concept maps will reflect the influence of each parent.
• Concepts will be more similar within families than among families.

TRANSFORMATIONS:
• Concept maps of each interview and qualitative evaluation of such.
• Qualitative comparison of parental maps and children's maps.

RECORDS:
• Series of interview tapes.
• Series of handwritten notes recorded during the interview relating to task results.

EVENT:
    A series of three individual interviews with each preschool child and two interviews with each parent on the concepts of food — what is it? how are foods grouped?

Figure 6.5 A vee heuristic that (1) defines each element involved in the process of knowledge construction (in italics) and (2) illustrates the plan for a theory-driven inquiry in nutrition education. From Achterberg, Novak, & Gillespie, 1985. Reproduced with permission from JNE.

cognitive structure). Thus, the psychology of meaningful learning underlies and gives rise to the epistemological process of knowledge construction. *Human Constructivism* is both a psychological and an epistemological phenomenon. This view is illustrated in the concept map in Figure 6.6.

Figure 6.6 is an exceedingly complex figure. Do not expect to understand all of the concepts and relationships represented in it with a single reading. Instead, use it as a "reference map" to see how ideas presented in this chapter and Chapter 5 interrelate with one another. Most of my graduate students have found that it takes them one to three years to feel comfortable with the ideas of "human constructivism," including some time needed to shake off old ideas

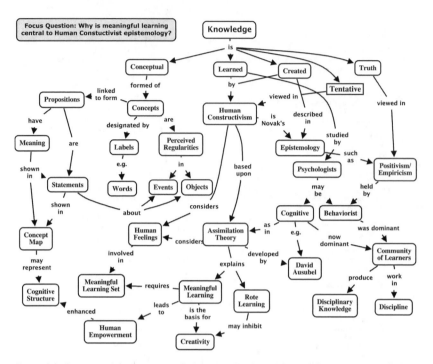

Figure 6.6 A comprehensive map of ideas involved in "Human Constructivism." This "conceptual road map" requires frequent reference as you progress through this chapter and seek to understand my views on how humans create knowledge. It combines elements from both the psychology of learning (Chapter 5) and epistemology, or the study of the nature of and creation of knowledge.

and attitudes that are positivistic in character. Our society is permeated with positivistic thinking, and it is not easy for one to move away from this. Behaviorist theories of learning may be almost dead in the world of psychology, but they are alive and well in schools and corporations. Neither positivist epistemology nor behaviorist psychology that is rooted in positivist epistemology will be expunged from schools and businesses in the foreseeable future.

Illustrated in Figure 6.6 is the idea that knowledge may be learned during the life-span of an individual and that new knowledge is created by "scholars" or communities of learners in disciplines. Increasingly, I expect that new knowledge creation will occur in business organizations. Piaget (1972, Chapter 2) hinted at the idea that the ontogeny of knowledge acquired by an individual is constructed in a way that is similar to the phylogeny of knowledge produced by generations of scholars. However, Piaget did not see learning as principally the acquisition of complex frameworks of concepts and propositions and hence his constructivist parallel between learning and knowledge creation was very different from what is illustrated in Figure 6.6. Moreover, Piaget tended to play down the role that affect or human feelings play in both learning and knowledge production, possibly in part as a result of his early training as a scientist, which was then and often is today explicitly positivistic in character (see Kitchener, 1986).

One of the ideas that grows out of the work of Toulmin (1972) is that knowledge is constantly evolving. We use current knowledge to design new inquiries and the product of these inquiries leads in time to new or modified concepts or principles, and more rarely, new theoretical or philosophical ideas. We can illustrate the evolving nature of knowledge with a "parade of Vees" as shown in Figure 6.7. For both the individual researcher, who is undergoing meaningful *learning* through the research, and for the discipline undergoing gradual modification through collective inquiries, the relevant "left side" of the Vee becomes modified over time. New knowledge and value claims modify old ideas and the process of knowledge construction continues. Vannaver Bush (1945) characterizes science as the "endless frontier," since new knowledge leads to new questions, and there is no end point where all the "answers" will be known. Collectively, and as individuals, scientists and scholars in every field will keep on learning—and modifying their theoretical/conceptual frameworks.

In some of our studies we used questionnaires and interviews to compare the learning approaches used by students who held constructivist as opposed to positivistic views on the nature of science. We found a strong trend toward meaningful learning for those students who held constructivist ideas and an inclination to prefer rote learning for those students who held positivistic ideas

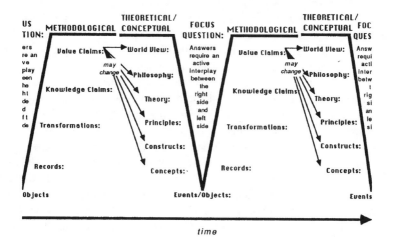

time

Figure 6.7 The "Parade of Vees" illustrating the constructivist view that we build new knowledge about events or objects based on what we now know, and this process goes on and on, evolving our ideas shown on the left side of the Knowledge Vee. As Bush (1945) famously pointed out, the process never ends.

(Edmondson and Novak, 1993). Songer and Linn (1991) reported similar findings. One of the reasons I believe it is difficult to move some students toward meaningful learning strategies is the deterrent effect of their positivistic thinking. This is one reason I believe learning tools such as concept maps are needed to help move all students to higher levels of meaningful learning.

The idea that new knowledge construction is nothing more than an extension of the meaningful learning process of those who create the knowledge has at once a great simplicity but also great complexity. It gives a simple explanation for how new knowledge is created, but it also necessitates an understanding of the psychological complexity of meaningful learning. There is in the view of human constructivism at once a simplicity and also a comprehensiveness that conforms to the "principle of parsimony" that has guided knowledge creators for several centuries.

The Principle of Parsimony

One other major influence on Western scientific thought was William of Occam. Writing in 1340, Occam stressed that explanations should be economical and simple, with no more constructions than are needed to explain an event or phenomenon; all unnecessary causes and explanations should be scrupulously removed. This principle of excising unnecessary causes became known as "Occam's razor." Sir William Hamilton (1853) stressed again the importance of Occam's canon and termed it the "law of parsimony." Hamilton rephrased the law this way: "Neither more nor more onerous causes are to be assumed than are necessary to account for the phenomena."

The history of physics and biology illustrates the power of parsimonious thinking. In biology, a half dozen or so major principles serve to give meaning to an almost infinite variety of observations. Evolution, gene theory, and complementarity of structure and function are a few of the constructions that meet Occam's criterion and which have served to advance our understanding of living systems. In contrast to physics and biology, psychology and education have been characterized by innumerable "principles" and theories each of which has at best dubious interpretive value over a very narrow range of phenomena. The field of education has been strikingly devoid of parsimonious explanations. One reason for this, in my view, is that educators have relied too heavily on psychologists for principles and theories. Until recently, most of the research done by psychologists has been what my colleague Ulric Neisser called "white lab coat psychology," done in the laboratory, usually with animals, and of almost no relevance to human learning in school settings. Educators must build their own *education* principles and theories that apply to humans in *educational settings*. And educators must seek to construct principles and theories that have wide-ranging power and relevance to educational events. Parsimony in theory building should always be a focal concern.

My enthusiasm for Ausubel's *assimilation* theory of cognitive learning has grown over the past four decades, partly because our research group sees increasing power and relevance of the theory to innumerable educational events in every domain of subject matter and for all age groups. In short, we observe enormous parsimony both in the relative simplicity of the theory and also in the enormous range of educative events to which it can be applied. The most important principle in Ausubel's cognitive learning theory is *meaningful learning*, that is, the principle that meaningful learning occurs when the learner *chooses* to relate new knowledge to prior knowledge, non-arbitrarily and substantively. Principles of subsumption, progressive differentiation, integrative reconciliation and superordinate learning further explain how *assimilation* of new knowledge occurs in meaningful learning in any educational setting. In our work in research and instructional innovation, we have found the principle of meaningful learning to be fundamental to understanding a wide range of phenomena occurring in educative events, which this book will seek to illustrate. Our research group has also seen growing power and parsimony in *A Theory of Education* (Novak, 1977a) as it has been applied and modified over the past three decades and evolved to the form presented here. It will, we hope, continue to evolve as it is used. I expect the evolution and application of the theory will accelerate rapidly as businesses seek to apply and adapt the ideas.

Improving Research Productivity

As an outgrowth of university faculty development seminars in which participants were taught how to use concept maps and the Vee heuristic to improve their teaching, with the suggestion that they try also to apply these tools to their research work, we found the tools to show marked success in facilitating new knowledge construction. More recently, my colleagues and I have been applying these tools in corporate settings with striking success. For example, in seminars with research directors at Procter and Gamble, we used concept maps and Vees to help groups design new products and to pinpoint gaps in available knowledge that needed to be filled through new, targeted research. The manager in charge of this program remarked, "You led the team to see better the nature of the new product and research that needs to be done in four hours than usually occurs in four months." Unfortunately, proprietary rights do not permit me to show examples of concept maps and Vees created with this and other companies. Increasingly corporations recognize the importance of understanding the process of knowledge construction.

One of our research projects involved a research team at Cornell University led by Professor Zobel. Concept maps and Vees were used to help the group see the global structure of the total research effort as well as to sharpen the definition in research work of individual team members. Figures 6.8 and 6.9 show examples from this project.

While the application of concept maps and the Vee heuristic to facilitation of research work is still in its infancy, we already see evidence of high promise

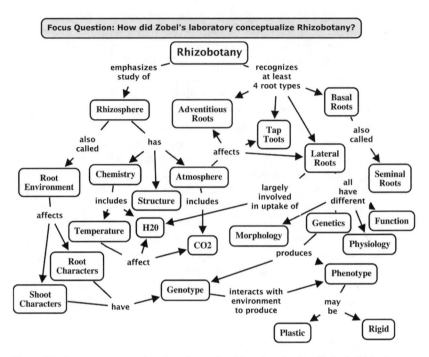

Figure 6.8 A concept map showing the major ideas involved in Zobel's Rhizobotany research group. From Matthews, 1995. Reproduced with permission.

of these tools for aiding in the creation of new knowledge, in both academic and for-profit corporations. As we shall see in Chapter 10, facilitating knowledge creation may be the key to economic survival of any nation.

Forms of Knowledge

Knowledge Versus Information

There is currently much discussion about various forms of knowledge. Nonaka and Takeuchi (1995) distinguish between knowledge and information:

> First, knowledge, unlike information, is about *beliefs* and *commitments*. Knowledge is a function of a particular stance, perspective, or intention. Second, knowledge, unlike information, is about *action*. It is always knowledge "to some end." And third, knowledge, like information, is about *meaning*. It is context-specific and relational. (p. 58; italics in original)

If one looks at Nonaka and Takeuchi's descriptions from the perspective of the Vee heuristic, it is evident that what they describe as information is essentially

FOCUS QUESTIONS
What can I understand about plant gravitropic responses,
specifically the interaction with temperature and carbon dioxide?

WORLD VIEW & PHILOSOPHY
• Understanding the effects of gravity on life is a
fundamental question of substantial, inherent
scientific value and provides a unique
environmental tool in our search to understand life.
• Plants are an integral part of the world as we know it,
so understanding them is important.
• We can construct knowledge about plant gravitropic responses.

VALUE CLAIM
• Temperature and carbon dioxide are two environmental stimuli
that affect plant gravitropic responses.
• Since different hybrids respond in different manners to both
temperature and carbon dioxide, then there may be a genetic
component that is somehow regulating or directing these responses.

THEORY
• Life on Earth has been exposed to the constant force of gravity.
• Gravity helped shape and continues to influence the structure,
function, and on-going evolution of all living organisms,
including plants.
• Plants use gravity to effect "normal" growth.

KNOWLEDGE CLAIMS
• Some areas of the gravitropic response are still under consideration.
• Ethylene, auxin, and calcium all play a role (and there may be others)
in a gravitropic response, but the roles are not well understood.
• Carbon dioxide is a competitive inhibitor of ethylene, so in high CO2
a gravitropic response may be inhibited.
• Temperature affects the gravitropic responses of some hybrids more
than others.
• Carbon dioxide affects the gravitropic responses of some hybrids
more than others.
• There are no significant differences in seed angles between treatments;
therefore the only variable in the experiment is temperature or CO2.
• Some significant differences between temperatures and carbon dioxide
level exist for initial shoot angle, final shoot angle, initial root angle, and
final root angle.

PRINCIPLES
• Gravitropic responses are not seen when plants are subjected
to microgravity conditions.
• On Earth, plants use a geotropic response to send roots "down"
and shoots "up".
• Plants must have within them 1) gravity sensors, 2) a means of
action, and 3) a means of translation between the sensors and
the action.
• Plants use gravity to produce "normal" growth, but sometimes
we see abnormal growth in gravity situations and we must be
able to explain this.
• Gravity sensing involves a pressure gradient created by both
starch granules and Golgi bodies.
• The translated signal begins with the cell producing ethylene,
which then regulates the transport of auxin; the signal may also
be affected by calcium.
• The mechanism of action is based on auxim movement.
• I will integrate new knowledge based on my previous
cognitive framework.

TRANSFORMATIONS
• Averages and standard deviation for all reps for each hybrid.
• AMMI analysis for genotype by environment interaction.

RECORDS
• 12 replications of 5 seeds each for each of 5 hybrids
(Cargill 4327, DeKalb 524, Eastland 541, HyTest 474, Pioneer 3751).
• Measurements are: seed angle, initial shoot angle, final shoot angle,
initial root angle, and final root angle.

CONCEPTS
• concept map • Vee diagram • pressure gradient • gravitropic
response • auxin • ethylene • carbon dioxide • plant hormones
• gravity • gravity sensors • Golgi bodies • starch granules
• endoplasmic reticulum • auxin sensitivity • hybrid

EVENT
Evaluation of maize seedling gravitropic response at various temperatures (17.5, 20, 25, and 30° C)
and at various carbon dioxide levels (.035%, 0.15%, and 1.5%).

Figure 6.9 A Vee diagram constructed in tabular form to show espistemological elements involved in a Ph.D study of plant gravitropic responses. From Matthews, 1995. Reproduced with permission.

"records," and knowledge is much more complex. Their description would be similar to what is shown on the Vee as "knowledge claims" and "value claims." Viewed from the perspective of the Vee heuristic, however, knowledge is really much more complex than they describe. Moreover, the Vee helps us to see more explicitly the processes involved in knowledge creation.

Tacit and Explicit Knowledge

Another distinction Nonaka and Takeuchi (1995) discuss at some length is *tacit* contrasted with *explicit* knowledge. They build on the earlier work of Polyani (1966) and characterize tacit knowledge as "subjective" knowledge and explicit knowledge as "objective" knowledge. The latter is the product of rational thought and may result from empirical studies. Explicit knowledge is knowledge we can easily show or explain to others, whereas tacit knowledge is knowledge we build up over our lifetime, and often we are at a loss to explain what we believe to others. For example, a skilled driver or golfer can have a difficult time explaining to another person how to drive or play golf as skillfully as he or she does. Experts in any field have a good deal of tacit knowledge that they do not know how to impart to others.

The principal challenge Nonaka and Takeuchi (1995) see facing corporations is how to capture, preserve and exchange tacit knowledge and how to transform tacit into explicit knowledge. We have found concept maps to be a powerful tool in these processes. In the field of medicine, we have found concept mapping very useful to clarify complex ideas. For example, we worked with an expert cardiologist, Dr. Andrews, who had developed a relatively non-invasive method for diagnosing coronary diseases but was having difficulty training other cardiologists to use his tools and methods. Through interviews with Dr. Andrews and study of a book he coauthored explaining his techniques, we constructed a comprehensive concept map of both his explicit and his tacit knowledge.

Once we had captured Dr. Andrews' tacit and explicit knowledge of "first pass functional imaging" for diagnosis of coronary problems and concept mapped this knowledge, it was relatively easy to design the Artificial Intelligence (AI) Program for training, and even lab technicians were achieving 93 percent correct diagnosis (on cases in the files) using the AI Program. Figure 6.10 shows the concept map prepared in this work.

More recently, Von Krogh and colleagues (2000, p. 83) offered a useful discussion on ways to share tacit knowledge. They suggest direct observation

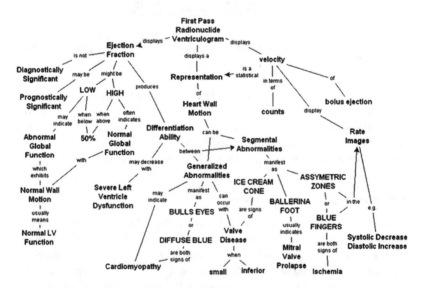

Figure 6.10 A concept map prepared from interviews with an expert in nuclear cardiology. This map was used to help design an artificial intelligence program to train MDs in using First Pass Functional Imaging technology. Reproduced with permission from A. Cañas.

of tasks done by colleagues, including discussion with the colleague, attempts at imitating the work of the colleague, and joint execution of tasks with colleagues. Their suggestions apply to all fields, not just the business community.

As in the case of our work with Dr. Andrews, we have found repeatedly in various projects that the challenge is not only to ascertain the tacit knowledge pertinent to a problem but also to find ways to preserve and share this knowledge. Concept maps have been found repeatedly to be the most effective way to do these things.

Declarative, Procedural, and Structural Knowledge

Declarative knowledge is usually described as knowledge or awareness of some object, event, or idea. Ryle (1949) describes this kind of knowledge as *knowing that*, and contrasts it with procedural knowledge or *knowing how*. Declarative knowledge is needed to construct procedural knowledge. Jonassen, Beissner and Yacci (1993) describe *structural knowledge* as that knowledge "that mediates the translation of declarative into procedural knowledge and facilitates the application of procedural knowledge." Their book goes on to describe various methods for representing, conveying, and acquiring structural knowledge, including discussion of our work on concept mapping.

While the declarative/procedural knowledge distinction is currently popular in psychological writings, I see this as of limited value. For one thing, it is more parsimonious to recognize that all knowledge is fundamentally concept-propositional in nature. Furthermore, the distinction between declarative and procedural knowledge is often ambiguous and at times purely arbitrary. As noted above, *information* may lack structure, but I regard all knowledge as possessing structure. In the three decades we have been working with knowledge-representation tools, we have not found any subject matter or field of inquiry where the structure of the knowledge has not been important. Certainly when it comes to knowledge creation, the quality of the structure of knowledge we possess is the critical variable.

Approaches to Knowledge Capture and Utilization

The Personal Interview

Over the years, we have found the personal interview to be the most powerful tool for capturing the knowledge held by an individual or groups of individuals. Personal interviews involve a one-on-one conversation between the interviewer and the interviewee. The key to successfully probing and capturing how the interviewee thinks, feels, and acts toward an idea, thing, or experience is for the interviewer to ask the type of questions that reveal as spontaneously as possible the interviewee's thoughts, feelings, and actions. This requires some experience and skill on the part of the interviewer. Numerous books and articles have been written on interviewing, including Piaget's prodigious works and writings that contributed enormously to the popularization of interviewing, and to our own early work with interviews. None of these works, however, were based on a specific theory of knowledge and complementary theory of learning, combined with knowledge-representation tools based on these theories. Since the early 1970s, we have used concept maps to design and interpret personal interviews. Since the late 1970s, we have used both concept maps and Vee diagrams to design and interpret personal interviews. See Figure 6.5 for an example of a Vee design for a research project dealing with pre-school and parents' ideas on nutrition.

We must be careful not to underestimate the complexity of ideas younger interviewees can deal with. Matthews (1980) found that, in interviews with children three to nine years old, some remarkably profound philosophical ideas were expressed. These ideas rated favorably with similar ideas expressed by great philosophers. For example, the question of the constancy of objects in differ-ent frames of reference has a long philosophical history. Matthews observed:

> One day John Edgar (four years), who had often seen airplanes take off, rise, and gradually disappear into the distance, took his first plane ride. When the plane stopped ascending and the seat-belt sign went out, John Edgar turned to his father and said in a rather relieved, but still troubled, tone of voice, "things don't really get smaller up here." (p. 6)

This and many other examples led Matthews to conclude that, although young children may have less language sophistication and fewer relevant experiences, they are capable of profound philosophical thinking. We found, in interviews with pre-school children and their parents, that, in terms of the number and variety of nutrition concepts expressed by the children, they were comparable to their parents, and in some cases, even more sophisticated than their fathers (Achterberg, 1985).

Market researchers seldom consider children's ideas regarding products other than toys or breakfast cereals, even though it is recognized that young children can influence parent product or service choices. Woodruff and Gardial's (1996) book, *Know Your Customer*, has no discussion on interviews with children, although they do give strong endorsement and preference to personal interviews over other research techniques. Lafley and Charan (2008) place the customer at the center of their model for effective businesses, but they do not discuss the importance of interviewing children and capturing in an explicit way their thoughts and feelings.

The design of good personal interviews involves several steps. First is the clear definition of a question or set of questions we hope the interviewees will answer. From the perspective of the Knowledge Vee, these are the "focus ques-tions." We must consider all of the elements on the left side of the Vee that are pertinent to our focus questions and relevant for our target population. For example, the concepts and principles relevant to interviewees of ages three to six or seven might be quite different than those for interviewees of ages eighteen to thirty.

A concept map should be prepared to organize the structure of knowledge the interviewer anticipates will be relevant to the focus questions and that will represent a good composite of the concepts and principles that may be expressed by the interviewees. For knowledge domains where the pertinent knowledge is clearly defined, this map may represent the knowledge structure held by experts, with the degree of sophistication dependent upon that of our target population. For example, a concept map for interviews on the question: "Why do things float?" is shown in Figure 6.11. While this would be too simplistic for interviews with physicists, it served very well as a template for interviewing school children and adults of all ages.

For domains of knowledge where there are no "right" concepts or principles, the task may be initially more difficult. If we want to know why people choose to buy or not buy a certain beverage most often, we can start with a preliminary concept map based on our own experiences, but it will very likely be necessary to modify this map substantially. In any case, we need to use an iterative process where we design interview questions based on a first approximation concept map, revise this after an interview or two, redesign the interview, try two or three more interviews, and repeat the process. My experience, based on teaching several thousand students, teachers, and professors how to interview, is that three to five cycles of design–try out–concept

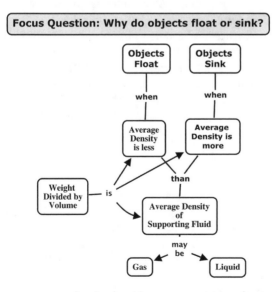

Figure 6.11 A concept map showing key ideas necessary to understand floating and sinking.

map–redesign are needed to achieve highly effective interviews. We have found that interviews with six to ten subjects from a given population provide essentially all of the concepts and principles that will be expressed and can serve as a basis for understanding the belief structure of that population on the questions posed. Zaltman and Higie (1993, p. 35) reported that 90 percent of the ideas held by consumers were captured in three to ten consumer interviews, with the number required varying with the product or service. In general, they conclude that there is little new insight to be gained after eight to ten customer interviews. Our interview strategies are only recently being applied in corporate settings.

Interviews should be conducted in a friendly, cordial manner. They should not be "interrogations" where questions are fired at the interviewee in rapid succession. Interviewees need some time to think to scan their memories and to formulate answers. In classroom settings it has been found that on average, teachers wait only 0.7 seconds before firing another question or moving to question another student. Rowe (1974) found that students give either no answers or superficial replies when "wait time" is 0.7 seconds or less. A wait time of 3–4 seconds is minimal, and questions that require some introspective thinking by the interviewee might best be followed with a "wait time" of 10–15 seconds or more. This will appear to be an "eternity" to the interviewer, so novice interviewers need to watch a clock during interviews. If you want to uncover what some people call customers' "unarticulated" concerns or desires, you need to use sufficient wait time and good follow-up questions to get this kind of "deep reflection."

There is always the question, "Will my interviews only reveal what I designed them to reveal and miss large and important segments of the interviewee's beliefs?" Our experience has been that this is unlikely if interviewers use good techniques, and sufficient iterations of interview design, concept mapping of interviewee responses, and redesign are employed. The latter process will show a quick reduction in interview modifications needed and a growing confidence that a relatively complete set of interviewee beliefs are being recorded. Detailed instruction on design, execution, and interpretation of interviews can be found in Novak and Gowin (1984, Chapter 7).

Questionnaires

The principal advantage of using questionnaire or survey forms is that they can be administered to much larger samples than is usually possible or feasible for interviews. Another major advantage is that *numbers* can be extracted from the response forms, and these can be used in various statistical, transformations, tables, graphs, etc. There is, in the general population, the idea that if you have large numbers and maybe two or three numbers after the decimal point, then the results must be "right". Sometimes this belief is strongly held by managers. The problem is that the individual's responses to each question and the totals of various combinations of responses may mean very little if we don't understand *why* the respondent chose to respond as he or she did! There can be significant *validity* problems in that the respondent's choices may not represent his or her real thoughts, feelings, or actions. And, neither the respondent nor the researcher can ask, "What do you mean by that (question or response)?" The questionnaire may also miss important topics, ideas, or feelings, further contributing to validity problems.

Looked at from the perspective of the Knowledge Vee, many sources of validity problems are possible. Was adequate consideration given in the questionnaire to ascertain the respondent's World View, Philosophy, Theories, Concepts and Principles? Were the focus questions the right foundation for design of the questionnaire? There may be high reliability for the *records* obtained from the questionnaire, but how *valid* are the records? No amount of statistical manipulation will add validity to the raw records. Even worse, there is always the danger of reification, that is, we may extract "factors" or correlation coefficients from our statistical transformations, but it is not easy to decide whether these are real or valid, and even more difficult at times to determine what they mean. For all of these reasons, my bias leans toward the power *and* cost-effectiveness of personal interviews combined with concept mapping when we want to understand a population's beliefs about anything.

All of the above notwithstanding, questionnaires can be used effectively *in conjunction with personal interviews*. In fact, the best way to design a questionnaire or survey form is to begin with a series of interviews as described above. Using the "knowledge claims" from the interviews as a starting point, questionnaire items can be designed. When this approach is used, much more *valid* results can be obtained. Furthermore, the Vees and concept maps generated from the interview process can help to interpret the *meaning* of the quantitative data extracted from the questionnaire responses. Another benefit of this approach is that the response rate from mailed questionnaires or other forms of distribution can be much better. We found this to be true in one of our studies. Because the survey instrument was designed from actual statements of the sample population's thoughts, feelings, and actions, the items of the survey "made sense" to most of the respondents, and may even have intrigued the respondents. Whereas typical response rates to mailed questionnaires are 20 percent to 30 percent, we obtained a 61 percent response rate to a mailed, very complex questionnaire on water conservation sent to a random sample of a city's water customers (Hughes, 1986). The questionnaire revealed a surprisingly good understanding of factors influencing groundwater contamination and toxicity, as was also true in the interviews done to design the questionnaire. Probably every reader has had the experience of receiving a questionnaire to complete where the items or choices just didn't make sense. Your response was probably the same as mine—into the rubbish it goes!

Focus Groups

A common practice in business is to gather a group of 15–20 consumers together and ask them as a group to express their thoughts, feelings, and actions regarding some product or service. Too often the results of these focus groups are difficult to interpret, and they have serious validity problems. For example, they are typically conducted during the working day, thus most participants are people (usually female or retirees) who do not have jobs during the day. It also requires a very knowledgeable, skillful leader, knowledgeable both regarding the topics of the focus group discussion and knowledgeable as well as skillful in leading such groups. The "generic" focus group leaders many companies employ are often limited in both pertinent knowledge and leadership skills. There are also the technical problems associated with video and/or audio recording of the sessions.

For focus groups, as for questionnaire studies, results can be improved by applying the personal interview strategies in preparation for the focus groups. However, it is likely that the the concepts and beliefs identified with focus group findings will be largely redundant for those found using interviews. They can serve, nevertheless, as a kind of cross-check on the interviews to see if patterns are similar.

Team Concept Mapping

One of the most useful roles concept mapping can play is to aid a group or team to capture, and come to consensus on, their collective knowledge regarding some question or set of questions of interest to the team. This may proceed in several ways.

In one of our early applications of the process, each staff member of a state school for girls was asked to concept map how they perceive their role in the school. The school was faced with significant budget reductions necessitating some redeployment and reduction in staff. There was a need to become more efficient and to raise the morale of the staff. After staff members completed the concept maps, the maps, with no names or other identification, were taped to the walls of a large meeting room. The staff then spent an hour reviewing all of the concept maps and taking notes. The subsequent discussion led to very productive suggestions on how operations and staff activities could be made more efficient. This led, in time, to substantial improvement in staff morale, student morale, and effectiveness of the school.

A different approach was used with a research team, the Rhizobotany Group at Cornell University, studying plant roots. After an orientation to concept mapping and opportunities for individual team members to construct a concept map dealing with their segment of the research program, the whole research team assembled to construct a "global map" for their area of plant science research. The professor in charge of the research group led the discussion, with one of my graduate students helping to facilitate the discussion and recording the ideas in the form of a concept map on the blackboard. The team used this map to help orient each team member as to where, in the larger domain of knowledge, each individual's research project fitted in. From time to time, revisions were made to the "global map," and individuals continued to refine their own maps as the research program progressed. Figure 6.12 shows the global map for the study of the biosphere as it was at the time we discontinued our work with the team. The professor in charge and most of the individual team members found the use of concept maps to be very helpful in guiding their research. Interestingly, a technician and a visiting foreign researcher made no effort to produce their own concept maps, and they saw little or no value in them. On the other hand, a new graduate student joining the research team saw immediately how the maps helped her to understand the research in progress with the Rhizobotany Group and to see how her own research questions could be designed to fit into and extend the knowledge structure the research team was developing (Novak and Iuli, 1995). She

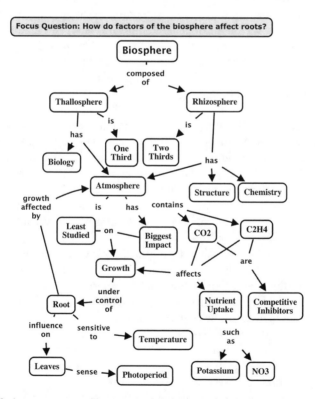

Figure 6.12 A concept map showing a global view of the study of the biosphere. Individual projects on root growth were seen to fit into this global knowledge structure.

reported that she had a better understanding of the research work being done by the team after a one-month association with the group than she had for the work of an entomology team she had worked with for two years. The concept map in Figure 6.8 and the Vee diagram in Figure 6.9 guided her Ph.D studies. In general, we have found that technicians have a good knowledge of how to perform tasks associated with the research, but little conceptual understanding of what the project seeks to accomplish in terms of knowledge discovery. Unfortunately, too many graduate students perform as poor technicians rather than as budding scholars. Much of this problem can be reduced by having graduate or other apprentices construct concept maps for the domain in which they are working.

A third method we have employed extensively in the corporate setting involves a somewhat different approach. We first work with a team leader who has responsibility for some area of technological or market development to define the key question or questions that are of most pressing concern, e.g., how can we double sales in five years of X products in the Japanese market? The team leader also works with one or more of our facilitators to develop a preliminary "global concept map" containing perhaps 8–12 concepts that he or she believes are the most general, most inclusive, and linking words to form some of the key propositions on the global map. This pre-teamwork preparation helps the team leader become oriented to the process of concept mapping and also builds confidence in the person for leading the whole team in the process of concept mapping.

We have found that it is useful to provide all team members some orientation to the theory of learning and theory of knowledge underlying concept mapping early in the process of team concept map building, or preferably in advance through readings and/or technologically mediated orientation materials. We developed a DVD orientation program for a very large consumer products company that included specific examples from some of the concept mapping projects completed with that company. A video presentation made by me to introduce concept maps to a group is available at: http://www.ihmc.us/movies/cmapIntro.mov

Our experience has been that the optimal size for "knowledge capture and mapping" teams is usually 12–20 members. The team needs to be large enough that most of the relevant knowledge and/or experience is represented in the group, but not so large as to make whole-team discussions difficult. As with all teamwork, optimal size of the team is not always easy to determine in advance. Moreover, the team leader may not have recognized the need for a member with a certain area of expertise until after the mapping process gets well along and the team knowledge map begins to show "knowledge gaps" that are now obviously pertinent but were not recognized earlier.

Subsequent to orientation of the team members, which may occur during the first half of the first day, the whole team discusses the focus question(s) and the tentative "global map" created by the team leader. We used to work with Post-its^{tm} of various sizes, using larger Post-its^{tm} for the large general concepts of the "global map" and smaller Post-its^{tm} for specific concepts. These were often mounted on large sheets of butcher paper, permitting the finished maps to be rolled up and saved, either for later review and modification or for transfer to electronic files via computer. We now more commonly use computer projectors either with the whole team or subteams and, using CmapTools, it is easy to create concept maps as the team's work progresses. It usually takes about an hour for the team as a whole to discuss, debate, and reach consensus on one or two good focus questions and the 8–12 concepts representing the top concepts of a global map. Usually this global map will contain a top concept and 3–5 "second level" concepts. The team is now divided into subteams, and a leader is selected for each subteam. These subteams now proceed to develop a concept map for their subdomain of the "global map." This process usually takes 2–4 hours. Ideally, a facilitator skilled in leading groups in concept mapping is available for each subteam.

After the subteams have developed a "prototype" concept map for their subdomain, a whole-team review of each of the subdomain maps is conducted, with the subdomain leader "walking" the whole team through his or her subdomain map. Each subdomain map is discussed, questions are raised, and suggestions for revisions are made. After all of the subdomain maps are reviewed, the whole team may meet to revise the focus question and top concepts. Then each subdomain team returns to extend, modify, correct, or in other ways, improve their map. This process may take one or two hours, depending on the difficulties encountered.

The next step is for the whole team to reassemble, either to review again each of the subdomain concept maps or to continue further development of a "global map" for the team. Suggestions are proffered as to how each subdomain map could be incorporated into a "global map," and how modifications of the original "global map" might lead to better inclusion of all of the knowledge captured up to this point. This process may be continued to the end of the first working day, or extend to a second day. Alternatively, the team may work over a period of weeks, exchanging ideas on how each subteam map can be improved and how the global map might be improved. Electronic communication of maps, revised maps, and suggestions can greatly facilitate this process.

Another step in the process is for the team to work both individually and as groups to see better and novel ways to integrate knowledge in each of the subdomains of the global map. In short, the team is doing a *creative* exercise in searching for better ways to organize the knowledge of their field and to seek new *intergrative reconciliations* between segments of the global map. Searching for significant "crosslinks" between segments of the global map will facilitate creative insights. These are the processes that lead to new *creative insights*, new ways to "break out of the box," to express an idea common in business (cf. Vance and Deacon, 1995). Here we come back to the significance of each team member recognizing and considering the important theoretical foundations underlying concept maps and their role in facilitating learning and creativity.

Concept maps can be used to capture and display knowledge a company has in "core competencies." These can be very helpful both in achieving and making available to all employees knowledge the company has in core competency areas and in identifying new core competencies that are needed and new market opportunities. Hamel and Prahalad (1994) present a four-section grid, with new and existing core competencies combined with new and existing markets (p. 227). Gaps in knowledge that could be useful often become obvious to teams constructing core competency concept maps, leading to suggestions for new core competencies that might be developed. The ease with which new crosslinks on core competency concept maps can be constructed permits identification of new market opportunities.

The Use of CmapTools and Computer Projectors. Recently we have had available for concept mapping the sophisticated software, CmapTools, created by the Florida Institute for Human and Machine Cognition. This software is available at no cost at: http://cmap.ihmc.us. Newer computer projectors are now much lower in cost, and they can also be used in rooms with reasonable ambient lighting. We have found that we can now capture the knowledge of individual experts or groups of experts in real time by using CmapTools and a computer projector. Our approach is to have a facilitator ask probing questions of the expert or group of experts, and as concepts and propositions are elicited, they are typed into a concept map on the computer by one person, whom we often call the "driver", and projected on the screen. Members of the group are free to comment and make suggestions, or ask for clarifications. Within an hour or two, it is possible to build an excellent concept map showing the knowledge of the expert or group of experts. Figure 6.13 shows an example of such a knowledge elicitation session conducted at the Florida Institute for Human and Machine Cognition.

Another advantage of this approach for knowledge elicitation is that it is relatively easy to teach people to be knowledge elicitors or facilitators, "drivers" or computer concept mappers, or team leaders to orient a team prior to a knowledge elicitation session. Using some of the ideas shown in Appendix I, we begin training sessions with an introduction to concept mapping for all participants. We have found a two-day training session is sufficient to demonstrate the approach, and to have several participants practice each of the latter roles.

To date, we have found the approach described above to be enormously helpful. The necessity for confidentiality with private corporation concept maps prevents me from showing many of the maps developed in recent years. However, we have used the above procedures to capture the expertise of people in many fields, and some of this work is described below.

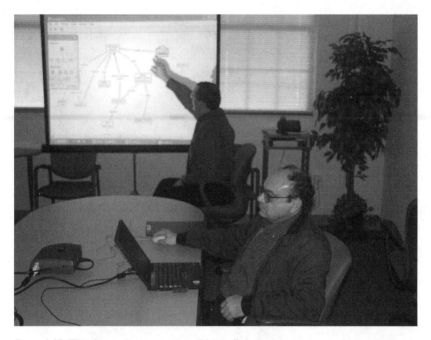

Figure 6.13 This figure shows a person "driving" the computer to produce concepts in boxes as the facilitator (at the screen) prods the expert(s) for ideas pertinent to the domain being elicited. This "driver" was one of the training group participants.

Capturing and Archiving Expert Knowledge

Most of the funding that IHMC has received to support improvement of the CmapTools software has come from federal organizations such a NASA, Department of Navy, and National Security Administration (NSA). Of course, the concept map produced by the latter group are strictly confidential, so none of these can be published. A primary objective of this work has been to capture knowledge from experts, many of whom are soon to retire and much of whose tacit knowledge would be lost. Thus we are using CmapTools both to facilitate capturing this knowledge in an explicit, concise form and to preserve or archive this knowledge for current and future use. Concept maps made by NASA are available to anyone. One of our colleagues at NASA, Geoff Briggs, has developed a large collection of concept maps to inform the public about the nature of Mars exploration (see: Briggs, et al., 2004). Figure 6.14. is the "Top Map" for a collection of concept maps that provide detailed information on Mars exploration. By clicking on icons on concepts in this and other concept maps in the collection, one can access subordinate maps that present more details, photos, videos, and other resources that provide additional information. The whole set of concept maps can be seen at: http://cmex.ihmc.us

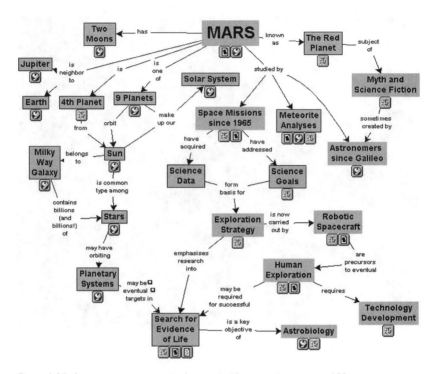

Figure 6.14 A concept map created to provide access to some 100 concept maps dealing with Mars exploration. Clicking on icons on concepts provides access to other concept maps and resources.

We are currently working with NASA to develop a set of concept maps that build the case for the importance to plan a NASA program for return to the moon. A former astronaut, US Senator, and geoscientist, Harrison Schmitt has been working with us to create these concept maps. He has also presented some of his arguments for returning to the moon and establishing colonies there in his book, *Return to the Moon* (2006). This set of concept maps will be available to the public when it is completed. A key argument in Schmitt's book is that the moon's surface contains unusually large quantities of Helium 3. If methods can be found to fuse Helium 3, an immense store of nuclear energy would become available supporting colonies on the moon, for use on earth, and in future space travel. When the set of expert concept maps are finished on this project, they will by posted on the IHMC CmapTools server under "Return to the Moon".

Another area where we have worked with experts is with the National Weather Service weather forecasting. Figure 6.15 shows an example of one of the concept maps created with weather forecasters. Other projects have been done with workers in nuclear power plants. Since no new nuclear power plants

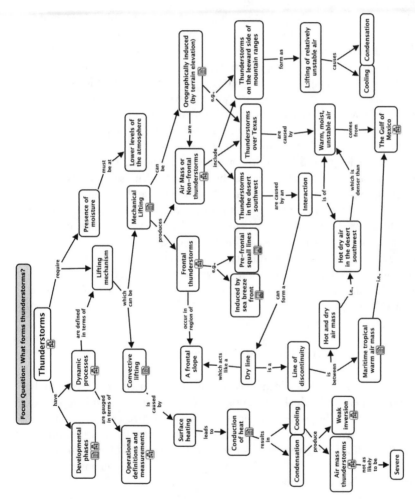

Figure 6.15 A concept map prepared with an expert in weather forecasting dealing with the nature of thunderstorms. Also shown are icons that access related sub-concept maps and other resources. By R. Hoffman, reproduced with permission.

have been built in the US for almost three decades, most of the workers soon to retire have knowledge that is "not in the books." This work has been led by Hoffman (Hoffman, et al., 2001; 2006) and more details on the work can be found in his publications.

My grandson, Christopher Durocher, is trained in photography and design, and he has found CmapTools a powerful way to present complex ideas in a holistic fashion. He presented his ideas as a poster at the Third International Conference on Concept Mapping in Tallin, Estonia in September, 2008 and it attracted the attention of a number of participants, including a team associated with theatrical productions. Figure 6.16 shows Durocher's poster with the theme or central concept of "Speed in Art". Clicking on icons of his concept map opens files with photos, video clips and other representations dealing with the central idea of speed in art, some of which are shown around the concept map. More conversations with people involved in theatrical productions expressed an interest in using CmapTools as one method of archiving the millions of pieces of information that go into the production of a major show, from costume design, music, set design, individual acts, etc. The visual display made possible with CmapTools helps the hundreds of persons involved in a production to see where they fit into the "big picture," and in turn suggests to them ways they can tailor their piece to better complement the theme of the show. Moreover, the knowledge archive created facilitates in a highly accessible way the design of future shows, where many of the same components are employed along with new components. While I know of no applications similar to this in the advertising world, it should be obvious that CmapTools can function in a similar way to produce advertising campaigns that center around a creative "concept".

Other Approaches to Knowledge Capture

Knowledge Vee. The Knowledge Vee has also been used very successfully as a tool to help individuals or teams capture, organize, and utilize knowledge more effectively. Some examples have been presented earlier. Compared with concept maps, using the Vee requires significantly more training, "incubation time," and reorientation in the way most people think about knowledge and knowledge creation. My guess is that it will take two or three decades before the power and utility of using the Knowledge Vee for knowledge capture and facilitation of thinking takes hold, even in the business community where management motivation may be high, but probably not their understanding of the nature of knowledge and knowledge creation.

Karoline Afamasaga-Fuata'i (2004) has used concept maps and Vees successfully in math classes and she has found that these tools significantly enhance students' conceptual understanding of mathematics. Moreover, students become more enthusiastic about mathematics, as might be expected when their understanding increases.

Mind Mapping. One of the earlier tools developed for capturing knowledge of individuals or groups is Buzan's Mind Mapping (Buzan, 1974). In this approach, one begins with a central idea in the center of a paper and then begins to link with lines relevant ideas radiating out from this key idea. As other subordinate ideas, these branch off and are connected with other lines. The outcome is a map such as that in Figure 6.17, prepared by Okada (2008).

It is also possible to include figures or other information in Mind Maps, and software is available to aid in the process of making Mind Maps. The simplicity of Mind Mapping has made the use of this tool very popular, and it is used in many schools and scores of corporations. Dissemination of this tool is also aided by many individuals and companies that sell consulting or training services for the use of this tool. It is perhaps the best known knowledge representation tool at this time. Partly for this reason, some of my colleagues find it useful to begin with a new group by constructing a mind map and then move the group to the more explicit knowledge structure that can be created using concept maps. This may be one approach you can use in your own work with concept maps. Kinchin and colleagues (2005) observed: "Whereas mind mapping helps rapid brainstorming of ideas and formation of simple associations with related concepts, concept mapping is a more reflective process and emphasizes the 'how' and 'why' of such links. The two tools may, therefore, be seen as complementary." (p. 11)

Other Approaches. There are, of course, many other approaches to knowledge capture, representation, and utilization. Some of these, in my opinion, are little more than gimmicks to stimulate discussions among group members and schemes to record information in pictorial ways. They obviously have some value, since some schools and companies spend thousands of dollars in staff time, materials, consulting fees, and other costs to employ these strategies. It has been my experience, and the experience of many who I have worked with in schools and businesses, that the value of most other "knowledge tools" pale in comparison to the value experienced using concept maps.

If the 1990s belonged to the businesses that were successful in utilizing Total Quality Management (TQM) and "reengineering" their operations, I believe the decades ahead will be dominated by those corporations who become most effective in using tools such as concept maps to help them organize, create, store, and access knowledge more effectively. TQM brought with it ideas such as "benchmarking" best practices and "just in time" inventory systems, but most of these activities were centered on *processes* of corporate functioning and not on knowledge creation, Similarly, reengineering also places emphasis on processes utilized, although there is also concern with mechanisms for providing leadership for process improvements (Hammer, 1993).

Figure 6.16 A concept map on "Speed in Art" produced to show how a wide array of representations can be combined to create a way to represent an "organizing concept" in the field of art. By C. Durocher, reproduced with permission.

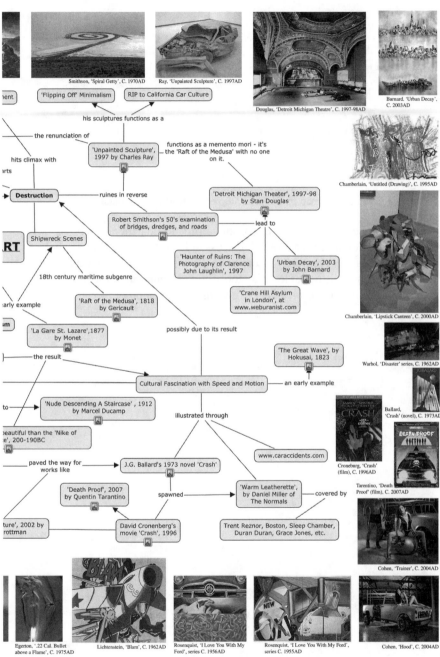

Smithson, 'Spiral Getty', C. 1970AD

Ray, 'Unpainted Sculpture', C. 1997AD

Douglas, 'Detroit Michigan Theatre', C. 1997-98AD

Barnard. 'Urban Decay', C. 2003AD

'Flipping Off' Minimalism

RIP to California Car Culture

Chamberlain, 'Untitled (Drawing)', C. 1995AD

Chamberlain, 'Lipstick Canteen', C. 2000AD

Warhol, 'Disaster' series, C. 1962AD

Ballard, 'Crash' (novel), C. 1973AD

Croneburg, 'Crash' (film), C. 1996AD

Tarentino, 'Death Proof' (film), C. 2007AD

Cohen, 'Trainer', C. 2004AD

his sculptures functions as a

the renunciation of

hits climax with

Destruction

Shipwreck Scenes

18th century maritime subgenre

early example

the result

'Unpainted Sculpture', 1997 by Charles Ray

functions as a memento mori - it's the 'Raft of the Medusa' with no one on it.

'Detroit Michigan Theater', 1997-98 by Stan Douglas

ruines in reverse

Robert Smithson's 50's examination of bridges, dredges, and roads

lead to

'Haunter of Ruins: The Photography of Clarence John Laughlin', 1997

'Urban Decay', 2003 by John Barnard

'Crane Hill Asylum in London', at www.weburanist.com

'Raft of the Medusa', 1818 by Gericault

'La Gare St. Lazare',1877 by Monet

possibly due to its result

'The Great Wave', by Hokusai, 1823

Cultural Fascination with Speed and Motion

an early example

'Nude Descending A Staircase' , 1912 by Marcel Ducamp

illustrated through

beautiful than the 'Nike of e', 200-190BC

paved the way for works like

J.G. Ballard's 1973 novel 'Crash'

www.caraccidents.com

'Death Proof', 2007 by Quentin Tarantino

spawned

'Warm Leatherette', by Daniel Miller of The Normals

covered by

ture', 2002 by rottman

David Cronenberg's movie 'Crash', 1996

Trent Reznor, Boston, Sleep Chamber, Duran Duran, Grace Jones, etc.

Egerton, '.22 Cal. Bullet above a Flame', C. 1975AD

Lichtenstein, 'Blam', C. 1962AD

Rosenquist, 'I Love You With My Ford', series C. 1956AD

Rosenquist, 'I Love You With My Ford', series C. 1955AD

Cohen, 'Hood', C. 2004AD

Figure 6.17 Sample mind map. In Okada, 2008, reproduced with permission.

By comparison with change in corporate practices, change in schools has been very modest at best, as we will discuss in later. My hope is that schools and universities will eventually incorporate the best we know about the facilitation of learning, the use of learning tools, and exploitation of the promise of the Internet. This book is my effort to encourage and empower such change.

Chapter 7

The Effective Teacher/ Manager

Integrating Thinking, Feeling, and Acting Constructively

As stated in Chapter 2, human beings experience concomitantly thinking, feeling, and acting. This is true for school learners and workers as well as for teachers and managers. I shall consider all of these as *learners* whether in a "work" context or a school context. The challenge is how to help students and workers integrate in a constructive manner these concomitant experiences. When learners do this successfully, the teacher's or the manager's experience is also positive, constructive, and rewarding. I also see managers as teachers in a "work" context and shall call them both *teachers*. When learners fail to achieve a constructive integration of their thinking, feeling, and acting, both teacher and learners lose, although the loss can be more serious for the learner. In the worst case, the bedlam that can result in the classroom or in the work-place can lead to great teacher or manager frustration or even dismissal from the job.

Teaching is a complex activity. This is evident in the thousands of research studies, such as those summarized in *The Handbook of Research on Teacher Education* (Houston, 1990; Saha & Dwarkin, 2009). Rowan (1994) compared teachers' work with work in other occupations and found that: "Teaching children and adolescents is complex work compared with other professions, and successful performance of this work requires high levels of general educational development and specific vocational preparation" (p. 13). As a complex activity, I believe it is imperative that teaching be guided by a comprehensive theory of education. However, in a study of foundation courses for teacher education, Bauer and Borman (1988) found no such courses listed in 508 courses from 100 college catalogs. The idea that teachers need a theory of education to guide their work is clearly an idea whose time has not come, at least not for most teachers in the United States. More recently, Wilson and Peterson (2006) point out that there is now general recognition that learning requires active construction of knowledge by learners, and that teachers need to structure their classrooms for individual and shared work. However, most studies of actual classroom teaching practices show that most classrooms do not utilize such practices or do so only infrequently.

The same, unfortunately, is true for management. This, too, is a complex activity, and while books abound on how to manage, *theory*-based ideas of management are hard to find. Those books that do deal with theoretical issues, such as the classic works of Argyris and Schon (1978) and Schon (1983), do not deal with a theory of learning or a theory of knowledge. Schon, for example, argues that effective practitioners must base practice on theory, but he does not describe a theory that is relevant nor give examples of the relationship between specific theories and specific practices such as teaching or management.

My theory is that *meaningful learning* must underlie the constructive integration of thinking, feeling, and acting if learners are to be successful and achieve a sense of empowerment—and also a sense of commitment and responsibility. The responsibility is to themselves as learners, to peers, and to the learning environment. I have discussed at length in earlier chapters what is required to effect meaningful learning, and this chapter will focus on the challenges the teacher (or manager) faces to achieve what I like to refer to as successful negotiation of meanings. While learning is an activity that cannot be shared, but is rather the *responsibility* of the learner, it is the teacher's responsibility to seek the best possible negotiation of meanings and an emotional climate that is conducive to learn meaningfully. Teachers must also recognize their role in negotiating meanings and for creating a favorable emotional climate to encourage such negotiation.

First and foremost, effective teaching requires that we constantly remain cognizant of the fact that only meaningful learning can lead to progressive differentiation and integration of cognitive structure and concomitant sustained enhancement of an individual's ego. This is shown in Figure 7.1. Second, and also exceedingly important, we must recognize that every teaching event should seek to achieve two purposes: (1) to enhance further differentiation of the learner's cognitive structure, and (2) to enhance the learner's sense of "I'm OK." These two attributes also underlie development of skills when combined with practice of the skill. I do not believe that there is ever an occasion when teaching or managing that deliberately assaults a learner's ego is justified, although this is commonly observed in schools and in job settings.

One can never overestimate the amount of knowledge and the extent of emotional sensitivity required to teach or manage effectively. Moreover, knowledge and emotional sensitivities must be brought together to achieve effective teaching and management skills, and a mastery in teaching or management takes time and constant effort. While people vary in their innate talents to effect constructive integration of thinking, feeling, and acting, as with all human talents, my thesis is that any person can become a much more effective teacher or manager through theory-guided efforts. Some of the key ideas I will address to help in this effort are shown in Figure 7.2.

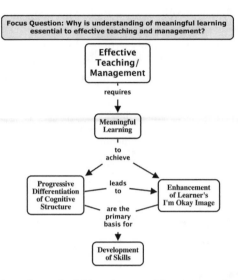

Figure 7.1 Facilitation of meaningful learning to achieve progressive differentiation of cognitive structure in a manner that leads to ego enhancement is essential.

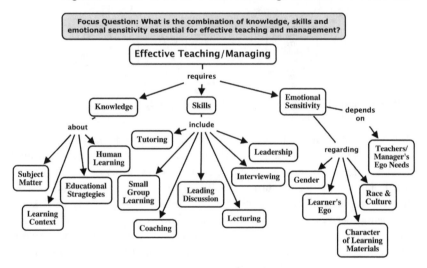

Figure 7.2 Necessary conditions for effective teaching/managing.

Teachers and Managers Need Knowledge and Emotional Sensitivity

Knowledge, as discussed earlier, is a well-organized framework of concepts and propositions. For effective teaching or managing, these frameworks must include knowledge of the subject matter to be learned, knowledge of alternative contexts for learning (even within the constraints of a poorly equipped shop, classroom, office, or school), knowledge about how humans learn, and knowledge about alternative evaluation and other educational strategies that can facilitate meaningful learning while recognizing the limitations the learners may possess and the context of the learning. In short, university programs in education *and* programs in management need to include instruction in a theory of education (Figure 7.3).

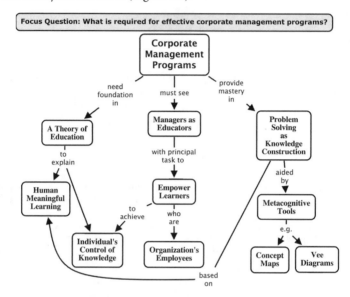

Figure 7.3 Effective management programs need to include ideas and tools from a theory of education.

Perhaps even more important, effective teaching and managing requires *emotional sensitivity* on the part of the teacher, a sensitivity to the emotional status and needs of the learner *and* a consciousness of his or her own emotional status and needs. Harris (1969), in his book, *I'm OK, You're OK*, shows in a practical way how all of us, to some extent, feel "not OK," since this feeling derives, in part, from early childhood experiences in the normal course of growing up. In the most deleterious early environments, the "I'm not OK" feelings can be so deeply rooted that a lifetime of antisocial actions, or actions that are personally destructive such as drug abuse, eating disorders, etc., may result. Because humans live in societies that are not ideally suited to engendering "I'm OK" feelings, where ethnic, cultural, racial, or gender biases may aggravate early "I'm not OK" feelings, the challenge to the teacher or manager is how to deal with the multiple ego needs of learners in constructive ways, constructive both to the learners and to the teacher or manager. It is now known that genes strongly influence social behavior in many animals (Robinson, et al. 2008), and genes also influence human social behavior (Lieberman & Eisenberger, 2009). We are finding that there are specific regions of the brain that are activated when we engage in value or moral judgments, indicating in part the evolutionary importance of value and moral judgments to human beings (Miller, 2008). Individuals' moral judgments are influenced by the groups they associate with, and Haidt (2007) found that people would agree or disagree with a moral statement depending on what group made the statement. We certainly see this when it comes to statements made by politicians! Recent studies suggest that social cooperation has evolutionary adaptive value and can be observed in other primates, especially bonobos (Miller 2007). Humans are uniquely capable to think about their social behavior and to learn how to modify their behavior (Gazzaniga, 2008). The challenge is to find ways to encourage constructive collaborations, and here we have much to learn.

Events in school can have a very damaging effect on children's development of self-confidence, and I cannot stress enough how important it is to consider the teacher's affect on children's positive ego development. Sternberg (1996), as Dean of Education, related his experience as a child growing up in schools that put inordinate emphasis on IQ scores:

> I was lucky, damn lucky, in a way few students are. In fourth grade, when I was nine years old, I ended up in Mrs. Alexa's class. Whereas my teachers in the early primary grades had all been older and deeply dug into the trenches of the testing field, Mrs. Alexa was fresh out of college and either didn't know or didn't care much about IQ test scores. She believed I could do much better than I was doing, and she expected more of me. No, she demanded more of me. And she got it. Why? Because I wanted to please her, even more than I had wanted to please my teachers in the first three grades (In fact, I would have proposed marriage to her on the spot if she hadn't been just a little too old and, inconveniently, already married). (p. 18)

My wife and I can relate to this. Our oldest son was also not the best on tests given in school, although he tested high on IQ tests given privately by a psychologist. Combined with the fact that he was left-handed, he had numerous difficulties in elementary grades, and we were advised by his fourth-grade teacher that we had to face the fact that he was "a bit retarded." Mostly, he was incredibly bored with school tasks that required him to do simple, repetitive tasks when his activities at home involved much more complex tasks. He did go on to complete a BS degree in architecture, an MBA degree at Cornell University, and in his early forties, an MS degree in computer science. Alas, our grandson showed the same proclivities. Fortunately for him, his parents recognized his unusual abilities, and also could afford to send him to exceptionally good private schools. The most outstanding feature of his schools, his parents and we agree, is that they have great concern for variation in individual aptitudes *and* in the positive ego development for their students. We experienced once again, as our grandchildren progressed through school, the enormous positive or negative effect teachers can have on children's ego development.

Knowledge relevant to teaching and managing becomes merged with emotional sensitivity in the skillfully guided educative event. For example, in conducting a discussion, still the most common educative event in most schools and corporate settings, an enormous set of ideas and feelings must be brought together. To illustrate, let us consider a relatively simple topic: Why do we have seasons?

The first consideration is: "What are the relevant concepts and principles needed to understand an answer to this question?" I have found that the preparation of a concept map for any topic to be taught is an enormously helpful way to begin, albeit at first this is time-consuming. But the time invested early in one's career, both to gain skill in constructing concept maps and in gathering the information needed for each topic, can pay off handsomely in a few years. Even very experienced teachers are often surprised at the fuzziness of their own ideas about a topic they may have taught for years when

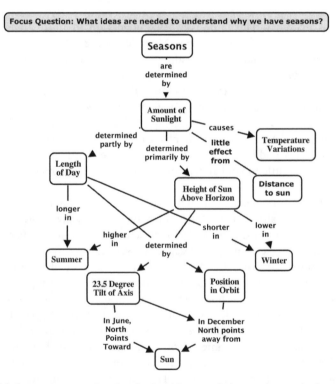

Figure 7.4 A concept map showing the key ideas needed to understand why we have seasons. Many people fail to understand the effect of the inclination of the earth on its axis as the primary cause of summer and winter in both hemispheres.

they take the time to concept map the topic (Novak, 1991). So I begin my example with a concept map on "seasons" (see Figure 7.4).

Although some regions of the earth have essentially no "seasons," that is, no major climate variations from month to month during the year, some regions experience "wet" and "dry" seasons. Most of us, however, think of seasons as colder or warmer—a bias that comes from living in a geographic area where this occurs. We might ask if any of our learners come from a region (or have relatives in a region) where temperature is not the major factor in seasons—a nice way to help foreign-born students feel participatory in our class, especially if they are encouraged to share their knowledge or experiences. We may also forget that it is summer in the northern hemisphere when it is winter in the southern hemisphere, because we live in the northern hemisphere. Again, sharing what New Year's Day may be like in the home or their relatives' home can be culturally sensitive *and* educative in terms of our knowledge goals.

The Problem of Misconceptions

Some of the knowledge about learning that should be brought to bear on this topic is that most of us develop *misconceptions* or limited conceptions about events in our lives. For example, most people believe that seasons are caused by how close the earth is to the sun. This belief may arise from the common experience that we feel warmer when we are close to a fire or a light bulb and less heat when we are further away. If we have also learned that the earth's orbit is not a perfect circle, this may reinforce our faulty belief because we now know that the earth will be closer to the sun sometimes during the year and further away at other times. We may not know, or have obliteratively subsumed, the factual details that the variation in the distance to the sun is only about 3 million miles from the average distance of about 93 million miles (or about 3 percent). Furthermore, the earth is actually *closer* to the sun when it is *winter* in the northern hemisphere, and summer in the southern hemisphere. One might ask, "How would you expect the temperatures in summers to compare at the same latitudes in the northern and southern hemispheres?"

The effective teacher or manager will know that people do not "change their minds" easily. The literature on faulty conceptions is enormous (see, for example, Novak & Abrams, 1993), and most of it points to one stark reality: Giving learners the "correct information" does not displace their faulty conceptions. It takes a lot of negotiation of meanings, a lot of shared experience to help learners reconstruct their "internal concept maps" to be congruent with the "expert's knowledge." We have found, however, that engaging students in building their own concept maps, showing (and negotiating) these in small groups, and reflecting on the "teacher's" map can be effective in helping learners reconstruct their knowledge frameworks (Feldsine, 1987; Trifone, 2005; Gorman, in review).

Knowledgeable teachers and managers know that it is not sufficient to "just give students the facts." Yes, they can memorize these if they are motivated to do so but, for most, it will not alter their *understanding* of seasons. For example, a videotape produced by the Harvard Smithsonian Center for Astrophysics, *A Private Universe*, shows that most (21 out of 23 interviewed) Harvard graduates, alumni and faculty could not give an adequate explanation of why we have seasons, *including a new graduate who recently completed a course in "The Physics of Planetary Motion"*. You can get a Harvard BS degree largely by memorizing "facts" presented (and tested for), but you may not get much education. Students need opportunities to *act on ideas*, to pretend they are the planet earth and orbit the sun (or maybe a bright light) tilted 23° from the North Pole, and pretend first they are in the northern hemisphere and then in the southern hemisphere. It takes a lot of "acting out" ideas to reconstruct faulty ideas, but what else is worth doing? Moreover, there can be some joy, humor, and excitement when learners are engaged in helping to come up with ways to act out ideas.

We see in this example the potential for merging much of the knowledge, emotional sensitivity, and skill that is necessary for helping learners take responsibility for their own meaningful learning. I shall refer back to this from time to time as one of my "paradigm cases."

Recently I had my car towed to the Nissan garage because it would not start. It was a Saturday morning, and a full crew of mechanics was not available. The mechanic who worked on my car was "almost positive the problem was an ignition module, since 95 percent of the time, cars with this problem had a faulty ignition module." I took his advice and replaced this part at a cost of $165. Unfortunately, my car would not start the next Monday morning and was towed to the garage again. A more experienced mechanic looked at the car on Monday and replaced a simple plug-in relay that controls the fuel injection motor (at $19). No more starting problems. Was I liable for the "misdiagnosis" of my problem? Technically, probably yes, but there is a lesson to be learned here. Inadequately educated mechanics can cost customers and/or the management problems, and money and frustrations for all concerned. In this case, the dealer refunded the first charge and suffered some losses, but he also gained a customer. I gave preference to this Nissan dealer when I later chose to buy another car.

In some five decades of work with teachers and managers, I have become very familiar with the limited *conceptual understanding* many teachers and managers (in school, university, and corporate settings) have regarding the subject matter they are charged to teach. This is not due to any intellectual shortcomings on their part, but is primarily a product of poor educational opportunities and little guidance for professional growth. For example, Fedock, Zambo and Cobern (1996) found that college science teachers involved in a special program for K-12 teachers not only gained new instructional strategies and skills, but also new insights about their subject matter. As one professor commented, "I never saw science as integrating with other facets of life. I had a very narrow perspective of science, being a cell biologist, but my perspective has broadened greatly, and I am amazed" (p. 17).

One of our studies (Kerr, 1988), based on intensive interviews with female scientists at Cornell University, illustrates the problem even outstanding students have had in acquiring subject matter knowledge.

> In her early education, it was the effort she put into these [science] projects that provided the meaning of learning. . . . The social institution, the school provided the meaning for those projects. . . . But it was not *her* meaning for learning that compelled her effort, only what the performance meant. At some point, *her* understanding of the meaning of science replaced performance. This did not occur until she was a senior undergraduate. What caused the switch?
>
> The first experience was discovering the conceptual foundation of evolution; ". . . it really is a passion. . . . [it] sort of made everything fall into place." (pp. 61–62)

Contrasting learning in biology with learning in physics, another scientist reported in Kerr's study commented: "I had a tendency to over-learn; over-study, because I probably never *did* know when I knew for certain." (p. 74)

Kerr also reported that biology was simple for her, but physics was not, and she got through physics by cramming it all into her head and hoping to pass on exams, but without coming to an intuitive feeling of what was involved. It was years before she had any intuitive feeling for some of those topics. She admits that there was always in the beginning memorizing and "then there is something that clicks. Or all of a sudden it fits. And you are not having to go back to proposition one to get to proposition ten" (pp. 74–75).

What Kerr is describing is the very difficult process of constructing a powerful conceptual framework for any domain of science when the teacher(s) fail(s) to help bring clarity to the concept and propositional structure necessary to have a "feeling" for the subject. While admittedly, each learner must construct his or her own conceptual frameworks, teachers can do much to facilitate this process.

In my experience, most teachers, especially novice teachers, focus on *teaching* activities and tend to ignore *learning* activities. They center attention on how to teach a given topic, rather than on what is required for a learner to learn the topic. This stems, in part, from teachers' limited knowledge of the learning process and implications for the teaching process. The long-term consequence for many teachers (especially professors in tertiary schools) is a growing cynicism toward learners and a manifest lack of empathy and emotional support for the struggle learners face in constructing and reconstructing their knowledge frameworks. The same problems prevail in business settings. Too often the focus is on covering topics for trainees to learn, often using

PowerPoint presentations. Employees dutifully try to capture and then memorize each of the highlighted points. What they fail to do is to build a *conceptual* understanding of the tasks to be mastered. In a recent study Kinchin (2006) points out the advantages of using concept maps in presentations over the use of typical PowerPoint presentations. When the instruction favors acquisition of a conceptual understanding of the topics, substantive learning takes place.

At first sight, concept mapping activities would seem to have little in common with production of PowerPoint presentations. Concept maps are constructed explicitly to illustrate the links between ideas and to highlight multiple ways of constructing concepts within a developing expert knowledge framework (Kinchin, 2006). Concept mapping is explicitly embedded within a constructivist approach to teaching with the aim of facilitating meaningful learning.

In contrast, PowerPoint is seen largely as a tool to deliver content (Szabo and Hastings, 2000) and, as such, can be seen as supportive of an objective stance to teaching. Typically PowerPoint presentations tend to overemphasize a linear structure of knowledge to the exclusion of alternative perspectives, as an authoritative voice that gives the definitive account. The linear structure of the templates supplied with PowerPoint drives teachers down a rigid sequential teaching pathway. Such an approach to teaching is complemented by a rote-learning approach by students (Hay and Kinchin, 2006). The tendency toward student passivity has been described as the "pedagogy of PowerPoint" by Tufte (2003), who has been highly critical of the software and what he sees as its negative impact on the quality of teaching and learning in higher education.

Kinchin and Cabot in a more recent study (2007) go on to report results from their research with dental students that showed that while 92 percent of the students preferred PowerPoint presentations for memorizing information, 95 percent preferred concept maps for making connections between major ideas. PowerPoint instruction can be effective when the evaluation centers on recall of specific information; it falls far short when compared with the use of concept mapping when understanding of subject matter, and subsequent ability to apply this knowledge in new contexts are the goal of learning.

Overcoming Misconceptions

Our research group has been studying the problem of student misconceptions since the early 1960s. We found in our early work the same kind of misconceptions in various science fields as had been reported by other researchers, and we also found that most teaching strategies failed to "correct" student misconceptions, even though they may learn the "correct" answers to questions dealing with these misconceptions. The fundamental problem with permanently overcoming misconceptions is that a learner must do more than learn the "correct" description or definition. Concept meanings are embedded in a matrix of concepts and propositions in the learner's cognitive structure, and one or two significant changes must occur. The pre-existing related concept meanings (i.e., propositions) must be "corrected" and/or new concepts and propositions must be assimilated into the relevant knowledge structure. Neither one of these events will occur with rote learning, since the latter does not involve active reorganizations of pertinent segments of cognitive structure. The learner must choose to engage in *meaningful learning* or relearning of relevant concepts and propositions. We and others have found the use of learner-constructed concept maps dealing with the domain of knowledge involved with misconceptions is the most effective way to overcome misconceptions (Novak, 1983).

Another way to describe the problem of misconceptions is that in some way the segment of cognitive structure containing the misconceptions is either limited or is missing important relevant concepts and propositions, or some of the relevant propositions are incorrect or inappropriate. This led me to suggest in 1983 that we might call misconceptions LIPHS, or Limited and/or Inappropriate Propositional Hierarchies (Novak, 1983). I thought this label better accounted for the real cognitive problem that underlies misconceptions, alternative conceptions, naïve notions, and other labels that appear in the literature on "misconceptions." In a later paper (Novak, 2002), I again reviewed some of the pertinent literature and emphasized that meaningful learning was the necessary process required if a learner is to overcome any given misconceptions. While current literature tends to support the latter views, and the important role that concept mapping can play in facilitating overcoming misconceptions (see Kinchin and others cited), there remains great resistance in many schools and universities to incorporate concept mapping as a standard part of instruction. Thus we see papers such as Bloom and Weisberg (2007) that well describe the problem, but do not offer a viable solution. Unfortunately, as noted earlier, in the USA the No Child Left Behind program enacted in 2001 with its emphasis on multiple-choice testing for factual recall has led to more instructional practices that emphasize memorizing "correct" answers than encouraging meaningful learning to remediate misconceptions and help learners build powerful knowledge structures. In effect, the No Child Left Behind program is encouraging instructional practices that result in *most* children being left behind. I would rename the NCLB program as the MCLBH program. But we must give due credit to those teachers and administrators that have tried to counter these negative effects of the NCLB program.

Problems in Organizational Settings

What I did not anticipate when I began working with corporations was that most administrators and managers have a surprisingly poor *conceptual understanding* of their organizations. Oh, they may know well the organizational chart showing who reports to whom. What they grasp only with fuzzy vision is how each member of the organization contributes to the overall operation of the organization. For example, when we interviewed and then concept-mapped how various members of the Cornell University Theory Center viewed their jobs, and how they felt about their jobs, we found some striking differences in perceptions of the organization between various individuals' perceptions and those of senior administrators. Figure 7.5 shows an example of one of these concept maps and describes some of the complexity of the organization's mission and functions. Prior to our preparing this map, the staff member was not clearly aware of some of the factors that were impacting her work as a manager of networking functions.

Shown in Figure 7.6 is the view of the Cornell University Theory Center held by the Director of the Center. This map was made by a class member in a course on "Application of Educational Theory and Methods to Corporations" from a lecture given by the Director to a local Rotary Club meeting. It was later reviewed and corroborated by the Director. Other class members interviewed individuals involved in administration in various subordinate positions. What we found is that their perceptions of the Theory Center, and their views on their work, were significantly at variance with that of the Director. We were not surprised to learn later that Cornell University did not get a continuing grant from the National Science Foundation to operate the Center, with one of the criticisms being poor management of the Center.

Our findings that managers do not understand what they are managing is not a new idea. Many years ago, Crosby (1992) tried to figure out operations at a missile plant where he was employed. He created a flow chart to help himself and observed:

> I spent about two weeks on the chart doing that in between chasing problems. I got all involved with laying it out on a long sheet of paper, using different shaped blocks for different missile and supply systems. It was a lot of fun. When the chart was about complete, I had one aspect I couldn't figure out, so I took it to my boss and asked him for guidance. "Where did you get this?" he asked. He was astounded that such a piece of paper existed. Everyone wanted copies, and I was an instant hero. (A little later my chart was classified "Top secret" which was one level above my clearance—so I never saw it again.) That is when I began to realize that hardly anyone knew anything about what was happening except in his or her own area of work. (pp. 5–6)

My work and the work of my students in recent years has shown examples similar to Crosby's in every organization where we have worked. We learned something else, too. The low-cost (or no-cost) student interviewer(s) may be very intimidating and embarrassing to the person who hired the expensive

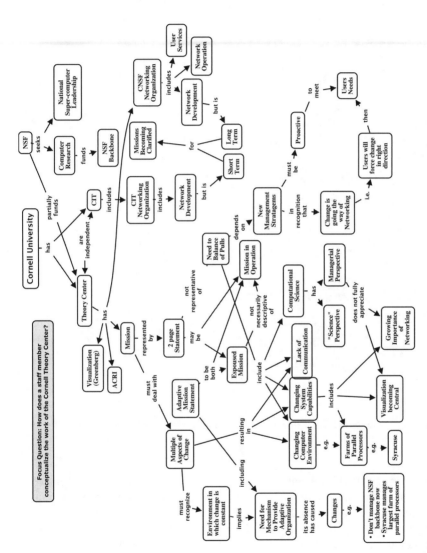

Figure 7.5 A concept map prepared from interviews with one of the Cornell University Theory Center staff members after modifications by the staff member.

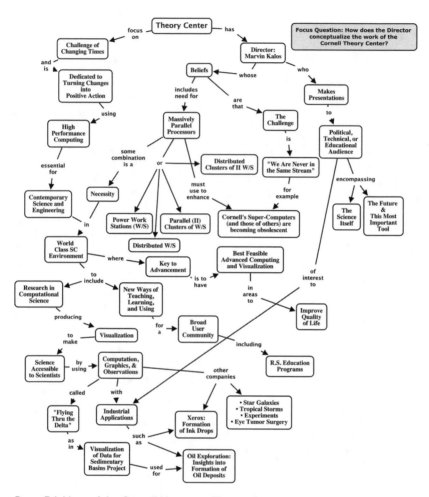

Figure 7.6 View of the Cornell University Theory Center held by the Director of the Center.

consulting firm. The student interviewer can learn more about the organization and organizational problems by interviewing and concept-mapping persons, from line workers to the chief executive officer, than may be revealed by very expensive consultants. Therefore, whoever contracted with the consulting firm does not want to be embarrassed and will try to have the student interviewer(s) removed or counsel based on their concept maps silenced. As Senge (1990) points out:

> It is no accident that most organizations learn poorly. The way they are designed and managed, the way people's jobs are defined, and most

importantly, the way they have all been taught to think and interact (not only in organizations, but more broadly) create fundamental learning disabilities. Learning disabilities are tragic in children. . . they are no less tragic in organizations. (p. 18)

Knowledge of a Theory of Education

Nobel Laureate Kenneth Wilson (Wilson & Davis, 1994) asserts in his book, *Redesigning Education,* that teacher training "requires them to know more about theories of teaching than about the subjects they teach, and whose training imparts those theories without giving them a chance to learn how to practice them effectively" (p. 83). While I agree with the latter assertion, my experience is that teachers learn almost nothing about a theory of education— at least not a theory that meets my criteria of a theory, namely that it has *explanatory* and *predictive* power for educative events. What teachers too often learn in conventional teacher education programs is a collection of rules or procedures, many of them *called* theories, none of which have the necessary comprehensiveness, explanatory power, and predictive power to guide the teacher in the hundreds of decisions that must be made in a single day of teaching. The combination of the invalid, unworkable, and non-parsimonious character of the theories usually presented lead experienced teachers to advise novice teachers to "forget all that theory stuff you learned in college." None of the award-winning elementary school teachers we interviewed in depth in one study to ascertain why they were so successful found their pre-service teacher education programs of value (Gerber, 1992). Partly this reflected the uselessness of many of the teaching methods courses that were taught two decades ago, and remain all too common today. However, these teachers do attend professional meetings, take *selectively* further university in-service education courses, and seek out conversations with experienced colleagues on theoretical issues. We found very high congruence between their *theoretical* beliefs and the ideas put forward in this book.

As noted repeatedly, teaching and managing are very complex activities. To illustrate this again, refer to Table 7.1 to see how teaching practices under the "traditional paradigm" differ from teaching practices under contemporary constructivist ideas.

In my work with pre-service and in-service teachers, I have seen my own work move from emphasis on procedures that are effective or ineffective, plus heavy emphasis on the need to understand the subject matter of the discipline (see, for example, Novak, 1963), to instruction that begins with basic ideas of *A Theory of Education* and combines tools and ideas from this work with subject matter. The response from my students has been increasingly positive. With experience in applying the theory and tools, they become strong proponents of these ideas and tools. Many go on to publish papers, textbooks, and other materials, in various languages, to "help

Table 7.1 A comparison of traditional and constructivist contexts for education as seen through the five elements of education[a]

Learner	Teacher	Curriculum	Context	Evaluation
Task is to acquire information (usually by rote learning).	Management and class control emphasized.	Fixed, textbook centered.	Schooling is good. Minor improvements may be needed.	"Objective" tests are the key to evaluation, with grades assigned "on a curve".
Emphasis on lesson planning focused on discipline, not learner's prior knowledge.	View that teachers cause learning.	Emphasis on coverage techniques.	Children should do as they are told.	Frequent testing helps students meet course objectives.
Failure regarded as lack of aptitude or motivation.	Motivation strategies emphasize clear statement of rewards and punishments.	View that knowledge is truth to be learned (i.e., memorized).	School curriculum is generally okay, but more emphasis on "basics" is needed.	Scores on standardized state publishers' tests are good criteria of success.
Use of "objective" tests validates view of learner as "empty vessel" to be filled with information.	Teacher charisma is a desired goal.	Little planning or regard for student's feelings.	Teachers should be rewarded according to standardized test scores received by their pupils.	Time-consuming evaluation methods are not worth the effort (e.g., essay exams, group project reports).
Group instruction validates view that failure is due to lack of aptitude.	Audiovisual aids, computers seen as information givers rather than as tools to help in meaning making.	Subject matter taught and testing should show close to one-to-one correspondence.	Years of service and college credits/degrees earned are primary basis for salary levels.	"Test item banks"—collections of test questions "covering" various subject matters—are a primary resource for teacher made tests, together with tests prepared by book publishers.
Rewards and punishments are principal motivators for learning.	Lecturing, test writing skills emphasized.	School, state, or university exams set the criteria for what is covered.	Educational theory and research is of little relevance and value to teachers or program planners.	Facts must be learned before understanding can develop; hence, tests should stress knowledge of facts.
	Little concern for curriculum development by teachers.	Publishers are responsible curriculum developers.	Administration should run the schools.	
Learner must make new meanings based on his/her prior knowledge.]	Emphasis on finding out what the learner already knows.	Emphasis on major conceptual ideas and skills.	Schooling emphasizing rote learning is "domesticating."	Progress of students should be monitored with files containing a broad range of performance indicators.

Learner	Teacher	Subject matter	Social milieu	Evaluation
Meaningful learning is primary basis for positive motivation and sense of empowerment.	Research and theory guide practice.	Recognition of diversity of learners and need for variety in learning resources.	Schooling emphasizing meaningful learning and creativity is empowering.	A broad range of evaluation measures is needed.
Teacher skills needed for appraising student's prior knowledge (e.g., concept maps, pretests, occasional interviews).	Clear distinction between topical or "logical" organization of subject matter and "psychological" organization. Use of concept maps to help with latter.	Efforts in student involvement in planning and executing instructional program.	Much of the school curriculum is anachronistic, and major revisions in curricula are needed.	Objective tests measure only a small percentage (about 10%) of aptitudes and achievement relevant to real-life application.
Learners need help to learn how to learn.	Techniques needed for helping students learn how to learn.	Emphasis on evolving nature of knowledge.	Teacher preparation should be viewed as lifelong with continuing efforts for appraisal and "renewal."	Evaluation measures should help students and teachers identify conceptual problems and work toward their resolution (e.g., concept maps).
Human potential is much greater than usually manifest.	Optimistic view of human potential.	Wide variety of learning approaches, with flexible evaluation.	"Career ladders" are needed to keep the most talented teachers in classrooms and help them to help their peers.	Evaluation should help students take responsibility for their own learning (e.g., use of journals, self-report measures, concept maps, etc.).
Feelings are important.	Lack of motivation seen as derived in large part from lack of meaning/understanding.	Confidence in meaningful learning as preparation for standardized exams.	Teaching practice should be theory and research based and evaluated.	Teachers should conduct occasional in-depth interviews with students.
Learning is the responsibility of the learner.	Teacher is responsible for sharing meanings with/between learners. Gaining skills is lifelong process.	Emphasis on empowering learners rather than "coverage" of material.	Major decisions should involve teachers, parents, and administration.	

Notes:

a These five elements are my modification of Schwab's (1973) "commonplaces": (1) learner, (2) teacher, (3) subject matter, and (4) social milieu. I have added (5) evaluation, because it plays a dominant, indeed, often a controlling role in schooling.

spread the word." Some of the tools, such as concept mapping, are becoming common in science textbooks, with Vee diagrams and applications in other disciplines progressing more slowly. Change in education is indeed a slow process.

An Illustrative Case

Although I will deal more extensively with the context element of educating in the next chapter, it is important to recognize the role that the teacher or manager plays in setting the context. A primary responsibility of the teacher is to set the agenda for learning. This can be done as thoughtlessly as proceeding with the next section of a highly prescriptive syllabus, which in the worst school settings is almost the only option for the teacher. Or it can be done as part of a thoughtful sequence of experiences growing out of the needs of the learners, the opportunities in the physical and cultural setting, and using the vehicle provided by the knowledge or subject to be studied.

We saw in the example of Rachel's inquiry about flowers using dirt an ideal context for learning, where Rachel raised the questions arising out of a context of real-world experience she chose to engage in that was also emotionally comfortable to her. While my wife set the learning agenda by inviting Rachel to weed flowers with her, she did not predetermine questions to be raised or the subject matter to be "covered." The result was a highly successful learning experience for Rachel (and for her grandmother as regards Rachel's interests), and one that laid a foundation for future learning.

The power of this kind of "contextualized" learning was illustrated six months later when, after watching logs burn in the fireplace, Rachel asked, "Where does wood go when it is burned?" Rachel, just past her fourth birthday, again illustrated her developing concept of conservation of substance, namely that wood cannot just disappear; it must go somewhere. I began to address her inquiry by reminding her of the question she asked her grandmother last summer, "Do flowers eat dirt?" Rachel recalled the question and also the answer that flowers and other plants used a little bit of the earth, but most of the plant comes from air and water. Although it is possible that Rachel had occasion to ask her question again and to review again this relationship of plant growth with dirt and air, her mother could not recall Rachel repeating this experience. The "remarkable" recall, by usual school standards, Rachel exhibited is actually not remarkable when children have the opportunity to learn answers to *their* questions in a context that makes sense to them. It was now easy to build on this framework of concepts and propositions and to suggest that when wood burns, the wood turns back into water and air (actually carbon dioxide) and some of the energy from the sun used to form the wood is now released as heat (and light) from the fire. The ash that remains is that little bit of "dirt" the tree needed to grow. "Do you understand now where the wood goes when it burns?" I asked. "Yes," Rachel replied confidently. "Can you explain it to me?" I asked. Rachel proceeded in her own words to give an accurate description of where wood goes when it burns, albeit she left out the bit about the stored energy from the sun being released as heat and light. Clearly *energy* was a concept that was not integrated well into her knowledge framework at this time. However, the idea that the volume of a substance must come and go somewhere, the idea of conservation of substance in this context, seemed to be solidly established in Rachel's answers. Contrast this with the poor performance of seventh- and twelfth-grade students shown in Figure 4.6.

A Twelve-Year Longitudinal Study of Concept Learning

During the 1960s there was a widely proclaimed view that young children could not learn *abstract concepts*. Part of the argument was based on Piagetian ideas that only "formal operational" students could learn ideas that required a kind of inferential reasoning. In Chapter 5, I discussed the difference between what Ausubel called primary abstractions and secondary abstractions. The former are concepts that derive directly from experience with concrete objects or particular events, whereas the latter derive from recognizing relationships among other concepts. While it is true that primary concepts must be formed before secondary abstractions are possible, I saw no inherent reason for this to be the case in a strictly age-related fashion, but rather more dependent on the quality of the learning experiences and the sequence of those learning experiences. My own experience with young children, including my own children, indicated that with proper conceptual preparation, even five- and six-year-old children could demonstrate remarkable understanding of *abstract concepts*, or secondary abstractions. While this is no longer an idea that goes against conventional wisdom, it was very much opposed by conventional wisdom in the 1960s. For example, Gelman (1999), in a recent paper posted on the Internet (http://www.project2061.org/tools/earlychild/context/gelman.htm),   Gelman makes these observations:

Four key themes have emerged from recent research.

- Theme 1. Concepts are tools and as such have powerful implications for children's reasoning—both positive and negative.
- Theme 2. Children's early concepts are not necessarily concrete or perceptually based. Even preschool children are capable of reasoning about non-obvious, subtle, and abstract concepts.
- Theme 3. Children's concepts are not uniform across content areas, across individuals, or across tasks.
- Theme 4. Children's concepts reflect their emerging "theories" about the world. To the extent that children's theories are inaccurate, their conceptions are also biased.

Gelman goes on to identify four myths that have been shattered by recent research:

- Myth 1. The sole function of concepts is to organize experience efficiently.
- Myth 2. There is qualitative change in children's concepts over time, with major shifts between four and seven years.
- Myth 3. Until about age 7, most children are unable to reason about abstract concepts or non-obvious features.
- Myth 4. Children's concepts start out perceptually-based, becoming conceptual with development.

In addition, Gelman goes on to say in the same paper that:

. . . Theories help concept learners in three respects:

- Theories help identify those features that are relevant to a concept.
- Theories constrain how (e.g., along which dimensions) similarity should be computed.
- Theories can influence how concepts are stored in memory.

Unfortunately, even today the above-mentioned prevailing mythology persists, and I shall revisit this issue. In the 1960s the mythology was so tightly held by administrators in major US funding agencies that it was impossible to get financial support for the kind of research we wanted to do from federal agencies.

It was my view that to understand science, children must very early on begin to build concepts of the particulate nature of matter, the nature of energy, and the role of energy and energy transformations as they relate to changes in matter. My experience with young children suggested that a reasonable understanding of these concepts was attainable with carefully developed instructional sequences. The problem was how to test this hypothesis in a wider school setting and, recognizing that most adults, including primary-grade school teachers, are very limited in their understanding of these ideas. I therefore chose to utilize a context for educating that we had developed with college botany students, namely audio-tutorial instruction (Postlethwait, Novak & Murray, 1969; 1972).

In audio-tutorial instruction, audiotape is used to guide the learner through a set of observations and manipulations of materials to explore ideas dealing with phenomena associated with these materials. For example, in the lessons designed for first- and second-grade children that we developed, children were guided in using batteries, wires, and light bulbs to explore the idea that electrical energy can be produced in the batteries, transmitted through wires, and transformed into heat and light in the light bulb. A series of some 60 lessons was developed, each requiring 15–20 minutes of hands-on activity on the part of the learner while guided through observations with audiotape, pictures, photographs, and, in some cases, 8-mm loop films. Figure 7.7 shows a photograph of a child in a carrel with one of our audio-tutorial lessons. Carrel units were placed in individual classrooms and teachers were asked to have their students, working one at a time, proceed through the lesson at least once during a two-week interval. In practice, many children performed each lesson more than once, and, in a few cases, as many as five or six times. There was high interest in the lessons.

While this represents a rather unusual context for teaching, it was a financially feasible method for organizing experience for learners without undue disruption of other classroom activities and the ordinary protocols of school operation. I will discuss in Chapter 8 some of the problems associated with school organization and the context for learning it normally creates, but it is important to note that even within those constraints, high-quality instructional segments can be incorporated into the student's experience. The lessons were highly popular with both students and teachers, although a few students missed a chance to study every lesson.

After some two years in design and development of our audio-tutorial lessons, we were prepared to conduct a study to test whether or not these lessons could produce learning at a sufficient level of meaningfulness that there would be facilitation of future science learning. While preliminary studies suggested that the lessons were successful in effecting student learning (Hibbard & Novak, 1975; Nussbaum & Novak, 1976), the real test of meaningful learning is long-term transfer in facilitation of future learning, even when the context for learning is changed.

Twenty-six lessons that we had developed were placed in a number of classrooms in Ithaca Public Schools, and every two weeks a new lesson was

Figure 7.7 A six-year-old student studying plant growth in a science carrel.

introduced into the carrel units. Depending on the pace at which the students proceeded through the lessons, classrooms continued working with these lessons throughout grades one and two (ages six to eight). Following a sequence of lessons, students were interviewed by project staff and subsequently transcripts of interviews and later, concept maps were prepared. As mentioned earlier, it was from this research study that the tool of concept mapping was developed as a method of representing changes in student knowledge structures. The students receiving the audio-tutorial science lessons in grades one and two were called "instructed students," since they received special instruction in basic concepts of science. There were 191 students in the latter group, and we followed them with occasional interviews throughout their tenure in Ithaca Public Schools.

In the second year of the study, operating in the same classrooms with the same teachers, we interviewed students who did not receive the audio-tutorial science lessons but were members of the same general population of students. This group of 48 students was followed throughout their tenure in Ithaca Schools. Students received science instruction sporadically through the remainder of the elementary grades, and as organized classes in grades 7, 8, 9, and 10, with smaller numbers continuing in chemistry and physics in grades 11 and 12.

By 1984, we had completed all of the data gathering for the study and began to analyze the results by comparing changes in conceptual understanding in one domain of science, namely the understanding of the particulate nature and behavior of matter. While early instruction included other conceptual domains, it was impossible with the staff resources and funding that we had to continue interviewing in all of these conceptual domains. Furthermore, this would have required such extensive interviewing that logistic and other practical problems would have resulted, as well as contamination of the initial learning experience by the extensive interview experience.

The findings of the study are summarized in Table 7.2 and Figure 7.8. What was remarkable is that the impact of this high-quality early science instruction, in the special education context we had created, had highly substantial effect on learners early in their school experience (that is, in grades 1 and 2) and the facilitative effect of this learning experience persisted for the next ten years. These findings are so remarkable that I had considerable difficulty in getting the paper describing the research published, having it rejected three times prior to publication. It is not uncommon, of course, to have difficulty with editorial review boards when research results challenge the conventional wisdom that prevails. These results were indeed challenging much of the conventional wisdom, even though the rigid constraints in cognitive functioning that was initially suggested by Piaget's work were now questioned by many researchers, as indicated in Chapter 4 and the above quotations from Gelman.

One might ask, "Why is it that there is little research that explores the effect of early instruction on later achievement of the *same students*?" The obvious answer is that such studies are exceedingly difficult to execute and require a long-term commitment on the part of the researcher. From the initial conception of the study that involved the design of the audio-tutorial lessons to the final publication of the study results in 1991, there was a span of more than twenty years. As much as I would have liked to repeat such a study, it was not possible during my active professional life. It should also be noted that this kind of study need not cost millions of dollars. The total investment in this research project, including graduate student stipends which provided support for their graduate study, would total less than $200,000. Funds were patched together from various sources, but the most useful continuing funding was from Shell Company's Foundation in small ($5000–$10,000) unrestricted grants made to me over most of the years of the study, and from small grants from Hatch Act funds available to the College of Agriculture at Cornell University.

Let us examine for the moment the meaning of the use of audio-tutorial instruction as a context for learning in conventional classrooms in conventional schools. First, the data clearly show that very substantial learning of highly abstract ideas was not only possible but achieved to a significant level. By the end of grade 2, when the audio-tutorial science instruction was completed, the majority of students had developed at least rudimentary ideas regarding the particular nature of matter and the fact that, as energy is added to the molecules of matter, we can move from a solid to a liquid to a gaseous state. These ideas appeared to be firmly established in their cognitive structures and some of the evidence for this was the persistence of key concepts and

Table 7.2 Analysis of variance for valid and invalid notions by method of instruction (Audio-tutorial or no Audio-tutorial instruction in grades 1 and 2) and by grades*

Source	df	Sum of squares	Mean square	F-ratio	Prob.
For Valid Notions					
Grade	3	143.938	47.979	3.6	0.015
Method	1	553.521	553.521	41.0	0.000
Interaction	3	75.187	25.062	1.9	0.138
Error	184	2480.83	13.482		
Total	191	3253.48			
For Invalid Notions					
Grade	3	90.729	30.243	16.0	0.000
Method	1	198.725	198.725	107.0	0.000
Interaction	3	23.636	7.878	4.3	0.006
Error	424	784.352	1.849		
Total	431	1097.44			

* From Novak and Musonda, p. 148. Copyright © 1991 by the American Educational Research Association. Reprinted by permission of the publisher.

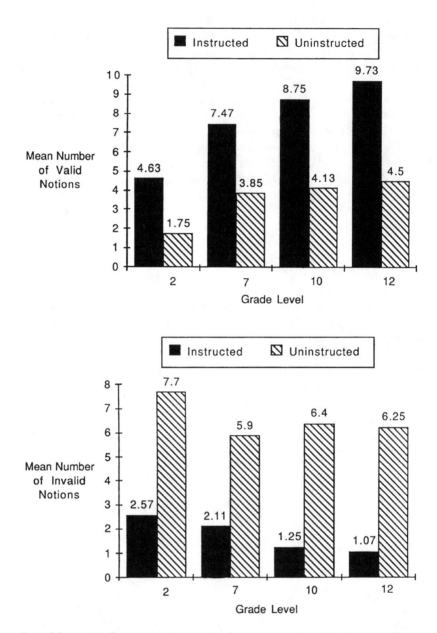

Figure 7.8 a and *b.* Bar graphs showing the frequencies with which "instructed" students (dark bars) and "uninstructed" (striped bars) evidenced valid notions about the structure of matter (upper figure) and invalid notions (lower figure). Note that only the instructed students show continuous improvement over the years. From Novak and Musonda, 1991. Reproduced with permission of AERA.

relationships throughout the remaining ten years of schooling. The data shown in Table 7.2 and Figure 7.8 indicate that students receiving the early instruction had *more than twice* as many valid conceptions of the particulate nature of matter, and less than half the number of invalid conceptions, when compared with their "uninstructed" counterparts. These are highly significant differences, both from the perspective of practical consequence and in terms of statistical significance. These are differences that exceeded my own expectations and certainly fly in the face of the conventional wisdom prevailing in the 1960s and 1970s. As pointed out in earlier, there have been more recent studies by others that point to the under-exploited learning capabilities of young children, but this was not the case when the study was designed and executed. Partly for this reason, I was unsuccessful in repeated efforts to obtain federal funding for the study. Wilshire (1990) addresses the problem that scholars who take positions that challenge conventional wisdom are often met with incredulity at best and banishment at worst. This has been true over the millennia and is likely to continue in the future. This may be one of the reasons why students of creative productivity identify the necessity for tenacity and the creative drive to persist in pursuing an idea even in the face of numerous obstacles (Gardner, 1994).

In recent years, there has been an increased interest in longitudinal studies of learning, partly because it is now widely recognized that new learning is highly dependent on related prior learning, especially if the assessment of new learning involves transfer of knowledge to new contexts or new problem solving. For example, the *The Canadian Journal of Science, Mathematics, and Technology Education* (Shapiro (ed.), 2004), *Research in Science Education* (Russell and Arzi (eds.), 2005), published special issues dealing with longitudinal studies in science education and papers in these issues have been widely cited. My papers (Novak, 2004; 2005) in these journals discussed some of the implications that derived from our 12-year longitudinal study, a study that has been a catalyst for a number of other longitudinal studies. Arzi and White (2007) published a 17-year longitudinal study of teacher's knowledge from pre-service to 17 years of professional development. They found that knowledge not used in teaching soon faded from teacher's memories. Since it is very difficult to do long-term longitudinal studies in education, or indeed in any field involving people, it is not surprising that there are so few in the literature. There is another message in our study cited here and that is that technology-mediated instruction, even of the more primitive nature of audio-tutorial instruction, can be effective in a conventional teaching context in a conventional school district. The potential of newly emerging hyper-media systems as a teaching context has yet to be explored and exploited, but I believe the results above suggest that well-designed hyper-media systems can have a profound effect on the facilitation of meaningful learning, whether in school settings, corporate education, home schooling, or independent study. I will discuss this further in later chapters, including recent work in Panama and Italy.

Teaching in the Context of a Counseling Environment

One of my graduate students, Joan Mazur (1989), worked in a drug rehabilitation program near Ithaca, New York. She was intrigued with the ideas we were presenting on obstacles to educating individuals, in her case, a problem of educating drug users to understand the deleterious effect of drug use to themselves and to society, and the motivations that led them to persistence in drug abuse. The persons with whom she worked were repeat drug offenders who were assigned to the treatment center as a last alternative to prison. They were cognizant of the fact that they were in a situation of last resort, but nevertheless often remained uncooperative and difficult to reach.

Mazur decided to try to teach concept mapping to her clients to see if this would be a way of creating both a cognitive and an emotional recognition of the reasons for their drug habits. While she met with resistance in acquiring this technique on the part of some of her subjects, she eventually was successful in getting all nine of her clients to develop concept maps of their drug habits and motivation for using drugs. A sample of one of these maps is shown in Figure 7.9.

These concept maps served as a basis for one-on-one counseling and also for group discussions on individuals' view of their habit. What Mazur found was that the concept maps were an important tool in facilitating the treatment of these patients and their discharge from the drug treatment facility. Ordinarily, the recidivism rate (re-incarceration rate) for drug abusers is about 94 percent nationwide. In the case of Mazur's clients, *none* of her nine subjects were readmitted for drug treatment three years after discharge, although one was imprisoned for other reasons. Clearly, the concept mapping that Mazur chose to use as a context for expressing thoughts and feelings about drug use was highly successful with her clients. Her colleagues at the drug treatment center have subsequently incorporated the use of concept maps in their treatment programs, but on a more limited basis. I am not aware of other drug treatment programs that are utilizing concept mapping with their clients, and this is unfortunate.

There have been other counseling settings in which my students have employed concept mapping, but the data I have from these students is largely anecdotal. It is my hope that this book and other writings will stimulate more research studies on the role that concept maps may play in counseling settings.

Emotional Sensitivity

When I was enrolled in teacher education courses, I cannot recall ever discussing the issue of the emotional needs of teachers and how these impact on their effectiveness. But what has become increasingly apparent to me over the years, both through experiences with my own children and in my efforts at teaching, is the *exceedingly* important role that teachers' and manager's ego needs play

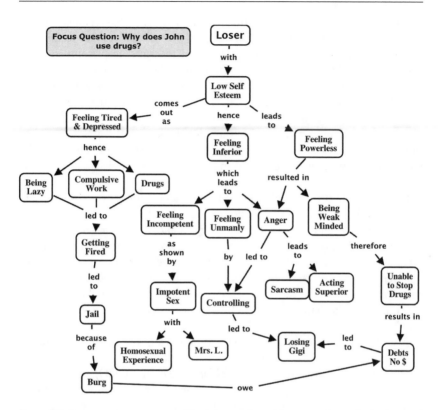

Figure 7.9 A concept map prepared by John to show his perceptions of why he used drugs. Reproduced from Mazur, 1989, with permission.

in how they organize the context for learning and how they operate in it. Those teachers and managers who do not have a strong ego perception of "I'm OK" often in subtle or explicit ways attack the ego of their students or workers.

The research on teacher education is almost devoid of citations of studies explicitly dealing with teacher ego needs and corresponding effects on their teaching activities. For example, a recently published book reviewing research on science teaching and learning, with some 575 large pages of reviews of research, has no entries in the index on ego or ego needs nor even on emotional needs of teachers and learners (Gabel, 1994). Similarly, an earlier review (Houston, 1990) of research on teacher education also fails to cite any work that deals with the recognition of teachers' ego needs and how they relate to effective or ineffective teaching practices.

Our parents and older siblings are our first teachers. As we see clearly in John's map (Figure 7.9), he suffered from very low self-esteem. In interviews he also indicated that his dad's ego needs led him to hold high expectations for John, and he also felt in competition with him. John has a Masters Degree in

Social Work and was successful in this work for a time. He has an older brother and a younger sister whose successful lives contributed to his feelings of inadequacy. His escape was drugs, which led to crime, imprisonment, and subsequently, a treatment center and work with Mazur. John's concept map shows clearly the "I'm not OK" feelings he had about himself. Counseling with Mazur and others at the clinic helped him to see that his feelings were *his* creation, and he could act to overcome these feelings, and in fact, had done so for a time as a successful counselor working with cases assigned to him. The starkness of his map made it possible to confront John with the reality and his perceived reality, and in time, to successful discharge from the program.

John's case, and thousands similar to him, show how destructive the ego needs of parents can be to their children. All of us, as parents, fail on occasion to give our children the ego support they need and, instead, act to gratify our own ego needs. Probably every reader of this book can recall one or more incidents of this with one or both parents. Those of us who have seen our children move on successfully into adulthood, and perhaps their own success-ful parenting, have the satisfaction of knowing that we probably succeeded much more often than we failed to help our children achieve a sense of "I'm OK; You're OK."

A problem now faced in many schools is bullying by students directed at other students. Although this has always been a problem to some extent, there has been increasing attention to the problem by Sweeney (2009) and others. In general, children raised by authoritarian parents—parents who are demand-ing, directive and unresponsive—are the most prone to act out bullying behavior. While there is a growing interest in the study of bullying and efforts in schools to ameliorate the problem, much more needs to be done.

Trust

In his book, *On Caring*, Mayeroff (1972) identifies a number of requirements for successful *caring*. He points out that caring is a process directed at helping others grow. It can apply to people, ideals, or ideas. The "major ingredients" of caring identified by Mayeroff include: (1) knowing, (2) alternating rhythms, (3) patience, (4) honesty, (5) trust, (6) humility, (7) hope, and (8) courage. All play a role, and all support each other in the caring process. Over the years, I have felt the emotions associated with all eight of these ingredients as I have sought to construct and care for the idea that a theory of education can guide and lead to improvement of education. My many students and visiting scholars have often and in many ways shared in this caring process. In turn, we have also cared for each other, employing all eight of Meyeroff's ingredients.

Perhaps most important, and often times most difficult, is trust. But, in many ways, trust is the fundamental process; it is the process that is required for all other processes to proceed. A recent study showed that classroom teachers are more effective at teaching sensitive issues such as pregnancy prevention and HIV than are experts brought in to teach these subjects. This research indicates that students have greater trust in the classroom teachers they know (Ohio State University, 2008). Mayeroff writes:

> Trusting the other is to let go; it includes an element of risk and a leap into the unknown, both of which take courage.
>
> The father (or mother) who "cares" too much and "overprotects" his child, does not trust the child, and whatever he may think he is doing, he is responding more to his own needs than to the needs of the child to grow. (p. 21)

This may indeed have been the case with Andrew's parents, and much of his good fortune may have been the true caring of Michelle Lucia who participated in and wrote *Andrew's Story* presented below. Michelle may have helped his parents move toward a more positive caring for Andrew.

What we saw in the case of John was a father who was too competitive and a mother who was too protective. We shall see a similar situation in the case of Andrew that follows. Andrew suffered from a visual deficiency that went undiagnosed for several years until one of my students helped to solve the problem.

Andrew's Story[1]

The Face of a Learning Disability

This is the study of one boy, one beautiful little boy who has been hurt by a system and by a society which accepts nothing less than perfection. His story, unfortunate though I believe this to be, will revolve in large part around his learning disability and the treatment he received in school, but this will remain, first and foremost, the story of this very real little boy.

Even more than Andrew's story, this will be my story as well; the story of a student who believed that she had the power and the insight to find answers that no one else had been able to.

For as long as can be remembered, Andrew has had trouble in school. It was said many times, with true confusion, that it was impossible that the boy we all knew outside of school was the same one said to be so "bad" inside school. In first grade, he was labelled as having attention deficit disorder and barely escaped undergoing an intensive treatment of ritalin. When in class, the teacher said he would refuse to read aloud and would

1 Quoted, with permission, from a paper by Michelle Lucia, who did the study and wrote *Andrew's Story* [abridged by me].

rarely complete assignments. At home, he and his parents would fight bitterly over his misbehavior in school and over his "refusal and excuses" about doing work. He was "socially passed" to the second grade. His teacher said she decided to pass him because of his "innate intelligence" and his ability to reason and problem solve orally.

[In a new private school,] the second grade teacher somehow came to the disastrous conclusion that Andrew was simply a "non-student;" one of those students who would struggle through school and amount to little later in life. Her comments on one report card of Andrew's read, "[Andrew] is a good boy deep down. He will never be a reader or a stellar student, but he will undoubtedly be a good person." It is hard to say on what actual evidence she based these opinions, but it seems clear from what is now known that she had not at any time sat down and talked to, listened to, or individually worked with Andrew. Again, Andrew received a "social pass" and, again, at a new public school, he struggled painfully through third grade only to receive a "social pass" to fourth grade. What this means is that, at fourth grade, Andrew was still a non-reader. What this also means is that, by fourth grade, Andrew had been to three schools and had missed out on any chance to develop lasting friendships. Always being the new kid and "bad" in class, Andrew was usually the subject of ridicule and ostracization. This means that not only was this little boy dealing with the frustration and pain of being a poor performer in school and the pain of his parents' disappointment in him, but he was also suffering the pain of being shut out socially.

In fourth grade, someone finally took notice of Andrew. His fourth grade teacher saw and questioned the pain and the frustration Andrew suffered and the energy he exerted trying to keep up with the class. This, she said, was not a lazy child, but in fact, this was a child who worked very hard and struggled greatly. Why? Such a simple question, and yet it took four years and myriads of consulted teachers to ask it. Why? Why was this little boy not learning? Why were his eyes tearing when he did his work? Why was this little boy suffering at school?

And that was quite literally all it took; just one question to change Andrew from a lazy and undedicated student to a wonderful child who was likely suffering from a learning disability. A series of unending, prolonged, and stressful tests and evaluations was immediately begun. Andrew was first tested for dyslexia and other well known disabilities. When those tests came back negative, it was as if the sky had fallen, again. The school board said things like, "See, it's not our fault. Your child is just not a good student . . ." And, Andrew was saying things like, "I don't try to be bad" and "I'm sorry." Andrew's parents were struggling to contain their disappointment at not having found an "easy explanation" and trying to decide how to go on, trying to learn what was left to do that hadn't been tried. The one person who refused absolutely to accept those results was Andrew's teacher. Taking quite a risk, she explained to Andrew's parents that it was likely that Andrew was, in fact, suffering from a learning disability and that the school had chosen to not identify or pursue it further as they would then be obligated, under the rights guaranteed students in New York State, to teach to his unique needs. She referred them to a psychoeducational consultant for private testing and recommended Andrew be tutored with a new reading method known as Orton-Gillingham.

Andrew's parents, again at great monetary sacrifice, sought out both the tutor and the consultant. Thirteen months after testing began, Andrew's parents, armed with the psychoeducational consultant and her report and an attorney, appeared before the school board and stated what were Andrew's needs and rights as a child diagnosed with scotopic sensitivity (see Figure 7.10).

In the presentation before the school board then, a list of requests was set forth: (1) Andrew should be labeled: "Learning Disabled," but for

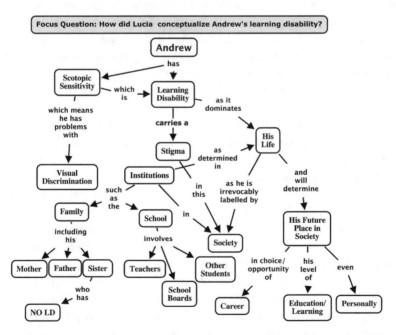

Figure 7.10 A concept map by Lucia showing her understanding of Andrew's problem. From Lucia, 1993. Reproduced with permission.

emotional reasons, should continue to be mainstreamed; (2) He should receive individual assistance within the school in the areas of reading and cursive writing; (3) His workload should be reduced through the prioritization of assignments, and he should be excused from "heavy writing assignments;" and (4) The school should support and see that he sees a scotopic sensitivity screener. It is important to note that not a single request, but for the last one made by the consultant or the parents, dealt specifically with the fact that Andrew does not see things correctly. Instead, the belief seemed to persist that Andrew just needed to "work harder."

The school board, just prior to Andrew's fifth-grade year, agreed to every request except the subsidizing of the screening. Andrew would be sent to a resource room for private help during desk work times and the staff would monitor and guide him in whatever ways possible. His workload would be lightened, and effort would be made to reduce the stress he now feels to get everything done "on time." Aside from the fact that Andrew's physical needs were not being addressed, hopes were high that the individual attention would help Andrew learn to read.

This is the point at which I [Michelle Lucia] came in as a researcher, the beginning of Andrew's fifth-grade year, following what was believed to be a victory with the school board and at a time when things seemed as if they would improve. What I had initially hoped to do in this study was to chronicle the struggle of a learning disabled child in this society, to spend time on the inadequate screening methods in detecting learning disabilities, and devise ways to improve them; to illustrate the inadequate training received by many of today's teachers in that it took four long years for a learning disability to be even suspected in this case, to construct ways to improve the competence of future teachers, and to close with the happy ending of Andrew's present success and well-being. I think it was maybe ten days before I realized that that would not be the story to be told; that in fact, Andrew's struggles are far from over and are of sufficient magnitude even today that just understanding them and their basis and magnitude would occupy the whole of my focus.

For even that early into the school year and into my study, it was evident that Andrew was not improving and was not being helped. What really happened and what is continuing to happen since the school board meeting is that Andrew is sent to this windowless room in the basement of the building a few times a day where he sits with three or four other children, usually kids who have been sent out of class for behavior problems, and a teacher or monitor who reads the paper and answers only questions asked of her. It is far from private tutoring, and it is anything but helpful. Andrew then returns to his classroom and sits in confusion because the teacher had started a new lesson while he was out of the room. Seeing what they believe is special treatment, Andrew is ridiculed and exiled from his peers, only to be left to suffer in the same way as five years before.

In the last two years, this woman [Andrew's mother] has championed and sometimes outright battled for her son with everyone from the principal and the school board to the parents of the kids who have teased him. She has watched her firstborn child suffer, seen him come home from school hungry because another child stole his lunch, cleansed his cuts from fights in school, and listened to him weep alone in his room. She has spent most of her free time at the library or on the phone and is, at this point, just about out of energy. She has pursued every lead she could find to the brink of bankruptcy and breakdown. The few options that are left for Andrew now, which will be discussed below are too unknown, not to mention expensive, for her to risk raising her hopes again.

The problem is not that Andrew cannot be taught to read by conventional methods, but that he cannot learn to read because he cannot discriminate between the letters of words.

One need not look very long at the rights of a child in Andrew's school district to know that Andrew has been denied many of his rights. Perhaps most crucial, Andrew's parents were denied the "Right to be Fully Informed." When the school pronounced Andrew as a "normal" student following the first set of tests, they did so with knowledge that this was not true, with knowledge that the erratic test scores and urgings of Andrew's teacher were signaling a disability. While this is not grounds for a history-making lawsuit, had the school board been up front in the meanings and possible interpretations of the test scores, Andrew and his parents may have been spared a bit of the disappointment and pain they suffered during the time when there were no explanations for Andrew's poor academic performance. It seems as if the school board had wanted Andrew's parents to internalize his difficulties, with the effect that responsibility would then be shifted away from the school.

There were other instances in which the school and/or the officials involved could be cited as denying rights, but this one sticks out most in that it is an example of bureaucracy at work, of an institution having forgotten its reason for being. Must we struggle to recall why we have schools at all? From their inception, we have had schools primarily to teach and educate children. In this instance, though, the school was not trying to teach and educate Andrew, but was trying to save itself the money, time, and effort it would be forced to expend in having and teaching a child with an uncommon learning disability.

The final information Bonnie (Andrew's mother) sent to me were two articles on scotopic sensitivity and a new, experimental way to treat those suffering from it. In essence, these articles explain the treatments Bonnie referred to as being too risky and expensive to try. I am not in a position to judge her for I have not suffered as she had, but in reading the information that she sent to me, I couldn't help but become hopeful and excited. The articles explain that research is necessary and continuing, but that the researchers at the Irlen Institute, a clinic committed to the treatment of perception-based learning disabilities, have so far found that by selectively reducing the input of certain light wavelengths, a specially designed filter allows the scotopic sensitive person to more effectively process information.

It is only fair to concede that, along with the potential for disappointment and the extensive testing involved, ten to nineteen hundred dollars is a lot to invest in such an experimental treatment.

After having evaluated the information sent to me [from the Irlen Institute], I did what any researcher must. I went to the libraries to gather information of my own. All in all, the libraries did nothing to further this study, except make very clear to me that Andrew had indeed been diagnosed with a newly recognized and unknown disability.

I next went to the Special Children's Center. Having previously been a volunteer there, many people knew me and were willing to talk with me about Andrew. Unfortunately, the results I obtained in terms of information were much the same as I had from the libraries, meaning the teachers and specialists at the Special Children's Center had little knowledge of or experience with scotopic sensitivity.

What I did gain from my visit to the Special Children's Center was an interview with Kelly, a five-year-old child diagnosed with dyslexia. What was so interesting in speaking with Kelly was the contrast between her and Andrew in terms of self-esteem, having adapted to a disability, and in prospects for the future. Kelly was diagnosed as dyslexic at age three, as soon as she was learning to read. Having been diagnosed so early, Kelly's parents were able to obtain for her the best possible education with the best trained staff and save her from the pain and embarrassment of having failed and suffered in school, which is a common way for a disability to be detected. As a result, Kelly is already reading at a second grade level. She is expected to steadily progress as she has been labeled dyslexic and will be treated and taught to as such. She is aware and accepting of the fact that she "reads different," and she is expected to be able to do and read and be anything that she hopes to. As is and will be further seen, Andrew, having been diagnosed later in life and having an uncommon disability, lives a life almost opposite to Kelly's.

Because of a restructuring within the school, Andrew's teacher in fifth grade is the same one who first suspected his disability in fourth grade. She was hesitant to meet with me, saying she'd already "become too involved," but agreed to talk with me on the phone. The two statements she kept repeating were, "Then why are we here?. . . . Why am I here?. . . . If not for each individual child, then why is there a school system?" She told me of the risk she was warned she was taking, by who she would not say, in voicing her "disgust with the bureaucracy and the 'evil' of the system," but says, at this point, she does not care. As I had been thinking, she says her termination would be, to her, a sign that she should speak out and confront a system which is willing to "so shamelessly sacrifice the individual for the majority."

From his mother, to his teacher, to the consultant, to his sister, we have seen how Andrew is viewed and treated by those around him, but where does Andrew fit in? How does Andrew see himself, his disability, his "future prospects?"

My bias should be apparent by this time, but Andrew truly is a beautiful and intelligent little boy. Speaking with him, one would never once think, "This child can't read. This child is dumb . . ." But, in listening to what Andrew says, one can see that is indeed what he thinks when he thinks of himself and school. Andrew does not understand that his performance in school is, in a sense, out of control, that no matter how hard he tries or how much effort he makes, he will not be able to learn and perform as well or as quickly as the other kids do. He has internalized five years of Fs and detentions, and ridicule so much so that it has, as it was inevitable that it would, become a part of who he is today. In the area of intelligence, it is clear that Andrew thinks himself a disappointment and a failure. When I would try to press him or urge him to express himself on this, on general issues concerning himself and school, he would say that he couldn't read, he was dumb, he was bad in school, and then he would get upset and refuse to say anymore.

I asked Andrew's parents if anyone had ever explained to him what was known of his disability, and their initial response was not much more than to stare at me blankly. "Of course, he knows it isn't his fault." "Does he?" More blank stares. At this point, I saw my first opportunity to help Andrew. Andrew's parents and I talked some more, and I was able to persuade them to talk with their son about exactly what was going on, while doing their sincere best to offer him the complete benefit of the doubt that he could understand what they were telling him. I retreated to the background and watched as, for two hours, Andrew and his parents really, and possibly for the first time, communicated with one another. His mother, in an already shaky voice, asked Andrew if he knew what a learning disability was and that he had one and what that meant. As was my suspicion, Andrew sat quietly and, after a long pause, shook his head no. While the meaning of this sank in to Bonnie, that her son had been blaming himself for not learning to read, that he had been suffering and taking the blame for something which was and is out of his control, Andrew's father did his best to explain scotopic sensitivity and what it means to be learning disabled to Andrew. While speaking, he made a comparison between Andrew's situation and that of his uncle who is paralyzed, and a flicker of understanding and then pain passed over Andrew's face. "I can't be smart?" was the first question he asked. The communication continued, and Andrew was finally told why he was seeing the consultant and having so many tests done and going to the resource room and what they were trying to do, things which should have been explained all along, but which were at least being said now. For two hours, I watched this family come together and mend. I saw a rollercoaster of emotions, from guilt to pain to joy, and I left as Andrew hugged and, in his own way, thanked his parents for giving him so much of themselves that day. Since that time, I have not seen or spoken with Andrew, but Bonnie has told me repeatedly of the breakthrough that was made that day. She cried for the pain that had been needlessly caused Andrew and which is now mending, told me of the questions Andrew is now asking, of his seemingly increased confidence in, for example, admitting and accepting his need for help. While this will not make everything "all better," while it will not make Andrew see correctly, it will allow him the confidence to ask questions, and it will give him some peace of mind in knowing and learning that there is justification and understanding as to his performance in school.

While things are still improving for Andrew at home, they remain much the same in school. [I wondered if there was something I could do to help.] For four days, I tried endlessly to get someone—anyone—from the Irlen Institute, as referred to above, to speak with me. Finally, after having spoken so often with me that she was able to recognize my voice, the receptionist concluded that I was not going to stop calling and put me through to one of the researchers. I wanted to know, as my advisor (Novak) and I had discussed, if there was a side of the spectrum or a certain color filter more likely to work or with which they had had a higher success rate. I wanted to know why it was necessary to spend thousands of dollars, why Andrew and his parents could not just sit down with a sample of colored overlays and ask Andrew if any of them were easier to read through. After a further test of my persistence, the researcher admitted the possibility of something as simple as a blue or purple overlay helping to ease Andrew's visual difficulties. He said the only way to find which color was suited for Andrew would be to test the full range of colors. The next day, the day before Thanksgiving, I found colored overlays and went home in anxious anticipation of meeting with Andrew, of him looking through one of the overlays and smiling because it did not hurt and the letters did not move. In fact, I went straight to Andrew's house when I got to town, rushed in, and related to Bonnie the details of my phone call to the Institute and spread the assorted overlays on the table. "No," she said. "No." She was sorry, but she would not allow me to try this. Too many times she had seen Andrew's hopes dashed and this, she did not believe, would be able to help Andrew to read, it was too easy. With my hopes crushed, as I knew that I could not push and that I had to respect whatever and all decisions Bonnie made in regard to her son, I left the overlays on her table and returned to Cornell, intending to tell the added story of a mother defeated by the system her son would now be left to battle alone.

Two days ago (December 8, 1993), I received a message on my answering machine: "Michelle," Bonnie said, "Green. We think that the green one was easier for Andrew. He read to us, Michelle. I'm sorry. I called today, the Institute. Tuesday, Andrew starts the official process then. I'm sorry. You should have been the one to see the smile on his face. We're thinking of you. Thank you." That is what Bonnie said.

There is a satisfying "postscript" to *Andrew's Story*. Andrew did get the help he needed for his vision, and with continuing support from his parents who helped him recognize his *physical* handicap and gave encouragement, Andrew began to progress well. By seventh grade, he had made the school honor role! His energy, enthusiasm, and joyful manner returned to that of his early childhood.

We see in *Andrew's Story* the tragedy of a "system" that was both incompetent and insensitive. Except for Andrew's fourth-grade teacher, a pattern of "blame the victim" is all too common in schools everywhere. I'm not sure what would have been Andrew's fate if he had not had the love, support, and wisdom of his former babysitter. Michelle took on this project as a means of applying ideas she learned in my course, *Learning to Learn*, but she went beyond the "requirements for credit"—she pursued Andrew's case with vigor, competence, and compassion. Michelle, I predict, will be a strong positive influence in the lives of many people in the future.

Andrew's Story is not unique. In *Learning Denied* (Taylor, 1991), the author related a similar story of a child struggling to survive in schools where too much incompetence and too much insensitivity persists. There are probably few graduates from any school system, especially males, who have not faced the ego assault that derives from such incompetence and/or insensitivity. While the majority of teachers work hard to help their students learn, and help them to feel good about themselves, most schools have too many teachers who fail on both accounts. We need to make greater efforts to help those teachers who struggle with the challenges they face, partly by improving "the system." While it is not easy to remove the incompetent teacher, more effort is needed to do this for the sake of our children and to improve the environment for other teachers (Bridges, 1986; 1992). We also need to set a higher standard for learning, for such standards are achievable if we effectively help students build their cognitive structures and skills—and contribute to their ego enhancement. Too often, schools, as Sedlak, Wheeler, Pullin, and Cusick document (1986), are *Selling Students Short.* The problem of incompetent teachers continues with no good solutions in sight. Today's (February 18, 2009) *New York Times* published an article on the problem, but the resource cited is a paper written in 1984. This illustrates how little progress we are making with this problem. A more recent major article by Matus (2009) details the procedures required to remove incompetent teachers. Matus points out that a survey of 20,000 administrators reported that 3–5 percent of teachers were incompetent and 13 to 20 percent are marginal, In Hillsborough and Pinellas counties in Florida, with over 20,000 teachers, only 16 were discharged in the last four years, or 0.08 percent. The sad reality is that the hard work and effectiveness of most teachers is diminished by those who are marginal or incompetent, and thousands of students suffer. A major reason for a rise in interest in Charter or Contract schools is that usually these school get to pick the teachers they employ.

Trust and Honesty in the Corporate Setting

It is often stated: "business is business, and you can't let personal feelings or friendship interfere." There is some truth in this, especially when it comes to dealing with poor performance, and even then, there may be extenuating circumstances that require special consideration. Apart from shared interests and enthusiasms, the characteristics that are fundamental in close friendships are unqualified trust and honesty between friends. If corporations wish to engender the strongest possible support from employees and customers, they, too, must create a relationship of unqualified trust and honesty.

In a conversation with a senior staff person in a large national accounting firm, I asked what role trust played in his company. He said (Novak, 1996A):

> I think there are people in our firm that clients really trust and turn to for advice; they truly believe them to be trustworthy business advisors. Then there are clients who will look at another professional in our firm and say that person is just a bag of hot air—and we have plenty of bags of hot air

in our firm. They can "talk the talk," but they cannot deliver; they cannot "walk the walk." They can be successful as long as they've got people beneath them that *can* deliver, at least most of the time.

I asked what kinds of relationships resulted between subordinates and senior people who could not "walk the walk." My interviewee responded:

> It can create some tension, but you have to recognize the fact that, let's say Partner A is very good at "talking the talk," and he can assure a client that Manager A is going to be engaged in doing the day-to-day work, and Manager A is recognized by the client as very competent, then Partner A can sell the work to the client. Manager A may not be full enough of himself nor have a large enough ego to walk into a room and *sell* the client, but in the end, it is Manager A who is responsible to see that the job is done right.

The situation described above is common in many organizations, not just accounting firms or other business settings, but also in academic and governmental settings. Yes, there is trust and respect in the situation described above, but there is also exploitation. Sometimes a fine line may exist between mutually beneficial collaborations and those that lopsidedly benefit only one individual or set of individuals. When the prevailing relationships in any organization become too lopsided and subordinates can no longer "cover" for their superiors, unfortunate consequences can ensue. Hamel and Prahalad (1994) describe a situation that developed at Motorola when top management lost the confidence of subordinates. They conclude:

> The lesson here is that setting corporate challenges requires great honesty and humility on the part of top management; honesty in portraying the magnitude of the task ahead; humility in admitting that it must bear its share of the responsibility for poor performance. Motorola is one of the most self-critical firms we know. Motorola's refusal to ever be satisfied with "good enough" shows up in its results. Unfortunately, in some companies, honest criticism is, particularly when it comes from subordinates, more likely to raise hackles than standards. (p 142)

In an interview with a senior executive in the construction industry, a somewhat different picture on trust emerged (Novak, 1996B):

Novak: How much trust is involved between you and your customers? Is this a big issue?

Exec.: Well, it depends; with some customers, trust is an important factor; with other customers—in the construction industry, it's a boom-and-bust industry, here today, gone tomorrow—so, I'm not sure that

| | trust is a wide component. I'm not sure that a lot of entities necessarily expect long-term relationships. |

Novak: How about between you and the employees and the other people that you deal with?

Exec.: There's a lot of different philosophies and styles, the kind of philosophy that trust is a very important factor, that you can't be very successful without developing a high degree of trust. There are a lot of people in the world that don't subscribe to that theory.

Novak: Yes, but I—it seems to me from what I've read, that the drift is where you get further with being trustworthy than seeing what you can get away with?

Exec.: That's the drift in the literature, but not in practice.

Novak: But, not in practice?

Exec.: In practice, you see all styles.

Novak: So, when you have an employee where the operating rule seems to be only do that that you have to and get away with everything you can get away with, how do you deal with that?

Exec.: You terminate them. If that's their core belief, you terminate them.

Novak: You do run into that?

Exec.: Yes, and—but, that's rare, because most people do want to do a good job, and they want to be successful.

One of the problems in the construction industry is that it is so often "boom or bust." When business is booming, hiring more and effective personnel is critical, but when business wanes, employees may be seen as expendable. The interview with this executive continued:

Novak: Do they want to develop a sense of confidence—that you have confidence in them?

Exec.: Yes, you know they want to do a good job, and they want to be recognized for doing good work.

Novak: Well, it would seem like that would call for building trust on the part of management and other important employees, but you don't see that happening in your company?

Exec.: Well, you see all types of styles, so that's why those books are written—because there are all types of styles, and they try to describe them. Amazing, isn't it? Some of the styles are highly discredited in the literature, but are very successful in industry.

Novak: What is a good example of "do anything you can get away with" type?

Exec.: Well, it's not so much "doing anything you can get away with," it's that the autocratic approaches are very prevalent in industry.

Novak: I read about Bill Gates—he doesn't operate that way?

Exec.: That's a different management style, but I believe the literature

	will tend to lead you to believe that the most effective style is the participatory, consensus-building, empowering style.
Novak:	Team building?
Exec.:	Team building, but in the real world, you see all styles; you see a lot of them that say they use autocratic approaches.
Novak:	How would you characterize the president of your company?
Exec.:	He's very old-school-management style. He believes that, on a regular and routine basis, go around and kick everybody in the ass.
Novak:	That's his idea on how you motivate them?
Exec.:	Yeah, you go in there and, you know, beat on them.
Novak:	I would think that a lot of people wouldn't respond well to that?
Exec.:	Well, it's—that's one reason why the company has about a 70 percent turnover rate.
Novak:	You mean per year?
Exec.:	Per year.
Novak:	Holy Smoke! Isn't that expensive?
Exec.:	You would think so [chuckle].
Novak:	Not only terms of recruiting and getting people up to speed, but in lost momentum?
Exec.:	I would say very expensive, but those expenses are all soft costs.
Novak:	And, your president is not going to change?
Exec.:	No, that's the way he learned the craft; that's the way that he learned management, the style he uses. You know, as I mentioned, people typically don't change.
Novak:	With over 70 percent turnover rate, that indicates there's not a lot of trust there in anything he says.
Exec.:	Yep. The thing that amazes me, there's these couple of long-term employees—been here 10–12 years—one employee has been here longer than anybody else at least, probably because he's not competent to go anywhere else, but the other one is very competent.
Novak:	Why does he live with it?
Exec.:	I think it's inertia. It would be easier to stay on than to make a move.
Novak:	How do you see honesty and trust related in the work you do?
Exec.:	I guess I have a different management style, and I think, clearly, honesty is no longer presumed. Trust is no longer presumed in any relationship, and it has to be developed. In the past, it may have been presumed. I certainly wouldn't presume anything until I had some evidence.
Novak:	The old Texas handshake is not the operating reality.
Exec.:	Yeah, and if you haven't got trust, I don't think you'll have efficiency and effectiveness, and when you don't, you don't, so, unfortunately, the lack of trust and honesty assumes there's a quick fix, short-term perspective. Although many, many organizations operate strictly with a lot of short cuts, short quick fixes, and it's hard to invest in

them over a long-term perspective. On a long-term, I wouldn't say
they have effectiveness.

Novak: Given the growing competitiveness in all markets, do you see a greater
and greater problem with that style, or will you still find a niche?

Exec.:   Well, the literature would certainly lead you to believe that that is a
problematic style, but it's so prevalent that you have to wonder, how
can it be so prevalent if it's so ineffective?

Novak: Yes, and still stay in business. Is there any data that you know of on
the styles that are represented by companies most likely to go belly
up versus those that survive? Well, in terms of trying to build trust
and a sense in honest relationships, what are some of the things that
you have to do to do that?

Exec.:   My own value is you have to be trustworthy, but be worthy of trust,
to develop trust and, as I was saying, you've got to be consistent in
your practice. You can't be "average." You have to establish a certain
degree of predictability so people understand what you're trying to
accomplish, and you're consistent with your approach—you're not
changing directions every minute.

We see a glimpse of the "real-world" context for business through this
executive's eyes. Obviously, contexts for educating and managing that may
deviate from the "textbook ideal" can succeed, at least for a time. It should be
noted that the executive quoted planned to leave the company as soon as a
suitable replacement could be recruited (and recruitment has been difficult),
and there is a real question as to whether or not this company can stave off
bankruptcy for another year. This executive did confirm something that is
common in the literature: to quote Peters (1994) who quotes Secretary of War
Henry Stimson, "The only way to make a man trustworthy is to trust him."
(p. 78). And now the same must be true for women. I believe that increasingly
the global, competitive environment we are in will require trust and honesty
on the part of both management and employees, for this is the best context for
creating and using knowledge.

In contrast to the management style described by the executive interviewed
above, we have business counselors such as Thaler and Koval (2006) who
promulgate *The Power of Nice: How to negotiate so everyone wins, Especially you!*

> Let us be clear: *Nice is not naïve.* Nice does not mean smiling blandly while
> others walk over you. Nice does not mean being a doormat. In fact, we
> would argue that *nice is the toughest four-letter word you will ever hear.* It
> means moving forward with the clear-eyed confidence that comes from
> knowing that being very nice and placing other people's needs on the
> same level as your own will get you everything you want. (pp. 3–4)

Thaler and Koval proceed to describe the importance of collaboration and
sharing ideas, giving examples of business success stories where being nice,

communicative, open, and honest lead to winning business successes. Increasingly we are seeing in the corporate world constructive sharing of positive feelings as well as ideas which lead to winning enterprises.

Facilitating Team Work

In recent years there has been much publicity regarding the importance of teams in industry. The Ford Taurus and Saturn automobiles are heralded as evidence of the payoff that comes from team efforts in industry. Driven, in part, by competition from Japanese auto companies, where team planning has been used extensively, American auto companies found that similar strategies can pay off.

Teams can be as small as two members or number into the hundreds. For example, "Team Mustang," which produced a new 1994 model, had 400 members, with "chunk teams" responsible for parts of the car, coordinating efforts through the larger team (White and Suris, 1993).

In school settings, team learning has become popularized under the label "cooperative learning." David and Richard Johnson and their associate Holubec (1995) have done much to help teachers and administrators understand and apply cooperative learning strategies. Their recommendations stress the importance of structuring group work in such a way that every student has a clear and defined role to play, assuring that all members of a learning group are actively engaged. Cooperative learning in school settings has been shown to facilitate learning to some extent and can also have positive effects on ego enhancement of learners. In our Conécate al Conocimiento Project in Panama, we have sought and obtained high cooperation among students, teachers, and administrators. This project will be discussed further in Chapter 10.

Using analogies from the world of sports, Martin (1993) describes how all corporations can benefit from "team think." As a starting point, he recommends that corporations define clearly their mission statement, philosophy, and yearly and long-term goals. These should be concise and understandable. He cites examples such as Shell Oil Company's mission statement, "To meet the energy needs of mankind" (p. 10); statements of philosophy such as "People come first" and "To treat our clients' interests as if they were our own" (pp. 14–15). Goals also need to be stated simply. Progress toward the goal should be measurable. Employees can contribute to reaching goals only if they know and understand the goals. Drucker (1993) states that, "The knowledge-based organization, therefore, requires that everyone take responsibility for that organization's objectives, contributions, and indeed, for its behavior as well" (p. 108). Drucker goes on to say:

> There is a great deal of talk today about "entitlement" and "empowerment." These terms express the demise of the command and control-based organization. But they are just as much terms of power and rank as

the old terms were. We should, instead, be talking about responsibility and contribution. For power without responsibility is not power at all; it is irresponsibility. (p. 109)

For every employee to perform responsibly, clear statement of mission, philosophy, and goals are not enough. There must be leadership that manifests concern for each employee and a reward structure that recognizes achievements. Salary alone is not enough. Special recognition programs, stock options, and a manifest interest in employee welfare by the leadership is necessary. Martin (1993) even recommends that termination should be done with care, consideration, compassion, and clarity. Kilts and colleagues (2007) advise: " Terminations should not be judgmental. There should be an attempt to help the person find something he will enjoy doing and do well" (p. 288). This, of course, sends a valuable message to employees who are not terminated.

In his book, *Winning*, Welch (2005) discusses the case of Arthur Anderson, at one time one of the most respected accounting firms in the world. In the 1980s the firm decided to enter the consulting business, and indeed this was very profitable for a time. By 1989, the company split off the consulting business, but staff shared the same office areas, and in time the rigid standards for integrity of the accounting firm eroded to the more free-wheeling standards of the consulting business. Welch observed:

> Arthur Anderson was founded almost a century ago with the mission to become the most respected and trusted auditing company in the world. It was a company that prided itself on having the courage to say no, even if that meant losing a client. It succeeded by hiring the most capable, highest-integrity CPAs and rewarding them for doing work that rightfully earned the confidence of corporations and regulators around the world.
>
> Then in the boom times of the 1990's arrived, and Arthur Anderson decided it wanted to start a consulting business; that's where the excitement was, not to mention the big money. The company started hiring more MBAs and paying them constantly increasing salaries that the consulting industry demanded.
>
> . . . There was a real cowboy mentality in the consulting industry, and the accounting side of Anderson felt the impact . . .
>
> Throughout most of the 90's, Arthur Anderson was a company at war with itself. . . . In these circumstances, how could people know the answer to questions like: "What really is our mission?" "What values matter most?" . . .
>
> Eventually, in 2002, the house collapsed, due in no small part to the disconnect between the mission and values. (pp. 22–23)

Welch goes on to describe a similar case for Enron Corporation. Indeed, the corporate graveyards became strewn with failed companies in the 2002–2009 period, and the failures continue as of this writing. Many of these failures were, at the core, a failure to maintain high levels of integrity and moral values. Unfortunately, many small investors, innocent of the machinations that went on, have suffered huge losses.

Aburdene (2005) also stresses the importance of "values driven" business.

> What do I mean by "values driven"? Simply this. If *values* more than income, demographics, geography or other factors profoundly influence your choices at the cash register, whether you purchase fair trade coffee, solar panels or that new Honda hybrid, you are a Conscious Consumer. (p. 92)

> Conscious Consumers are categorized as "LOHGAS" (Lifestyles of Health and Sustainability) customers. By 2005, 63 million Americans—or 30 percent of the adult population—were part of the LOHAS market says the Natural Marketing Institute, a marketing research firm specializing in the LOHAS customer. (p. 93)

With growing public awareness of the fragility of the world environment, global warming, and the fact that non-renewable natural resources are finite, we are likely to see values-driven consumer decisions increasing substantially above the 30 percent cited above.

Teams as Learning Groups

Whether in school or corporate settings, the central purpose of teams is to learn how to do something better. This brings into play all of the factors discussed in earlier chapters, as well as principles that will be included in subsequent chapters. Consistent with the learning principle, "The most important thing influencing learning is what the learner already knows," we bring into play both the richness and diversity of knowledge, skills, and attitudes of the various team members—and also the problems associated with each person's idiosyncratic view of the world. To capitalize on the diversity represented in the team, we need to begin by reviewing the mission, philosophy, and goals relative to the work to be done and to reach some consensus on the tasks at hand. Leadership in this early process could be by a more experienced or more senior team member. However, every team member can and should play a leadership role in some capacity.

In my classes, I have frequently used teams with four to six members, and then, after the goals were agreed upon, each team subdivided into subteams of two or three persons to tackle specific aspects of the whole team's program. When class schedules allow for two or more projects to be undertaken, I insist that persons who played a smaller leadership role in the first project accept a larger leadership role in the second or third project. Often students are themselves surprised how well they can play leadership roles in team settings. My role in the program is similar to that of a head coach for an athletic team. I help to define goals and procedures for the teams and subteams, and then work with teams individually as they progress in their project. Valadares (2008) also has found that teamwork produced better learning in high school physics.

In the corporate setting, most of my "coaching" work has been to help team members understand the nature of knowledge and nature of learning and to assist them in organizing their knowledge using concept maps and Vee diagrams. Almost without exception, the latter tools are new to all team members, so there is commonly a half-day "coaching" session needed to help them understand and learn how to use these tools.

Using Concept Maps and Vee Diagrams

With a relatively small investment of time, school students and corporate employees can acquire sufficient skill in concept mapping and Vee diagramming to use these tools to advance their learning. Although it would seem to make sense to begin by using the Vee, since this tool can incorporate concept maps as part of the "left side" and "right side" of the Vee, our early experiences in a junior high school setting indicated that students (and teachers) can be overwhelmed with the Vee if it is presented before concept mapping skills are acquired (Novak, Gowin, and Johansen, 1983). With relatively few exceptions, we have found this to be true with high school, university, and corporate learners as well. Some of the reasons for this were discussed in Chapter 6. On the other hand, we have found that it only takes most people an hour or two to gain enough skill in concept mapping to build a reasonably good "first cut" concept map for a given knowledge domain. Therefore, we have found it highly useful to use concept maps for team problem solving even when none of the team members have had prior experience with this tool.

Some of our most successful work has been in corporate settings, since effective team problem solving has become so overwhelmingly important in the highly competitive corporate environment. In most cases, we have been very successful in capturing the essential knowledge structure for any problem area in as little as a half-day session. Sessions running two or three days have permitted refinement of preliminary concept maps and discussion of alternative strategies that were suggested by the concept maps. Participants find an all-day concept mapping session a real "brain drain," but they typically come away highly motivated. There is a natural excitement and stimulation to seeing "the big picture" of a problem area laid out in front of you. For example, a participant in one of our corporate sessions observed:

P: I was really enthusiastic, especially the day we worked through the mapping and started seeing some of the concepts come out because those were questions that I've had. I've been with the company for 4 years, and I have worked on these compounds for 1 year, and so I started seeing concepts coming out that I had been questioning people about that had been working in the field for a while. You know, it's like "okay now, how do you know that you need to call this the hydrophobe?. . . . which activator?" Some of this concept started coming out, and I think this would have a real value for onboarding new hires. We could have real value for onboarding people into the team that haven't worked on these compounds before or even the idea of taking the compounds and applying them in a new area for new products.

Commenting on the value of concept maps for communications with other team members on other projects, this participant said:

P: Concept maps would be very useful for each team that I interact with because I interact with teams on totally different projects, like 3 or 4 different projects. Each team is at different stages of development, but it would be nice to be able to say, for instance, now what are we going to do to get this product to market? What are the things we have to fill in our maps to have the knowledge, and to gain the confidence of, to present to managers that this is our recommendation, this is our technical recommendation, this is what we want to go with. Or for instance, having something that's further upstream when we're still under the development stage, talking with someone about, hey, now this is what we think this interaction is, or we don't quite understand this interaction? Do you have any feedback? Do you have any data that can help us make this connection here?

Commenting on the value of the experience, this participant said:

P: I thought that it was actually very informative because I've only worked in the area for a year, and it was very good to work with a group of people, technologists who had worked in the area for say 10–15, 20 years and to *start seeing the concepts that they have intuitively held in their minds start to come out onto the map and to the paper.* (emphasis added)

We cited in the previous chapter the valuable role concept maps played to help a new research team member understand the knowledge the Rhizobotany Group was using to guide their research. In corporate work, I have found that the knowledge structure necessary to understand and resolve problems is often an order of magnitude more complex than that which is needed in academic research programs. Is it any wonder that corporations often waste so much time and resources in trying to create and bring to market superior products or services? Although we have experienced an increasing interest from corporations in the use of concept maps, this movement has been slower than I expected. In part this is a reflection of the inertia that exists in corporations to try new ideas or approaches; in part it is the result of corporate practices that require bringing in consultants to sell new ideas. The Institute for Human and Machine Cognition (IHMC) now offers at no cost CmapTools for use by corporations, and there are now private consultants who will offer training programs for corporate staff. We may see an acceleration in corporate application of concept mapping tools and related ideas. Corporations as diverse as Cirque du Soleil and EDS have expressed interest in the tools. Perhaps in 10–20 years from now, there will be many major corporations that will find value in using concept maps, and the psychological and epistemological ideas that give them more meaning. There are nothing more disempowering to an employee than feelings of stupidity, and especially for new employees or new members joining project teams, these are all too often the feelings they do experience. One advantage in using CmapTools either in facilitation of individual's learning or in facilitating group problem solving and knowledge creation is that we have at the end of the process an explicit artifact that represents the achievement concisely. Paavola and colleagues (2004) stress that: "In contemporary society, human work is increasingly constituted by creation of knowledge artifacts" (p. 573). However, they do not discuss the best ways to create and preserve these artifacts.

Once team members are comfortable with making and using concept maps, it is not difficult to help them understand and use the Vee heuristic. Part of the value in employing the Vee is that it helps to keep in front of participants those global ideas that are too easily ignored. The corporate mission statement can easily be modified, if necessary, to provide a good world view for any project. The statements on corporate philosophy or fundamental beliefs may also contribute to the world view and/or to the philosophy, theory, and major principles guiding project work in the company. Consideration of Value Claims early in project planning can help to clarify what the major value(s) is/are that the work seeks to achieve. For example, the Ford "Team Mustang" may have written: "The new Mustang will be fuel efficient, high performance, and fun to drive." Considering the Knowledge Claims in advance could help to define tasks of "chunk teams," e.g., "The fuel injection system will have these performance characteristics. . . ."

As with concept maps, the Vee representing the knowledge creation work to be done by a team can be drawn on a single page. Posted in team members' work areas, it could help them to keep "the big picture" of the job to be done in clear view. It also can serve to provide imagery and language to help workers communicate with one another, addressing questions such as, "Are those measurements you propose to make really supported by the theory and principles x, y, and z, and will they be valid?" Or, another example, "Are the value claims we believe we can make, based on our data, consistent with our assessment of customer wants?" As a project progresses, there will be a need to prepare Vees for each subteam, and perhaps, for each of several studies undertaken by subteams. Even with these multiple Vees, there remains a basic

Table 7.3 Functional backgrounds of Product Development Team Members. From Nonaka and Takeuchi, 1995, p. 77*

Company	Sales			Quality				
(Product)	R&D	Production	Marketing	Planning	Service	Control	Other	Total
Fuji Xerox (FX-3500)	5	4	I	4	I	I	I	17
Honda (City)	18	6	4	—	I	I	—	30
NEC (PC 8000)	5	—	2	2	2	—	—	II
Epson (EP101)	10	10	8	—	—	—	—	28
Canon (AE-1)	12	10	—	—	—	2	4	28
Canon (Mini-Copier)	8	3	2	I	—	—	I	15
Mazda (New RX-7)	13	6	7	I	I	I	—	29
Matsushita Electric (Automatic Home Bakery)	8	8	I	I	I	I	—	20

* Reprinted by permission of Oxford University Press.

simplicity and connectedness, since all of the subproject Vees will contain many of the same elements, such as the operative World View guiding the work.

The problems of communication among team members can be over-whelming. Most project teams in corporations involve 10 to 30 or more members, drawn from a variety of backgrounds and "corporate cultures." Table 7.3 illustrates this diversity for eight company projects (from Nonaka and Takeuchi, 1995, p. 77).

We can see from Table 7.3 that constructive interaction among team members with such diverse backgrounds would not be easy, and indeed, we observed this to be the case at Kodak in the example cited in Chapter 6. By contrast, I have observed the enormous facilitating effects the use of concept maps and Vee diagrams can have in both academic and corporate settings.

The communication problem is common in most organizations. This problem is being addressed by groups such as the Institute for Research on Learning (IRL), where the idea of a "community of practice" has been developed. Peters (1994) asserts:

> Becoming a member of a community of practice is literally a requirement of modern-day job success. Non-members, IRL researchers insist, can't

succeed in an age of knowledge. IRL has examined everything from airline operations centers to insurance companies. In the latter, for example, new insurance claims processors become effective to the extent that they are accepted into (and wish to join) a local community of practice. IRL's Etienne Wenger claims that a knowledge-age organization is nothing but "an ensemble of interconnected communities of practice." (p. 174)

Waitley (1995, p. 164) goes so far as to assert there is "no creation without communication." The "bottom line" is that, in any team project setting, better methods for improving communications among members are needed. There is little "hard" data to support this claim, but there is an abundance of "soft" data from many different sources that do support the claim. In time, I believe we shall see good empirical evidence that concept maps and Vee diagrams can facilitate team communications and team effectiveness in creating new knowledge and new useful products. These tools, when wisely applied, will markedly alter the context for teaching and learning needed for knowledge creation.

Friedman in his book, *The World is Flat* (2005), presents a compelling case that we have moved from the Information Age to a new world where virtually anything can be made anywhere and shipped anywhere primarily because there are virtually no boundaries on knowledge and knowledge utilization. Another important factor has been the enormous expansion of the Internet and free open-source software that has allowed exponential growth in the use of the Internet and transfer of information, Friedman observes:

> My bottom line is this: Open-source is an important flattener because it makes available for free many tools, from software to encyclopedias, that millions of people around the world would have had to buy in order to use, and because open-source network associations—with their open borders and come-one-come-all can challenge hierarchical structures with a horizontal model of innovation that is clearly working in a number of areas. Apache and Linus have each helped to drive down costs of Internet usage in ways that are profoundly flattening. (pp. 102–103)

Tapscott and Williams (2006) concur with Friedman and point out:

> Today everything from customer relationship management (CRM) to enterprise resource management (ERM) to content management and business intelligence—basically any enterprise management application you can think of—is becoming available in open source. (p. 85)

The changes that are occurring in our ability to gather and share information in schools or organizations continue at an accelerating pace. These changes are creating new contexts for educating and management and now permit fundamental changes in the way we teach in schools and the way we do business. Some of these changes will be examined in the next chapter.

Tapscott and Williams' case is illustrated in recent work by Procter and Gamble reported by the Vice President for Knowledge and Innovation, Larry Huston and a colleague (2006). When it was suggested that printing popular pictures on Pringles™ might increase sales, they searched the literature and found a researcher/baker in Italy had developed a method for printing pictures on bread. Working with this baker, it was relatively easy to adapt the technology for use with Pringles, and this led to double-digit growth in sales of Pringles. Procter and Gamble now routinely searches the literature for research relevant to its interests, saving millions of dollars in R&D development costs. Currently Huston is working with researchers in India and other countries to prepare comprehensive concept maps dealing with diabetes, eye care and other areas of health care. Many scholars in India, China, and other countries are finding that they can sell their knowledge to interested parties anywhere in the world, and remain at home to continue their research. We shall see much more of this kind of "flat world" knowledge creation and utilization in the future. We shall also see how dependent innovation is on high levels of education and investment in top-flight researchers. Kao (2007) points out how the latter kinds of investment have made Singapore a premier innovative nation, with the economic prosperity such investment brings.

The P&G Pringles example serves as a good illustration of what is required in a *Forward-Focused Company* as suggested by Harper (2001). Harper indicates that a Forward Focused Company not only is a learning organization, but that "Learning organizations do not spend all their time developing new knowledge. They recognize there is no reason to reinvent the wheel if the knowledge they need already exists. Learning organizations develop knowledge networks so they can access critical information" (p. 51). The problem of organizing information in a digital age is enormous and there are no easy answers (Borgman, 2007). Nevertheless, we have found the use of concept maps to be a powerful tool to help both with knowledge capture and knowledge archiving. Increasingly in the future we see the use of CmapTools as a powerful resource for collaboration and sharing of knowledge (Cañas, et al., 2001).

As noted earlier, CmapTools provides a patented search function that allows one to search from a concept in a given concept map, and the software recognizes the links to the given concept and "contextualizes" the search. This means that the resources identified on the Internet or other concept map files are much more likely to be of value, and one need not sift through dozens or hundred of "hits' to find a resource identified as pertinent either in the pool of concept maps on the IHMC servers or on the Web. There is a growing interest in the use of CmapTools in corporations, and I expect this will accelerate.

Chapter 8

The Context for Education/ Management

The Importance of Context

Education and management are events that always occurs in a specific context. The context includes emotional, organizational, physical, and cultural characteristics, and each of these include other factors. One of the reasons education or management are too often ineffective, or even destructive, results from a limiting context. Some of the complexity of the context is shown in Figure 8.1.

As with all other concepts in my theory of education, each of the concepts shown in Figure 8.1 interrelate with all the others, some in more significant ways than others. For example, the audio-tutorial lessons we developed for elementary school science lessons, described in the previous chapters, created a special context (an equipped carrel unit) within a traditional classroom within

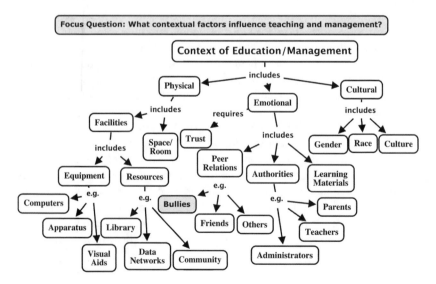

Figure 8.1 The variety of factors involved in creating the context for education and management.

a traditional elementary school in a representative New York State school system. Our primary motivation for developing these lessons was to exercise careful control over the knowledge presented, but important secondary goals were to utilize a wide range of hands-on materials, apparatus, and visual aids, to allow some learner control over the pace of instruction and to use examples that were emotionally neutral or positive for students, and also culturally sensitive. Certainly we fell short of the ideal, but the significant, enduring positive effects on students' achievement indicated that we had a measure of success exceeding that of typical elementary school science classrooms. An anecdotal comment made by one of our cooperating teachers was, "About the only time George really seems to pay attention in class is the fifteen to twenty minutes a week he spends in the science carrel." Our evaluation interviews indicated that George was indeed engaged in learning in the carrel, since his performance exceeded that of most of his peers. Kahle and her colleagues (Kahle, et al., 1976) found that the most striking difference between high school students using audio-tutorial biology lessons and their classmates receiving conventional instruction was their substantially higher class attendance rates. These kind of findings attest to the fact that the best form of motivation comes when learners recognize that they are learning something meaningfully. This so-called *cognitive drive* motivation is far more beneficial to learners or workers than the transitory motivation that arises from superficial rewards in common practice.

With the explosion on new technology now accruing and increasing access to electronically-mediated learning in contexts where the learners can increasingly exercise their preferences, we may see in time radical changes in the way education is delivered and selected. School-age children spend much more time with computer games and other electronic media than do most adults (Stansbury, 2008). A limiting factor in the use of newer electronic resources for learning is that teachers are often reluctant to use resources that their students use routinely. Devaney (2009) reports that some students prefer online learning to conventional schooling, such as the Insight School of California–Los Angeles program that can lead to a high school diploma. I sometimes wonder what I would have chosen if I had this option 70 years ago? One of my goals for this book is to guide the process by which education can be improved for the more traditional as well as electronically-mediated contexts.

The Emotional Context

The Importance of Feelings

When do people begin to be cognizant of how they feel, and how others around them are feeling? According to Dunn (1987) and Lewis (1995), children begin to manifest recognition of how they feel within their first year of life. By age 20 months, they evidence clearly not only concern for themselves but also concern for the feelings of others. For example, an older sibling may give a crying baby her or his pacifier or a favorite toy. The meanings human beings construct for events include feelings. Penfield (1952) found that when electrodes placed in the brain were used to stimulate specific regions of the brain, the subject not only recalled the details of some event but also the feelings that were experienced during the event. Human beings integrate their thinking, feeling and acting in some form for every experience they have. More recent research (Niedenthal, 2007) indicates "that perceiving and thinking about emotion involve perceptual, somatovisceral, and motoric reexperiencing (collectively referred to as 'embodiment') of the collective emotions in one's self. The embodiment of emotion when induced in human participants by manipulation of facial expression and posture in the laboratory, causally affects how information is processed." Increasingly we are seeing research studies that confirm the idea that thinking, feeling, and acting interact to produce the meaning of experience. The challenge is how to use this knowledge to improve learning in school and corporate settings.

Can people learn to enhance their positive feelings about themselves and become more sensitive and more concerned with the feelings of others? The answer from many sources is a resounding yes. However, caring, sympathy, concern, responsibility, and commitment are not simply the unfolding of our genetic endowment as we grow older; they are traits that need to be learned and practiced—with learning and practice continuing throughout our lifespan.

Harris (1969), in his popular book, *I'm OK—You're OK*, drew on the earlier work of Berne (1964) to describe *transactional analysis* (TA), a technique used by many psychiatrists and others to help people understand their own feelings and the feelings of others. The theory behind TA is that we all experience feelings of "You're Ok, I'm not OK" as we move through infancy and early childhood. The basic unit of TA is when one person says or does something to another person. Berne defined three emotional states he labeled as Parent, Child, and Adult. The Parent state is that huge store of "recordings" we have from our growing-up experiences with parents and other "authority" persons. The recordings: "don't touch that; you might break it;" "wear your coat and cap when you go out today—it's cold;" "don't associate with John or Mary because they are nasty people;" etc. The admonitions may or may not have validity, but they are recorded as *truth* and we are supposed to feel bad or inadequate if we violate them. The Child, on the other hand, is the records we make of our *feelings* when we are subjected to Parent transactions. They lead to feelings of "You're OK; I'm not OK." By ten months, children begin to have sufficient control that they can act on their environment and achieve a certain amount of control over their environment. The child begins to "record" ways he or she can consciously control his or her environment, including using smiles or kisses to get adult approval. The child begins to develop his or her Adult. The Adult is the rational person who can achieve rational control over events and people. The feelings of the Adult move toward "I'm OK, You're OK."

Too often teachers or managers issue instructions with little or no rationale, or a rationale that is patently fraudulent. They are acting as Parent, and elicit in students or subordinates feelings of Child. This is obviously not the way to empower people to achieve their best performance. And yet, a few hours' observation in almost any classroom or work setting will probably reveal multiple instances of Parent transactions eliciting Child feelings and actions. Of course, we all offer and experience Parent, Child, or Adult transactions from day to day in our lives, but most of us manage to maintain an Adult emotional posture most of the time. When we deviate widely from this, as under periods of great stress, we may become candidates for the psychiatrist's care.

It is a constant challenge for the teacher/manager to interact with others in ways that will do nothing to diminish their "I'm OK" image and do everything possible to enhance their image. The most robust criterion is at once simple and profound: How can I organize the transaction so that it may become an optimal meaningful learning experience? As Maslow (1984) pointed out, emotional needs of individuals need careful consideration. This will be a theme stressed in this chapter, as it has been in other chapters.

The Art of Loving

At first blush, you might think I am referring to the sexual act of making love. While I believe the latter is important, and there are whole sections in most bookstores dealing with sex, I wish to discuss the kind of loving Fromm (1956) stresses in his book, *The Art of Loving*. In his chapter on "The Theory of Love," Fromm states:

> Envy, jealousy, ambition, any kind of greed are passions; love is an action, the practice of human power, which can be practiced only in freedom and never as a result of a compulsion.
>
> Love is an activity, not a passive affect; it is a "standing in," not a "falling for." In the most general way, the active character of love can be described by stating that love is primarily *giving*, not receiving. (p. 18)

By giving, Fromm is not referring only or even primarily to material things. When one seeks to help someone else enhance his or her "I'm OK" image, that is *giving*. The truly loving (giving) person is attractive to others not by the material things they offer, but by the understanding, compassion, and search for meaning they offer. It is not surprising that many of us have at least on some occasions experienced the love of an effective teacher or an effective manager.

Fromm discusses another important concept of love: *fairness*.

> Fairness means not to use fraud and trickery in the exchange of commodities and services, and in the exchange of feelings. "I give to you as much as you give to me," in material goods as well as in love, is the prevalent

ethical maxim in capitalist society. It may even be said that the development of fairness ethics is the particular contribution of capitalist society.

   The reasons for this fact lie in the very nature of capitalist society. In
pre-capitalist societies, the exchange of goods was determined either by
force, by tradition, or by personal bonds of love or friendship. In capitalism, the all-determining factor is the exchange on the market. Whether we
deal with the commodity market, the labor market, or the market of
services, each person exchanges whatever he has to sell for that which he
wants to acquire under the conditions of the market, without the use of
force or fraud. (pp.108–109)

However, Fromm goes on to express his skepticism that fairness and other
concepts of love can operate in a capitalistic society: "The *principle* underlying
capitalistic society and the *principle* of love are incompatible" (p. 100).

   People capable of love, under the present system, are necessarily the
   exceptions; love is by necessity a marginal phenomenon in present-day
   Western society. Not so much because many occupations would not
   permit of a loving attitude, but because the spirit of a production-
   centered, commodity-greedy society is such that only the non-conformist
   can defend himself successfully against it. Those who are seriously concerned with love as the only rational answer to the problem of human
   existence must, then, arrive at the conclusion that important and radical
   changes in our social structure are necessary, if love is to become a social
   and not a highly individualistic, marginal phenomenon. The direction
   of such changes can, within the scope of this book, only be hinted at.

   Our society is run by a managerial bureaucracy, by professional politicians; people are motivated by mass suggestion, their aim is producing
   more and consuming more, as purposes in themselves. All activities are
   subordinated to economic goals; means have become ends; man is an
   automaton—well fed, well clad, but with out any ultimate concern for
   that which is his peculiarly human quality and function. If man is to be
   able to love, he must be put in his supreme place. The economic machine
   must serve him, rather than he serve it. He must be enabled to share
   experience, to share work, rather than, at best, share in profits. Society
   must be organized in such a way that man's social, loving nature is not
   separated from his social existence, but becomes one with it. If it is true, as
   I have tried to show, that love is the only sane and satisfactory answer to
   the problem of human existence, then any society which excludes, relatively, the development of love, must, in the long run, perish of its own
   contradiction with the basic necessities of human nature. Indeed, to speak
   of love is not "preaching," for the simple reason that it means to speak of
   the ultimate and real need in every human being. That this need has been
   obscured does not mean that it does not exist. To analyse the nature of

love is to discover its general absence today and to criticize the social conditions which are responsible for this absence. To have faith in the possibility of love as a social and not only exceptional individual phenomenon, is a rational faith based on the insight into the very nature of man. (pp. 111–112)

Much as I admire what Fromm has written on the "Art of Loving," and I know of no recent books or articles as cogent and powerful as his work, I believe he may be wrong about the incompatibility of capitalism and loving (as he saw it). With the emerging globalizations of businesses and the constantly increasing competitive pressure, there is a growing number of economists and other writers who see business success *over the long term as requiring* those elements that Fromm sees as necessary for *loving*. Fromm may have been right for capitalism up to the 1990s, but now we have entered what Drucker (1993) calls the *Post-Capitalist Society*. In this society, knowledge and knowledge creation become the principal resources for increasing profitability. But how do you create knowledge and enhance the utilization of knowledge at all levels of a corporation? Certainly not by "top down" dictates from the management. As Drucker observes:

> *The knowledge-based organization therefore requires that everyone take responsibility for that organization's objectives, contribution, and, indeed, for its behavior as well.*
>   This implies that all members of the organization must think through their objective and their contributions, and then take responsibility for both. It implies that there are no "subordinates;" there are only "associates." Furthermore, in the knowledge-based organization all members have to be able to control their own work by feedback from their results to their objectives. All members must ask themselves: "What is the one major contribution to this organization and its mission which I can make at this particular time?" It requires, in other words, that all members act as responsible decision makers. All members have to see themselves as "executives." (p. 108, emphasis in original)

The community that is needed in post-capitalist society—and needed especially by the knowledge worker—has to be based on *commitment and compassion*. . . . (p. 174)

And, how does Drucker believe we get commitment and compassion from the corporate workers?

> "Loyalty" from now on cannot be obtained by the paycheck; it will have to be earned by proving to knowledge employees that the organization which presently employs them can offer them exceptional opportunities

to be effective. Not so long ago, we talked about "labor." Increasingly, now, we are talking of "human resources." This implies that it is the individual knowledge employee who decides in large measure what he or she will contribute, and how great the yield from his or her knowledge can or should be. (p. 66)

In knowledge and service work, partnership with the responsible worker is the *only* way to improve productivity. Nothing else works at all. (p. 92)

It is interesting to observe that increasingly all companies, including WalMart, Publix and other grocery chains, and most other companies refer to all workers, including those who only stock shelves, as Associates. Apparently there is value in this since it has become so common.

Drucker is not the only economist calling for a new view of capitalism. Virtually every leading economist is telling us that we have entered a truly new era. For example, Nonaka and Takeuchi (1995) show the necessity for commitment and responsibility at all levels of the organization:

For any organizational knowledge creation on a global scale to succeed, the following three conditions must be met. First, top management of the participating organizations should show strong commitment to the project. This visible support provides the first step in persuading project members to commit themselves to the project. Second, assigning capable middle managers to the project as "global knowledge engineers" is critical. . . . Third, participants in the project should develop a sufficient level of trust among themselves. Building trust requires the use of mutually understandable, explicit language and often prolonged socialization or two-way, face-to-face dialogue that provides reassurance about points of doubt and leads to willingness to respect the other party's sincerity. (p. 222)

Waterman (1995), in his book, *What America Does Right*, makes a similar observation:

What makes top performing companies different, I would urge, is their organizational arrangements. Specifically:

- They are better organized to meet the needs of their *people*, so that they attract better people than their competitors do and their people are more greatly motivated to do a superior job, whatever it is they do.
- They are better organized to meet the needs of *customers* so that they are either more innovative in anticipating customer needs, more reliable in meeting customer expectations, better able to deliver their product or service more cheaply, or some combination of the above. (p. 17)

Furthermore, to succeed, corporations need to acquire a new view of "customers" and their needs. It is necessary to recognize that we need to dialogue with customers to come to understand their needs:

> Most customer's needs are tacit, which means that they cannot tell exactly or explicitly what they need or want. Asked "What do you need or want?," most customers tend to answer the question from their limited explicit knowledge of the available products or services they acquired in the past. This tendency points to the critical limitation of the one-way questionnaire format employed in traditional market research. (Drucker, 1993, p. 234)

Lafley and Charan (2008) go much further with their focus on the customer as "boss."

> The overarching principle for game-changing innovation that delivers sustained organic growth and profits, no matter whether your business is consumer products, services, or business-to-business industrial products, is placing the consumer or customer at the center of this framework. While many say they are "customer centric," few actually put the customer at the center of the innovation process. (p. 10)

Lafley and Charan illustrate their focus on the customer as the driving force for "game-changing" innovation as shown in Figure 8.2. They go on to explain each of the eight "drivers of innovation." For example:

> P&G is purpose-led and values-driven. Billions of people around the world are striving to improve their lives through accessible and affordable products and services. Our purpose is to improve their lives in small but meaningful ways with brands and products that continually deliver superior performance, quality, and value better than the best competition. (p. 11)

To facilitate enhanced consumer input, P&G instituted in 2002 a consumer immersion program where employees at all levels of the company were encouraged to live in consumers' homes, eating meals with the family, shopping with them and observing all aspects of their use of consumer products. They also instituted a program called *Working It* where employees worked behind the counters of small shops where they had direct contact with shoppers and a chance to get time-of-purchase comments from customers. Some of the observations in these programs led to new products or different packaging to meet better the needs of different segments of the market. These immersion programs with consumers led to the identification of *tacit* consumer needs or wants that would not have been identified by the usual methods of surveying consumers' wishes.

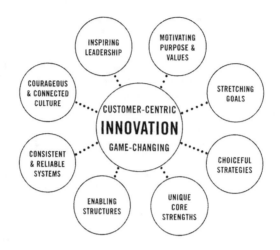

Figure 8.2 "Game Changing" innovation requires "Customer-centric" attention to eight primary drivers with guidance from the customer. From Lafley and Charan, 2008, p.11. Reproduced with permission from Random House.

Under Lafley, P&G also instituted a vigorous program of seeking innovation and R&D ideas from outside the company. Already noted was the example where P&G built on a baker's technology in Italy to print pictures on bakery products and applied this to Pringles™. Many other companies now employ "knowledge mining" practices developed by P&G to capitalize on creative work being done in other companies and in other countries. India and China with their huge and increasingly educated populations are emerging as a major source of ideas and technology for companies in other countries.

In my work with P&G during 1993–1998, we worked with teams from groups varying from R&D groups to marketing groups to groups with both R&D and marketing people, as noted earlier. Teams were first taught how to make concept maps, including some of the ideas underlying concept maps (e.g. Novak & Gowin, 1984; Novak and Cañas, 2006a), and then we proceeded to mine their knowledge for a given problem. We quickly found that it was important to identify a team leader for each project and to work with the team leader prior to a team session to identify a good focus question. This often required several hours, but in turn this saved 1–2 hours when meeting with the team. It was still common that the focus question and three to five concepts identified for the "top" of a team map had to be modified by the team, but the advanced preparation did save time. Usually a team could master the concept mapping process in an hour or two, and we could build a prototype team map for a project within 2–3 hours. Often we would identify subgroups to work on a section of the developing team map for which the subgroup had expertise. Subsequently the team would review subgroup concept maps and these would be merged into a revised "global" team concept map. Often these team maps and subgroup concept maps were done using Post-Its™ on butcher paper, and then later P&G staff would render the Post-Its™ into a computer-generated concept map and the latter was circulated to team members for further comment and refinement. According to Huston (2004), who was Vice President for Knowledge and Innovation at the time, the team work was greatly facilitated by the concept mapping process and led to many significant, profitable innovations.

I would go further than saying corporations need to place the customer as "boss." I believe the successful corporations of the future will become the *educating corporations.* They will seek to negotiate meanings with customers to understand better their needs, and to help educate consumers on the best way for them to meet their needs. If the company is truly an *educating company,* it will seek to make its products the best for the consumer's needs. The efforts P&G have made toward this goal, as described by Lafley and Charan (2008), are laudable; later I will spell out what it means to be an *educating* company.

Peer Relations

For many students, a major motivation for going to school is to be with their friends. In fact, a major incentive for expelled or dropout students to return to school is to be with their friends. However, when schooling fails for a substantial percentage of students, their friends may not be found in schools but in shopping centers, in street gangs, or, in worst cases, in prisons. Dropouts in high percentages come from families that move frequently, making establishment of school friendships difficult (US Dept. of Ed., 2001). The challenge to educators is to encourage peer relationships that build mutual trust and a sense of caring and being cared for. Some of the growing popularity of "cooperative learning" (Johnson & Johnson, 1988; Slavin, 1982) approaches in classrooms is recognition that students can assist each other in a learning task structured as a team effort. There may be competition between groups, which can add motivation to excel, but the criteria for high performance in the groups must be structured so that no group is unwarrantedly disadvantaged. A variety of strategies for achieving this have been promulgated by the writers cited and by many others.

One strategy I have found effective in building trust and encouraging positive peer relationships is concept mapping. When done individually and shared with a group, concept maps can show that all learners see a view of the larger conceptual picture and that no one has the "perfect" map of the domain. The individuals who are more ego secure, or more in need of recognition, will usually offer their maps early in a discussion, but as realization builds that each person has something to contribute, all members of a class or cooperative learning group will express ideas. It is a bit like the proverbial story of the blind men and the elephant—each "saw" a piece of the whole and collectively the group can construct a better "picture" of the knowledge domain. After constructing individual concept maps, members of a coopera-tive learning team can work together to construct a "team map," and a healthy competition may occur as individuals vote on which team map (with names omitted) "wins the prize." A similar process is effective with Vee diagrams.

When sensitivity is used in structuring cooperative learning groups, the results can reduce bias favoring male or female gender, race, or cultural differ-ences, and personality differences. Gorman, at Northbridge, Massachusetts High School, has used white boards and erasable markers successfully with teams of students in physics. Since computers are available to the class on a limited basis, students usually first create concept maps on the white boards and later rebuild them using CmapTools. Figures 8.3 and 8.4 show examples of the work done by two teams. When computer time is available to the class, student teams collaborate to produce digital versions of their concept maps. Gorman's strategy could be useful to teachers in any school that lacks adequate computer resources. Gorman bought 4 × 8 white panels from a home supplies store and cut these to produce the inexpensive white boards. He has shown that students making concept maps outperform similar students not doing concept mapping (Gorman, in review).

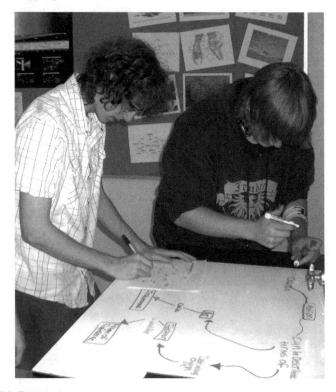

Figure 8.3 Two students working on a white board to create a concept map in high school physics. Reproduced with permission from J. Gorman.

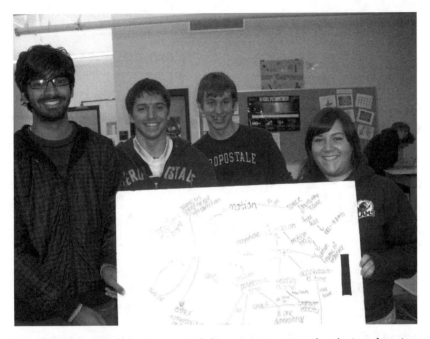

Figure 8.4 A four-student team created this concept map on the physics of motion. Teamwork has been met with enthusiasm from the students in laboratory and other studies as well as in building concept maps. Reproduced with permission from J. Gorman.

Personality factors are complex and their influences on learning are equally complex. There have been numerous studies in education dealing with such factors as intrinsic versus extrinsic motivation tendencies, internal versus external "locus of control," i.e., beliefs about who controls my destiny, me or other forces, and dogmatic versus open-minded characteristics. A recent study found that for more than 7500 subjects followed from birth, 10-year-olds who tested higher with regard to locus of control (i.e., they believed they control their fate) were less likely to be obese at age 30, less stressed, and less likely to describe their health as poor (Norton, 2008). The fundamental issue is, however, how an individual seeks to achieve an ego status of "I'm OK." Education and employment practices that encourage peer relations that enhance the "I'm OK" feelings of all should be the goal of the contexts we construct.

Peer relations in the workplace are perhaps as important as in schools. In one of our studies we found that dissatisfaction with peer relations between two staff members was the result of failure to understand clearly both their own job characteristics and their associates' job characteristics (Fraser, 1993). When we prepared concept maps describing each staff member's job (see Figure 8.5) and these were shared, Gwen could see why Catherine was performing as she did and vice versa. In a matter of minutes, they resolved

(a)

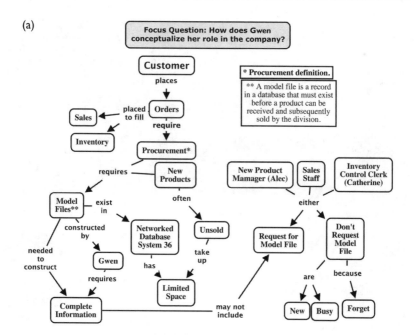

Figure 8.5 Concept maps showing the job characteristics and feelings as seen by two staff members in a computer sales office. When Gwen (a) and Catherine (b) [opposite] shared their maps with each other, conflicts were quickly resolved.

conflicts that had festered for some two years, and six months later, both staff members reported continuing satisfaction with their peer relationships.

In the corporate setting, constructing concept maps to better understand a problem, search for new problem solutions, and to seek better ways to organize and represent knowledge can lead to improved peer relations as a consequence of the empowerment conferred to all team members. The latter application was discussed earlier and in Chapter 6.

Evaluation practices can enhance or damage peer relations in either work settings or school settings. Higgins (1995, pp. 205–206) points out in his book, *Innovate or Evaporate*, that corporations that promote innovation need a variety of approaches to recognize and reward creativity. Money alone is not the solution.

As we shall see in Chapter 9, we need to place less emphasis on evaluation practices that place individuals in direct competition with their peers and more emphasis on practices that can be mutually ego-enhancing to groups of students or employees. Moreover, we need to emphasize evaluation of the *feeling* aspect of an educational experience much more than we currently do in most settings. Questions relating to how a learner feels toward their peers and how they believe their peers feel toward them can be informative and productive.

(b)

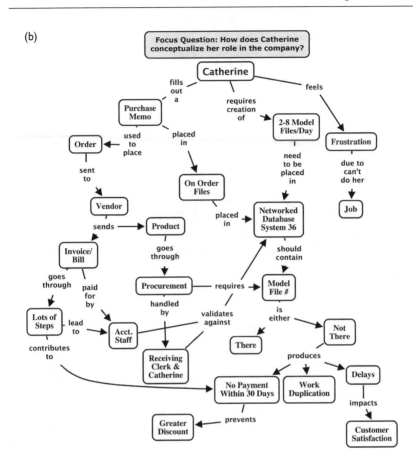

Learning Materials

Learning materials carry the potential for strong positive (ego-enhancing) or strong negative (ego-destructive) effects. For example, learners who have had negative experiences with mathematics may respond negatively to a learning task where mathematics is involved even when they are in a comfortable physical or cultural context and have considerable knowledge about the subject. What does an educator do when the level of understanding of a domain we desire *requires* understanding mathematical ideas? The solution may not be easy, but usually we can find another pathway.

Conceptual Opaqueness. A key problem in learning mathematics is that most instructional materials are *conceptually opaque*, that is, they do not present the concepts and concept relationships needed to understand the *meaning* of the mathematical ideas involved. This is almost a universal problem, beginning

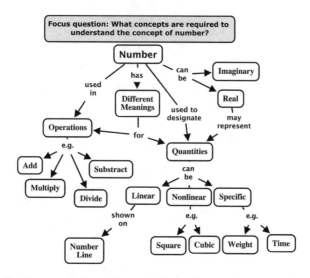

Figure 8.6 Key ideas needed to understand the mathematical concept of *number*.

in early grades and continuing in many college math courses. What is usually presented are *procedures* for obtaining answers to problems.

To illustrate concepts in mathematics, let us begin with Figure 8.6, which shows the key concepts needed to understand the concept of *number*. It also illustrates some of the sources of confusion in math problem solving. For example, many people do not understand clearly that numbers used to designate *units*, such as pounds, inches, or hours, have a separate meaning from numbers used to perform *operations*, such as add, multiply and divide. While 2 + 2 may equal 4 as an *operation*, 2 hours plus 2 minutes equals 122 minutes when the *units* are considered, not 4 hours or 4 minutes.

Professor Henderson, a colleague at Cornell University and distinguished senior mathematician, who helped me prepare Figure 8.6, said he only recognized the sharp distinction I have described late in his career. It is obviously not obvious that the concept *number* has two distinct meanings, one to represent units and another used in operations such as addition or division. Baroody and Benson (2001) address the question of when mathematics instruction should begin, and they conclude that number instruction can be started between the ages of 1½ and 3 years and should include the ideas of numbers as a *property* (or counting operation) and number as a *collection* (or number of units). The failure to understand clearly the differences in the very elementary concepts in Figure 8.6 is one of the reasons mathematics is so confusing to so many people. The problems multiply as we move into more advanced mathematics and applications of mathematics in sciences and other fields. The long-term result is "math anxiety" experienced by so many people, but most research studies on math anxiety fail to consider the "conceptual opaqueness" of almost all instruction in mathematics or fields using mathematics. I believe if we made strong efforts to make mathematics as "conceptually transparent" as suggested in Figure 8.6, it could become one of the easiest and most emotionally rewarding subjects people could study. At this writing, only a very small minority of the mathematics education community agrees with me, but these numbers (people units) are increasing. With our recent book on the use of concept maps in mathematics (Afamasaga-Fuata'ī, 2009), it is my hope that there will be increasing focus on mathematical concepts that underlie math problem solving.

Another issue that is receiving increasing attention is that math instruction that focuses on the abstract or symbolic ideas is more effective than instruction that emphases multiple concrete examples of math problems (Kaminski, et al., 2008). While concrete examples may promote initial learning, abstract examples significantly enhance transfer of knowledge to novel problems.

Another problem that we face to improve mathematics education is that algebra is a necessary foundation for most higher math studies and functions as a "gatekeeper" to further studies (Mervis, (2007b). Unfortunately, most algebra courses in junior high school emphasize drill and practice on standard problems, rather than conceptual understanding of algebra. Caldwell and his colleagues at the University of North Florida implemented a program to teach junior high school teachers to use CmapTools as an integral part of their algebra instruction. For more information contact Bill Caldwell at: <wcaldwell@unfal>

There remains today a mystique that the only learning that is of value is learning that derives from *discovery* by the learner of the concepts, principles, or relationships we seek to teach. Thus, the context for learning becomes one of extensive manipulation of materials, "experimentation" and practice of "the Scientific method." As noted in Chapter 5, most so-called discovery learning can be just as rote, just as meaningless, as poor reception learning. It is true that the extensive didactic methods of much schooling in the twentieth century, and even today, results in little usable knowledge. For example, Thorndike (1922) reported that math students who worked textbook problems such as squaring $(x + y)$ could not square $(B_1 + B_2)$. The solution is not necessarily dependent upon students working with graph paper or models; it does require that teacher and learner seek to identify and comprehend meaningfully the concepts and principles involved. This is as true for learning in the workplace as it is for learning in classrooms. For example, the failure of two engineering teams working on the Mars Orbiter to make sure they were using the same units resulted in the crash of the $125 million Mars Orbiter in 1999 when one team submitted computations in English units and another submitted computations in metric units. Not only was much money wasted, but the Mars exploration program lost the 10 months' time it took the Orbiter to reach Mars and the time required to replace the Orbiter.

What I have described as the problem of conceptual opaqueness is evident at this time in almost every field of study. In my early school years, I had a substantial dislike for history, for it was presented as little more than memorizing dates, names, and places. In later years when I recognized that history was a tapestry of human experiences, the toil and suffering of the poor and oppressed and the aggrandizement by the rich and powerful and similar relationships, I found history exciting, easy, and satisfying to study, and even dates, names, and places were easy to remember when they were fitted into the tapestry of human experiences over time.

There have been a few notable efforts to organize content in a way that made learning the content fun and exciting. Cannon's (1932) *Wisdom of the Body*, Bonner's (1962) *The Ideas of Biology*, Commoner's (1971) *The Closing Circle*, Dethier's (1962) *To Know a Fly*, and Muller's (1958) *The Loom of History*, are a few of the books that brought excitement into my education. Commoner's book, for example, presents five metaphors which, if understood, explain why it is important to work to sustain and improve our environment; one of these, "There is no such thing as a free lunch," applies not only to ecology, but to many domains of knowledge. Metaphors can be very powerful for building communications. In *Metaphors We Live By*, Lakoff and Johnson (1980) show how so much of our thinking and acting can be explained by common metaphors. Metaphors can be powerful tools for organizations as well as for individuals. Nonaka and Takeuchi (1995, pp. 15–16) describe the "Tall Boy" metaphor used by Honda to mobilize a team to create a new car ideal for cities.

In 1963, the National Science Teachers' Association's (NSTA) Committee on Curriculum held a conference to identify the "big ideas" of science that could serve as the organizing ideas for curriculum design from grades in kindergarten through college. Seven "conceptual schemes" were identified (Novak, 1964) and promulgated by NSTA. The work attracted considerable attention and some strong criticism, but the idea of using foundational major concepts as one set of superordinate concepts to be developed and elaborated upon over the years never took hold. For one thing, behavioral psychology and associated emphasis on "behavioral objectives" dominated school learning ideas in the 1960s and beyond. The powerful ideas of Ausubel's (1962; 1963) cognitive learning theory had just been put forward and were then not generally known in the United States (or now, for that matter!). The powerful tool of concept mapping had not yet been developed; it was difficult to show how powerful superordinate ideas could be used to facilitate meaningful learning of the myriads of concepts and principles of science. Science learning for most students remains today largely the memorization of "facts" and problem-solving procedures, most of which are forgotten six months after they are studied.

Despite the many years of effort of the Social Sciences Education Consortium, headquartered in Boulder, Colorado, to promulgate basic concepts of social sciences that could serve as the foundations for school studies in this field, most social science classes remain largely the memorization of isolated "facts." It is difficult to find programs or textbooks that emphasize the kind on "big ideas" of history discussed by Muller (1958), or the major intellectual achievements in any of the social sciences and humanities. This lack of focus on conceptual understanding is also reflected in the fact that few concept maps dealing with the humanities or social sciences can be found in the hundreds of thousands of concept maps on the CmapTools server (http://cmap.ihmc.us), other than for the field of psychology.

Probably every reader of this book has experienced courses where understanding basic concepts played little or no role. You may recall how emotionally unrewarding these experiences were, except for the extrinsic reward of teacher approbation and high grades—if you played along with this meaningless game. For those learners who do not, disapproval by parents, teachers, and peers, or even ridicule, can have dire emotional consequences creating many "learning disabled" (read "school disabled") people, school dropouts, and, in worst cases, criminals.

The Physical Context

The Sameness of School Facilities

Working with a team of colleagues, we completed a nationwide study in 1971 of *exemplary* school science facilities and programs (Novak, 1972). Nominations for exemplary facilities were sought from various school leaders, architects and equipment companies. Some 600 schools were nominated and after screening by phone calls or visits by local colleagues, 140 schools were selected as showing the most promise. Each of these were visited by one or more members of our study team, and some schools were visited two or three times.

The most striking finding was that even most of the schools nominated as exemplary were, in most respects, highly traditional and similar in both facilities and programs. The typical pattern was schools with an auditorium, gymnasiums, many rooms for 25–30 students, a library/learning center, and administrative quarters. The room facilities usually included fixed laboratory benches, either at the room perimeter or in a rear section of a room, and two-student tables or arm-tabled chairs. Less than a dozen facilities and programs departed radically from this arrangement with "open-space" arrangements for multiple groups, carpeted floors, furniture that could be arranged in many configurations, student project space, and supply and materials centers.

It was this latter kind of facility we recommended for new or remodeled schools with two important provisos: (1) extensive staff education was needed for new curriculum development, building skills in using these flexible facilities, acquiring skills in managing more interactive student and staff relations; and (2) support staff, equipment centers and a different curriculum were needed. Most schools that attempted to build new, more open and flexible facilities failed to provide the staff education and support needed to make successful use of the facilities. Many reverted to traditional patterns "walling-up" open spaces with cabinets and bookcases and bolting down furniture. The study illustrated an important thesis of this book: you cannot improve education by modifying only one element of the five elements of education. In some cases, students and staff felt that the new facilities were worse than the old.

Little has changed in most school facilities since 1971. A more recent report by Arzi (1998) called for a need for more flexibility in facilities, the same kind of problem described in my 1972 report. The major addition has been computer laboratories, usually by taking over standard classroom space. Little has changed in the instructional programs, although we are hearing less and less about "behavioral objectives" and more about the need for students to construct their own knowledge. Although the more recent report on science facilities published by NSTA gives more space to the role of computers in learning, and more emphasis on "inquiry learning" (Motz, Biehle, & West, 2007), the typical classroom facilities illustrated are similar to those found in schools 40 years ago. For most students, schooling is still memorizing information in preparation for frequent "objective" quizzes and multiple-choice tests. The No Child Left Behind program enacted by Congress in 2001 and signed by President Bush in January, 2002 may have done more to exacerbate the problem than to diminish it (Hanushek and Raymond, 2005). This may account for the fact that 20 percent of US schools have failed to improve test scores by 2007 (Hoff, 2008). It is an exceptional classroom in an exceptional school where activities that foster meaningful learning are the common educative events, unlike what we described earlier in Silesky's high school in Costa Rica. While groups such as the Partnership for 21st Century Skills (2009) call for schools similar to what we recommended in our 1972 report, they give no examples of schools designed and operating in this way. Related problems will be discussed further in other chapters.

The "Ideal" Learning Environment for Education

From the standpoint of the physical context for education, the "ideal" depends upon what we hope to teach and the strategies we select to use. For the teaching of a foreign language, the ideal context might be a tutorial approach in a marketplace setting in the culture where the language is spoken. Here learners could see, smell, feel, and hear all that is associated with the language. Obviously this is not possible for most learners, especially those in traditional classrooms where the dull memorization of English word synonyms and rules of grammar predominate. The creative teacher, even in a traditional school, can find ways to use visual aids, food samples, plays, audio- and/or videotapes and other resources to help approximate "the real thing." For over three decades, Marli Moreira (1977) has found the use of concept maps helpful to facilitate understanding and syntax in foreign language teaching, especially in real-world settings. In more recent years, a number of educators have reported on the facilitation of meaningful learning that can be achieved using concept maps. (see Proceedings at : http://cmc.ihmc.us).

If one is teaching science, some aspects of physics, for example, might be brought to life in a playground with slides, teeter-totters, swings, and pulleys. In the classroom, we can use models of these things, visual aids, and computer simulations. Much good mathematics could also be taught in this setting.

The issue at the core of our concern is how to help learners experience the regularities coded by the concept labels and concept relationships we seek to teach. Recall again the relationships between the psychological constructions we seek to help learners make and the epistemological origins of these constructions. Remember, the universe is made up only of events and objects (or "happenings" and "things" may be better descriptors for young children). The language we use to code regularities and relationships in those events and objects takes on greater meaning the closer the educative experience duplicates or models the world we seek to understand. Some of the most advanced applications of computers for education is in pilot training. All airline pilots obtain at least some of their education "flying" aircraft using computer simulations. It is not only very expensive to fly large jet planes to practice flying skills and the application of knowledge in special situations, but it is clearly impossible to practice emergency routines that may occur just prior to or during crash conditions. In a personal interview with an airline pilot of one of the major airlines, this captain comments on the very high quality of the training programs for her airline (Novak, 1997).

There is a growing international movement toward providing every child with their own laptop computer and access to high-speed Internet service. For example, Peru is working with the One Laptop Per Child Program to provide over a half million computers to school children (Talbot, 2008). The project has numerous problems, including problems with Internet connections in this mountainous country, but they are making progress. In Panama, we are working with project Conécate al Conocimiento to train teachers in the use of computers, CmapTools, the Internet, and meaningful learning strategies. The project seeks to train all fourth-, fifth- and sixth-grade teachers in 1000 schools throughout Panama (see: http://www.conectate.gob.pa). So far the project is progressing well, albeit there are problems with the technology, transforming teaching, and providing the continuing teacher aid that is needed. More will be presented on this project in Chapter 10.

At time of writing we stand on the brink of what I believe to be a revolutionary advance in our ability to use electronic resources to provide a good simulation of almost any learning environment. Computer arcades in shopping malls already illustrate the wide range of sights, sounds, and feelings we may experience with electronic devices, and there may already be some devices that emit smells as well. The exponentially growing capabilities of computer-driven simulations, as illustrated in Wii games, would suggest that we are only years away from creating extraordinary learning environments electronically. Long before this book is as old as my first *Theory of Education* (1977), I predict we shall see this extraordinary capability manifested, not just in some homes and shopping malls but in all businesses, homes and maybe eventually in most schools.

Although the quality of online courses varies widely, the fact is that enrollments in these courses has increased dramatically. For example, in 2002 some 1.6 million students were enrolled in online courses in post-secondary degree-granting programs and the number enrolled grew to some 3.5 million students by fall 2006 (Allen and Seaman, 2007). In contrast enrollment regular programs grew from 16.6 million in 2002 to 17.6 million in 2006. Thus enrollment in online courses grew 117 percent while enrollments in regular programs increased 6 percent. While this kind of differential in growth rate cannot continue indefinitely, there is every reason to believe an increasing percentage of post-secondary students will be learning online. An example of opportunities that are being created is MIT's announcement (December, 2007) that all 1800 of this distinguished university's courses are available online at no cost, including video talks, lecture notes, etc. Of course, to get official MIT University credit for these courses, there are some costs. Other groups, such as the Apollo Group, offer programs for other educational levels (www.apollogrp.edu).

The open question is, "Can schools as we know them (at all levels) continue to exist when such an extraordinary learning opportunity can be brought into the home?" It can be argued that humans are social beings and learning at home with electronic devices is asocial. But we do not need to be in social settings 16 hours each day. Moreover, pairs, teams, and network groups can interact together with many constructive social exchanges. Many of the *negative* social exchanges that now occur in schools could be reduced or avoided. Given the potential educative power of *well-designed* electronic educational packages, three or four hours of online learning would be all that would be needed to achieve much higher levels of achievement than learners experience in schools today. Better learning in schools is what I seek as a primary goal, but I am also interested in seeking improvements in online learning.

The central issue then becomes, "How do we create these *well-designed* electronic learning resources?" The short answer is: "We build them on the basis of a solid *theory of education*." I believe the theory put forth in this book is more than adequate for the task, and the theory will improve as it is applied, tested, and revised. What evidence do I have to assert this? Not much, but then there has not been a great deal of effort to design and evaluate such theory-based educational experiences, or the theories that have been applied in the past have had major shortcomings, for example, theories based upon behavioral psychology or Piaget's developmental psychology. What we sought to do in our 12-year longitudinal study (Novak and Musonda, 1991) is one research study that illustrates the power or technologically mediated instruction, but that was done 20 years ago before modern computers and the Internet were available. More recent work by Marcia Linn (2000; 2004) and her colleagues illustrate some of the new opportunities to facilitate learning using modern media. And I refer again to Silesky's school (Chapter 1) and the remarkable successes they have had even with limited technology.

Let us examine again what was achieved and evaluated in our 12-year longitudinal study of science concept learning. We provided 191 first- and second-grade children some 15 hours of carefully designed, theory-based audio-tutorial lessons dealing with basic concepts of science, including concepts of matter, energy, living things, and human anatomy and physiology. While audio-tutorial lessons have some advantages over electronically delivered learning experiences, such as working with real things in real demonstrations, they also have severe limitations compared with electronically-mediated lessons. The latter can provide virtually unlimited access to visual (still and motion) images, *learner-selected* sequences of text and images, interactive experiences where successive materials offered depend on prior materials selected and/or evaluation information, and easy updating by the addition or deletion of materials. But even with their limitations, the audio-tutorial lessons provided to many of the students enough development in understanding basic science concepts that the mean achievement for students receiving this instruction was much greater than that of "uninstructed" students for the balance of their schooling (refer again to Figure 7.8). Remember that this instruction was given only in grades 1 and 2 (six- to eight-year-old children). One can only speculate on what achievement would be possible if such quality instruction were given from grades 1 through 12. To date, I am not aware of any school or school district that involves students in using concept mapping and a focus on meaningful learning from grades 1 to 12.

There is an ominous side to the possibilities suggested. Children in the most affluent homes may be the only recipients of this kind of learning opportunity in their homes. A new kind of school with new kinds of home, school, workplace, and community relationships needs to be created. These changes are not likely to occur as a smooth transition with equality and justice for all. Is it too early to begin to plan for this transition?

The Cultural Context

Heredity and Environment

Is nature (heredity) more important than nurture (environment) in forming who we are and what we can do? The finest seeds will not produce healthy plants without proper nutrients and light. The child with the best possible genetic endowment will be severely limited in development in a poor environment. The issue is, "How can we capitalize on the genetic endowment of every individual by creating the most favorable environment?" As with most important issues, there are no easy solutions.

There is the need to consider the physical environment as well as the emotional environment. Obviously, the child of an alcoholic or drug-abusing mother will be damaged in developing his or her potential due to the deleterious effect of drugs on fetal development. Less obvious, but in some cases more significantly, the child may suffer from strong negative and little positive emotional support from *both* parents who are drug addicted. Nutrition and health care may be additionally limiting factors in childhood when drug costs and drug impairment compete with food purchases and preparation. For these problems we must look to long-term societal changes that are at the root of the problem, albeit heredity has been shown to be a factor in drug addiction and mental health. Radical improvement in education can contribute to better retention of drug users and their children in educational programs, but at best this is a long-term solution to the problems. Quick-fix attempts at outlawing drugs (already "on the books"), imprisoning drug dealers, and interdicting drug supplies are, at best, only moderately successful, with no evidence that these by themselves can solve the problem. Programs for nutrition supplements (such as federally funded Women, Infants, and Children Programs) can be helpful, but they, too, are not the long-term solution to the problem. In the end, our best hope for radical reduction in these problems is radical improvement of educational programs, including new kinds of programs based on a viable theory of education.

There are those who believe that some races are, on average, better endowed genetically than others—Hitler, Jensen (1969), and Herrnstein and Murray (see *The Bell Curve*, 1994). For Hitler, there was a political agenda that required and fed this belief, and for Jensen, and Herrnstein and Murray, there is the press of the academic publication game that drives some people to take controversial positions to gain recognition (or notoriety?). There certainly are genetic differences among the races, in skin color, for example, but to assert that "mental tests" demonstrate hereditary differences between the races is to illustrate naïveté both as regards psychometric issues of testing and issues associated with differential performance on tests of any kind. I will deal with some of these issues in Chapter 9. Many scholars, including Keddie (1973), *The Myth of Cultural Deprivation*, Kamin (1972), *The Science and Politics of IQ*, and Gould (1981), *The Mismeasure of Man*, have shown that the arguments made to assert genetic differences in mental capabilities between races are naïve at best. Sternberg (1996) provides one of the best summaries of the "myths and truths about intelligence" issues I have seen. The April 1995 issue of *Educational Leadership* presented papers by Molnar (1995) and others critical of the Herrnstein and Murray book.

The "nature–nurture" debate has gone on for decades, and it is not likely to be resolved in the near future. Those who argue that heredity accounts for most of the variance in human abilities and performance tend to look at data in ways that support their position, whereas persons who argue that nurturing, better homes and better schools can profoundly influence aptitudes and performance look at different data in different ways. It is difficult to argue that inferior heredity is why Michigan has the lowest high school graduation rates (33 percent for black males and 74 percent for white males), and why in Detroit more black males graduate than white males (17 percent vs. 20 percent) (from Mrozowski, 2008). Bronfenbrenner and Ceci (1994), in their "bio-ecological model" see heredity as playing a significant role, but they also see a synergistic effect where an enhanced environment early in development leads to progressively greater enhancement in abilities and performance as the child matures. One of the problems for society is that this early, pre-school environment is not easily augmented. Bronfenbrenner, who is credited with a major role in creating the Head Start Program for pre-school children in the United States, has long argued that more concern and attention must be paid to ways to improve family life, especially for pre-school children. This remains a daunting social challenge. One recent study shows that pre-school programs can significantly improve cognitive control over executive functions, such as focusing on critical information, avoiding distractions, etc. (Diamond, et al., 2007). Such programs obviously give an advantage to children who receive them. Sternberg comments:

> It is always tempting to value most what we ourselves possess—and, in the process, to scapegoat other groups. It is happening in ethnic wars around the world. And one might argue it happens when Herrnstein and Murray (1994) cheerfully note that most readers of their book are members of the cognitive elite (p. 47) and other elite groups. We need to remember that, over time and space, those at the higher rather than the lower end of the various intellectual spectra have been those most likely to be persecuted or scapegoated. However it is defined, intelligence is only one attribute of human beings and one attribute leading to certain kinds of success, but tests of intelligence can, at best, provide measures of certain cognitive skills (Keating, 1984); they are not measures of human worth. (Sternberg, 1996, p. 15)

Gender Issues

With regard to gender, there are again obvious genetic differences, in hormonal levels and associated secondary sex characteristics such as breasts and facial hair, but no obvious differences in intellectual capacity. Scholars such as Gilligan (1982), Belenky and colleagues (1986), and Keller (1985) have shown that in personality and social characteristics, there appear to be patterns of differences between males and females that are innate. But the influence of environment is also evident and may account for much of the gender differences observed in Western cultures, since some of these patterns are not observed in other cultures. Best (1983) has shown that even by grade 1 (six years old), boys manifest different patterns of action toward girls, other boys, and their teacher than are manifested by girls. However, these patterns of differences mirror the patterns of the adults of our culture, and they can be modified by appropriate educational intervention.

In her book, Best (1983) describes the actions and attitudes toward the teacher and school tasks as strikingly different patterns for boys and girls. While in kindergarten, both girls and boys sought affection from their teacher. By the end of grade 1, this pattern began to shift for boys who now sought affection and approbation from their peers. By grade 2, membership and status in peer groups were far more important for boys than girls. Best reported that in one classroom where the teacher was ill from March until June and a succession of substitute teachers presided, nine of the twelve girls showed lower achievement in June than in January, and the other three showed no change.

> What was astonishing, however, and not only to me but to all those with whom I discussed it, was the finding that the academic achievement of the boys had not suffered any adverse affects whatsoever from the teacher's long-term absence. Eight of the twelve boys had scores in the same range in June as they had had in January. And four had even higher scores. None had suffered learning setbacks. All those who lost ground in the teacher's absence were girls. (p. 13)

Best explains the result as a consequence of the independence of the boys on need for teacher approval for achievement, with greater reliance on peer approval as supporting achievement.

There is also a hidden message here that Best does not discuss but is implicit in the gender differences observed. Boys more than girls socialize more toward becoming autonomous learners—the consequence being, over time, that boys more often than girls take charge of their own meaning making. Sometimes the boys overtly reject the teacher's agenda, especially when it requires work that they see as meaningless, or as what they classify as "women's work," such as household chores. The long-term net result is that boys more than girls seek to excel in those things seen as "man's work"—and these tend to be the jobs and professions that are most rewarded by society.

There is a downside to the male tendency to identify more with peers than with their teachers. Best reported (p. 49) that boys who were rejected by their peer group experienced a reduction in school achievement rather than substantial increases. The pressure on boys to be "part of the gang" is severe, for better and worse.

In an effort to study a curriculum that included discussion of gender issues, Best (1983) worked with the fourth-grade students, discussing issues of sex-role stereotypes, supplying them with vocabulary to discuss sex, and attitudes toward gender. Her initial reaction was that her efforts over the school year were not successful in changing attitudes or behaviors. However, when the students returned to school after the summer holiday, Best observed:

There seemed to have been an incubating effect in process during the summer hiatus. Seeds had apparently been planted the year before that were now beginning to bud. Only now, in fifth grade, did the boys and girls I was working with begin to talk to one another. But when they did, it proved to be a critical event. They seemed now to be ready to leave the stereotypes behind them and work toward new ways to relate to one another. (p. 141)

We see in Best's work a study of how the school context can reinforce the gender stereotypes of the society. We also see that modifying the curriculum to include frank and sustained discussion of issues of sexism and stereotyping can have a strong positive effect. Best reports (Chapter 12) that the language used in fifth grade expressed repeatedly the recognition by boys and girls that common stereotypes were invalid at best and often the reverse of reality. Once again the power of high-quality meaningful learning experiences shows payoff not only in the knowledge acquired by the students but also in the attitudes and values expressed by the learners.

While Benbow and Stanley (1982) puzzled over observed gender differences in mathematical reasoning, where the gap between males and females appears to increase with schooling, we found some evidence to support the thesis that females socialize into playing the school game (that is learning by rote) more than males, and this leads in time to significant gender differences favoring males in mathematical or science reasoning tasks (Ridley and Novak, 1983). In most cases, gender differences in cognitive abilities tend to be exaggerated (Hyde, 1991). There are ways that schools can help to reduce gender bias and gender stereotypes. The American Association of University Women's report (1995) *Growing Smart: What's Working for Girls in Schools*, has many suggestions for schools to recognize and deal with gender problems. There are, of course many factors that influence gender differences in achievement and no simple answers are available. A recent summary of research on gender differences (Ellis, et al., 2008) indicates that gender differences in math achievement are declining, partly as a result of changes in our society.

In our society, traits associated with masculinity are often seen as desirable and traits associated with feminity are seen as less desirable. As Gilligan observes:

The repeated findings of these studies is that the qualities deemed necessary for adulthood—the capacity for autonomous thinking, clear decision-making, and responsible action—are those associated with masculinity and considered undesirable as attributes of the feminine self. The stereotypes suggest a splitting of love and work that relegates expressive capacities to women while placing instrumental abilities in the masculine domain. Yet looked at from a different perspective, these stereotypes reflect a conception of adulthood that is itself out of balance, favoring the separateness of the individual self over the connection to others, and leaning more toward an autonomous life of work than toward the inter-dependence of love and care. (p. 17)

The impact of culture on the thoughts, feelings and attitudes of people is also profoundly severe in the business world. Tannen (1994), in her book, *Talking from 9 to 5*, describes well the different patterns in the way males and females express their thoughts and feelings. Some years ago, Gilligan (1982) described how women speak "in a different voice."

"I have a very strong sense of being responsible to the world, that I can't just live for my enjoyment, but just the fact of being in the world gives me an obligation to do what I can to make the world a better place to live in, no matter how small a scale that may be on." Thus while Kohlberg's (male) subject worries about people interfering with each other's rights, this woman worries about "the possibility of omission of your not helping others when you could help them." (p. 21)

Tannen takes this gender difference further and shows how, in the business world, men do not express the world they see in the same way as women.

Amy was a manager with a problem: She had just read a final report written by Donald, and she felt it was woefully inadequate. She faced the unsavory task of telling him to do it over. When she met with Donald, she made sure to soften the blow by beginning with praise, telling him every-thing about his report that was good. Then she went on to explain what was lacking and what needed to be done to make it acceptable. She was pleased with the diplomatic way she had managed to deliver the bad news. Thanks to her thoughtfulness in starting with praise, Donald was able to listen to the criticism and seemed to understand what was needed. But when the revised report appeared on her desk, Amy was shocked. Donald had made only minor, superficial changes, and none of the necessary ones. The next meeting with him did not go well. He was incensed that she was now telling him his report was not acceptable and accused her of having misled him. "You told me before it was fine," he protested.

Amy thought she had been diplomatic; Donald thought she had been dishonest. The praise she intended to soften the message "This is unacceptable" sounded to him like the message itself: "This is fine." So what she regarded as the main point—the needed changes—came across to him as optional suggestions, because he had already registered her praise as the main point. She felt he hadn't listened to her. He thought she had changed her mind and was making him pay the price.

...Amy delivered the criticism in a way that seemed to her self-evidently considerate, a way she would have preferred to receive criticism herself: taking into account the other person's feelings, making sure he knew that her ultimate negative assessment of his report didn't mean she had no appreciation of his abilities. She offered the praise as a sweetener to help the nasty-tasting news go down. But Donald didn't expect criticism to be delivered in that way, so he mistook the praise as her overall assessment rather than a preamble to it. (Tannen, 1994, pp. 21–22)

Whether the differences between the "voice" of men and women are, in part, genetic or entirely a consequence of the socialization differences for males and females, the consequences are that real differences do exist in how males and females converse and how they interact with others. Given that management has been dominated for most of history by males, women who seek to succeed in management face what is called a "glass ceiling." Tannen describes it this way:

Here is a brief explanation of how conversational-style differences play a role in installing a glass ceiling. When decisions are made about promotion to management positions, the qualities sought are a high level of competence, decisiveness, and ability to lead. If it is men, or mostly men, who are making the decisions about promotions—as it usually is—they are likely to misinterpret women's ways of talking as showing indecisiveness, inability to assume authority, and even incompetence. All the conversational-style differences discussed thus far can work against women who use them in an office setting. For example, a woman who feels it is crucial to preserve the appearance of consensus when making decisions because she feels anything else would appear bossy and arrogant begins by asking those around her for their opinions. This can be interpreted by her bosses as evidence that she doesn't know what she thinks should be done, that she is trying to get others to make decisions for her.

Again and again, I heard from women who knew they were doing a superior job and knew that their immediate co-workers knew it, but the higher-ups did not. Either these women did not seem to be doing what was necessary to get recognition outside their immediate circle, or their superiors were not doing what was necessary to discern their achievements and communicate these upward. The kinds of things they were doing, like quietly coming up with the ideas that influenced their groups and helping those around them to do their best, were not easily observed in the way that giving an impressive presentation is evident to all.

Even so small a linguistic strategy as the choice of pronouns can have the effect of making one's contributions more or less salient. It is not uncommon for many men to say "I" in situations where many women would say "we." One man told me, "I'm hiring a new manager; I'm going to put him in charge of my marketing division," as if he owned the corporation he worked for and was going to pay the manager's salary himself. (Tannen, 1994, pp. 1336–37)

Tronto (1993) observes that the perception of women as caregivers places them at a disadvantage in our competitive male-dominated society. Women are not supposed to be the aggressors, but rather the supporters of males in competitive situations.

A more recent report by Swiss (1996) found in a survey of 325 women that 65 percent indicated attitudes of senior management influenced gender inequity "to a great extent" and 68 percent indicated that their compensation had been limited by their gender. These and other findings indicate that American businesses still have a long way to go to eliminate gender inequities.

Working women also face other stresses. In a 2008 survey by the AFL-CIO, the pressures on women are both economic and family pressures. Working women also need a break. They are talking to their co-workers more than their children or friends, they are extremely busy and have little time for themselves, and 37 percent say they work during their breaks or have no breaks. After work and family responsibilities, a plurality of respondents say they have an hour or less to themselves a day (11 percent none, 34 percent less than an hour). A quarter say they have two hours to themselves, 16 percent have three hours, 10 percent have somewhere between four and six hours, and only 4 percent have more than six hours to themselves. Respondents in their 30s and 40s are particularly likely to say they only get an hour or less to themselves a day (58 percent and 53 percent respectively), as are those who are parents (72 percent). In spite of their lack of personal time, they are most likely to say they would work another job if they had free time.

In the sciences similar gender differences favoring men have been reported. Sonnert and Holton (1996) comment on a conversation with a female scientist who observed:

> "Men . . . stood in the hallways and found the great men and went over to them and shook their hand or asked them to have a drink with them or something, and women couldn't do that in my day . . . They took themselves very seriously and they said anything that came into their head. I call it 'professor talk', and I found that a waste of my time."

Sonnert and Holton remarked,

> "Professor talk" may indeed be a waste of time in terms of exchanging research information or gaining scientific insights. But it may be anything but wasteful in terms of its hidden agenda. What other respondents called a "bull session" or "chatty self promotion" may have the function of a bonding ritual. And the social bonds thus forged may have beneficial effects on a scientist's research and career. (p. 68)

Whatever one may conclude about the pros and cons as regards differences in male and female styles of interaction, the undeniable fact is that gender does play a powerful role in setting the context for teaching and learning in any organizational setting. Gender bias continues in many covert and overt ways. However, when President Lawrence Summers, President of Harvard University, suggested in a speech to a private audience in January, 2005 that men innately had a greater ability for the sciences and mathematics, the uproar from faculty and various groups that followed led to his resignation in the summer.

Race

As noted earlier, there have been repeated attempts to associate intellectual potential (and other traits) with genetic racial differences. Usually the motivation has been to establish the superiority of the dominant race, also the majority race, over the minority race. There is political motivation behind this, as Kamin (1972), Gould (1981), and others have noted, but the sustaining force for these kinds of prejudices is a problem of ego needs, especially of males, to feel "I'm OK," and perhaps also "You're Not OK." Rooted in childhood, and too often in early experiences in school, these emotional needs tend to persist into adulthood and beyond. In some cases, they become overwhelming, leading to drug abuse and a variety of antisocial or pathological actions. Because they are often emotionally deeply rooted, racial biases or prejudices are not easily modified. Objective data or rational discourse is often not sufficient to reduce or eliminate racial biases or prejudices. Even distinguished scholars such as Nobel Laureate James Watson, co-discoverer of the structure of DNA and a Nobel Prize-winner, asserted that African-Americans were in some respect genetically inferior. The consequence was that Watson was soon asked to resign as Chancellor of Cold Spring Harbor Laboratories in 2007. It was too embarrassing for the Laboratory Board for this distinguished geneticist to be continued in his post.

Perhaps even more than gender, race plays a role in shaping the interaction between individuals, and the effect is typically deleterious to the minority members in any national or local context. The literature on this issue is voluminous, and any effort to cull key points from this literature would probably prove deficient. I shall not deal with it extensively, not because race is not important, but rather because I believe that many of the problems and issues that have race as a root cause can best be dealt with by applying the ideas and tools presented in this book. Undoubtedly the 2008 election of Barack Obama as the first Black American president will have a significant impact on race relations and perceptions, but at this writing, it is too early to predict what these may be.

The Organizational Context

Democratic versus Authoritarian

School organization varies from country to country, state to state, and city to city. The degree of autonomy for individual schools varies considerably, although in general, schools must follow state or national mandates regarding curriculum, certification of personnel, salary and retirement compensation, tenure, and graduation requirements. Within most schools, there are also relatively rigid structures; although individual teachers have some autonomy in selecting learning materials, instructional strategies, and evaluation, for the most part they must follow dictates imposed upon them. Even in so-called "alternative schools" that pride themselves on their freedom and inventiveness, what is commonly observed is more cosmetic than substantive. Ted Sizer, former Dean of Education at Harvard University and a leading proponent of school reform, describes most school reform as similar to fine-tuning a Model T Ford. What is really needed are truly substantive reforms, and these are very difficult to achieve (see O'Neil, 1995).

Some states and some school districts in the US have tried to employ "for-profit corporations" to run "privatized" schools. However, the reports to date on "contract" or "for-profit" schools are not overwhelmingly favorable (see, for example, Ferrell, Johnson, Jones & Sapp, 1994). While some proponents of contract schools have recently issued positive reports on contract schools (Roland, 2009), it is hard to discern the degree of bias in these reports. The distinction between contract schools and charter schools is sometimes blurred, but in general contract schools are operated by for-profit organizations under contract with state or local schools, whereas charter schools are non-profit schools that received funding from local schools but operate under an independent charter. The problem, as I see it, is that most school reform does not deal with truly fundamental issues, namely, *how do we modify our teaching and administrative structure to help teachers help learners take charge of their own meaning making?* To achieve this, there needs to be a *new vision* for education, and leadership that helps to create and share the vision with parents, students, teachers, and administrators. This cannot be done by authoritative "top down" administration, but for most schools, this remains the overwhelming characteristic of "school reform."

A controversial problem in many schools is the placement of students into different "tracks." Parents, whose children qualify for "high" or "honors" tracks, usually defend the practice, and often they are the most vocal at school board meetings. The evidence regarding "tracking" is that, while students in honors or high tracks may benefit, students in lower tracks may suffer, both socially and academically (Gamoran, Nystrand, Berends, & LePore, 1995). The net effect over time is a widening gap in achievement and opportunity between students in high versus low tracks. Apart from the inequalities in achievement that result from tracking, there are also the social consequences, including segregation of peer groups. It is evident that it is not a desirable condition in a democracy and for future economic development where "low track" students will need to become skilled technicians in an increasingly sophisticated job market.

Currently, the new enthusiasm for school reform is so-called site-based management (SBM). In theory, SBM encourages parents, teachers, administrators, and sometimes students, to plan, collaboratively, programs that will meet student needs. In practice, what occurs is that constraints of union contracts, state legislative requirements, funding restrictions, and ordinary resistance to change subvert most efforts at truly positive reform.

The overriding problem in all school reform issues comes in dealing with teacher unions. Some 85 percent of public school teachers are unionized, and rules and procedures negotiated by unions determine, to a large part, how schools will operate. Moore (1996) cites examples such as the following:

> In Michigan, a group of young teachers wanted some extra training in math. Since their school system couldn't afford to pay the teachers for the training, the teachers agreed to do the training without pay. Veteran teachers protested, pointing out that the union contract forbids unpaid work. The training never took place. (p. 260)

Moore goes on to identify 12 satirical steps for "How Unions Can Ensure Excellence in Education." His steps included: (1) Protect mediocre and incompetent teachers by rewarding longevity, not performance; (6) Abolish quality-based incentives, and oppose quality by opposing all measures of quality; and (10) Build your program on gimmicks, not substance. At Cornell University, Bacharach (Bacharach & Mitchell, 1985) studied factors that influence decision making in schools, and he concluded: "Three principal factors are determinant, union contracts, union contracts, and union contracts." For better or worse, the reality that exists now regarding the context for school education is overwhelmingly determined by union contracts. There are some 15,000 "independent" school districts in the United States, but for most of them, the operating policies will be determined in union contract negotiations.

For many reasons, systemic change has been slow and is likely to continue to be slow. As one teacher put it:

> My conclusion is this: If *systematic* changes are made in schools, site-based management [SBM] might succeed. So far, that has not happened. At Wilson Magnet, a school with a reputation for making SBM work, the teachers can't even get enough people to run in-site elections to fill out our numbers. By now, most of us have figured out the drawbacks: trying circumstances and long hours for minuscule results. (Geraci, 1995, p. 52; italics added)

The overriding problem is that schooling in America, and I would include much of tertiary education, is a huge bureaucracy, run autocratically mostly from the top down. State legislative actions, partly under pressures from strong teachers' unions, are more designed to preserve the autocracy than to modify it in significant ways. Millions of parents have simply given up on public *and* private schools and are doing "home schooling." Financially difficult as this is in most cases, without the benefit of tax revenues, endowments, or other sources of income, parents who choose to do home schooling seek to take back from the bureaucracy, to the extent that laws allow, responsibility for education of their own children. It is for them, in regards to schooling, similar to the early American frontier days, when each family had to be almost completely independent. Important differences now, of course, are the huge reservoir of knowledge available in libraries, museums, nature centers, and exhibits, and electronically through the Internet. There has been a continuing increase in the number of children home schooled, and this group now exceeds 2 million. (See Google or Yahoo for latest figures.)

Corporations suffer from the same "top-down" autocratic management as do schools. In fact, in many ways, they have been the model followed by schools. The problem is that such organizations are poor for empowering people in the organization to learn, and to facilitate learning by the organization. Senge (1990) describes such organizations as *learning disabled*—and, the disability is widespread, if not universal. Senge (p. 17) points out that one-third of the firms in the Fortune "500" in 1970 had vanished by 1983. These were large companies, many of whom were at one time leaders in their industry. They failed, according to Senge, because the organization did not know how to learn:

> But, what if high mortality rate is only a symptom of deeper problems that afflict *all* companies, not just the ones that die? What if even the most successful companies are poor learners—they survive, but never live up to their potential? What if, in light of what organizations *could* be, "excellence" is actually "mediocrity?"
>
> It is no accident that most organizations learn poorly. The way they are designed and managed, the way people's jobs are defined, and most importantly, the way we have all been taught to think and interact (not only in organizations, but more broadly) create fundamental learning disabilities. These disabilities operate despite the best efforts of bright, committed people. Often the harder they try to solve problems, the worse the results. What learning does occur takes place despite these learning disabilities—for they pervade all organizations to some degree.
>
> Learning disabilities are tragic in children, especially when they go undetected. [Consider Andrew's case.] They are no less tragic in organizations, where they also go largely undetected.
>
> (Senge, 1990, p. 18, emphasis in original)

Senge is not alone in his analysis. Nonaka and Takeuchi (1995) also see corporations as poor learners, and poor creators of new knowledge. They argue that corporations need a new management organization they describe as "middle-up-down" where new ideas flow freely "up" and "down" the organizational structure. Peters (1992) has also called for the need to "demolish the corporate superstructure" (p. xxxii) if real, sustained change is to be effected. Higgins (1995) advises bluntly in his book, *Innovate or Evaporate*, that corporations need to become much better at developing constructive innovations, in short, much better at learning. Lafley and Charan (2008) have a number of useful suggestions to help organizations learn, as were noted earlier.

Organizations can learn. As Nicolini and Meznar (1995) state, two things are required: "1) the modification of organizational cognitive structures (which constitute a form of cognition in action), and 2) the process of representation, formalization, and normalization of such knowledge" (p. 743). Change in corporations also involves feelings. As Kotter (2002) states: "People are sensitive to the emotions that undermine change, and they find ways to enhance those feelings. This is true throughout all eight stages of a process that helps organizations leap forward" (p. 180). The ideas and tools described in this book are a way to achieve positive feelings toward change.

Schools, too, are poor as learning organizations. In a "conversation" with Senge regarding schools, O'Neil (1995) relates:

> The Fifth Discipline explains the characteristics of "learning organizations." Schools are considered to be institutions of learning, but are most of them learning organizations?
>
> Definitely not. A learning organization is an organization in which people at all levels are, collectively, continually enhancing their capacity to create things they really want to create. And most of the educators I talk with don't feel like they're doing this. Most teachers feel oppressed trying to conform to all kinds of rules, goals and objectives, many of which they don't believe in. Teachers don't work together; there's very little sense of collective learning going on in most schools. By the way, I also disagree with your assumption that schools are institutions of learning for students.
>
> Why is that?
>
> We say school is about learning, but by and large, schooling has traditionally been about people memorizing a lot of stuff that they don't really care too much about, and the whole approach is quite fragmented. Really deep learning is a process that inevitably is driven by the learner, not by someone else. And it always involves moving back and forth between a domain of thinking and a domain of action. So having a student sit passively taking in information is hardly a very good model for learning; it's just what we're used to.

Katzenbach (1995) and his colleagues at McKinsey and Company combined their experiences consulting with companies to identify characteristics of truly effective change leaders. Some of the outstanding characteristics they found for real change leaders (RCLs) were:

> RCL's establish individual—and team—accountability measures by doing two simple things:
>
> 1. Establishing measures, assessments, and goals that put real meat behind the change effort, and link it to performance priorities that people can understand.
> 2. Avoiding "the activity trap," in which lots of measured actions are viewed as surrogates for results. (pp. 40–41)

In both schools and corporations, assessment of performance and learning in truly valid ways is not easy. These problems will be addressed in the next chapter.

And, just as schools are caught up with archaic organizational bureaucracies, so are most corporations. But there is one important difference—in today's global economy, the corporation that does poorly in reorganizing, in learning as an organization, will soon disappear. Therein lies some hope for new leadership in the world for better ways to organize and operate to make organizations far better learning environments. From changes in corporations and their new insights may arise new promise for schooling in America—and in the whole world.

Chapter 9

Evaluation and Rewards

The Importance of Evaluation

From the time we are born, we are weighed, measured, and evaluated in various ways until we die. In fact, even before birth our heartbeat, fetal position, and other characteristics may be evaluated. Those who are highly weight conscious may stand on the scales several times per day—or fear the day they must be weighed. Being evaluated may not involve much thinking for the moment, but most of the evaluations we face will involve thinking, feeling, and acting to varying degrees. And when we die, many religions hold that we face the eternal judgment, a judgment based upon the life we have led.

In the world of work, we also face evaluations of various kinds, some of which lead to advancement in position, usually with higher earnings and/or higher status and privileges. Some rewards may be special recognition or increased opportunity for self-expression and creative pursuits. While this chapter will focus on evaluation issues common in school settings, many of these also apply in work settings. Conversely, rewards and recognitions apply in school settings, albeit, they are usually not monetary. Key ideas regarding evaluation and rewards are shown in Figure 9.1.

Too often evaluation is equated with "testing," that is, the kind of paper-and-pencil tests we take in school, or to qualify for a driver's license. The latter may also require *performance* evaluation as we try to parallel park and do the other tasks required, at least to some criterion level of skills with perhaps 70 percent or better success. Performance evaluation occurs in schools also, especially in schools of dance, music, art, and design, but also in science laboratories, language classes, and increasingly in all kinds of classes.

Using the Vee heuristic as a framework to understand the role of evaluation, we see that the fundamental problem in measurement is to obtain *valid and reliable* measures of key variables involved in the event we are observing. In education, we can never observe and measure all relevant variables (e.g., the subject's mood at the moment of test taking) but we must strive to measure what we believe are the most important, relevant variables. Here is where A Theory of Education can be helpful in deciding on *what* to record. Specific

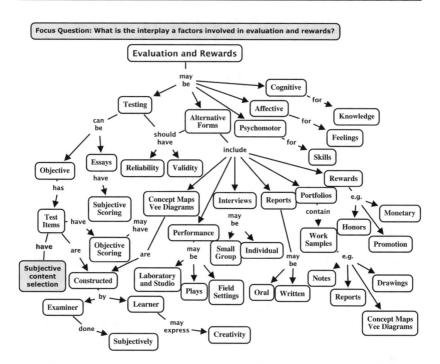

Figure 9.1 Key ideas that must be considered regarding evaluation and rewards.

concepts and principles relevant to the event (shown on the "left side" of a Vee diagram for the event) will assist us in determining key variables and appropriate measures of these variables. Refer to Figure 9.2 and note that measurement is a way to make records of events. These may be transformed using statistics or other tools; however, the claims derived can be no better than the quality of the records we make. This is one reason why evaluation is so important.

Measurement

One of the reasons the natural sciences have advanced more rapidly than the social sciences is that the measurement of significant variables in the social sciences is much more difficult than in the natural sciences. Furthermore, the social sciences have been "theory-poor" and hence we have not been clear on what are the key variables that influence human thinking, feeling, and acting, to say nothing about how to measure these variables appropriately. A theory of education, including a theory of learning, can do much to bring clarity and specification to the assessment of human characteristics and thus contribute to the advance of measurement in education, business, and in the social sciences in general.

According to *A Theory of Education*, the most important factor influencing

THE KNOWLEDGE VEE

CONCEPTUAL/THEORETICAL
(Thinking)

METHODOLOGICAL
(Doing)

WORLD VIEW:
The general belief and
knowledge system
motivating and guiding
the inquiry.

FOCUS QUESTIONS:
Questions that serve
to focus the inquiry
about events and/or
objects studied.

VALUE CLAIMS:
Statements based on
knowledge claims that
declare the worth or
value of the inquiry.

**PHILOSOPHY/
EPISTEMOLOGY:**
The beliefs about the nature
of knowledge and knowing
guiding the inquiry.

KNOWLEDGE CLAIMS:
Statements that answer the
focus question(s) and are
reasonable interpretations
of the records and trans-
formed records (or data)

THEORY:
The general principles guiding the inquiry that explain
why events or objects exhibit
what is observed.
between concepts that explain
how events or objects can be
expected to appear or behave.

TRANSFORMATIONS:
Tables, graphs, concept
maps, statistics, or other
forms of organization of
records made.

STATISTICS

CONSTRUCTS:
Ideas showing specific relationships between concepts,
without direct origin in events
or objects

RECORDS:
The observations made
and recorded from the
events/objects studied.

CONCEPTS:
Perceived regularity in events
or objects (or records of events
or objects) designated by a label.

MEASUREMENT

EVENTS AND/OR OBJECTS:
Description of the event(s)
and/or object(s) to be
studied in order to answer
the focus question.

Figure 9.2 The Vee heuristic can serve to illustrate ideas presented in this chapter.
Measurement provides us with records, and statistics are one tool we can
use to construct claims.

humans is the extent to which meaningful learning has occurred and well-
differentiated, hierarchical cognitive structure has developed. Most of this
learning is "domain specific," that is, it relates to knowledge in specific subject
matter areas. There is also some learning that transcends knowledge domains
and concerns what we know about learning strategies, problem-solving strategies and similar "metacognitive" knowledge, and this has been ignored or
only poorly measured in the past. In recent years, their has been a growing
interest in metacognition or learning about how humans learn about learning
(Kuhn, 2000).

Based on my theory, our central concern in evaluation of cognitive learning should be with the ability of the test instrument to assess the quality of the conceptual and propositional *frameworks* held by the subject, or the extent to which knowledge is learned substantively and non-arbitrarily, which is the case in meaningful learning. Test items that require no more than recall or recognition of specific information may be adequate for evaluation of rote learning but they fail to assess the extent to which functional conceptual frameworks have been established or modified by the learner. It is the latter that influence and give power for future learning, problem solving, and creativity.

Records are often transformed to produce graphs tables or charts, often with the use of statistical tools. These transformations also need to be guided by theory.

"Testing"

The "Objective Test"

Every student in education programs learns that there are "objective tests" and "subjective tests." Multiple-choice or true–false tests are examples of objective tests, and short-answer or essay exams are examples of subjective tests, the latter being subjective because the evaluator must make a subjective judgment on the accuracy and appropriateness of the response. What is seldom discussed is the *highly subjective* process by which "objective test" items are constructed. The test-maker *chooses* the specific subject matter content to be covered, the exact wording of the question, and the exact wording of the choices in multiple-choice exams. While there are strategies for evaluating the extent to which various domains of subject matter are sampled by a given objective test, and item analysis techniques for identifying test items that may have a faulty structure, the bottom line is that the test-maker *subjectively* decides what will be accepted as "correct" answers. Only the scoring is objective; that is, the testee must choose the "right" answer as judged by the test writer or the answer is marked wrong.

Let us consider for a moment what this means. In general, it means that the meaning of the content tested must be expressed in the *exact words* of the test-maker. If the testee constructs his or her meanings in a somewhat different, but equally valid, form, the answer chosen may be "wrong." Look at this example from a national achievement test:

Is each of the following foods rich in protein?

(a) lettuce   yes   no
(b) fruit   yes   no

The "correct" answer is "no" for each of these items since the bulk of these two foods is water and, compared with meats or eggs, the amount of protein per serving is low (poor). However, a student may know that lettuce and fruits are made of cells and that except for the cell walls and the water and sugars in the cells much of the remaining substance in these foods is protein. This would be good reasoning, but it could lead to the "wrong" answer. This is the kind of reasoning that Hoffman (1962) argued goes unrewarded in his book, *The Tyranny of Testing*. The kind of thinking that is rewarded is rote memorization of the "four food groups" and that a high level of protein is found in the meat and eggs group, while the fruit and vegetable group is high in fiber and vit-amins. Too often, objective tests, even those that are comparatively well designed, tend to encourage verbatim, non-substantive and arbitrary memor-ization of information. The typical teacher-made test too often penalizes the meaningful learner who has constructed their idiosyncratic but valid mean-ings for a domain of knowledge. Unfortunately, national standardized tests and textbook tests are not much better, and Holden (1992) reported that "95 percent of the items in school math tests rely on 'lower level thinking skills' such as memorization, and fail to measure 'higher order' functions that are involved in creative problem solving" (p. 541). In reviewing proposed new test items recently for a national exam, I raised the same concerns with the test-makers.

Two of the concepts of measurement that enter into testing are reliability and validity. Reliability is the extent to which a test assesses a given domain of knowledge consistently. A test is reliable when individuals with the same fund of knowledge obtain the same scores, or if a given individual obtains the same score when the exam is repeated with no change of knowledge occurring between tests. Obviously, the conditions needed for these situations are almost impossible to establish, so more commonly reliability is estimated by methods such as computing the correlation between frequency of correct answers on even-numbered items with the answers on odd-numbered items. Unfortunately, if subjects were guessing on answers for all items, we could get a high correlation between frequency of right or wrong answers on odd, com-pared with even, items, but the reliability coefficient obtained would have little value for assessing the reliability of the test.

Validity is the extent to which test items assess the competencies they are intended to assess. There are no easy ways to establish the validity of a test. A common practice is to solicit "expert" judgment on individual items or the test as a whole. While this practice has merit, it is very difficult to judge the validity of a given test item or test without knowing what specific instruction was given, the prior knowledge of testees before instruction, and the condi-tions or context in which the test was or will be given. Another method of assessing test validity is to determine the correlations of scores on the test with scores on some other test that is *assumed* to be a valid test of the same or similar abilities. Thus we may see claims that a given achievement test is valid because it has significant correlation with IQ test scores. There are at least two problems with this kind of *correlational* validity. First, even relatively low correlations (commonly r = 0.2 to r = 0.4) may be *statistically* significant with large sample groups. But we need to recognize that the amount of variation in test scores that one test predicts for another test is only equal to the correlation coefficient squared, or 4 percent to 16 percent in our example. What accounts for the remaining 84 percent to 96 percent of variation in test scores? God only knows. A second problem is that a high correlation coefficient (say r = 0.8 to 0.9) only means that the two tests tend to be measuring the same competencies, but both could be measuring poorly the true competencies we seek to assess. We are back to a judgment call on the validity of both tests. Typical multiple-choice tests often show serious validity problems (cf. Glanz, 1996; Burton, 2005).

Another problem that is too often ignored by educators is that the distribution of scores on any test is a function of the competence of the testees and the *item difficulties. Item difficulty* is the percentage of testees who pass a given item, now sometimes referred to as *item ease*. A test item with a high percentage of testees answering correctly has a high-ease value (and a high item difficulty value). Based on experience with a set of test items administered to similar sample groups over time, it is possible to establish item ease values that will show stability for a pool of test items. We can then select test items that will produce almost any score distribution we desire. Figure 9.3 shows the score distribution using a test with many items with a low-ease index, and Figure 9.4 shows the expected score distribution *for the sample group of testees* if many items have a high-ease index. In practice, tests are usually designed to produce a "normal curve," using test items with items having a range of ease indices from relatively low to relatively high.

Selection of items with various ease values can affect the validity of a test.

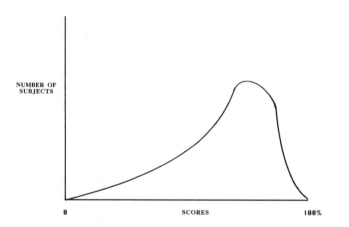

Figure 9.3 Score distribution obtained when many test items are easy, i.e., have high "ease values" or "item difficulty" values.

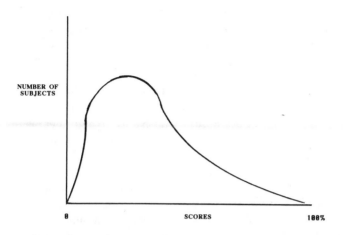

NUMBER OF
SUBJECTS

0   SCORES   100%

Figure 9.4 Score distribution obtained when many test items are hard, i.e., have low "ease values" or "item difficulty" values.

For example, if we construct a test with test items of relatively low-ease values, the test can be a good (valid) measure of the excellent and good testees but a poor measure of the competencies of the average or below-average testees (see Figure 9.4). We are not assessing well their relative competencies, relative to others in their group. Their scores are "bunched up" at the low end of the distribution. On the other hand, such a test might have higher validity for selecting the "top" 10 percent of a group who should receive "gifted" programs. The reverse selection of items might be effective for selecting students to receive remedial help (See Figure 9.3).

Given the wide recognition of problems with conventional testing, one would expect that there would be a concerted effort to write better tests. The problem is that test items that require higher levels of understanding and thinking are usually missed by most students, with the result that these items have near zero *discriminability*. That is, they fail to separate those students who know more from those students who know less for a given sample of students. Tests made up with such items would give essentially a chance score distribution and lack both validity and reliability. In 1956, Bloom proposed a "taxonomy" of educational objectives, wherein test items that measure only rote recall of specifics were rated as 1.0 level items and items that required "synthesis" or "evaluation" were rated as 5.0 or 6.0 items, respectively. Most studies of the "taxonomy levels" of most tests show that overwhelmingly, the tests' items rank only one or two on Bloom's taxonomy. For example, a million dollar study supported by the National Science Foundation found that close to 95 percent of test items used in school math tests relied on "lower level thinking skills" and failed to measure higher-order functions that are involved in creative problem solving (Holden, 1992). There also exists what I like to refer to as the "psychometric trap"—tests items that require higher levels of thinking will usually show very low percentages of students passing, and thus produce results that show little or no discriminability among students. And hence these items must be rejected. Thus usually we cannot use tests with many difficult test items and we end up perpetuating the testing problems decried by so many thoughtful and critical observers.

As noted earlier, the USA No Child Left Behind (NCLB) program enacted by Congress in 2001 had the goal that 100 percent of US students would reach proficiency in math and English by 2014. This has led to a great emphasis in schools for improving test scores. However, as one recent report observes (de Vise, 2008):

> Maryland officials removed a section of multiple-choice questions from state reading and math tests this year, shortening each from roughly three hours to two and a half. They did not publicly announce the change, although the 24 school-system superintendents were apprised in a June 2007 memo.
>
> These changes could easily account for the jump in performance observed in Maryland schools. Many similar issues with state exams testing for math and English proficiency have been reported as states seek to meet NCLB standards. (p. C01)

Another illustration of problems with using typical "objective" tests for judging student or school performance is that change in the selection of test items can make major changes in test scores. Mooney (2008) reported that when elementary and middle-school proficiency tests were redesigned to make them more rigorous, the number of students scoring "proficient" plummeted. In some schools, passing rates fell by 50 percent–60 percent, falling into the teens. Needless to say, students, parents, teachers and school officials were not pleased that the State had changed the tests so markedly. No doubt there will be changes in future State exams to make them less "rigorous."

There are other ways to make objective tests more effective. Much research has been done on common misconceptions (or faulty conceptions) of students, especially in sciences and mathematics (Helm & Novak, 1983; Novak, 1987; Novak & Abrams, 1993). These studies have identified concepts and concept relationships that interfere with or do not permit valid interpretations of certain events. It is possible to design multiple-choice test items that give alternative answers that are wrong, but appear valid to testees with specific misconceptions. The result can be a test that can produce below-chance scores (below 20 percent on five-choice, multiple-choice items) for testees and still have high validity and reliability. For example, Sadler (1995) found that when test items in astronomy were developed using as alternative answers statements of common misconceptions held by students, even items with low difficulties can be very discriminating. Furthermore, he found that when student performance on a given item is plotted against student ability, students of low ability may actually perform better than students of nearly average ability. This pattern was repeated on the majority of the 47 test items given to a large sample of school students. What the data indicate is that, as students gain some pertinent information, they may actually strengthen their misconceptions and perform more poorly (see Figure 9.5). The data also call for careful sequencing of concepts taught to minimize that latter problem and enhance overall achievement. Objective test data can be useful in curriculum design when the kind of sophisticated item analysis is done as is illustrated in Sadler's work.

Figure 9.5 Average ability students may perform more poorly than low ability students on test items that are designed to include as choices common misconceptions that arise from partial knowledge of what causes day and night. From Sadler, 1995. Reproduced with permission.

Likert Scales

A common type of testing where there may not be right or wrong answers but rather expressions of feelings or attitudes was devised by Likert (1932). In this form of testing, testees are given statements to which they may reply on a scale, usually 1–5 or "strongly agree" to "strongly disagree." For example, one of the Likert scales we devised dealing with preferences for learning approaches contain these items:

I try to relate new material, as I am reading it, to what I
   already know on that topic: SD D U A SA
(SA = meaningful learner)

I prefer to follow well tried out approaches to problems
   rather than trying anything too adventurous.   SD D U A SA
(SA = rote learner)

While I am studying, I often think of real-life situations
   to which the material I am learning would be useful. SD   D   U   A   SA
(SA = meaningful learner)

I find I tend to remember things best if I concentrate
   on the order in which the teacher or book presented
   them.   SD   D   U   A   SA
(SA = rote learner)

Key: SD—Strongly Disagree; D—Disagree, U—uncertain A—Agree, SA—
Strongly Agree

It is not easy to determine why a given individual chooses to agree or disagree with a statement, but validation of Likert scales can be achieved by doing interviews on a sample of the target population to ascertain whether or not the testees' belief structure is being accurately assessed by the test items. Our experience, in a variety of studies using Likert scales, is that they are at best limited in their validity for assessing individuals' beliefs about their learning preferences, views on the nature of science, tendency to believe they control their destinies, and similar attitude or preference measures. Nevertheless, compiling the direction of preferences of an individual on ten or more Likert items can have predictive validity on, for example, how that person will approach learning in a given domain. Bretz (1994) found that students with Likert-scale preferences for rote-learning approaches described their learning strategies as essentially rote in interviews, and the reverse was true for students who showed meaningful learning preferences in a college chemistry course designed to help students understand and approach the science of chemistry. Meaningful learners generally performed better in the course than rote learners, especially on those test items that required novel applications of knowledge.

Likert scales were first developed to assess feelings and they continue to be useful in this way. For example, Alaiyemola, Jegede, and Okebukola (1990) used tests of student anxiety to study the effect of concept mapping on the reduction of anxiety. They found that students using concept mapping showed very significantly lower anxiety toward science study compared with non-mapping students, after a six-week treatment of learning selected science topics. While these feelings may not generalize to study of other science topics, the findings do point to the positive affective results from use of a strategy that can facilitate meaningful learning. We see affirmation here of the theory put forth in this book.

Up to this point, I have focused on tests for cognitive learning and tests that involve feelings or affective learning. There are also tests for our actions or psychomotor learning, but these are usually quite different in character. Figure 9.6 illustrates the range of concepts and principles involved in measurement, and I shall turn next to other forms of evaluation, some of which are

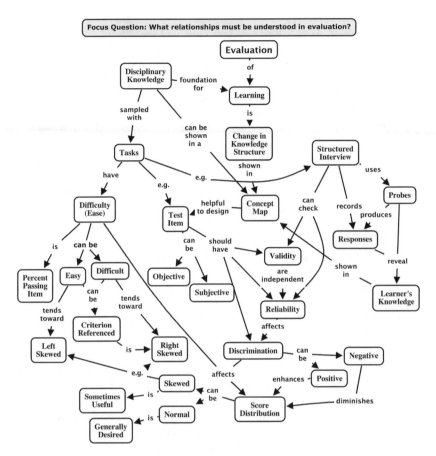

Figure 9.6 Key concepts and relationships necessary for understanding evaluation.

commonly called *alternative assessment* which will be discussed later (see, for example, Herman, Aschbacher & Winters, 1992).

Other Forms of Evaluation

Performance Evaluation

Perhaps the most common performance evaluation faced by people in developed countries is the test for a driver's license. Usually a written test is first required and the knowledge needed to pass this exam, together with test-taking skills, have only limited relevance to the driving test. Skillful, experienced drivers sometimes fail the written portion of the exam. This suggests, in part, a need to improve the kind of written exams given to qualify for a driver's license. Since thinking, feeling, and acting must be constructively integrated to be a skillful driver, or to perform any psychomotor task skillfully, it should be possible to design written tests that better match the cognitive and attitudinal attributes associated with skillful driving.

Music, art, architecture, photography, dance, and all sports are domains where performance evaluation predominates and usually identify the distinguished from the undistinguished performer. But it is important to recognize the crucial supporting role that cognition and affect or feelings play in skillful performance. The successful performers must get their thoughts and feelings organized, as Herrigel (1973) so nicely described in *Zen and the Art of Archery*.

One of our graduate students, Nadborn (see Novak & Gowin, 1984), found that when his junior varsity basketball team developed concept maps to better understand and communicate, their game performance went from a previous 3 win and 8 loss record to a 8 wins and 3 losses. Smith (1992) found that when students in nursing were asked to prepare concept maps and review a Vee diagram for each week's instruction in nursing skills, they performed seven out of ten skills significantly better than students not using these learning tools. Ben Amar Baranga (1990) found that fifth-grade students who prepared concept maps prior to writing stories and poems performed at levels much beyond the typical student performance at that age. In the latter case, the students even wrote a successful play that they performed for their school and for other schools that requested to see the play.

The use of metacognitive tools for enhancing performance is still an uncommon event, and I believe this is a highly promising area for research and educational development. For more than a decade, we have been working with research teams with each member employing concept maps and Vee diagrams to conceptualize their research. The results suggest substantial enhancement of research productivity. Given the importance of knowledge creation in both academic and corporate settings (Drucker, 1993), research that shows substantive enhancement in new knowledge production by individuals instructed in the use of metacognitive tools could be even more exciting than the results that have been found in enhancement of school learning.

One of the fields in which performance testing has been utilized commonly is in the health sciences. Some of our work with nursing students was discussed above. On the surface, it would appear self-evident that performance tests would have high validity, since they require subjects to perform the kind of tasks that subsequent application of their learning will necessitate. However, testing is always to some extent a contrived experience, and when one takes into account the problems of scoring or ranking performance, this type of evaluation can also be problematic. Swanson, Norman, and Linn (1995) present a concise synopsysis of "lessons" that have been learned from work in the health professions. Their "lessons are shown in Table 9.1

It is evident from the issues cited in Table 9.1 that performance testing is not without its problems. Whether in the school or the workplace, more care and attention is need when performance testing is used for assessment,

Table 9.1 Lessons learned in the health professions regarding performance testing. From Swanson, et al., 1995. Reproduced with permission from Sage

Lesson 1:	The fact that examinees are tested in realistic performance situations does not make test design and domain sampling simple and straightforward. Sampling must consider both context (situation/task) and construct (knowledge/skill) dimensions, and complex interactions are present between these dimensions.
Lesson 2:	No matter how realistic a performance-based assessment is, it is still a simulation, and examinees do not behave in the same way they would in real life.
Lesson 3:	Although high-fidelity performance-based assessment methods often yield rich and interesting examinee behavior, scoring that rich and interesting behavior can be problematic. It is difficult to develop scoring keys that appropriately reward alternate answers that are equivalent in quality, both because of poor consensus on scoring keys and because of scoring artifacts resulting from variation in response style.
Lesson 4:	Regardless of the assessment method used, performance in one context (typically, a patient case) does not predict performance in other contexts very well. In-depth assessment in a few areas results in scores that are not sufficiently reproducible for use in high-stakes testing.
Lesson 5:	Correlational studies of the relationship between performance-based test scores and other assessment methods targeting different skills typically produce variable and uninterpretable results. Validation work should emphasize study of threats to the validity of score interpretation, not general relationships with other measures.
Lesson 6:	Because performance-based assessment methods are often complex to administer, multiple test forms and test administrations are required to test large numbers of examinees. Because these tests typically consist of a relatively small number of independent tasks, this poses formidable equating and security problems.
Lesson 7:	All high-stakes assessments, regardless of the method used, have an impact on teaching and learning. The nature of this impact is not necessarily predictable, and careful studies of (intended and unintended) benefits and side-effects are obviously desirable but rarely done.
Lesson 8:	Neither traditional testing nor performance-based assessment methods are a panacea. Selection of assessment methods should depend on the skills to be assessed, and generally, use of a blend of methods is desirable.

especially when the assessment is the basis for determining promotion or rewards of any consequence.

Concept Maps

I have shown in earlier chapters examples of concept maps that we have used in our research and teaching projects. Concept maps were developed by our research group to meet a need for an evaluation tool that could show easily and precisely changes in students' conceptual understanding. I now routinely use concept maps as an evaluation tool in my own courses. Figure 9.7 shows an example of a concept map prepared by a student in my course, Theory and Methods of Education.

What is evident in Figure 9.7 is that an enormous amount of knowledge is represented. My approach is to provide students with a list of 20–30 concepts and ask them to map these, adding at least 10 or 20 more concepts of their choosing. This, of course, is a fairly demanding task, and I often give these as "take home" exams. The construction of the map requires considerable creativity in organizing the structure of the map, selecting important, relevant concepts to add to the map and searching out salient "crosslinks," indicating

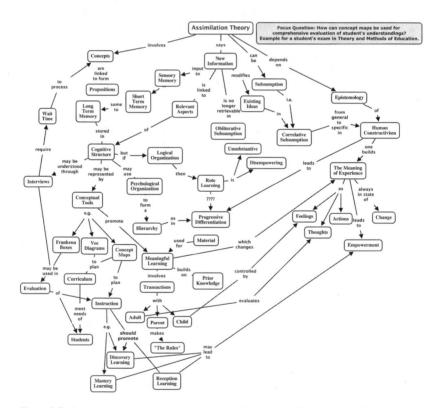

Figure 9.7 A concept map constructed by a student for a mid-term exam in my course, Theory and Methods of Education. Thirty concepts were provided as a starting point, and students were asked to organize these and additional concepts to show their learning in the course. Consider how many multiple choice questions would be needed to test for all the ideas included in this map, to say nothing about the relatively good creativity shown in building the map.

relationships between concepts in different sections of the map. Needless to say, the map becomes an important *learning* experience for my students, as well as a unique evaluation experience. A common comment I receive from students is: "I thought I knew all the concepts needed for your test, but when I began concept mapping them, I realized that what I knew was not sufficiently precise and clear for me to incorporate it properly into a concept map." Of course before using concept maps for assessment, one must give students weeks of practice and constructive feedback in building smaller concept maps, and maps of the size shown would be inappropriate for elementary school students. Those teachers in secondary schools and tertiary schools who use comprehensive concept mapping assignments for end-of-year evaluations report positive results both in terms of comprehensiveness in evaluating learning and in terms of students' affective responses.

One of the problems of traditional "testing" is that true–false or multiple-choice exams can never sample more than a small portion of the relevant knowledge considered in the instruction. Try to guess at how many multiple-choice questions would be required to evaluate students' ability to understand and relate all the concepts and propositions shown in Figure 9.7. Furthermore, there would be no opportunity for students to show how they organized their knowledge nor the creativity demonstrated in selection of additional concepts included in the map organization. In my view, concept maps are the most powerful evaluation tool available to educators, but they can be used only when they are also first used to facilitate learning. Perhaps by 2050 we shall see widespread and worldwide application of this tool in business and also in education.

Concept maps have been used successfully in virtually every field of study. For example, Walker and King (2003) found that successive maps prepared by students in bioengineering show more valid concepts and more precise use of vocabulary. Similarly, Quinn and colleagues (2003/2004) found that successive maps drawn by biology students showed greater complexity and evidence of understanding. Baroody and Bartels (2001) showed that understanding, or lack of understanding, of mathematics concepts could be well seen in mathematics concept maps drawn by students.

There are the issues of reliability and validity that need to be addressed with use of concept maps. The validity issue is relatively transparent since it is obvious that the fundamental characteristics of constructivist learning is exemplified in a well-constructed concept map. For any competent evaluator, it is relatively easy to see whether propositions indicated on the map are valid and to determine whether the superordinate/subordinate nature of concepts in the structure makes sense.

It is now generally agreed among researchers that changes in learners' conceptual frameworks may be most thoroughly evaluated by use of clinical interviews. The problem is that use of interviews for evaluation requires skilled interviewers and relatively costly interviewer time. There remains the problem of the interpretation of the knowledge expressed in interviews; in fact, it was this problem which led our research group to devise the concept mapping tool. We have also developed a variety of scoring algorithms to give numerical scores to concept maps, permitting statistical tests and comparison with other tests (Novak & Gowin, 1984, pp. 34–37). Scoring a concept map, when scoring criteria have been established, requires only three to ten minutes, depending on the complexity of the map (Lancaster, et al., 1997. If interviews remain the "gold standard" for evaluation of cognitive structures, how does the concept map compare. Edwards and Fraser (1983) showed that concept maps constructed by students were as revealing of their knowledge structures as clinical interviews of students. Over the past two decades, in dozens of studies by our research group and other researchers, concept maps have been shown to be reliable assessment instruments (Åhlberg & Ahoranta, 2008; Shavelson, et al., 1994; Ruiz-Primo & Shavelson, 1996; Ruiz-Primo, et al., 1998; Ruiz-Primo, 2000; Shavelson & Ruiz-Primo, 2000; Ruiz-Primo, et al., 2001).

An obvious advantage in using concept maps for evaluation is the ease with which new tests can be devised. By simply adding or subtracting one-third or more concepts from the list of concepts to be mapped by students, a "new" test has been devised. As already noted, it is comparatively easy to cover large domains of knowledge with opportunity for creative expression. While there is some subjectivity in scoring the maps, the great freedom given to individuals to demonstrate their idiosyncratic meanings for the subject matter removes an important source of bias and subjectivity that is present when the *test writer chooses* the specific content and form in which answers must be selected. One of the powerful attributes of using concept maps for instruction and evaluation is the extent to which they encourage meaningful learning and discourage rote learning. In one of our studies, Gurley-Dilger (1982) asked her school psychologist to interview members of her class regarding their thoughts and feelings on her use of concept maps with instruction in high school biology. The following are some quotations from the psychologist's interview:

> Given a choice, well I probably wouldn't do it. I don't like doing 'em, but . . . the map shows out the more important things.

> I always use my maps. If you just read the book it's different 'cause you might not see the main point of the chapter and how it all fits together. Concept maps are easier to understand. It puts it a different way than the book says it. It gives you the concepts in your own way. They're worth the time—it's easier to learn, for me.

> I can't use concept maps. I'd rather read the chapter over and over. Concept maps are more work. It's different than memorizing—it's all related.

Concept maps are hard to study from. When you're doing it though, you're sorta studying it. If ya make 'em good they can help you. They make ya read the book. I'd rather not do them. (Gurley-Dilger, 1982, p. 155)

It is difficult to overemphasize the problems that are created with years of schooling where assessment is primarily by multiple-choice or true–false tests and require little more than rote memorization. Kinchin (2001) observed in his paper, "If concept mapping is so helpful in learning biology, why aren't we all doing it," there is both strong resistance to meaningful learning, and many teachers see no problem with a focus on memorization of information. He states: "concept mapping is seen as a tool that may support learning within an appropriate teaching ecology. Such an ecological perspective may require, for some, a re-conceptualization of the teacher's role in which teaching, learning, and change are seen as integrated components of effective teaching" (p. 1257). We have noted in Chapter 1 how difficult this was in Silesky's school in Costa Rica, but with sustained leadership, he was able to overcome the predisposition of students and teachers to engage in predominantly rote learning. Trifone (2005) found similar resistance to change in his study with high-ability high school students:

Specifically, the findings revealed that concept mapping may play a supportive role in contributing to a more meaningful approach to learning biology, as indicated by positive and statistically significant effects on students' test performance, as well as adaptive and statistically significant fall-to-spring changes in motivational and learning strategy use profiles in direct relation to the level of mapping proficiency. This dichotomous relationship appears to be a consequence of whether learners' perceive that concept mapping can provide them with a more effective learning strategy than those utilized in the past and, more importantly, upon their willingness to put in the requisite time and effort to develop proficiency in using mapping to take a more self-regulated and meaningful approach to their learning. Thus, it behooves the educator interested in using concept mapping to consider students' receptiveness to using concept mapping and encourage them to perceive the value of becoming sufficiently proficient in its use. (p. 122)

We see that in general students recognized the value of concept maps both as a learning tool and a tool evaluating their learning. Also evident is that it is "hard work" to construct your own meanings and many students prefer just to memorize information. After years of school practices that emphasize the latter, it is not surprising to see that students find taking responsibility for constructing their own meanings to be challenging—but most also see this as rewarding. Unfortunately, we have found some of the greatest resistance to use of concept maps among medical students for whom meaningful learning is essential if they are to perform competently. Their previous successes with rote mode learning approaches make them very insecure and fearful in moving to meaningful learning strategies. The fact is that the Medical College Admission Test (MCAT) requires almost no synthesis and evaluation of information and does not help to encourage high levels of meaningful learning (Zheng, et al., 2008). In fact, the latter team found that very few test items in college biology or first-year medical school exams require higher levels of thinking suggested in Bloom's Taxonomy, discussed earlier. Students often seek the path of least resistance, so if they are not required to learn with sufficient clarity of meanings that they can use knowledge for novel problem solutions or other forms of synthesis and evaluation, they often settle for near rote leaning, and thus fail to build powerful, functional knowledge structures. Nevertheless, concept maps have been used successfully with veterinary medicine students and others and have proven to be useful for assessment (Edmondson, 2000).

The use of CmapTools software not only greatly facilitates concept mapping, it also facilitates assessment. For example, if the instructor prepares an "expert" concept map for a domain of knowledge, CmapTools can show how each student's concept map compares with the "expert" concept map, providing a list of concepts and propositions included in each student's map and the differences between the student and expert maps; this makes it easier to check on the quality and completeness of student's maps. The *History* tool in CmapTools when turned on will show steps in the construction of a concept map, allowing one to see how the learner progressed. When used with a collaborative team, the tool will show which student contributed each item in the concept map. This tool is also of value for cognitive research studies that seek to analyze pathways of thinking for different types of learners or for any given group of learners.

In our work in Panama, we found the need to have a more systematic way to assess the quality of concept maps made by teachers and their students. In order to identify strengths and weaknesses in our training programs that included the development of concept mapping skills, we developed a taxonomy dealing with the structure of concept maps produced and a rubric dealing with the quality of ideas or meanings expressed in the maps. The taxonomy dealing with general structure of the concept maps we call the topological taxonomy and the rubric dealing with the quality of meanings we call the "semantic" rubric. Using ideas from Bloom's (1956) taxonomy for classifying test items, who used a scale from 1 to 6, ranging from simple factual recall to synthesis and evaluation, we developed similar scales, but with criteria specifically pertinent to concept maps. A topological taxonomy and a semantic rubric were developed (Cañas, Novak, Miller, et al., 2006; Beirute and Miller, 2008; Miller & Cañas, 2008). A brief summary of these scoring schemas are described below:

Topological taxonomy

The topological taxonomy classifies concept maps according to five criteria: concept recognition, presence of linking phrases, degree of ramification, depth, and presence of crosslinks. These criteria consider progressively more complex topological entities, beginning with concepts, passing through propositions, and ending with the complete concept map. We note that in order to apply the first criterion, one must consider content. Therefore, this would appear to be a semantic criterion—and it is. However, the ability to recognize individual concepts is so basic to being able to build up rich, interconnected, flexible concept map topologies that this criterion is included among the structural criteria. In other words, the focus is not on what is actually said, but on whether the mapper is able to recognize concepts in their original context and depict the way in which they are related to one another. Once nodes (concepts) have been placed in a map, they are related to one another to form larger graphic structures, usually triads, by means of any form of symbolic representation—this is the linking phrase. Ramification occurs when several relationships emanate from the same node or make use of the same linking element; this event is usually thought to be related to Ausubel's (1968) notion of "progressive differentiation;" hierarchical depth refers to the number of levels of concepts nested under the root (main) concept of the map. Though this nesting may indeed be evidence of conceptual subsumption, the two are not to be confused; this topological criterion considers only the number of levels, not what concepts are placed in each of them. The last criterion deals with crosslinks. From the perspective of spatial organization, crosslinks, when accompanied by all the other elements mentioned above, lead to topological entities of greater overall complexity. They are thought to be associated with "integrative reconciliation," another fundamental principal of Ausubelian theory.

Semantic Scoring Rubric

The semantic scoring rubric used to evaluate the maps consists of six semantic criteria: concept relevance and completeness, correct propositional structure, presence of erroneous propositions, presence of dynamic propositions, number and quality of crosslinks, and presence of cycles. As before with the topological taxonomy, in this semantic rubric content is considered at different, increasingly complex, levels. The first criterion involves the level of individual concepts, what one might call the "atomic" level of meaning present in a concept map; criterion 2 moves up a notch, to the "molecular" level, which involves being able to construct and express coherent units of meaning in the form of propositions; continuing to higher levels, criterion 4 looks at the sophistication of the relationship established between concepts in a proposition along a static–dynamic scale; further up, criterion 3 ascertains the veracity of those units, relative to external objective standards, that is, in relation to contextual elements; finally, criteria 5 and 6 involve the entire concept map; in our metaphor, this might be the level of "matter," where individual strings of meaning present in a concept map are tied together, as the mapper draws from his or her life's experiences to generate an integrated, coherent whole (Beirute & Miller, 2008, p. 465).

We have found that mentors in our program in Panama could use the above rating schemes with high consistency and that the schemes also correspond to the patterns in concept mapping skills observed in teachers and students. This taxonomy and rubric should be useful to anyone who wants to use concept maps as an assessment tool, as well as a learning tool. Using the topological criteria, we have found that concept maps can be scored reliably by computer, and this represents a step toward assessing concept maps with large populations and for other purposes (Valerio, et al., 2008). While the use of semantic criteria for computer scoring may be some years off, at least the taxonomic criteria can be applied as a first indicator on quality of concept maps. Other studies using concept maps for assessment can be found at the CmapTools web site (http://cmap.ihmc.us). Many examples of concept maps in virtually every field can also be found at this website and at: http://www.cmappers.net, where, given search items, the topological taxonomy is used as a means of retrieving relevant maps.

While it is difficult to use concept maps for assessment on a state or national scale when concept mapping is not used as a learning tool, inclusion of a sample concept map along with a "skeleton" concept in exams is one way to begin. If standardized tests began using concept maps for assessment in this manner, the practice would encourage teachers to use concept maps in teaching. Moreover, as computers become more common in classrooms and Internet access increases, there will be added incentives to use free CmapTools software to enhance learning and improve assessment. Figure 9.8 shows the increasing downloads of CmapTools, an indication that we may be on the path of more universal use of this tool for learning and assessment. The reader can see the worldwide locations of downloads of CmapTools in the past 24 hours at: (http://pictor.ihmc.us/geolookup/).

Vee Diagrams for Evaluation

As with concept maps, Vee diagrams are both a tool to facilitate learning and a tool for evaluation. Their use is especially appropriate when the focus of interest is on an event, such as a demonstration, performance, laboratory or field event, or any creative event. For example, in some of my courses I ask students to construct a Vee diagram for their class project. The usual events I ask them to create are interviews with subjects on any topic they choose with any kind of sample group they choose. Figure 9.9 is an example of a Vee diagram created by one of my students. The left side of the Vee draws heavily

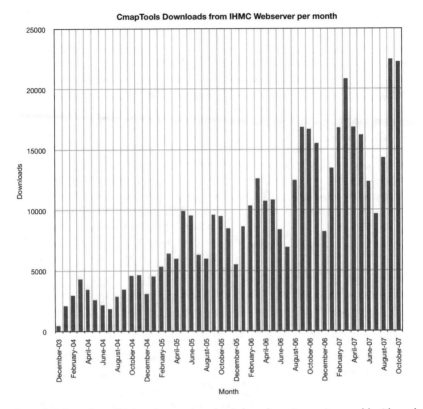

Figure 9.8 Free CmapTools software downloads have been increasing world-wide and this trend is expected to continue.

on the theory, principles, and concepts I teach in my course, as well as other items that are relevant to the specific inquiry, and the right side represents the activities they engage in as part of the inquiry.

Vee diagrams help learners recognize the complexity and also the basic simplicity of the knowledge construction process. If done thoughtfully and with reflection, they help learners see that every element interacts with and influences every other element and all are necessary for understanding how and why we constructed the knowledge claims and value claims for the focus question(s). Vees can be very successfully employed in group settings. They allow for creative expression, partly by the selection of salient elements on the left side, in construction of the focus question(s), description of the event(s) observed, and description of the elements on the right side. While the basic form of the Vee is given, and hence students often report that Vees are easier to construct than concept maps, the Vee is more comprehensive. In fact, one can incorporate a concept map in the Vee to represent concepts, constructs,

Vee-diagram summary of
results of inquiry

CONCEPTUAL

WORLD VIEW
One will enjoy life to
greater capacity if open-
minded.

PHILOSOPHY
Humans are both
rational and irrational
as they acquire knowledge
from various sources.

THEORY
Meaningful learning is
the basis of understanding
one's perceptions.

PRINCIPLES
Positive feelings,
attitudes and values are
rooted in meaningful
learning.
Better education on a
subject will allow for better
judgments.

CONSTRUCTS
Dairy products maintain
the qualities of milk itself,
but are more concentrated
in general.

CONCEPTS
Milk, dairy products, ice
cream, cheese, sour cream,
yogurt, calcium, water,
vitamins and minerals, fat,
cholesterol, protein, sugar,
media, parents, perceptions,
taste, health, skim, 2%, 1%,
chocolate milk.

FOCUS QUESTIONS:
Where do consumers
of different ages learn
most about the benefits
and drawbacks of dairy
products?
What do they know?
What are their
perceptions?

EVENTS/OBJECTS
Interviews on the
subject of milk and dairy
products: middle-aged,
college-aged, teenagers,
children. Questions focus
on where perceptions
have been gained and
what the perceptions are.

METHODOLOGICAL

VALUE CLAIMS
An understanding of
where people gain percep-
tions of the healthfulness
of dairy products can lead
to better education on the
subject.

KNOWLEDGE CLAIMS
Regardless of the age of
interviewee, milk is
perceived overall as "good
for you."
Middle-aged people
have some faulty percep-
tions about milk, possibly
due to a lack of research
and advertising on the
subject during their youth,
or lack of interest in the
subject.
College-aged people and
teenagers have a wide
range of opinion and
knowledge on the subject.
Children have some
faulty perceptions derived
from a variety of sources.

TRANSFORMATIONS
Concept map of each
interviewee indicates
where perceptions have
been gained, where there
are gaps in knowledge, and
show the different perceptions of the age groups.

RECORDS
Series of interview
tapes, notes, concept maps.

Figure 9.9 A Vee diagram prepared by a student in my course to illustrate her research on consumers' ideas about dairy products.

principles, and theory on the left side of the Vee, and another concept map to represent the knowledge and value claims on the right side (see Figures 6.3 and 6.4).

The very comprehensiveness of the Vee may explain in part why Vee dia-grams are currently less popular than concept maps, both as a learning tool and as an evaluation tool. As noted in Chapter 6, the pervasive positivism in schools and even in research laboratories tends to make use of the Vee as a learning and evaluation tool less attractive to many. Using the Vee heuristic with enthusiasm requires a commitment to constructivism, not only of the "trivial" kind that recognizes learners must construct their own knowledge, but also the "radical" kind (to use von Glasersfeld's (1984) terms) that recognizes the tentative and evolving nature of knowledge.

Referring again to the work of Gurley-Dilger, the following are some quotations from interviews with her students by her school psychologist when discussing Vee diagrams:

> I don't like them. I'd rather have lab questions. They're easy. I guess you understand what you're doing better with a Vee.

> You learn the stuff you need to talk about on the left side. The Vee helps me remember 'cause I write it all out. I don't mind Vees. They're easy and don't take a lot of time.

> I get more out of lab using a Vee. Not these lab questions. Vees are easy once you get used to it. Questions you could just skim, Vees make you tie everything together and work on it. (Gurley-Dilger, 1982, Table V-10, p. 160)

We see again that students regard construction of their own meanings to be challenging—but also rewarding. In the several dozen studies carried out by our research group at Cornell University and increasingly by colleagues at other universities and school systems, similar results are being reported not only in science learning but also in the study of literature (Moreira, 1977; Baranga, 1990), mathematics (Afamasaga-Fuatai, 1985, 2009; Kahn, 1994), and other fields.

Reports as Evaluation Tools

In all of my courses, I require each student to prepare oral and/or written reports, using data from an inquiry designed by the student. Typically, reports count 40 percent to 50 percent of the grade with concept maps and other work assignments comprising the remaining 50 percent to 60 percent. In smaller classes (30 or fewer) I usually require oral reports partly because I believe students need more opportunity to prepare and make presentations to a group. Their oral reports on their project work is typical of the kind of reports they may need to make in almost any "white collar" employment and increasingly in "blue collar" employment as well. In many cases, students advise that the report in my class was the first oral one to be given since they had entered Cornell University 2–3 years ago. Oral reports consume class time, so one must consider the value of time used this way, compared with other class activities. Written reports require considerable time for students to prepare and for the evaluator to read. For educators working with large groups (50 or more) both oral and written reports may be impractical unless special time allowances are made or competent assistance in evaluation is available.

It is necessary to provide learners with clear and sufficient guidance as to how to prepare their reports and how to deliver it. Samples of reports done by previous groups (with names deleted) can be helpful as well, and I usually make available both exemplary reports and reports that might have been improved, including remarks that indicate why the reports were evaluated as they were. I also use videotape to illustrate good oral presentations (with permission of the presenters). As with any evaluation, ambiguity regarding the standards for excellence have negative attitudinal consequences and diminish performance. If we want learners to demonstrate clearly their successes in constructing meanings and presenting their new meanings, they need guidance and assistance, as well as practice to do this well.

One form of report could be a poster, created either by an individual or by a team. Regarding their use at Procter and Gamble, Lafley and Charan (2008) observe:

> P&G "does" posters—yes posters—as a way to conduct innovation reviews. This approach could hardly be more low-tech. If anything, it has the feel of a grade school science fair. Each team creates a single poster that simply lays out the key ideas and technology for innovation, relevant consumer research data, the business potential, key timing and milestones, and the key issues the team is facing. Why posters? Because these reviews are often full of scientists, and posters force the scientists to speak in terms the senior management can understand. If they can understand it, so can the business unit, and eventually the consumer. They also drive focus and simplicity—to distill the innovation to a simple set of ideas. The posters are placed on stands around the room, so the group is on its feet and gathers around a poster to have a thoughtful conversation. One or two people from the team go through the data and add their own remarks. Often the discussion also involves show-and-tell where people get to touch and use a key product or key technology element. (pp.178–179)

One can raise validity issues regarding reports. While some innovations introduced as posters can be later judged in terms of additional revenue for the new or improved product, many innovations make contributions that are a small part of a new product and the judgment of the value of the ideas introduced in a poster is more subjective. There is the obvious concern with the bias of the evaluator, but there are also issues regarding the comparative skills of individuals to deliver written and/or oral reports. We face decisions that we must recognize as *value* decisions that must be confronted in assessment. How can we raise the level of written and oral expression of learners unless we require written and oral expression in our evaluation programs? There are ways to recognize individual differences in these abilities and to ameliorate the potentially disempowering effects of unrealistic standards for learners who come from cultures where written and oral expression *in English* is inordinately demanding. To evade or ignore these issues is to shortchange the futures of our students or workers and also to contribute to a decline in the competence and competitiveness of the American workforce. The long-term result is a lowering in the standard of living enjoyed by Americans, a trend already in progress and contributing to a growing sense of frustration and lowered aspirations of American youth (see, for example, Marshall & Tucker, 1992; Senge, 1990). As a result of the global financial meltdown in 2008–2009, additional stresses have been placed on the economic future of the US and other countries (Jubak, 2009). What remains at issue is whether the US will have the intellectual resources needed to benefit from the economic upturn that will eventually occur?

Portfolio Evaluation

In brief, portfolios are collections of learners' work used to demonstrate their competencies. They may include artwork, compositions, music (written or recorded), videos of performance, concept maps, Vee diagrams, and a host of other products of learner's efforts. The validity issue disappears when portfolios allow for a full range of evidence of the learner's thinking, feeling, and acting. In practice, portfolios may be required that present a more restricted sample of work, and hence selective bias is introduced.

As noted earlier, CmapTools permits relatively easy construction of digital portfolios. When we look to assessment of these portfolios, a few criteria that can be used include:

1. The quality and comprehensiveness of the "backbone" concept map, to which icons to open other resources are attached.
2. The number and variety resources integrated into the portfolio.
3. Quality of the resources in terms of illustrating key concepts.
4. Originality of resources, especially those produced by the portfolio maker
5. The quality of written and/or oral presentation of the project.

Each of the above items might be rated on a scale of 1 (very low) to 10 (very high).

When portfolios are produced by teams, there can be a class or school competition, with each portfolio rated by all students, assuming arrangements are made for all students to view all of the portfolios. Students can often be very candid and constructive evaluators of portfolios.

The reliability-of-assessment issue hinges upon the extent to which the learner has the resources to produce consistently the work samples requested and the competence of the evaluator to judge the work samples. One must consider carefully these issues when portfolios are employed as a substantial element in the evaluation process. Race, culture, socioeconomic status, and gender differences could introduce highly significant biases, both in opportunity to produce portfolio materials and in their evaluation. Nevertheless, because they are "real" work samples of the learner and can bear a close relationship to the kinds of competencies required in "real-world" settings, portfolios need to be included as at least part of any comprehensive evaluation programs.

Martin, Miller, and Delago (1995) report on a study done in California involving some 500 science teachers and reviewed 4000 portfolios. Teachers attended two statewide portfolio training and development sessions, as well as regional implementation meetings, and they also participated in scoring portfolios. Students were asked to submit three portfolio entries dealing with real-world applications of science concepts. Criteria for scoring portfolios were established, and in general there was good consensus between two independent raters for each portfolio. They found that female students obtained higher scores than males, in contrast to score averages on a multiple-choice type test, where male students scored slightly higher. Ethnicity did not show differences between performance on portfolios and other measures of performance, although there were not sufficient numbers of portfolios submitted by African-Americans to make statistical comparisons. Portfolio scores correlated $r = 0.3$ with multiple-choice test scores in chemistry, and $r = 0.4$ with biology test scores. Thus, some 84 percent to 91 percent of variance in portfolio scores was not accounted for in multiple-choice test scores. Clearly, portfolio performance gave students a good alternative way to express their understanding of science.

Unfortunately, using portfolios as an evaluation tool, as well as a method of instruction, requires more work on the part of the teacher. Students often need more guidance, schedules need to allow for library work or work off of the school premises, and grading cannot be done by simply comparing answers with those on a scoring key. Unless use of portfolios is adopted as part of a school's policy and standard curriculum, it is not likely to be adopted and continued over time.

A variant on typical portfolio evaluation is the use of computers to generate electronic documents that combine information, pictures, video clips, etc., into a composite electronic "portfolio." Krajcik, Spitulnik, and Zembal (1998) reported good success with using this technique with high school science students and pre-service teachers. Of course, this form of instruction/evaluation requires that students have access to relatively good computers, Internet connections, and instructors competent to guide them. The potential for such instruction and evaluation will increase exponentially, with advances in computers and information highways. Moore's Law that indicates computer power will double every 18 months continues to operate (Brock, 2006; Service, 2009). However, we are looking at instructional practices that will require more resources and teachers motivated and competent to lead this kind of work. The Internet is also providing learning at home and enrollment in "distance education" degree programs (Novak, 2002). It will probably be a few decades before these capabilities become commonplace in public schools.

Authentic Assessment

There has been substantial criticism in recent years of traditional "testing" practices, together with documentation on the low predictive validity of "tests" as indicators of "real-world" performance or competency. This has led to a call for more "authentic assessment." Wiggins (1989) identifies a number of characteristics of authentic tests, as shown in Table 9.2. Reviewing these characteristics, one would have to conclude that "authentic testing" is certainly the way to go. The problem is that it is extraordinarily difficult to implement the kind of evaluation program that would achieve many of these characteristics. Portfolios and performance tests would have some of these characteristics, but as we have seen earlier, these are not easy to implement, nor are they trouble-free. Puckett and Black (1994), who cite Wiggins' work, provide a good handbook of practices, but they also have no easy answers to achieve authentic assessment. It should be evident that most of the criteria in Wiggins' table apply as well in corporate settings.

While concept maps and Vee diagrams are no panacea for authentic assessment, they satisfy many of the criteria for such evaluation, and if they are also used as instructional tools, they can be highly effective at any level of schooling. They can also be effective in business settings when used in conjunction with various forms of data collection regarding consumer knowledge and interests, or as "self check" tools for individuals or teams working on any form of project. I expect we shall see the use of these tools increase slowly, but by the mid twenty-first century, I would not be surprised to see them used widely.

Evaluation problems are pervasive, profound, and in many ways, intractable. As a "fifth element" involved in educating, evaluation cannot be treated casually, for faulty evaluation practices can negate some of our best efforts at organizing and delivering knowledge to learners. It can also have devastating effects on individual's ego, and in some cases, irreparable harm can be done. My counsel is that one can never take too seriously how best to evaluate achievement and accomplishment. Mintzes, et al. (2000) provide many examples of effective authentic assessment methods.

Table 9.2 Characteristics of authentic tests

A. Structure and Logistics
1. Are more appropriately public; involve an audience, a panel, and so on.
2. Do not rely on unrealistic and arbitrary time constraints.
3. Offer known, not secret, questions or tasks.
4. Are more like portfolios or a *season* of games (not one-shot).
5. Require some collaboration with others.
6. Recur—and are *worth* practicing for, rehearsing, and retaking.
7. Make assessment and feedback to students so central that school schedules and policies are modified to support them.

B. Intellectual Design Features
1. Are "essential"—not needlessly intrusive, arbitrary, or contrived to "shake out" a grade.
2. Are "enabling"—constructed to point the student toward more sophisticated use of the skills or knowledge.
3. Are contextualized, complex intellectual challenges, not "atomized" tasks, corresponding to isolated "outcomes."
4. Involve the student's own research or use of knowledge, for which "content" is a means.
5. Assess student habits and repertoires, not mere recall or plug-in skills.
6. Are *representative* challenges—designed to emphasize *depth* more than breadth.
7. Are engaging and educational.
8. Involve somewhat ambiguous ("ill-structured") tasks or problems.

C. Grading and Scoring Standards
1. Involve criteria that assess essentials, not easily counted (but relatively unimportant) errors.
2. Are not graded on a "curve," but in reference to performance standards (criterion-referenced, not norm-referenced).
3. Involve demystified criteria of success that appear to *students* as inherent in successful activity.
4. Make self-assessment a part of the assessment.
5. Use a multifaceted scoring system instead of one aggregate grade.
6. Exhibit harmony with shared schoolwide aims—a *standard*.

D. Fairness and Equity
1. Ferret out and identify (perhaps hidden) strengths.
2. Strike a *constantly* examined balance between honoring achievement and native skill or fortunate prior training.
3. Minimize needless, unfair, and demoralizing comparisons.
4. Allow appropriate room for student learning styles, aptitudes, and interests.
5. Can be—should be—attempted by *all* students, with the test "scaffolded up," not "dumbed down," as necessary.
6. Reverse typical test-design procedures: they make "accountability" serve student learning (Attention is primarily paid to "face" and "ecological" validity of tests).

From "Teaching to the Authentic Test" by Wiggins (1989), *Educational Leadership*. Copyright © 1989 by ASCD. Reprinted with permission of the Association for Supervision and Curriculum Development. All rights reserved.

Chapter 10

Improving Education in Schools and Corporations

A Basis for Optimism

Are Improvements in Education Possible?

In 1977, I observed in *A Theory of Education* that change in education was much like Brownian motion, as Toffler (1971) described it: constantly churning but going nowhere. I asserted then, and I would assert even more forcefully now, that this characterization is likely to persist unless educators in every educational setting. businesses as well as schools, seek to base change on a comprehensive theory of education. As noted in Chapter 1, in spite of enormous increases in per-pupil expenditures on school education (even in inflation-corrected dollars), there is little evidence that schooling is improving in terms of the usual criteria of success, namely various achievement test measures. Moreover, we have noted repeatedly the limitations of standardized achievement testing and argued repeatedly that more powerful, more demand-ing standards of achievement are needed. One of the reasons I believe we have been making so little progress in improving education is that when our evaluation methods measure little more than trivial achievements, it is difficult to discern changes in programs that produce truly substantive changes in human understanding. We can and we must move toward the wider use of better evaluation measures. Fortunately, there has been some progress, even with more traditional multiple-choice tests.

It may have been argued that military expenditures restricted our opportun-ities to invest in education during the Cold War, but for a time, military expenditures have declined enormously, especially in constant dollars, or as a percentage of our gross domestic product (GDP). However, for the USA, the costs of the wars in Afghanistan and Iraq have caused military expenses to soar after 2002. In addition, the economic chaos that occurred in 2008 has caused trillions of dollars in US debt and at this writing, we are still not certain when the economy will turn the corner. The economic problems have spread world-wide and now are making it difficult for many countries to invest more in education. Health care costs have soared far beyond inflation and now represent a new financial crisis; how much of these costs are a product of poor health education and preventive care and/or inadequate education of health care professionals? Welfare and crime costs, too, are at least partly a result of failed educational programs. With a prison incarceration rate in the United States of 0.615 per thousand, we lead other industrialized nations with six to eight times as many prisoners on a per capita basis. While the overall crime rate has been declining since its peak in 1993, the number of homicides involving black male juveniles as victims rose 31 percent and as perpetrators by 43 percent between 2002 and 2007 (Page, 2009).

Crime prevention and incarceration together with Social Security and health care payments are the big-ticket items in our budget and the budgets of all developed countries. Without radical improvements in education of all kinds, none of these costs will be contained, let alone reduced. Add to the equation that since 1980 the USA has moved from the largest creditor nation to the largest debtor nation and the fiscal crisis is nothing short of frightening.

Another fact of life that permeates our lives now, but was just beginning in 1977, is the globalization of the economy. For centuries, countries have traded products and their banks have exchanged currencies. But these trades were comparatively a mere trickle in the world flow of money, goods, and services compared with that which is occurring now and what we can expect to occur in the next two or more decades. In the United States and in other countries there have been numerous free trade agreements that have markedly increased the extent of market globalization. The European Union (EU) has grown much more integrated since its founding in 1993, and trade between the 27 EU countries has increased markedly. This has been facilitated by acceptance of a common currency (the euro) among the majority of EU states, and the EU now accounts for some 30 percent of the world's gross domestic product. We are rapidly moving to a time when any product, good, or service can be produced almost anywhere and sold everywhere—if the price is right. The importance of this for business can only be conjectured at this time. As Marshall and Tucker (1992) pointed out, we have entered a new economic era:

> One of America's most important advantages in the 19th and early 20th centuries was its extraordinary store of raw materials and cheap energy sources. But the steady advance of technology after the Second World War has greatly diminished our natural advantage in raw materials ... The extent to which ideas, skills and knowledge are being substituted for natural resources is suggested by the fact that 50 to 100 pounds of fiber glass cable (made from sand) transmits as many telephone conversations as one ton of copper wire ... Thus human resources-ideas, skills and knowledge (have) replaced natural resources as a major source of production and wealth. (pp. 34–35)

We have not seen the last shock wave to run through the economies of the world. Nanofabrication, the new emerging technology that permits building products atom by atom from relatively inexpensive raw materials, is just in its infancy. Since the sequencing of the human genome in 2003 and subsequent refinements of our genetic knowledge, we also enter a new era for drug production and "individually tailored medication" that will in the next decade or two revolutionize health care. Nobody can predict how economies will adjust to these emerging technologies, but the message is clear: The old economic rules no longer apply and the number one source of wealth in the future will be new knowledge. This is being illustrated today as nations rush to find new, clean energy sources in a world where energy increasingly is in short supply, especially energy sources that do not contribute to global warming. Service (2008) describes how new research is producing microbes that can convert non-food plant sources into oil, innovation that can radically alter the energy picture in the next decade. We see this as illustrative of what Drucker (1993) asserted:

> The basic economic resource—the means of production, to use the economist's term—is no longer capital, nor natural resources (the economist's "land"), nor "labor." *It is and will be knowledge.* The central wealth-creating activities will be neither the allocation of capital to productive uses, nor "labor"—the two poles of nineteenth- and twentieth-century economic theory, whether classical, Marxist, Keynesian, or neoclassical. Value is now created by "productivity" and "innovation," both applications of knowledge to work. (p. 8)

Educated in the sciences, I had grown to believe that the enormous advances in the sciences and in associated technologies were derived from the explanatory and predictive power that the theories constructed by scientists permitted. Yes, some of these theories have been modified or discarded over time, but they were useful to advance the sciences when they were created. True, people do not behave as do atoms or molecules, but there are regularities in the ways people and organizations are structured and the ways in which they function. I believed it should be possible to construct a theory of education that would have explanatory and predictive power in 1977, and I am convinced now that audacious attempt has been vindicated. When *A Theory of Education* (Novak, 1977a) was first published, a close friend and respected scholar, Ned Bingham, wrote to me saying that "the theory explained why, what I had learned that worked in 40 years as an educator, worked." The late scholar, Ralph Tyler, was kind enough to write a gracious foreword to the book. Despite these good words, and translations of the book into Spanish and Portuguese, and just recently into Basque, *A Theory of Education* has not had a major impact on education in the United States or in most countries. There appears to be more recognition of the value of our theoretical views and resulting tools and practices in Spanish-speaking countries and Italy, as evidenced in part by the three Honorary Doctorates I have received from universities in these countries. The theory has had a major impact on my research program and programs of some of my colleagues in this country and abroad.

There is the saying that nothing succeeds like an idea whose time has come. In retrospect, it seems clear to me now that educators were not ready for, nor did they desperately need, a theory of education. Older educational practices, rooted largely in the now discredited behavioral psychology (see Brown, 1994) seemed to be good enough to carry on the business of education, not only in schools but also in the professions and in corporations. But, as another saying goes, we are in a new ball game. The accelerating globalization of the world economies is putting new demands on education of all people. As Marshall and Tucker (1992) observed:

> The new forms of work organization will not work unless management understands that it is just as important for front-line workers to learn constantly and to put that learning to work as it is for management. By learning enough to take over many functions previously reserved for management, they not only contribute directly to great productivity improvements, but they also reduce the compartmentalization of the organization, which once again increases the organization's learning capacity. In all these ways, the learning organization makes possible gains in quality and productivity that are not achievable in any other way. And, ultimately, it makes it possible for modem societies to substitute ideas, skills, and knowledge for physical resources. (p. 102)

It is not enough for individuals in an organization to learn. The organization as a whole must also be a learning organism. Commenting on the fact that one third of the Fortune 500 companies in 1970 had vanished by 1983, Senge (1990) observed:

> What if high corporate mortality rate is only a symptom of deeper problems that afflict *all* companies, not just the ones that die? What if even the most successful companies are poor learners—they survive but never live up to their potential? What if, in the light of what *could* be, "excellence" is actually "mediocrity"? It is no accident that most organizations learn poorly. The way they are designed and managed, and the way we have all been taught to think and interact (not only in organizations but more broadly) create fundamental learning disabilities. (pp. 17–18)

The ideas and tools presented in this book are as relevant to individual learners as to organizations that seek to learn. They are now being applied to some organizations in the United States and abroad.

To return to the question in the title of this section, I believe that the examples presented in this book suggest a resounding "yes!" to the question,

"Are improvements in education possible?" I have tried to show how theoretical ideas can guide and accelerate the process of improvement of education in every kind of setting. Furthermore, I believe the economic pressures will force substantive changes in schools in the next few decades. Schools cannot do this alone, and corporations cannot become highly effective knowledge creating and knowledge utilizing organizations without better schools. A new partnership in creating, sharing, and using new educational ideas is needed. An overview of the ideas presented in this chapter is shown in Figure 10.1.

Improving Organizations

School Organization

In most countries, school policies are established by the national government. In the United States, responsibility for education is delegated to the states, with the exception of special programs such as school lunch programs. States provide financial support together with support from local communities and also set policies on licensure for teachers, administrators, and other school personnel. In general, licensure policies deal with college course credit hours rather than broad intellectual competencies and skills. Thus certain courses are required for various specializations. This rigidity in licensure policies is perhaps the major deterrent to creative programs for educators, but the rigidity of schools of education and other agencies preparing educators can be equally stagnating. There are efforts to break away from these conventions, such as the Coalition of Essential Schools, headquartered at Brown University. Some states have relaxed restrictions to allow for experimental programs in Essential Schools, and some colleges are collaborating to modify preparation programs for staff in these schools. For the vast majority of schools in the United States, innovations and variation in preparation of the staff and in instructional programs are modest at best.

School Reform

When the National Commission on Excellence in Education published, in 1983, its report, *A Nation At Risk: The Imperative for Educational Reform*, many schools, organizations, and state bureaucracies cited the report as justification for radical changes in schools. So, more than two decades later, what has happened? At best, the results have been modest, and in some school districts, the situation has gotten worse. Sarason (1993) in his book, *The Predictable Failure of Educational Reform*, observed that the long-standing educational structures, coupled with the needs of various groups to defend their power, stifled reform efforts. Sarason offered ideas on how educators can make significant reforms that produce substantial, long-lasting results, but still, such changes are slow in coming. The September 1993 issue of *Educational*

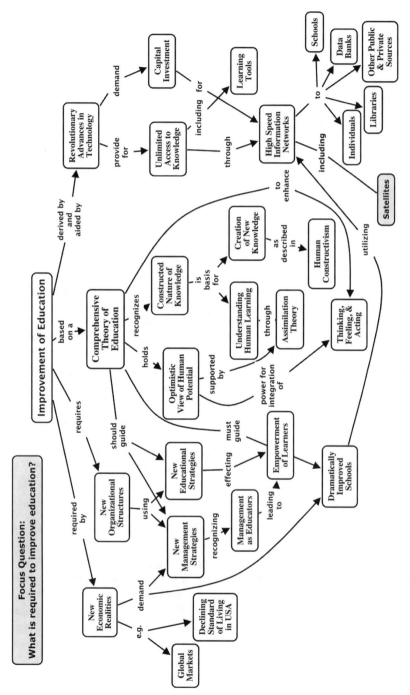

Figure 10.1 A concept map showing key ideas presented in this chapter.

Leadership published a series of articles dealing with system change, and I cite some articles in this issue.

What happened in most states after publication of *A Nation at Risk* (National Commission on Excellence in Education, 1983) was that legislation was passed that required higher standards for teacher certification and prescribed standards for student achievement in basics, and testing to assess if the standards were being met. Of course, such legislation did little to change the system. College courses for teachers, patterns of instruction well established in the classroom, curriculums, and textbooks—all these remained substantially the same. There was little new learning taking place either on the part of teachers or administrators. In short, little was happening to change the organization.

In the area of science and mathematics, the National Science Foundation (NSF) launched a program in 1990 to encourage systemic reform. This program recognized that many of the previous NSF programs to improve textbooks and teacher education dealt only with parts of the education enterprise. Other factors operating in schools tended to dilute these efforts at best and in some cases totally undermine them. Systemic reform has as its goal to deal with most of the factors that affect the quality of school science and math instruction (Lawler, 1994). Based on competitive proposals, the NSF selected 25 state programs and a number of urban systems to receive support for innovative programs involving teacher enhancement, equipment purchases, new evaluation procedures, and use of TQM strategies such a benchmarking and feedback from customers: that is, parents, students, and employers.

Unfortunately, the 100 million dollars allocated annually to this program was a mere drop in the bucket of funding that would be needed to reform schooling in America, although the intent was to provide model programs. If these funds were used for only two or three truly model programs in school districts, there might be a chance that, over time, some revolutionary change might be effected, but given the politics of Washington, this would be impossible to fund and sustain. Moreover, the approach even in best cases is similar to TQM and reengineering efforts in corporations, modifying largely the mechanics by which science and mathematics is taught and evaluated but not modifying substantially how the schools empower teachers and students to create and use new knowledge. The pessimistic view I took regarding curriculum reforms in science and mathematics in the 1950s and 1960s (Novak, 1969) was based on my belief that those programs failed to recognize and apply new knowledge on teaching and learning processes, and the evidence (Clune, 1998) is that the urban and state systemic reform efforts funded by NSF in the 1990s have not done better. Too little of what was done incorporates the kind of ideas and activities suggested in our books, *Teaching Science for Understanding* (Mintzes, Wandersee, & Novak, 1998), *Assessing Science Understanding* (Mintzes Wandersee and Novak, 2000), and *Aprendizaje Significativo: Tecnicas y aplicaciones* (Gonzales & Novak, 1996). It is again another case of doing mostly more of the same does not result in substantively improved learning.

Part of the problem has been the lack of leadership with the vision and talent to bring absolutely valid educational improvement. Brandt (1993) cited the example of the superintendent for Edmonton, Alberta, Canada, who used his status and 20 years of experience to turn power over to individual schools and gave them control over 87 percent of the school budget. Individual school principals would work with teachers, parents, and community groups to modify instruction and programs. Such leadership is rare, however, and most school superintendents' tenure is only 3 to 5 years. Even with changes that confer more power for local control, schools can do little to change teacher preparation, quality of textbooks, and collective bargaining practices, and a host of other factors that influence day-to-day classroom instruction. Feynman's (1985) scathing critique of the way in which textbooks for schools in California are selected would be equally valid in many states today.

Beginning in 1979, a group of school leaders formed a group that became known as the Coalition of Essential Schools. This group sought to effect changes in their individual schools and exchange ideas on things that work and things that were unsuccessful. There are now hundreds of schools loosely attached to the Coalition, but only 50 or so are really doing things significantly different from the mainstream (O'Neil, 1995a). With leadership from Ted Sizer, former Dean of Education at Harvard, and funding from a variety of foundations, the Coalition continues to encourage improvement in schools. Even with substantial foundation contributions, the Coalition has had relatively modest successes, and some notable failures.

In a *Wall Street Journal* article, Stecklow (1994) noted that evaluation data on the success of the schools is mostly anecdotal. Admittedly, it is not easy to do valid evaluation studies for schools that try to do truly innovative things, and a proposal to fund such a study was turned down by Exxon Foundation, one of the Coalition supporters. As noted in Chapter 9, good evaluation programs can do much to advance good school programs, and poor evaluation programs do the reverse.

In an interview with Peter Senge, O'Neil (1995b) reported:

> Nothing will change, no matter how fascinated you are by a new idea, unless you create some kind of a learning process. A learning process is a process that occurs over time whereby people's beliefs, ways of seeing the world, and ultimately their skills and capabilities change. It always occurs over time, and it's always connected to your domain of taking action, whether it's about relationships or about your professional work. Learning occurs "at home," so to speak, in the sense that it must be integrated into our lives, and it always takes time and effort. (p. 23)

The kind of systems thinking Senge (1990) recommended is difficult to implement when so few components of the system can be controlled and changed through the learning of the people involved in the system. The success of Otto Silesky's school discussed in Chapter 1 is a case where the leadership succeeded in enlisting the efforts of all teachers to achieve remarkable results. Current information on Coalition Schools can be obtained at: http://www.essentialschools.org/. Given the slow progress of school improvement, there has been growing support for privatizing schools, that is, using public funds to contract with for-profit organizations to educate children. There have been private schools for many years, but these are schools where the parents pay the tuition and fees. On the whole, private schools have enjoyed inordinate success by criteria such as that a high proportion of students in private schools come from homes where economic and social resources are much better than average. Needless to say, these schools tend to do better than the average public school. Could private schools operated by for-profit corporations achieve similar results for all children?

One form of privatization has been the formation of charter schools. Bierlein and Mulholland (1994) described charter schools in this way:

> In its purest form, a charter school is an autonomous educational entity operating under a contract negotiated between the *organizers* who manage the school (teachers, parents, or others from the public or private sector), and the *sponsors* who oversee the provisions of the charter (local school boards, state education boards, or some other public authority). Charter provisions address such issues as the school's instructional plan, specific educational outcomes and their measurement, and management and financial issues.
>
> A charter school may be formed from a school's existing personnel and facilities or from a portion thereof (for example, a school-within-a-school); or it may be a completely new entity with its own facilities. Once approved, a charter school is an independent legal entity with the ability to hire and fire, sue and be sued, award contracts for outside services, and control its own finances. Funding is based on student enrollment, as it would be for a school district. With a focus on educational outcomes, charter schools are freed from many (or all) district and state regulations often perceived as inhibiting innovation—for example, excessive teacher certification requirements, collective bargaining agreements, Carnegie units, and other curriculum requirements. (pp. 34–35, emphasis in original)

In theory, charter schools have the opportunity to innovate in ways that would not be possible in regular public schools. In practice, many of the constraints that operate to impede truly innovative programs in public schools also operate in charter schools and similar private schools. Partly for this reason, a recent University of Illinois study (2009) reported that public schools outperformed private schools in mathematics. As Molnar (1994) observed in his article, "Education for Profit: A Yellow Brick Road to Nowhere":

> Privatization seems attractive because it provides a comforting illusion of change without the sacrifices that would be necessary to bring about real improvement. It helps perpetuate the myth that the fundamental problems of urban schools are caused by bureaucracies, incompetence, and the self-interested greed of unions instead of crushing poverty, racism, and a lack of jobs. (p. 71)

More recent reviews of charter schools by Dingerson and colleagues (2008) indicate problems continue. On one hand, Jay Mathews (2008), who visited many charter schools, found that some were strongly outperforming neighborhood public schools. He saw promising results in schools managed by the Knowledge is Power organization. On the other hand, only two of 31 charter schools operated by White Hat Management made federal benchmarks for adequate yearly progress in 2006–2007. A report by Glod and Turque (2008) indicated that a study involving 1903 children in the Washington, DC area for whom public funds were used to enroll them in charter schools performed no better after two years than their public school peers. While it is likely that the charter school movement will continue to be controversial, there is evidence that they can stimulate changes in public school, and nearly everyone agrees that significant improvements in public schools is needed.

Home Schooling. An alternative some parents choose is to educate their children at home. Sometimes parents choose this option for religious reasons, but increasingly, parents seek to offer more education quality and opportunity than they believe can be provided by public, private, or parochial schools. They often do so at considerable personal and financial sacrifice because they continue to pay for public education but may receive no tax relief nor other support for their home school. In some cases, a home–public school partnership is established, where children use school facilities and participate in sports and other extracurricular activities. An advantage to public schools is that they typically receive state aid for local home-schooled children, but do not have the full burden for educating these children.

Home schooling is becoming an increasingly popular option with some two million children now receiving their education through such schools. With growing opportunities for learning via the Internet and other media sources, we are likely to see the popularity of home schooling continue to increase. If tax dollars are provided to parents for home schooling, either in direct funding or as tax credits, the growth in home schooling could accelerate greatly. There is a certain security, if not outright complacency, in maintaining the status quo in schools.

Most parents believe their local schools are doing an adequate or very good job in educating their children. By the standards of their own past experience in schools, their beliefs may be justified. By the standards required for graduates to compete in the new global economic scene, the standards are far short of the mark. For the one fifth of our students who drop out of school, schools have clearly failed them, and yet these people will need employment. Even for those who graduate from high school or college, the reports on their intellectual competencies are grim. For example, an article in the local newspaper reports that 46 percent of 1994 high school graduates who entered public colleges read below the eighth-grade level and 60 percent of students entering Florida colleges are below this level (Moloney, 1996). In science and math, eighth-grade students ranked 17th and 28th, respectively, when compared with students in 40 other developed countries (Hegarty, 1996).

Why? Why are schools performing so poorly? There are, of course, many difficult and complex societal issues involved, as we noted previously. Changing demographics with some urban schools almost 100 percent non-White, nonnative-born who speak various languages; drug abuse with both parents and students; physical safety in schools threatened with knives and guns-just to name a few. There are no easy solutions to any of these problems. And yet, I see the overriding failure in schools contributing to the problems listed is the failure to empower learners to take charge of their own meaning making. Why? For one thing, most school administrators with whom I have worked do not understand what is required for the latter condition to occur in their schools. They are either uneducated or badly educated in understanding how humans learn and how to organize school experience to empower learners. In three decades of teaching at Cornell University, I have had only one student in school administration enroll and complete my course in Theory and Methods of Education. Most of the leadership in school administrations remains largely blind to the revolutionary changes that have taken place in understanding how humans learn and the nature and structure of knowledge. In reviewing recent textbooks on school administration, only two of six books have any information on student learning, and this was only 1½ pages in one book and one half-page in another. Administrators who are concerned with empowering learners are rare indeed, and those who do care feel themselves trapped by the system.

Although I am a perennial optimist in my belief that the world can be made a better place for everyone, I see little hope for public schools in the United States working their way out of the organizational and political problems they are in within the next 10 years. I am much more optimistic that we can see changes along the lines suggested in this book in some foreign countries and in corporate America. Spain, for example, has as a national education commitment and determination to move forward on helping learners learn how to learn and to make school learning meaningful. The Spanish Ministry of Education and Science (MEC) published in 1989 the *White Book for the*

Reform of Education, putting forth an agenda for improvement of education that placed a central emphasis on the need to encourage meaningful learning. Unfortunately, promising and in some ways visionary as this White Book is, the transformation of teaching and learning in Spanish schools and colleges is no more easily done than are major educational overhauls in any country. Nevertheless, some countries, such as the Scandinavian countries, are succeeding and their students excel in a variety of evaluations, year after year.

Corporate America, especially the for-profit organizations, have pressures public schools do not face to a significant degree at this time: They must compete to survive. They cannot tap the public purse by increasing taxes to pay for their failures. Although I fear the near-term consequences of using taxpayer funds to support private schools, it seems to me inevitable that this will occur increasingly in some states. To date, no state has legislation to provide taxpayer support to home schools, although some expenses for home schooling are tax deductible. For one thing. it would be difficult for states to assure that funds to home schools were not being misused. However, if parents who home school do get some assistance from state funds in the future, their growth might be explosive. I expect to see increasing pressures in the US for taxpayer support for schools other than public schools in the future. Public schools in many areas may have to die before they can be born again with the central commitment not sorting successful from unsuccessful learners, but rather empowering all learners. The organizational structures of most states, localities, and schools in the United States are simply not prepared for, nor organized to seek, empowerment of learners as an overriding commitment.

For-Profit Organizations

As already noted in the quote from Senge, for-profit corporations are also learning-disabled. For decades I found my overtures to introduce *A Theory of Education* (Novak, 1977a) ideas to American business silently rejected. Often very junior corporate executives hearing of our work at a conference or seminar would respond with great enthusiasm and ask if I would be willing to visit with their colleagues. The calls never came. I am sure that when the junior executives spoke about our efforts to understand learners and knowledge, the senior officers saw little or no relevance to issues that were important to them. As Senge said, American business corporations have been learning-disabled. All of this has changed since the early 1990s, not dramatically, but in significant ways. Some corporate executives, again especially in foreign countries, are interested in theory-based methods and tools for improving learning in corporations and in facilitating knowledge creation (see earlier text on work with Procter and Gamble, p. 109).

One evidence of the changing Zeitgeist is illustrated with our book, *Learning How to Learn* (Novak & Gowin, 1984). When it was published in 1984 none of the many Japanese publishers translating books by Cambridge

University Press were interested in translation rights. In 1990, a prominent publisher in Japan approached the Press for translation rights to the book and published this in 1992. During the 1980s when the United States was moving from the largest creditor nation to the largest debtor nation, Japan was doing the reverse. As Prestowitz (1988) observed, we were trading places. Part of the problem was and is with research productivity. To quote Prestowitz,

> the United States gets very little bang from its R & D bucks. It not only spends less on commercial research and development as a percentage of gross domestic produce [1.6 percent of our GNP versus 2.9 percent for Japan], but it gets less out of what it spends. We must strive for a more rational organization of our R & D programs. . . ." (p. 106).

Yes, we must improve our capability for creation of new knowledge. What Prestowitz did not say, but Drucker (1993) and others are saying, is. "In the knowledge society (we are now in), people have to learn *how to* learn. Indeed, in the knowledge society, subjects matter less than the students' capacity to continue learning and their motivation to do so" (p. 201, italics added). I believe the Japanese see this, and I am told by the author of the translation that the Japanese version of *Learning How to Learn* is being well received (Yumino, 1994). Will Japan pick up the learning how to learn ball and run with it while American schools and corporations languish? I hope not. Or maybe the leadership will come from China, India or other emerging economic powers. Zakaria (2009) suggests this may be the case.

Corporate Learning. Almost every book or article published in recent years on ways to improve business success has as a key claim that corporations must become better at learning, not only learning by upper management, but by everyone in the organization. Senge (1990) proposed that organizational learning required five component technologies:

1. *Systems thinking*—ways of thinking that help people see the whole pattern of factors involved in any given problem domain. For example, to develop a truly revolutionary automobile, all the component factors—powertrain, body, suspension, customer's wants, and so forth, must be considered together with the interactions of these components with one another.

2. *Personal mastery*—"the discipline of continually clarifying and deepening our personal vision, of focusing our energies, of developing patience, and of seeing reality objectively" (Senge, 1990, p. 7). Part of the process of gaining personal mastery is employing systems thinking, and becoming more effective in the following component technologies.

3. *Building better mental models*—we all come to a new task with some kind of model of how the thing or process works. Often our mental models inhibit new learning. For example, most teaching interns come to their practice teaching experience with the mental model that teaching is lecturing, for this is

the model they have seen in most of their school and university classes. It takes time and practice for them to see that guiding teams, cooperative planning with students, and critiquing computer activities are what make excellent teaching. In the corporate setting, dealing with stomach acid and heartburn can be modeled as providing compounds to neutralize the acid as with Tums or Rolaids, or we can conceive a new, more effective model where stomach acid secretion is diminished, as with Zantac, Tagament, or Axid. Our conceptual frameworks underlie our mental models, and the challenge is how to enrich, modify, and/or substitute new conceptual frameworks to achieve new problem solutions.

4. *Building shared vision*—partly because each individual holds his or her own mental models, and often these are not clearly evident to the person or the group, it can be very difficult to create a shared vision in schools or corporations. One of the reasons positive change in schools is so difficult is that there is so little shared vision as to what constitutes good education and an exemplary school.

We saw in Chapter 8 (see Figure 8.5) the problems we identified at one major corporation and the concept maps that showed little evidence of a shared vision. Senge (1990) observed:

> When there is a genuine vision (as opposed to the all-too-familiar "vision statement"), people excel and learn, not because they are told to, but because they want to. But many leaders have personal visions that never get translated into shared visions that galvanize an organization. All too often, a company's shared vision has revolved around the charisma of a leader, or around a crisis that galvanizes everyone temporarily. But, given a choice, most people opt for pursuing a lofty goal, not only in times of crisis, but at all times. What has been lacking is a discipline for translating individual vision into shared vision—not a "cookbook," but a set of principles and guiding practices. (p. 9)

What Lafley and Charan (2008) present in their book is not only a clear vision that Lafley brought to Procter and Gamble where all aspects of the organization was to see the customer as the driver for innovation, but also the many practices that were introduced to make every employee a participant in achieving this vision.

5. *Team learning*—All of us work in teams, even the prairie pioneer farmer worked with his family and neighbors as teams. Senge (1990) asserted. "Team learning is vital because teams, not individuals, are the fundamental learning unit in modern organizations" (p. 10). We all know that teamwork is essential in most sports. Martin (1993) used the sports model as the basis for his book, *Team Think: Using the Sports Connection to Develop, Motivate, and Manage a Winning Business Team*. Martin emphasized that business teams need a leader or coach, and he argued that "To be an effective manager, you must

become a leader" (p. 34); and he contrasted the old style manager with the team leader thus:

- A manager administers, a leader innovates.
- A manager maintains, a leader develops.
- A manager plans, a leader sets a direction.

Senge (1990) emphasized the importance of dialogue and genuine thinking together as essential to effective learning by the team. I would be more specific and say that the team must effectively negotiate old and new meanings held by team members and work to modify and improve the conceptual frameworks of all team members. In sports, the goal of the team is generally clear, for example, to score the most touchdowns, field goals, and conversions possible. Peters (1992) suggested that corporations need more participation in management by all members of the organization. In school learning or business, teams need leaders to help define the goals and lead (guide) the team. This requires skill and understanding above all of Senge's five component technologies. Senge (1990) observed:

> Despite its importance, team learning remains poorly understood. Until we can describe the phenomenon better, it will remain mysterious. Until we have some theory of what happens when teams learn (as opposed to individuals in teams learning), we will be unable to distinguish group intelligence from "groupthink," when individuals succumb to group pressures for conformity. Until there are reliable methods for building teams that can learn together, its occurrence will remain a product of happenstance. This is why mastering team learning will be a critical step in building learning organizations. (p. 238)

My contention is that team learning needs to be seen as basically an educational problem. The tools and ideas presented in this book have been effective in team learning, as well as in aiding individuals to gain mastery in both school and corporate settings.

Hamel and Prahalad (1994) distinguished between vision and foresight. Industry foresight helps managers answer three critical questions. Hamel and Prahalad cautioned that vision, vanity, and foresight are not the same:

> Visions that are as grandiose as they are poorly conceived deserve to be criticized, as do companies that seem to prefer rhetoric to action. All too often, "the vision" is no more than window dressing for a CEO's ego-driven acquisition binge. Chrysler's purchase of an Italian maker of exotic sports cars and its acquisition of a jet aircraft manufacturer were driven more by the ego and whim of the company's erstwhile chairman, Lee Iococca, than by a solid, well-founded point of view about what it would

take to succeed in the automotive business ten years hence. They were a side trip. Any vision that is simply an extension of the CEO's ego is dangerous. On the other hand, it is equally simplistic and dangerous to reject the very notion of foresight simply because some corporate leaders can't distinguish between vanity and vision. (p. 75)

Katzenbach (1995) and his associates found that the real change leaders in successful companies they studied had an effective working vision that served the following functions:

> *Give meaning* to the changes expected of people;
> *Evoke clear and positive mental images* of what "it should be like around here";
> *Create pride, energy, and a sense of accomplishment* along the way; and
> *Link change activities and business-performance* results. (p. 66)

In addition to providing a shared vision, Lafley and Charan (2008) also emphasize that change leaders must *inspire* all members of the organization.

> Since the process of innovation has inherently uncertain outcomes and is riddled with risk, leaders of innovation *inspire and redirect emotional energy of knowledge workers*, both individually and on teams. They are patient if things don't go as planned, not getting frustrated if a team takes longer to work through qualifying a prototype with a customer. In fact, they know when to encourage a team to go off for further exploration to ensure they have considered all possibilities. And they know when to converge and go on to the next stage of development.
>
> Through their participation in innovation project reviews, they inspire individuals and teams to see new possibilities by asking questions unique to the innovation: What haven't you noticed? What can be connected that hasn't connected? How can you harness the diverse thinking of both internal and external people? Overall, they inspire people that they can do it, that they can make the breakthrough. (Italics in original, pp. 267–68)

If we see management as essentially the task of educating or teaching, we can apply much of what has been presented in the earlier chapters as the tools and ideas needed to build, share, and execute a more powerful vision for schools and corporations.

The Promise of New Technologies

The Internet

The Internet originated as a governmental network called ARPANET, which was created in 1969 by the Defense Department so that defense contractors and researchers could continue communications after a nuclear attack. Computer resources were distributed in various locations so that destruction of some would still permit communications with others. Proven to be popular with scientists and computer specialists, the network evolved into what is now called the Internet. It is a loose collection of commercial and noncommercial computer networks tied together by telecommunications lines. When federal funding for ARPANET was discontinued in 1989, the Internet was born, with support from various user groups.

Initially, the Internet served primarily to provide electronic mail service to research organizations, computer companies, scientists, and graduate students. More recently it has served to carry information from Web services set up by organizations or individuals. The availability of free software needed to browse websites has made access to the Internet popular with anyone who owns a computer with sufficient power to use the Web services. The World Wide Web, or www, is now accessed by millions of people all over the world. However, in some countries even today, especially in Africa, Internet access and bandwidth available is only 1 percent or 2 percent of the world average (Juma and Moyer, 2008). This highly limits access to information and ability for collaboration via the Internet.

As personal computers continue to become more powerful and/or less expensive, use of the Internet will continue to expand. The major limitation for home and school use now is the speed with which information can be transmitted. There are also limitations on the availability of Internet access in many countries, especially in remote locations. Transfer of large quantities of information over Information Highways, except for locations with direct fiber optic cable connections, is currently slow and not appropriate for good two-way video transfer. Undoubtedly, there will be great strides and maybe new breakthroughs in solving the problem of transferring huge amounts of information between computers in the next decade. However, even with current capabilities, there are extraordinary opportunities for gaining new knowledge via the Internet. Most schools and businesses today are far from utilizing the resources that already exist. With universities such as MIT posting all their courses and study guides on the Internet, a whole new range of educational opportunities are emerging. As Tapscott and Williams (2006. p. 25) observe: "Today a promising student in Mumbai who has always dreamed of going to MIT can now access the university's entire curriculum online without paying a penny in tuition fees." While learning via the Internet is still in its infancy, there can be no doubt that new opportunities that are arising will in time significantly impact the way many students learn.

Two-Way Video Conferencing

Current computer technology and Internet capabilities already allow for two-way video conferencing. IChat and Skype, both free software available to anyone, allow dialogue and video exchange between students or experts located in classrooms or offices almost anywhere in the United States, as well as in other countries. Now that I have substantially limited my travel commitments, I frequently use IChat or Skype software to deliver lectures or participate in other ways with students and professors in the USA and all over the world. For schools, this can mean access to many new knowledge resources, as well as collaboration on research projects between students located in different schools. For children in home-school programs, the new resources could give each child unprecedented opportunities for learning and collaboration.

In the corporate world, opportunities for two-way video conferencing can also afford new ways for teams to collaborate, including collaboration between members at almost any location on the globe. As the globalization of business continues to increase, video conferencing and other knowledge exchange forms will undoubtedly increase exponentially. Currently computer linked "white boards" allow conference teams to interact with electronic pens that record marks on both the originating and remote white boards. These records are also stored in computer files and can be retrieved, modified, and printed out. Thus, conferencing can proceed in real time, or individuals and groups can work on documents whenever their schedules permit.

New Forms of Curriculum Development

Across the years, curriculum development has meant production of new text-books, study guides, and course syllabi. For example, the numerous federally funded "alphabet programs" to improve science and mathematics education in the United States in the late 1950s and 1960s were mostly focused on the production of such materials. The Physical Science Study Committee (PSSC), Biological Sciences Curriculum Study (BSCS), Elementary School Science (ESS) and the Minnesota Math and Science Teaching (MMST) projects were all federally funded curriculum projects of this kind. None of these, however, were based on a theory of education, and the theories of learning, when considered, were either Piagetian developmental theory or behavioral psychology (Novak, 1969). Except for the BSCS, most of the curriculum development groups have become history, along with the materials they developed. The several billions of federal dollars that were invested in developing these materials and training teachers to use them now show little or no impact on the quality of science and mathematics teaching in the United States, or in other countries where the materials were adapted. Similar results occurred in the social sciences, where politically sensitive materials that were developed were widely criticized, and soon dropped from schools. Educators and publishers continue to develop and offer to schools new books and syllabi, now often including CD-ROM visual materials to extend the print materials. No doubt this kind of work will continue well into the twenty-first century. But there are new opportunities for developing curriculum materials made possible by the technology revolution that is taking place. Because learning is necessarily idiosyncratic and meaning making must be done by the individual learner, the best curriculum development is that which the learner constructs.

A first step toward this kind of curriculum development is illustrated in the work of Krajcik and his associates at the University of Michigan (Krajcik, Spitulnik, & Zembal, 2000). With both high school students and pre-service teachers, they have developed strategies to aid learners in developing individualized curriculum artifacts on computers that combine text Internet resources, visuals (including videos), and other resources that illustrate some major concept in science. The development of the computer-based montage or artifact of materials is guided by a teacher, but the end result is created by the learner. Furthermore, future students can review artifacts created by previous students, modify, and build on these and develop new materials.

A New Model for Education

As CmapTools software evolved over the past decade at the Florida Institute for Human and Machine Cognition (IHMC), the new capabilities together with the explosive growth of the World Wide Web make possible what we call a New Model for Education (Novak, 2004; Novak and Cañas, 2006b). Figure 10.2 summarizes key features of our New Model.

Expert Skeleton Concept maps. The idea here is that it is helpful to a learner to provide some ideational scaffolding that can aid in constructing a concept

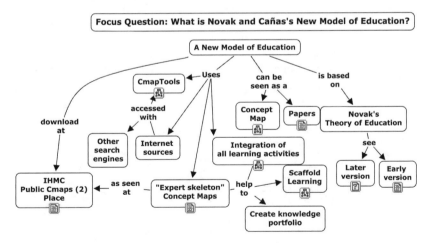

Figure 10.2 An overview of the Novak & Cañas New Model for Education. When viewed online, attached resources can be viewed by clicking on resource names.

map for a given domain of knowledge. By providing a small concept map, perhaps with 6–12 concepts and appropriate linking words, we can activate recall of pertinent concepts known by the learner and/or model appropriate structuring of these concepts. This skeleton map can also function as an advance organizer for proceeding to build a more detailed knowledge model by supplying ideas, at least some of which would be familiar to the learner. Since it is also common that learners have some misconceptions or faulty knowledge structures, the expert skeleton map can encourage rethinking already-held propositions. An expert skeleton concept map may also contain several suggested concepts in what we refer to as a "Parking Lot." These are concepts that the learners might incorporate into the concept map, thus providing them some further scaffolding of learning. Figure 10.3 illustrates an expert skeleton concept map (Figure A) and the example with some concepts in a Parking Lot (Figure B).

Adding Resources to Concept Map to Build a "Knowledge Model"

Starting with Figure A or B above, individuals or groups of students can search their own memories or the Internet for additional concepts to be added and linked in properly. Furthermore, learners can search the Internet using the CmapTools "Search" tool and other materials will be identified that are pertinent to the map, and these can provide additional concepts and propositions. Further searching can be done using Google or other search engines. Pictures, texts, video clips and other resources can be added to build what we call a "Knowledge Model" about US Government. CmapTools provides the option of saving concept maps as part of a Knowledge Model. To add these resources when using CmapTools, the map-maker only needs to drag the icon for the resource to the appropriate target concept and an icon will be added that permits later retrieval of the resources by simply clicking on the icon and selecting the resource name. Pictures, videos, text, URLs and digital resources

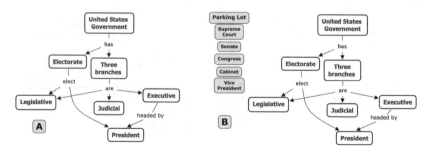

Figure 10.3 Two examples of "expert skeleton" concept maps that can help to scaffold learning, with a "Parking Lot" shown in figure B that can give additional scaffolding.

can be added to the Knowledge Model. The resources become part of the files for the Knowledge Model, and all of these are transferred along with the concept map if the Knowledge Model is moved to another folder or server. In general, we recommend that learners work in teams of two to four in building Knowledge Models, since much good learning takes place as teams discuss what should be added and how new concepts and propositions should be added. If the "Recorder" tool in CmapTools is turned on, a record of each addition will be kept, including an identification of the individual making the addition. Learners can also attach notes to parts of the map with suggestion or queries to be responded to by other team members. Figure 10.4 shows an example of a developing knowledge model that can be created.

Integrating All Forms of Learning Experiences

Lest I be accused of suggesting that most classroom time should be used building concept maps, I want to point out that all of the good learning practices should be used, and probably no more than 15–20 percent of class time should be the actual building of concept maps. Figure 10.5 shows that a concept mapping-centered classroom, whether in a school or a corporate training program, should involve the full array of learning activities. The difference when employing A New Model for Education is that all of the various activities are made conceptually explicit and are linked together through an evolving knowledge model where the evolving concept map foundation evolves with and integrates the learning activities. Furthermore, the learner and the teacher or manager has a product to observe, evaluate, and preserve. Any future related learning could begin with this knowledge model, facilitating further meaningful learning. Figure 10.5 illustrates the various learning activities that can be integrated in building the knowledge model.

Books still play an important role in the New Model classroom, but instead of buying classroom sets of textbooks, that are usually somewhat out of date when they are printed, books become one of many resources for learners to use both in the classroom and in the library. More time is spent in organizing learning teams and in preparing oral, poster, or written reports. Learning becomes a highly collaborative enterprise, both with local students and with students in remote locations. Permission can be given to others to view only, or view and edit concept maps, and the latter would normally be done when individuals are collaborating. Concept maps also can be emailed by simply dragging the Cmap file from a person's Cmap folder to an email message. The receiver can move the file into her or his Cmap files and save or modify the map. The teacher's role changes from disseminator of information to director of learning activities and supervisor of assessments. The New Model applies to all school disciplines, and ideally, learners would build knowledge models for every subject matter domain. For example, Figure 10.6 suggests that knowledge models might be built for history topics. In Costa Rica, pre-school children are

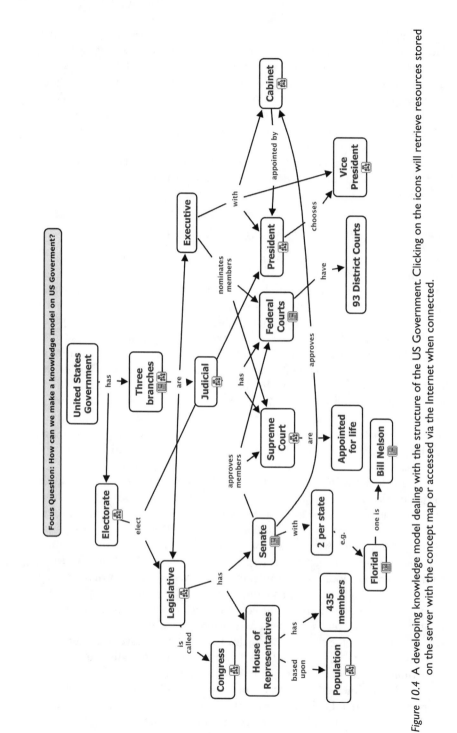

Focus Question: How can we make a knowledge model on US Government?

Figure 10.4 A developing knowledge model dealing with the structure of the US Government. Clicking on the icons will retrieve resources stored on the server with the concept map or accessed via the Internet when connected.

Figure 10.5 A concept map can serve as the foundation for a knowledge model that incorporates all types of classroom activities from early pretesting to experimentation and other research to written and/or oral reports.

Figure 10.6 Knowledge models can be constructed for History, and every other subject matter domain, and include linkages to knowledge models in other disciplines.

building concept maps using images of concepts plus words as shown in Figure 10.7. Older children often build concept maps using both Spanish and English words to label concepts, and this has helped them learn English. Ideally, instruction utilizing the New Model would begin in pre-school and continue through high school. Imagine the quality of learning records each learner would build over a lifetime of learning, and the learning artifacts that could be stored on servers, or on DVDs for portability. Needless to say, some in-service training is needed to implement the New Model in conventional schools.

In spite of the fact that per-student expenditure in the US now exceeds $10,000 per year in many states, or $200,000 per classroom of 20 students, much of this money is spent for remediation programs, busing, administration, and other costs. In spite of the fact that something less than $5000 would be needed annually to provide first-class computer and Internet facilities in each classroom that would be needed to fully implement our New Model, such classrooms are almost non-existent at this time in the US. The picture is much worse in developing countries. Nevertheless, there are some schools and teachers that are moving in the direction of implementing our New Model. Otto Silesky's school in Costa Rica is one example, and note again the impressive results his school is achieving.

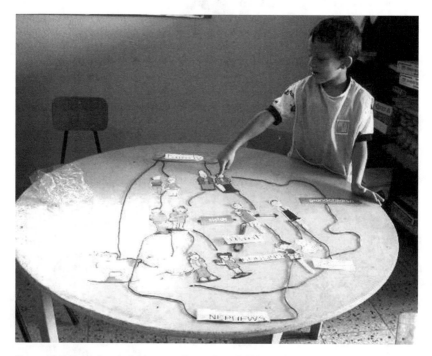

Figure 10.7 Pre-school children in Costa Rica build concept maps using images and words. This map shows family members. By L. Beirute, reproduced with permission.

In Northbridge, Massachusetts I have been working with the Principal and James Gorman to move toward implementing the New Model in Gorman's classes. Figures 8.3 and 8.4 showed examples of work his students are doing using white boards, since his class time on computers is limited. Nevertheless, Gorman and his school principal. Ms. Johnson, are working toward implementing the New Model in their school.

Valitutti (2006) and his colleagues in Urbino, Italy have been working to integrate the New Model in elementary schools. Figure 10.8 shows children working with plant leaves in their study of changes that occur in autumn. In Figure 10.9 we see children working with crayons and paper to build concept maps that are later transferred into computer-based concept maps, due to limited computer and Internet facilities.

One of the most ambitious projects underway is "Conécate al Conocimiento," which involves training all grade 4–6 teachers in 1000 public schools in Panama to use CmapTools, new technologies, and to move toward meaningful learning strategies. The project is now in its fifth year and progressing on schedule. The project has had strong support from President Torrijos and his cabinet, and they have visited project schools on several occasions. Teachers are brought to Panama City for a two-week training program and most of their school principals also participate. They have found that by the end of the two-week training program, there is little

Figure 10.8 Elementary school children in Urbino studying leaves collected on a field trip. By G. Valitutti, reproduced with permission.

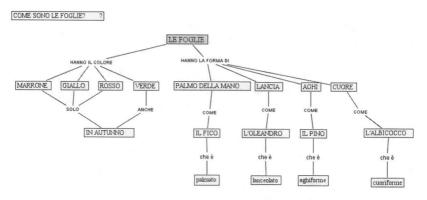

Figure 10.9 A concept map created by children in Urbino using CmapTools following study of autumn leaves. By G. Valitutti, reproduced with permission.

difference in the quality of the concept maps prepared by teachers who had never used computers prior to the training program compared with those from teachers who had prior computer experience, such as the use of email (Miller, et al., 2006; 2008). Follow-up visits to the teacher's schools to help teachers and assess progress show that while some teachers and schools still lacked the facilities to implement features of the New Model, many others were doing remarkably well. When one considers that some of the classrooms in rural Panama are outdoor classrooms such as shown in Figure 10.10, it is remarkable how far facilitation of learning is occurring by using modern technology and training teachers to use new methods. Other examples from this project are shown in Figure 10.11 and Figure 10.12. These are typical of the classrooms and activities that are occurring in all nine provinces of Panama. To the best of my knowledge, no other country has mounted such an ambitious program to bring computers, the Internet and constructivist teaching practices to almost all the elementary schools in the country. Progress of this project can be tracked at: http://www.conectate.gob.pa

It would be naïve to assume that because theoretical and empirical evidence supports the idea of schools and corporations moving to implement the New Model makes sense, this will happen in the near future. Unless we can get the kind of political leadership required for such a transformation in educating, we must be content with slow but hopefully continuing change from the current status, where the majority of learners are swimming in a sea of meaninglessness in "education" programs, to the future of education driven on solid theoretical grounds that engages all that today and tomorrow's best practices and technologies have to offer. But to borrow a phrase from the title of President Obama's book (2006), *The Audacity of Hope*, I choose to have the audacity to believe that educating in the future can be transformed into experiences that empower learners for commitment and responsibility. The

Figure 10.10 Children in rural Panama work on computers and the Internet in open classrooms. By J. Barrios, reproduced with permission.

closer we come to achieving such educating, the greater will be our chances for high levels of achievement of these goals.

The Customer as Teacher and Learner

What will be the new wave of change that flows through the corporate world? In the 1980s, it was TQM with the idea that using various strategies for systematic evaluation of customer needs, product quality, and manufacturing efficiencies could lead to enhanced productivity. To some extent, these strategies, first introduced by Deming in the United States, but implemented widely by Japanese corporations, showed promise. American companies, especially the automobile industry, sought to implement many of these strategies, and management consultant firms rushed to spread the gospel. TQM is essentially a management approach providing guidelines on how to manage people and resources. In the 1990s, a new gospel emerged: The rush was to become, in the words of Nonaka and Takeuchi (1995), the knowledge-creating company. Both application of TQM and emphasis on knowledge-creation strategies have contributed to business competitiveness. In fact, the latter movement is now very much in progress and, hopefully, this book will contribute to increased effectiveness in knowledge creation by corporations. Today

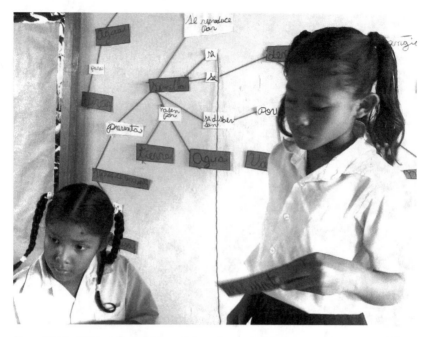

Figure 10.11 Children in Panama collaborating to build a concept map poster. These may be later transferred into computer based concept maps. By J. Barrios, reproduced with permission.

Figure 10.12 Children in Panama building concept maps using CmapTools. By J. Barrios, reproduced with permission.

the emphasis appears to be on promoting innovation, and the Lafley and Charan (2008) book epitomizes this effort.

So what does the future hold? Who will be the new leaders, and what will be the new strategies? Minkin (1995) identified 100 global trends he saw based on his experience and consulting practices. Among his predictions are that small entrepreneurs will become more numerous, with younger people and more women swelling the ranks of small business managers. J. Moore (1996) in his book, *The Death of Competition*, observed:

> Not that competition is vanishing. In fact, it is intensifying. But competition, as most of us have routinely thought of it, is dead—and any business manager who doesn't recognize this is threatened. Let me explain. The traditional way to think about competition is in terms of offers and markets. Your product or service goes up against that of your competitor, and one wins. You improve your product by listening to customers, and by investing in the processes that create it.
>
> The problem with this point of view is that it ignores the context—the environment—within which the business lies, and it ignores the need for co-evolution with others in that environment, a process that involves cooperation as well as conflict. Even excellent businesses can be destroyed by the conditions around them. They are like species in Hawaii. Through no fault of their own, they find themselves facing extinction because the ecosystem they call home is itself imploding. A good restaurant in a failing neighborhood is likely to die. A first-rate supplier to a collapsing retail chain—a Bradlees, Caldor, or Kmart—had better watch out. (p. 3)

Hamel and Prahalad (1994) in their book. *Competing for the Future*, argue that:

> Competition for the future is competition for opportunity share rather than market share. It is competition to maximize the share of future opportunities a company could potentially access within a broad opportunity arena, be that home information systems, genetically engineered drugs, financial services, advanced materials, or something else. (p. 31)

One of the methods they see as necessary to increase opportunities is to move decisively into markets, preempting the competition. For example:

> In a reversal of such [previous] misfortunes, P&G managed to preempt its Japanese rival, Kao, in the race to take super-absorbent diapers to world markets. In 1985. Kao surprised P&G by launching a technologically advanced, superabsorbent diaper in Japan. The new diaper quickly overtook Pampers as the market leader. But with little distribution or brand power outside Asia, Kao could do little to capitalize on its

innovation in global markets. Thus, P&G was able to launch its own version of a superabsorbent diaper around the world with virtually no opposition from Kao. In the end. it was P&G, more than Kao, that profited from the new diaper technology. While global distribution power alone can't substitute for a lack of competencies in other areas it is an absolutely critical multiplier of the returns to innovation. (pp. 246–247)

Another trend Minkin (1995) identified is changes in when and how we learn. He saw education and entertainment as merging, with the development of new technologies:

The decline of learning in the United States and its ripple effect on the economy and society leads many of us to believe that education can no longer be entrusted to the educational or governmental bureaucracies but instead requires a major shift in focus: The answer to when will we learn? is when "edutainment," the combining of education and entertainment, through interactive multimedia, saturates the classroom and corporate training rooms. Interactive education will be a huge business as global competition, new technology and other forces continue to provide occupational growth in areas requiring more training and education. (pp. 126–127)

Regarding the need to learn from our customers, J. Moore (1996) observed that we can learn most from early adopters. Sometimes they are the most educated, most advantaged individuals, but not always. For an example, from a relatively primitive setting:

The ideal customers are those who will tolerate a primitive version of the final offer, knowing that, even in the rudimentary form, the value is sufficient to improve their lives or businesses. Somalians nicely fit the bill. They will patiently wait days to get a phone call because the alternative is not talking to certain people at all. Moreover, they will provide useful feedback about the service and how to improve it, and they will often contribute to its improvement by creating support systems of their own. Finally, even though they are early adopter customers, they are representative enough of other sorts of customers that any information gleaned from them can be applied more broadly. (pp. 120–121)

Not all marketing specialists see the job as educating and learning from customers. Some such as Hayden (2007) "break down the marketing and sales process into a series of simple steps so you will know exactly where to begin to get clients today. It organizes the steps into a process system built around three powerful elements: effective personalized marketing strategies;

an action-oriented 28-day program; and suggestions for managing the fear, resistance, and procrastination that may hinder your marketing efforts" (p. 8).

No doubt that Hayden's methods would improve over trying to market with no or limited information, but it is hard to see where his approach would win in international competition for global markets.

It is difficult to project how satellite Internet access will affect schools and businesses in the next 10 years. Changes in capabilities and costs are changing so rapidly that the only certainty is that use of satellite Internet access will increase over time. The success of the Global Positioning System (GPS) developed by the US military and now available to all provides the information needed to identify a precise location anywhere on earth. Those who have used a GPS device in a car, plane or boat recognize how powerful this form of communication can be.

As corporations move toward seeing customers as both teachers and learners, they need to take cognizance of several principles from the theory of education presented in this book that should guide their programs. This we know about education:

1. There must be motivation to learn. No learning will take place unless the learner chooses to learn.
2. We must understand and engage the learner's existing relevant knowledge, both valid and invalid ideas.
3. We must organize the conceptual knowledge we want to teach.
4. Learning takes place in a context and we must consider what will be a facilitative context for educating.
5. Learning can be aided by a teacher who is knowledgeable and sensitive to the learner's ideas and feelings.
6. Evaluation is necessary to assess progress and further motivate the learner.

These six principles are fundamental for any substantive learning to occur. We shall review briefly the meaning of each of these principles as they pertain to marketing research and advertising programs. Each of the six principles influences action on all of the other principles, so there is an interconnectedness that needs to be recognized.

1. Motivation derives from some unsatisfied need or desire on the part of the learner. There are both thinking or cognitive aspects and feelings or affective aspects to customer's needs and desires. Market research must probe carefully how the target population for a given product or service *thinks and feels* about that product or service.

Although there are many ways to assess consumers' thoughts and feelings, the most powerful is the personal interview. The design of the interview is critical and is best done through an iterative sequence of identifying concepts and feelings that are pertinent to the product or service, concept mapping this knowledge, designing questions based on these concept maps that probe the customer's thoughts and feelings, concept mapping the thoughts and feelings of individual customers and customers taken collectively, then redesigning the interview based on the insights from the concept maps. Usually three to five iterations of this process will produce excellent interview protocols.

Zaltman and Higie (1993) at Harvard University and my students and I at Cornell University have found that a sample of 6 to 10 representative customers given carefully designed, executed and evaluated interviews can give a relatively complete and reliable picture of an individual's thoughts and feelings on any topic, product, or service for a given target population. Thus we can assess the underlying motivational factors of customers toward any product or service. The concept maps prepared from interviews can also be used to design more effective questionnaires that can be distributed to large numbers of customers and provide an additional data source. For more on these techniques, see Novak and Gowin (Chapter 7, 1984).

2. Well-designed interviews properly conducted will provide knowledge of the ideas and feelings held by customers. We must recognize that these are the conceptual glasses through which the customer sees his or her world. New information will be interpreted by the customer based on these ideas. Therefore, we need to build advertising copy and illustrations that will make sense to the customer based on the knowledge and feelings they have. However, we must be careful not to strengthen misconceptions and work toward replacing these with more valid ideas. There is a large body of literature that deals with this problem, some of this cited earlier.

3. For any product or service, it is possible to create a concept map representing the knowledge of experts and customers that is pertinent to understanding the properties, merits, and value of the product or service. This knowledge should be competently concept mapped and used as a basis for steps 1 and 2. These concept maps also help to communicate ideas between R&D teams and marketing personnel. They serve as a foundation for creative work by R&D and marketing staff.

4. *Context*, or the setting in which learning will take place, needs to be carefully considered. Copy and visuals appropriate for a package or store display may need to be quite different from those in home mailings or television. If consumer interviews are well designed and well executed, they will provide information on various contexts in which consumers learn about products or services. Lafley and Charan (2008, p. 48) describe two programs introduced by P&G in 2002: an *immersion program* wherein employees live in the homes of consumers for several days, as part of the family, and a *working it* program wherein employees work behind the counters in small shops. The success of these programs derive from the opportunity to learn from customers in a very real world context.

5. Gender, culture, race, age, education, economic status, and other customer attributes must be recognized and treated with sensitivity. A person

offended by product or service presentations as regards any of these will not be a customer, at least not for long. The source for information pertinent here is once again carefully designed and executed personal interviews and the concept maps developed from these interviews.

6. Information that provides the customer with a means to evaluate the value of a product or service needs to be provided. The customer needs a way to assess if they are getting what they want and what they are paying for. Similarly, the company needs a way to assess if they are providing what the customer wants and their comparative degree of satisfaction with the product or service.

There is, of course, much detail that could be added to the hows, whys, and wherefores for each of these ideas. Nevertheless, the items presented are complete—in terms of what we know about the basic components involved in teaching and learning with our customers. They are the essential ingredients for any corporation that wants to become an educating corporation.

The Road Ahead

Gates (1996) described well where we are and where we are likely to go in the near future as regards developments in technology and its application in business and education. What he did not discuss is what new knowledge and tools regarding the teaching and learning processes may bring, nor how the potential radical changes that will take place in how corporations create and use knowledge will change the world we live in. The latter is what I have attempted to present in this book. Gates did see education as important:

> Education is not the entire answer to the challenges presented by the Information Age, but it is part of the answer, just as education is part of the answer to a range of society's problems. H.G. Wells, who was as imaginative and forward-looking as any futurist, summed it up back in 1920. "Human history," Wells said, "becomes more and more a race between education and catastrophe." Education is society's great leveler, and any improvement in education goes a long way toward equalizing opportunity. Part of the beauty of the electronic world is that the extra cost of letting additional people use educational material is basically zero. (p. 293)

As we approach the time when any person can get any information at any time, anywhere—for little or no cost—we enter a whole new realm of possibilities for education. Yes, the invention of the printing press in 1460 made access possible to the great books for at least all of the more affluent. We now are on the brink of a period when almost everything known can be accessed—free—by almost anyone. The problem is, how do we use this potential to improve the lives of human beings the world over? As I have noted repeatedly, information does not automatically translate into knowledge, and what is required is the empowerment of people to access and use this information to construct new meanings. This is the principal challenge we face. I believe we now know many things to achieve a much higher level of meaning making by all people. At the present time, on a scale of 1 to 10, I believe most schools and corporations are only operating at a level of 2 or 3, in terms of capitalizing on what we know about knowledge, learning, ego-enhancement, and personal empowerment. There is much to be done in applying this knowledge and something like our New Model for Education more broadly, perhaps to achieve a 6 or 8 in educational effectiveness. There is also much to be done in creating new knowledge about learning and knowledge creation. My hope is that this book may contribute to this enterprise.

Appendix I
How To Build a Concept Map

1. Identify a focus question that addresses the problem, issues, or knowledge domain you wish to map. Guided by this question, identify 10 to 20 concepts that are pertinent to the question and list these. Some people find it helpful to write the concept labels on separate cards or Post-its™ so that they can be moved around. If you work with computer software for mapping, produce a list of concepts on your computer. Concept labels should be a single word, or at most two or three words.

2. Rank order the concepts by placing the broadest and most inclusive idea at the top of the map. It is sometimes difficult to identify the broadest, most inclusive concept. It is helpful to reflect on your focus question to help decide the ranking of the concepts. Sometimes this process leads to modification of the focus question or writing a new focus question.

3. Work down the list and add more concepts as needed.

4. Begin to build your map by placing the most inclusive, most general concept(s) at the top. Usually there will be only one, two, or three most general concepts at the top of the map.

5. Next select the two, three, or four subconcepts to place under each general concept. Avoid placing more than three or four concepts under any other concept. If there seem to be six or eight concepts that belong under a major concept or subconcept, it is usually possible to identify some appropriate concept of intermediate inclusiveness, thus creating another level of hierarchy in your map.

6. Connect the concepts by lines. Label the lines with one or a few linking words. The linking words should define the relationship between the two concepts so that it reads as a valid statement or proposition. The connection creates meaning. When you hierarchically link together a large number of related ideas, you can see the structure of meaning for a given subject domain.

7. Rework the structure of your map, which may include adding, subtracting, or changing superordinate concepts. You may need to do this reworking several times, and in fact this process can go on indefinitely as you gain new knowledge or new insights. This is where Post-its™ are helpful, or better still, computer software for creating maps.

8. Look for crosslinks between concepts in different sections of the map and label these lines. Crosslinks can often help to see new, creative relationships in the knowledge domain.

9. Specific examples of concepts can be attached to the concept labels (e.g., golden retriever is a specific example of a dog breed).

10. Concept maps could be made in many different forms for the same set of concepts. There is no one way to draw a concept map. As your understanding of relationships between concepts changes, so will your maps.

Appendix II
Procedures for Teaching VEE Diagramming

1. Select a laboratory or field event (or object) that is relatively simple to observe and for which one or more focus questions can be readily identified. Alternatively, a research paper with similar features can be used after all students (and the teacher) have read it carefully.
2. Begin with a discussion of the event or objects being observed. Be sure that what is identified is the event(s) for which records are made. Surprisingly, this is sometimes difficult.
3. Identify and write out the best statement of the focus question(s). Again, be sure that the focus question(s) relate to the events or objects studied and the records to be made.
4. Discuss how the questions serve to focus our attention on the specific features of the events or objects and *require* that certain kinds of records be obtained if the questions are to be answered. Illustrate how a different question about the same events or objects would require different records to be made (or a different degree of precision).
5. Discuss the source of our questions, or our choice of objects or events to be observed. Help students to see that, in general, our relevant concepts, principles, or theories guide us in choosing what to observe and what questions to ask.
6. Discuss the validity and reliability of the records. Are they facts (i.e., valid, reliable records)? Are there concepts, principles, and theories that relate to our record-making devices that assure their validity and reliability? Are there better ways to gather more valid records?
7. Discuss how we can transform our records to answer our questions. Are certain graphs, tables, or statistics useful transformations?
8. Discuss the construction of knowledge claims. Help students to see that different questions could lead to gathering different records and performing different record transformations. The result may be a whole new set of knowledge claims about the source events or objects.
9. Discuss value claims. These are value statements such as X is better than Y, or X is good, or we should seek to achieve X. Note that value claims should derive from our knowledge claims, but they are not the same as knowledge claims.

10. Show how concepts, principles, and theories are used to shape our knowledge claims and may influence our value claims.

11. Explore ways to improve a given inquiry by examining which element in the Vee seems to be the weakest link in our chain of reasoning, that is, in the construction of our knowledge and value claims.

12. Help students see that we operate with a constructivist epistemology to construct claims about how we see the world working, and not an empiricist or positivist epistemology that proves some truth about how the world works.

13. Help students see that a world view is what motivates or guides the investigator in what he or she chooses to try to understand, and controls the energy with which he or she pursues the inquiry. Scientists care about value and pursue better ways to explain rationally how the world works. Astrologers, mystics, creationists, and others do not engage in the same constructivist enterprise.

14. Compare, contrast, and discuss Vee diagrams made by different students for the same events or objects. Discuss how the variety helps to illustrate the constructed nature of knowledge.

References

Aberdene, P. (2005). *Megatrends 2010: The rise of conscious capitalism.* Charlottsville, VA: Hampton Roads Publishing Co, Inc.

Achterberg, C.L., Novak, J.D., & Gillespie, A.H. (1985). Theory-driven research as a means to improve nutrition education. *Journal of Nutrition Education,* 17(5): 179–184.

Afamasaga-Fuataĩ, K. (1998). *Learning to solve mathematics problems through concept mapping & vee mapping.* National University of Samoa, Samoa.

Afamasaga-Fuataĩ, K. (2004). Concept maps and vee diagrams as tools for learning new mathematics topics. In Canãs, A.J., Novak, J.D. & Gonãzales, F.M. (Eds.), *Concept maps: Theory, methodology, technology, Proceedings of the First International Conference on Concept Mapping* (Vol. 1, pp. 13–20). Navarra, Spain: Dirección de Publicaciones de la Universidad Pública de Navarra.

Afamasaga-Fuataĩ, K. (Ed.) (2009). *Concept mapping in mathematics: Research into practice,* New York: Springer.

Åhlberg, M., & Ahoranta, V. 2008. Concept maps and short-answer tests: Probing pupils' learning and cognitive structure. In Cañas, A., Reiska, P., Åhlberg, M., & Novak, J.D. (Eds.) (2008). *Proceedings of the Third International Conference on Concept Mapping* (Vol. 1, pp. 260–267). Tallinn, Estonia & Helsinki, Finland.

Alaiyemola, F.F., Jegede, O.J., & Okebukola, P.A.O. (1990). The effect of a metacognitive strategy of instruction on the anxiety level of students in science classes. *International Journal of Science Education,* 12(1): 95–99.

Allen, E.I., & Seaman, J. (2007). *Online nation: Five years of growth in online learning.* Needham, MA: Sloan Consortium.

American Association of University Women. (1995). *Growing smart: What's working for girls in schools,* Washington, DC: AAUW.

Anderson, J.R. (1983). *The architecture of cognition.* Cambridge, MA: Harvard University Press.

Anderson, J.R. (1990). *The adaptive character of thought.* Mahwah, NJ: Lawrence Erlbaum Associates.

Anderson, J.R. (2000). *Learning and memory: An integrated approach.* New York: John Wiley.

Argyris, C. & Schon, D. (1978). *Organizational learning: A theory of action perspective.* Reading, Mass: Addison-Wesley.

Arzi, H.J., & White, R.T. (2007). Change in teachers' knowledge of subject matter:

A 17-year longitudinal study. *Science Education.* Published online 14 December 2007 in Wiley InterScience (www.interscience.wiley.com).

Arzi, H.J. (1998). Enhancing science education through laboratory environments: More than walls, benches and widgets. In Fraser, B., & Tobin, K.G. (Eds.), *International handbook of science education* (pp. 595–608). Dordrecht, Netherlands: Kluwer Academic Publishers.

Ausubel, D.P. (1962). A subsumption theory of meaningful verbal learning and retention. *Journal of General Psychology,* 66: 213–224.

Ausubel, D.P. (1963). *The psychology of meaningful verbal learning.* New York: Grune and Stratton.

Ausubel, D.P. (1968). *Educational psychology: A cognitive view.* New York: Holt, Rinehart and Winston.

Ausubel, D.P., Novak, J.D., & Hanesian, H. (1978). *Educational psychology: A cognitive view* (2nd ed.). New York: Holt, Rinehart, and Winston. Reprinted, 1986, New York: Werbel and Peck.

Bacharach, S.B., & Mitchell, S. (1985). Strategic choice and collective action: organizational determinants of teacher militancy. *Research in Industrial Relations.*

Baranga, C.B.A. (1990). *Meaningful learning of creative writing in fourth grade with a word processing program integrated in the whole language curriculum.* Unpublished masters thesis. Ithaca, NY: Cornell University, Department of Education.

Baroody, A.J., & Benson, A.P. (2001). Early number instruction. *Teaching Children Mathematics,* 8(3).

Baroody, A.J., & Bartels, B.H. (2001). Assessing understanding in mathematics with concept mapping. *Mathematics in School,* 30(3): 1–3.

Bartlett, F.C. (1932). *Remembering.* Cambridge: Cambridge University Press.

Bascones, J., & Novak, J.D. (1985). Alternative instructional systems and the development of problem solving skills in physics, *European Journal of Science Education,* 7(2): 253–261.

Bauer, L., & Borman, K. (1988). *A reviewof educational foundations courses offered in U.S. Colleges and universities.* Unpublished manuscript, University of Cincinnati. Cited in Houston, W.R., *Handbook on teacher education.* New York: Macmillan.

Beirute, L., & Miller, N.L. (2008). Interaction between topology and semantics in concept maps: A neurolinguistic interpretation. In Cañas, A.J., Reiska, P., Åhlberg, M., & Novak, J.D. (Eds.), *Proceedings of the Third International Conference on Concept Mapping,* Vol. 2. Tallinn, Estonia & Helsinki, Finland.

Belenky, M.F., Clinchy, B., Goldberger, N.R., & Tarule, J.M. (1986). *Woman's ways of knowing: The development of self, voice, and mind.* New York: Basic Books.

Benbow, C.P., & Stanley, J.C. (1982). Consequences in high school and college of sex differences in mathematical reasoning ability: A longitudinal perspective. *American Educational Research Journal,* 14: 15–71.

Berne, E. (1964). *Games people play.* New York: Grove Press.

Best, R. (1983). *We've all got scars: What boys and girls learn in elementary school.* Bloomington: Indiana University Press.

Bierlein, L.A., and Mulholland, L.A. (1994). The promise of charter schools. *Educational Leadership,* 52: 34–35; 37–40 (September).

Bloom, B.S. (1956). *Taxonomy of educational objectives—The classification of educational goals. Handbook I: Cognitive domain.* New York: David McKay.

Bloom, B.S. (1968). *Learning for mastery, UCLA evaluation comment,* 1 (2), 1.

Bloom, B.S. (1976). *Human characteristics and school learning*. New York: McGraw-Hill.

Bloom, B.S. (1981). *All our children learning: A primer for parents, teachers, and other educators*. New York: McGraw-Hill.

Bloom, P. (2000). *How children learn the meanings of words*. Cambridge, MA: MIT press.

Bloom, P., & Weisberg, D.S. (2007). Childhood origins of adult resistance to science. *Science*, 316: 996–997. May 19.

Bonner, J.T. (1962). *The ideas of biology*. New York: Harper.

Borgman, C.L. (2007). *Scholarship in a digital age*. Cambridge, MA: MIT Press.

Bowen, B.L. (1972). *A proposed theoretical model using the work of Thomas Kuhn, David Ausubel and Mauritz Johnson as a basis for curriculum and instruction decisions in science education*. Unpublished doctoral thesis. Ithaca, NY: Cornell University, Department of Education.

Brandt, R. (1993). Overview: A consistent system. *Educational Leadership*, 51(1): 7 (September).

Bretz, S. (1994). *Learning strategies and their influence upon students' conceptions of science literacy and meaningful learning: The case of a college chemistry course for non-science majors*. Unpublished doctoral thesis. Ithaca, NY: Cornell University, Department of Education.

Bridges, E.M. (1986). *The incompetent teacher: The challenge and the response*. Philadelphia, PA: Falmer Press.

Bridges, E.M. (1992). *The incompetent teacher:Managerial responses*. Philadelphia, PA: Falmer Press.

Briggs, G., Shamma, D.A., Cañas, A.J., Carff, R., Scargle, J., & Novak, J.D. (2004). Concept maps applied to Mars exploration public outreach. In Cañas, A.J., Novak, J.D., & González, F. (Eds.), *Concept maps: Theory, methodology, technology. Proceedings of the First International Conference on Concept Mapping* (Vol. I, pp. 109–116). Pamplona, Spain: Universidad Pública de Navarra.

Brock, D.C. (Ed.), (2006). *Understanding Moore's Law: Four decades of innovation*. Philadelphia: Chemical Heritage Press.

Bronfenbrenner, U., & Ceci, S.J. (1994). Nature-nurture reconceptualized in developmental perspective: A bioecological model. *Psychological Review*, 101(4): 568–586.

Brown, A.L. (1994). The advancement of learning. *Educational Researcher*, 23(8): 4–12.

Brown, J.S., Collins, A., & Duguid, P. (1989). Situated cognition and the culture of learning. *Educational Researcher*, 18(1): 34–41.

Burton, R.F. (2005). Multiple-choice and true/false tests: myths and misapprehensions. *Assessment & Evaluation in Higher Education*, 30 (1): 65–72.

Bush, V. (1945). *Science: The endless frontier*. Washington, DC: U.S. Government Printing Office.

Buzan, T. (1974). *Use your head*. London: BBC Books.

Cañas, A.J., & Novak, J.D. (2008). Concept mapping using CmapTools to enhance meaningful learning. In Osaka, A., Shum, S.B., & Sherborne, T. (Eds.), *Knowledge cartography*. London: Springer Verlag.

Cañas, A.J., Novak, J.D., Miller, N.L., Collado, C.M., Rodríguez, M., Concepción, M., et al. (2006). Confiabilidad de una Taxonomía Topológica para Mapas Conceptuales. In Cañas, A.J., & Novak, J.D. (Eds.), *Concept maps: Theory, methodology, technology. Proceedings of the Second International Conference on Concept Mapping* (Vol. 1, pp. 153–161). San Jose, Costa Rica: Universidad de Costa Rica.

Cannon, W.B. (1932). *The wisdom of the body.* New York: W.W. Norton & Company.

Carey, S. (1985). *Conceptual change in childhood.* Cambridge. MA: MIT Press.

Cech, S.J. (2008). AP Trends: Tests soar, scores slip. *Education Week,* 27(24): 1, 13.

Ceci, S.J., & Williams, W.M. (2007). *Why aren't there more women in science? Top researchers debate the evidence.* Washington, DC: American Psychological Assosication.

Chi, M.T.H. (1983). Network representation of a child's dinosaur knowledge. *Developmental Psychology,* 19 (1): 29–39.

Chomsky, N. (1972). *Language and mind.* New York: Harcourt, Brace and Jovanovich.

Clery, D. (1994). Element 110 is created, but who spotted it first? *Science,* 266: 1479.

Clune, William (1998). *Toward a theory of systemic reform: The case of nine NSF Statewide systemic initiatives.* Madison WI: Nationals Center for Improving Science Education, Reseach Monograph No. 16.

Commoner, B. (1971). *The closing circle: Nature, man, and technology.* New York: Knopf.

Crosby, P.B. (1992). *The eternally successful organization.* New York: Mentor Books.

Cullen, J.F., Jr. (1983). *Concept learning and problem solving: The use of the entropy concept in college teaching.* Unpublished doctoral thesis. Ithaca, NY: Cornell University, Department of Education.

De Vise, D. (2008). *No single explanation for MD test score bump.* WashingtonPost.com: Web archive.

Dethier, V.G. (1962). *To know a fly.* San Francisco, CA: Holden-Day.

Devaney, Laura, (2009). Why some students choose virtual schools. *eSchool News.* P.14, January.

Diamond, A., Barnett, W.S., Thomas, J., & Munro, S. (2007). Preschool program improves cognitive control. *Science,* 318: 1887–1888, November 30.

Dingerson, L., Miner, B., Peterson, B., & Walters, S. (Eds.) (2008). *Keeping the promise: The debate over charter schools.* Milwaukee, WI: Rethinking Schools.

Donaldson, M.C. (1978). *Children's minds.* New York: Norton.

Drucker, P.F. (1993). *Post-capitalist society.* New York: Harper Business.

Dunn, J. (1987). Understanding feelings: The early stages. In Brunes, J., & Haste, H. (Eds.), *Making sense.* New York: Methuen.

Edmondson, K.M. (2000). Assessing science understanding through concept maps. In Mintzes, J.J., Wandersee, J.H., and Novak, J.D. (Eds.), *Assessing science understanding: A human constructivist view* (pp. 15–40) San Diego, CA: Academic Press.

Edmondson, K.M., & Novak, J.D. (1993). The interplay of scientific epistemological views, learning strategies, and attitudes of college students. *Journal of Research in Science Teaching,* 32 (6): 547–559.

Educational Policies Commission. (1961). *The central purpose of American education.* Washington, DC: National Education Association.

Edwards, J., & Fraser, K. (1983). Concept maps as reflectors of conceptual understanding. *Research in Science Education,* 13: 19–26.

Ellis, L., Wersinger, E.M., Field, E.M., Hetsroni, A., Pellis, S. Karadi, D.G., Geary, D., Palmer, C.T., & Hoyenga, K.B. (2008). *Sex differences: Summarizing more than a century of scientific research.* Boca Raton, FL: CRC Press.

Fedock, P.M., Zambo, R., & Cobern, W.W. (1996). The professional development of college science professors as science teachers. *Science Education,* 80(1): 5–19.

Feldsine, J.E., Jr. (1987).Distinguishing student's misconceptions from alternative conceptual frameworks through construction of concept maps. In Novak, J.D. (Ed.), *Proceedings of the second international seminar on misconceptions and educational strategies in science and mathematics.* Ithaca, NY: Cornell University, Dept. of Education.

Ferrell, W.C., Johnson, J.H., Jones, C.K., & Sapp, M. (1994). Will privatizing schools really help inner-city students of color? *Educational Leadership,* 52 (1): 72–75.

Feynman, R.P. 1985. *"Surely you must be kidding, Mr. Feynman": Adventures of a curious character.* New York: W.W. Norton.

Fields, G. (2008). The high school dropout's economic effect: Mayors go door to door, personally encouraging students to stay in the game for their own good—and for the sake of the city. *Wall Street Journal,* October 21.

Flavell, J.H. (1985). *Cognitive development* (2nd ed.). Englewood Cliffs, NJ: Prentice Hall.

Ford, K., Cañas, A., Jones, J., Stahl, H., Novak, J.D., & Adams-Weber, J. (1991). ICONKAT: An integrated constructivist knowledge acquisition tool. *Knowledge Acquisition Journal,* 3: 215–236.

Fraser, K. (1993). *Theory based use of concept mapping in organizational development: Creating shared understanding as a basis for the cooperative design of work changes and changes in working relationships,* Ph.D. dissertation, Ithaca, NY: Cornell University.

Freire, P. (1985). *The politics of education: Culture, power and liberation.* South Hadley, MA: Bergin and Garvey.

Friedman, T. (2005). *The world is flat: A brief history of the twenty-first century,* New York: Farrar, Straus & Giroux.

Fromm, E. (1956). *The art of loving.* New York: Harper & Row. New York: Avon Books edition, 1973.

Gabel, D. (1994). Learning: Alternative conceptions. In Gabel, D.L. (Ed.), *Handbook on research in science teaching* (pp. 177–210). New York: Macmillan.

Gage, N. L. (1963). *Handbook of research on teaching. A project of the American Educational Research Association.* Chicago, IL: Rand McNally.

Gamoran, A., Nystrand, M., Berends, M., & LePore, P.C. (1995). An organizational analysis of the effects of ability grouping. *American Educational Research Journal,* 32(4): 687–715, (Winter).

Gardner, H. (1983). *Frames of mind: The theory of multiple intelligences.* New York: Basic Books.

Gardner, H. (1994). *Creating minds.* New York: Basic Books.

Gates, B. (1996). *The road ahead.* New York: Penguin Books.

Gazzaniga, M. (1989). *Mind matters: How mind and brain interact to create our conscious lives.* Boston, MA: Houghton Mifflin.

Gazzaniga, M. (Ed.). (1995). *The cognitive neurosciences.* Cambridge, MA: MIT Press.

Gazzaniga, M.S. (2008). *Human: The science behind what makes us unique.* New York: Ecco.

Gazzola, V., Aziz-Zadeh, L., and Keysers, C. (2006). Empathy and the somatotopic auditory mirror system in humans. *Current Biology,* 18: 1824–1829, September 19.

Gelman, S.A., (1999). *Dialog on early childhood science, mathematics and technology education: A context for learning. Concept Development in Pre-school Children.* (http://www.project2061.org/tools/earlychild/context/gelman.htm)

Georgi, H. (1996). Quoted in, Glantz, J. (1996). How not to pick a physicist? *Science,* 274: 710–712.

Geraci, B. (1995). Local decision making: A report from the trenches. *Educational Leadership*, 35(4): 50–52. December–January.

Gerber, J.A. (1992). *Promoting excellence in elementary school teaching: Theory driven practitioners.* Unpublished doctoral dissertation. Ithaca, NY: Cornell University, Department of Education.

Getzelz, J.W., & Jackson, P.W. (1962). *Creativity and intelligence: Explorations with gifted students.* New York: Wiley.

Gilligan, C. (1982). *In a different voice: Psychology theory and women's development.* Cambridge, MA: Harvard University Press.

Glanz, J. (1996). How not to pick a physicist? *Science*, 274: 710–712. (November).

Glasser, W. (1994). *The control theory manager.* New York: HarperCollins Publishers, Inc.

Glod, M., & Turque, B. (2008). Report finds little gain from vouchers. *washington post.com*, June 17, P. B06.

Goleman, D. (1995). *Emotional intelligence: Why it can matter more than I.Q.* New York: Bantum Books.

Gonzales, F.M., and Novak, J.D. (1996). *Aprendizaje significativo: Tecnicas y aplicaciones.* Madrid: Ediciones Pedagogicas.

Goodlad, J.I. (1984). *A place called school: Prospects for the future.* New York: McGraw-Hill.

Gorman, J. (in review). Knowledge modeling and portfolios in the sciences. Submitted to *The Physics Teacher.*

Gould, S.J. (1981). *The mismeasure of man.* New York: Norton.

Gowin, D.B. (1970). The structure of knowledge. *Educational Theory*, 20 (4): 319–328.

Greeno, J.G. (1998). The situativity of knowing, learning, and research. *American Psychologist*, 53(1): 5–26, January.

Grove, E.A. (2008). Organizing the source of memory. *Science*, 319: 288–289, January 18.

Gubrud, A.R., & Novak, J. (1973). Learning achievement and the efficiency of learning the concept of vector addition at three different grade levels. *Science Education*, 57(2): 179–191.

Guilford, J.P. (1959). Three faces of intellect. *American Psychologist*, 14: 469–479.

Guilford, J.P., & Christensen, P.R. (1973). The one-way relationship between creative potential and IQ. *Journal of Creative Behavior*, 7(4): 247–252.

Guiso, L., Monte, F., Sapienza, P., & Singales, L. (2008). Culture gender and math. *Science*, 320: 1164, 30 May.

Gurley-Dilger, L.I. (1982). *Use of Gowin's vee and concept mapping strategies to teach responsibility for learning in high school biological sciences.* Unpublished doctoral thesis. Ithaca, NY: Cornell University, Department of Education.

Hagerman, H. (1966). *An analysis of learning and retention in college students and the common goldfish (Carassius auratus, Lin).* Doctoral thesis. Lafayette, IN: Purdue University.

Haidt, J. (2007). The roots of morality. *Science*, 316: 998–999, 18 May.

Halpern, D.E. (1989). *Thought and knowledge: An introduction to critical thinking*, 2nd ed. Hillsdale, NJ: Lawrence Erlbaum Associates.

Hamel, G., & Prahalad, C.K. (1994). *Competing for the future.* Boston, MA: Harvard Business School Press.

Hamilton, W., Sir (1853). *Discussions on philosophy* (2nd ed.). London: Longman, Brown, Green.

Hammer, M., & Champy, J. (1993). *Reengineering the corporation: A manifesto for business revolution.* New York, NY: HarperCollins Publishers, Inc.

Hangen, J. (1989). *Educational experience as a factor in bulimia and anorexia.* Unpublished masters thesis. Ithaca, NY: Cornell University, Department of Education.

Hanushek, E.A. (1981). Throwing money at schools. *Journal of Policy Analysis and Management,* 1: 19–41.

Hanushek, E.A. (1989). The impact of differential expenditures on school performance. *Educational Researcher,* 18(4): 45–65.

Hanushek, E.A. (1996). School resources and student performance. In Burtless, G. (Ed.), *Does money matter? The effect of school resources on student achievement and adult success.* Washington, DC: Brookings Institute Press.

Hanuschek, E.A., Costrell, R.M., & Loeb, S. (2008). What do cost functions tell us about the cost of an adequate education? *Peabody Journal of Education,* 83(2): 198–223.

Hanushek, E.A., & Raymond, M.E. (2005). Does school accountability lead to improved student performance? *Journal of Policy Analysis and Management.* 24(2): 297–327.

Harper, S.C. (2001). *The forward-focused organization: Visionary thinking and breakthrough leadership to create your company's future.* New York: American Management Association.

Harris, T. A. (1969). *I'm OK—You're OK; A practical guide to transactional analysis.* New York: Harper & Row.

Hay, D.B., & Kinchin, I.M. (2006) Using concept maps to reveal conceptual typologies. *Education and Training,* 48(2&3): 127–142.

Hayden, C.J. (2007). *Get clients now: A marketing program for professionals, consultants, and coaches.* New York: AMACOM.

Hedges, L.V., Laine, R.D., & Greenwald, R. (1994). Does money matter? A meta-analysis of studies of the effects of differential school inputs on student outcomes. *Educational Researcher,* 23 (3): 5–14.

Hegarty, S. (1996). Science, math study renews call for reform. *St. Petersburg Times,* p 1A: 10A (November 21).

Helm, H., & Novak, J.D. (1983). Overview of the international seminar on misconceptions in science and mathematics. In Helm & Novak (Eds.), *Proceedings of the international seminar on misconceptions in science and mathematics* (pp. 1–4). Ithaca, NY: Cornell University, Department of Education.

Herman, J.L., Aschbacher, P.R., & Winters, L. (1992). *A practical guide to alternative assessment.* Alexandria, VA: Association for Supervision and Curriculum Development.

Herrigel, E. (1973). *Zen in the art of archery.* New York: Vintage Books. Translated by R.F.C. Hull.

Herrnstein, R.J., & Murray, C. (1994). *The bell curve.* New York: Free Press.

Hibbard, K.M., & Novak, J.D. (1975). Audio-tutorial elementary school science instruction as a method for studying of children's concept learning: Particulate nature of matter. *Science Education,* 59(4): 559–570.

Higgins, J.M. (1995). *Innovate or evaporate.* Winter Park, FL: The New Management Publishing Co.

Hoff, D.J. (2008). More schools facing sanctions under NCLB. *Education Week*

Online, Dec. 19. http://www.edweek.org/ew/articles/2008/12/18/16ayp.h28.html? tmp=206215354

Hoffman, B. (1962). *The tyranny of testing*. New York: Crowell-Collier Press.

Hoffman, R.R., Coffey, J.W., Ford, K.M., & Carnot, M. (2001, October) STORM-LK: A human-centered knowledge model for weather forecasting. In *Proceedings of the 45th Annual Meeting of the Human Factors and Ergonomics Society*, Santa Monica, CA: HFES.

Hoffman, R.R., Coffey, J.W., Ford, K.M. and Novak, J.D. (2006). A method for eliciting, preserving, and sharing the knowledge of forecasters. *Weather and Forecasting*, 21: 416–428.

Hofstadter, D. (2007). *I am a strange loop*. New York: Basic Books.

Hogan, K., & Pressley, M. (Eds.). (1997). *Scaffolding student learning: Instructional approaches and issues*. Cambridge, MA: Brookline.

Holden, C. (1992). Study flunks science and math tests. *Science*, 258: 541, 23 (October).

Houston, W.R. (Ed.). (1990). *Handbook of research on teacher education*. New York: Macmillan.

Howe, K.R. (1995). Wrong problem, wrong solution. *Educational Leadership*, 56(6): 22–23 (March).

Hughes, B.F. (1986). *Knowledge, beliefs and actions of Elmira Water customers related to groundwater, contamination of groundwater*. Unpublished M.S. Thesis, Ithaca, NY: Cornell University.

Huston, L. (2004). Personal communication.

Huston, L., & Sakkab, N. (March, 2006). Connect and develop: Inside Procter & Gamble's new model for innovation. *Harvard Business Review*, 84(3): 58–66.

Hyde, J.S. (1991). How large are cognitive gender differences? *American Psychologist*, 36(8): 892–901.

Hyde, J.S., Lindburg, S.M., Linn, M.C., Ellis, A.B., & Williams, C.C. (2008). Gender characteristics characterize math performance. *Science*, 321: 494–495, 25 July.

Ichijo, K., & Nonaka, I. (Eds.) (2007). *Knowledge creation and management: New challenges for managers*. New York: Oxford University Press.

Jensen, A.R. (1969). How much can we boost IQ and scholastic achievement? *Harvard Educational Review*, 39: 1–123.

Johnson, D.W., Johnson, R.T., Holubec, E.J. (1988). *Cooperation in the classroom* (Revised Ed). Edina, MN: Interaction Book Co.

Jonassen, D.H., Beissner, K., & Yacci, M. (1993). *Structural knowledge: Techniques for representing, conveying, and acquiring structural knowledge*. Hillsdale, NJ: Lawrence Erlbaum Associates.

Jubak, J. (2009). US living standards in jeopardy. *Jubak's Journal*, 16 Jan, Access at: http://articles.moneycentral.msn.com/Investing/JubaksJournal/us-dilemma-how-to-grow-faster.aspx

Juma, C., & Moyer, E. (2008). Broadband Internet for Africa. *Science*, 320: 1261, 6 June.

Kaestle, C.F. (1993). The awful reputation of education research. *Educational Researcher*, 22(1): 21–31.

Kahle, J.B., Douglas, C.B., & Nordland, F.H. (1976) An analysis of learner efficiency when individualized and group instructional formats are utilized with disadvantaged students. *Science Education*, 60(2): 245–250.

Kahn, K.M. (1994). *Concept mapping as a strategy for teaching and developing the Caribbean Examinations Council (CXC) mathematics curriculum in a secondary school*.

Unpublished Ph.D. thesis. Barbados, W.I.: Faculty of Education, The University of the West Indies.

Kamin, L. (1972). *The science and politics of IQ.* Potomac, MD: Lawrence Erlbaum Associates.

Kaminski, J., Stoutsky, V.M., & Hackler, A.F. (2008). The advantage of abstract examples in learning math. *Science,* 370: 454–455, 25 April.

Kao, J. (2007). *Innovation nation: How America is losing its innovative edge, why it matters, and how we can get it back.* New York, Free Press.

Katzenbach, J.R. (1995). *Real change leaders.* New York: Times Books.

Keating, D.P. (1984). The emperor's new clothes: The "new look" in intelligence research. In Sternberg, R.J. (Ed.), *Advances in the psychology of human intelligence* (Vol. 3, pp. 221–254). Hillsdale, NJ: Lawrence Erlbaum Associates.

Keddie, N. (Ed.). (1973). *The myth of cultural deprivation.* Baltimore, MD: Penguin Books.

Keller, E.F. (1983). *A feeling for the organism: The life and work of Barbara McClintock.* New York: W.H. Freeman.

Keller, E.F. (1985). *Reflections on gender and science.* New Haven, CT: Yale University Press.

Kerr, P. (1988). *A conceptualization of learning, teaching and research experiences of women scientists and its implications for science education.* Unpublished doctoral thesis. Ithaca, NY: Cornell University, Department of Education.

Kilts, J.A., Manfredi, J.F., & Lorber, R. (2007). *Doing what matters: How to get results that make a difference: The revolutionary old-school approach.* New York: Crown.

Kinchin, I. (2001). If concept mapping is so helpful to learning biology, why aren't we all doing it? *International Journal of Science Education,* 23(12): 1257–1269.

Kinchin, I.M. (2006) Concept mapping, PowerPoint, and a pedagogy of access. *Journal of Biological Education,* 40(2): 79–83.

Kinchin, I.M., & Hay, D.B. (2005) Using concept maps to optimize the composition of collaborative student groups: A pilot study. *Journal of Advanced Nursing,* 51(2): 182–187.

Kinchin, I.M., & Cabot, L.B. (2007) Using concept mapping principles in PowerPoint. *European Journal of Dental Education,* 11(4): 194–199.

Kinchin, I.M., DeLeij, F.A.A.M., & Hay, D.B. (2005) The evolution of a collaborative concept mapping activity for undergraduate microbiology students. *Journal of Further and Higher Education,* 29(1): 1–14.

Kirschner, P.A., Sweller, J., & Clark, R.E. (2006). Why minimal guided instruction does not work: An analysis of constructivist, problem based, experiential, and inquiry based learning. *Educational Psychologist,* 41(20): 75–86.

Kitchener, R.F. (1986). *Piaget's theory of knowledge: Genetic epistemology & scientific reason.* New Haven, CT: Yale University Press.

Klausmeier, H.J., & Harris, C.W. (1966). *Analysis of concept learning.* New York: Academic Press.

Koshland, D.E. (2007). The Cha-cha-cha theory of scientific discovery. *Science,* 317: 761–762, August 10.

Kotter, J.P. (2002). *The heart of change: Real life stories of how people change their organizations.* Boston, MA: Harvard Business School Publishing.

Kouzes, J., & Posner, B.Z. (2006). *A leader's legacy.* San Francisco, Jossey-Bass.

Kozulin, A. (1990). *Vygotsky's psychology: A biography of ideas.* New York: Harvester Wheatsheaf.

Krajcik, J., Spitulnik, M.W., & Zembal, C. (1998). Using hypermedia to represent student understanding: Science learners and preservice teachers. In Mintzes, J., Wandersee, J., & Novak, J.D. (Eds.), *Teaching science for understanding* (pp. 229–259). New York: Academic Press.

Kuhn, D. (2000). Metacognitive development. *Current Developments in Cognitive Science,* 9: 178–181.

Kuhn, T.S. (1962). *The structure of scientific revolutions.* Chicago, IL: University of Chicago Press.

Kuncel, N.R., & Hezlett, S.A. (2007). Standardized tests predict graduate students' success. *Science,* 315: 1080–1081, February 23.

Lafley, A.G., & Charan, R. (2008). *Game changer: Now you can drive revenue growth and profit growth with innovation.* New York: Crown.

Lakoff, G., & Johnson, M. (1980). *Metaphors we live by.* Chicago, IL: University of Chicago Press.

Lancaster, K.J., Smiciklas-Wright, H., Ahern, F., Achterberg, C., & Taylor-Davis, S. (1997) Evaluation of a nutrition newsletter by older adults. *Journal of Nutrition Education,* 29 (3): 145–151 (May).

Lawler, A. (1994). NSF takes leap into school reform. *Science,* 266: 1936–1938, 23 (December).

Lewis, M. (1995). Self conscious emotions. *American Scientist,* 83 (January–Febraury), 68–78.

Lieberman, M.D., & Eisenberger, N.I. (2009). Pains and pleasures of social life. *Science,* 323: 890–891, February 12.

Likert, R. (1932). A technique for measurement of attitudes. *Archives of Psychology,* 40 (whole issue).

Linn, M.C., & Hsi, S. (2000). *Computers, teachers, and peers: Science learning partners.* Mahwah, NJ: Lawrence Erlbaum Associates.

Linn, M.C., Davis, E.A., & Bell, P. (Eds.) (2004). *Internet environments for science education.* Mahwah, NJ: Lawrence Erlbaum Associates.

Lutz, W., Cuaresma, J.C., & Sanderson, W. (2008). The demography of educational attainment and economic growth. *Science,* 319: 1047–1048 (February 22).

Macnamara, J.T. (1982). *Names for things: A study of human learning.* Cambridge, MA: MIT Press.

Mandler, G. (1967). Verbal learning: Introduction. In Mandler, G., Mussen, P., Kogan, K., & Wallach, M.A., *New Directions in Psychology III,* by pp. 3–50). New York: Holt, Rhinehart, and Winston.

Marshall, H., & McCombs, B.L. (1995). Learner-centered psychological principles: Guidelines for the teaching of educational psychology in teacher education programs. *NEP 15- Newsletter for Educational Psychologists,* 19 (1): 4–8.

Marshall, R., & Tucker, M. (1992). *Thinking for a living: Education and the wealth of nations.* New York: Basic Books.

Martin, D. (1993). *Team think: Using the sports connection to develop, motivate and manage a winning business team.* New York: Penguin Books—Dutton.

Martin, M., Miller, G., & Delago, J. (1995). Portfolio performance: Research results from California's Golden State Examinations science portfolio project. *The Science Teacher,* 62 (1): 50–54, (January).

Martin, B.L., Mintzes, J.J., & Clavijo, I.E. (2000). Restructuring knowledge in biology: Cognitive processes and metacognitive reflections, *International Journal of Science Education* 32(3): 303–323.

Marton, F., & Säljö, R. (1976a) On qualitative differences in learning, 1: Outcome and process. *British Journal of Educational Psychology*, 46: 4–11.

Marton, F., & Säljö, R. (1976b) On qualitative differences in learning, 2: Outcome as a function of the learner's conception of the task. *British Journal of Educational Psychology*, 46: 115–27.

Maslow, A.H. (1984). *Motivation and personality.* New York: Harper & Row.

Mathews, J. (2008). Few solutions in book on charters. *Washington Post.com*, May 6, p. 1.

Matthews, G.B. (1980). *Philosophy and the young child.* Cambridge, MA: Harvard University Press.

Matthews, G.B. (1984). *Dialogues with children.* Cambridge, MA: Harvard University Press.

Matthews, L. (1995). *Gravitropic responses of five maize Zea mays.* Unpublished Ph.D. study. Ithaca, NY: Department of Education, Cornell University.

Matus, R. (2009). It takes a lot to dismiss a teacher. *St. Petersburg Times*, (March 29), pp. 1A, 6–7A.

Mayer, R.E. (2004). Should there be a three-strikes rule against discovery learning? *American Psychologist*, 59(1): 14–19.

Mayeroff, M. (1972). *On caring.* New York: Harper & Row (1971). New York: Barnes & Noble Books (1974). New York: Harper Perennial (1990).

Mazur, J.M. (1989). *Using concept maps in therapy with substance abusers in the context of Gowin's theory of education.* Unpublished masters thesis. Ithaca, NY: Cornell University, Department of Education.

McGrory, K. (2009). *Report: Costly plan failed to improve schools.* Miami Herald, http://www.miamiherald.com/news/miami-dade/story/1049341.html

Mervis, J., (2007a). Researchers fault US report critiquing education programs. *Science*, 316: 1267 (June 1).

Mervis, J. (2007b). US expert panel sees algebra as key to improvements in math. *Science*, 318: 1534–35 (December 7).

Miller, G.A. (1956). The magical number seven, plus or minus two: Some limits on our capacity for processing information. *Psychological Review*, 63: 81–97.

Miller, G. (2007a). A surprising connection between memory and imagination. *Science*, 315: 312 (January 19).

Miller, G. (2007b). All together now—pull. *Science*, 317: 1339–1340 (September 7).

Miller, G. (2008). The roots of Morality. *Science*, 320: 734–737 (May 9).

Miller, N.L., Cañas, A.J., & Novak, J.D. (2006). Preconceptions regarding concept maps held by Panamanian teachers. In Cañas, A.J., & Novak, J.D. (Eds.), *Concept maps: Theory, methodology, technology. Proceedings of the Second International Conference on Concept Mapping* (Vol. 1, pp. 469–476). San José, Costa Rica: Universidad de Costa Rica.

Miller, N.L., & Cañas, A.. (2008). A semantic scoring rubric for concept maps: Design and reliability. In Cañas, A.J., Reiska, P., Åhlberg, M. & Novak, J.D. (Eds.), *Concept mapping: Connecting educators. Proceedings of the Third International Conference on Concept Mapping* (Vol. 1, pp. 60–67). Tallinn, Estonia: Tallinn University.

Ministry of Education and Science, Spain. (1989). *Li̇bio blanco la reforma del sistema educativo* (White Book for the Reform of the Educational System). Madrid, Spain: Ministry of Education.

Minkin, B.H. (1995). *Future in sight*. New York, NY: Macmillian Co.

Mintzes, J., Wandersee, I., & Novak, J. (Eds.) (1998). *Teaching science for understanding: A human constructivist view*. San Diego: Academic Press.

Mintzes, J., Wandersee, I., & Novak, J. (Eds.) (2000). *Assessing science understanding: A human constructivist view*. San Diego: Academic Press.

Moll, L. C. (Ed.). (1990). *Vygotsky and education: Instructional implications and applications of sociohistorical psychology*. Cambridge, UK, and New York: Cambridge University Press.

Molnar, A. (1994). Education for profit: A yellow brick road to nowhere. *Educational Leadership*, 52 (1): 66–71 (September).

Molnar, A. (1995). The bell curve: For whom it tolls. *Education Leadership*, 52(7): 69–70 (April).

Moloney, W.J. (1996). Reading at the 8th-grade level in college. *St. Petersburg Times*, p. 18A (December 11).

Mooney, J. (2008). Test scores plummet as State raises standards. *The Star-Ledger* (October 26).

Moore, J.F. (1996). *The death of competition*. New York, NY: Harper Collins Publishers, Inc.

Moore, R. (1996). Teachers unions. *The American Biology Teacher*, 58 (5): 260–262.

Moreira, M.M. (1977). *The use of concept maps and the five questions in a Brazilian foreign language classroom: Effects on communication*. Unpublished doctoral thesis. Ithaca, NY: Cornell University, Department of Education.

Motz, L.L., Biehle, J. and West, S.S. (2007). *NSTA guide to planning school science facilities, Second Edition*. Arlington, VA: NSTA Press.

Mrozowski, J., (2008). DPS grade rates low for black males. *detnews.com*, July 28.

Muller, H.J. (1958). *The loom of history*. New York: Harper.

National Commission on Excellence in Education. (1983). *A nation at risk: The imperative for educational reform*. Washington, DC: US Government Printing Office.

National Research Council (NRC). (1996) *National science education standards*. Washington, DC: National Academy Press.

Nicolini, D., & Meznar, M.B. (1995). The social construction of organizational learning: Conceptual and practical issues in the field. *Human Relations*, 48 (7): 727–746.

Niedenthal, P.M. (2007). Embodying emotion. *Science*, 316: 1002–1005 (May 18).

Nonaka, I., & Takeuchi, H. (1995). *The knowledge-creating company*. New York: Oxford University Press.

Nonaka, I., & Toyama, R. (2007). Why do firms differ? In Ichijo, K., & Nonaka, I. (Eds.), *Knowledge creation and management: New challenges for managers*. New York: Oxford University Press.

Nordland, F.H., Lawson, A.E., & Kahle, J.B. (1974). A study of levels of concrete and formal reasoning ability in disadvantaged junior and senior high school science students. *Science Education*, 58 (4): 569–575.

Norton, A. (2008). *Self confident children may be healthier as adults*. New York: Reuters Health (June 19).

Novak, J.D. (1958). An experimental comparision of a conventional and a project centered method of teaching a college general botany course. *Journal of Experimential Education*, 26: 217–230.

Novak, J.D. (1994). A view on the current status of Ausubel's Assimilation theory of learning, or "La teoria dell'appendimento per assimilation di D. P. Ausubel. Le proopsettive attuali." *CADMO (Giornal Italiano di Pedagogoa sperimentale, Didattica Doc imologia, Tecnologia dell'Instrusione)*, 2(4): 7–23. Also in Novak, J.D. (Ed.), *Proceeding of the Third International Seminar on Misconceptions and educational Strategies in Science and Mathematics* (August 1–4, 1993). Published electronically, Internet. Access: misconceptions.mannlib.cornell.edu (users need to have access to GOPHER program).

Novak, J.D. (1963). What should we teach in biology? *NABT News and Views*, 7(2): 1. Reprinted in *Journal of Research in Science Teaching*, 1(3): 241–243.

Novak, J.D. (1964). Importance of conceptual schemes for science teaching. *The Science Teacher*, 31(6): 10.

Novak, J.D. (1969). A case study of curriculum change: Science since PSSC. *School Science and Mathematics*, 69: 374–384 (May).

Novak, J.D. (1972). Facilities for secondary school science teaching. *The Science Teacher*, 39(3): 2–13.

Novak, J.D. (1977a). *A theory of education*. Ithaca, NY: Cornell University Press.

Novak, J.D. (1977b). An alternative to Piagetian psychology for science and mathematics education. *Science Education*, 61(4): 453–477.

Novak, J.D. (1983). Can metalearning and metaknowledge strategies to help students learn how to learn serve as a basis for overcoming misconceptions? In Helm, H., & Novak, J.D. (Eds.), *Proceedings of the International Seminar on Misconceptions in Science and Mathematics* (pp. 118–130). Ithaca, NY: Cornell University.

Novak, J.D. (1987). *Proceedings of the Second International Seminar on Misconceptions and Educational Strategies in Science and Mathematics Conference, June 1987*. Ithaca, NY: Department of Education, Cornell University.

Novak, J.D. (1991). Clarify with concept maps. *The Science Teacher*, 58(7): 45–49.

Novak, J.D. (1993). Human constructivism: A unification of psychological and epistemological phenomena in meaning making. *International Journal of Personal Construct Psychology*, 6: 167–193.

Novak, J.D. (1996a). Personal interview with a senior manager of a prominent accounting firm.

Novak, J.D. (1996b). Personal interview with a senior executive of a firm in the construction industry.

Novak, J.D. (1997). Personal interview with a senior airline captain.

Novak, J.D. (2002). Meaningful learning: The essential factor for conceptual change in limited or appropriate propositional hierarchies (LIPHs) leading to empowerment of learners. *Science Education*, 86(4): 548–571.

Novak. J.D. (2004). Reflections on a half century of thinking in science education and research: Implications from a twelve-year longitudinal study of children's learning. *Canadian Journal of Science, Mathematics, and Technology Education*, 4(1): 23–41.

Novak, J.D. (2005). Results and implications of a 12-year longitudinal study of science concept learning. *Research in Science Education*, 35(1): 23–40.

Novak, J.D., & Abrams, R. (eds.). (1993). *Proceedings of the Third International Seminar on Misconceptions and Educational Strategies in Science and Mathematics*. Held at Cornell University in Ithaca, NY, on August 1–4, 1993.

Novak, J.D., & Cañas, A.J. (2006a). *The theory underlying concept maps and how to construct them* (Technical Report No. IHMC CmapTools 2006–01). Pensacola, FL: Institute for Human and Machine Cognition.

Novak, J.D., & Cañas, A.J. (2006b). The origins of the concept mapping tool and the continuing evolution of the tool. *Information Visualization Journal*, 5(3): 175–184.

Novak, J.D., & Gowin, D.B. (1984). *Learning how to learn*. New York: Cambridge University Press.

Novak, J.D., Gowin, D.B., & Johansen, G.T. (1983). The use of concept mapping and knowledge Vee mapping with junior high school science students. *Science Education*, 67(5): 625–645.

Novak, J.D., & Iuli, R.I. (1995). Meaningful Learning as the foundation for constructivist epistemology. *Proceedings of the Third International History, Philosophy and Science Teaching Conference*, Vol. 2. Minneapolis, MN: University of Minnesota, College of Education.

Novak, J.D., & Musonda, D. (1991). A twelve-year longitudinal study of science concept learning. *American Educational Research Journal*, 28(1): 117–153.

Novak, J.D., & Wandersee, J.H. (1990). Co-Editors, Perspectives on concept mapping: Special issue of *Journal of Research in Science Teaching*, 28(1) (January 1991). New York: John Wiley & Sons.

Nussbaum, J., & Novak, J.D. (1976). An assessment of children's concepts of earth utilizing structured interviews. *Science Education*, 60(4): 535–550.

Ohio State University (2008, August 5). Teacher-student relationships key to learning health and sex education. *ScienceDaily*. http://www.sciencedaily.com/releases/2008/08/080804114258.ht

Okada, A. (2008). Personal communication.

O'Neil, J. (1995). On lasting school reform: A conversation with Ted Sizer. *Educational Leadership*, 52(5): 4–9 (April).

O'Neil, J. (1995). On schools as learning organizationa: A conversation with Peter Senge. *Educational Leadership*, 52 (7): 20–23 (February).

Paavola, S., Lipponen, L., & Hakkarainen, K. (2004). Models of innovative knowledge communities and three metaphors of learning. *Review of Educational Research* 74(4): 557–576.

Page, C. (2009). Youth crime surge. *Washington Times*, Jan. 10. http://www.washingtontimes.com/news/2009/jan/10/youth-crime-surge/

Papalia, D.E. (1972). The status of several conservation abilities across the life span. *Human Development*, 15: 229–243.

Penfield, W. (1952). Memory mechanisms. A.M.A. *Archives of Neurology and Psychiatry*, 67: 178–198.

Perkins, D.N. (1992). *Smart schools: Better thinking and learning for every child*. New York, NY: The Free Press.

Peters, T.J. (1992). *Liberation management*. New York, NY: Alfred A. Knopf, Inc.

Peters, T.J. (1994). *The Thomas Peters seminar: Crazy times call for crazy organizations*. New York, NY: Vintage Books.

Piaget, J. (1926). *The language and thought of the child*. New York: Harcourt Brace.

Piaget, J. (1972). *Psychology and epistemology*. New York: The Viking Press. Translated by A. Rosin.

Pines, A.L., Novak, J.D., Posner, G.J., & VanKirk, J. (1978). *The clinical interview: A method for evaluating cognitive structure* (Research Report #6). Ithaca, NY: Department of Education, Cornell University.

Pinker, S., (2007). *The stuff of thought: Language as a window into human nature*. New York: Viking Penguin.

Polyani, M. (1966). *The tacit dimension*. New York: Doubleday.

Postlethwait, S.N., Novak, J.D., & Murray, H.T., Jr. (1969). *The audio-tutorial approach to learning through independent study and integrated experiences* (2nd ed.). Minneapolis, MN: Burgess.

Postlethwait, S.N., Novak, J.D., & Murray, H.T., Jr. (1972). *The audio-tutorial approach to learning through independent study and integrated experiences* (3rd ed.). Minneapolis, MN: Burgess.

Prestowitz, C.V., Jr. (1988). *Trading places*. New York: Basic Books.

Puckett, M.B., & Black, J.K. (1994). *Authentic Assessment of the young child: Celebrating development and learning*. New York: Macmillan.

Quinn, H.J., Mintzes, J.J., & Laws, R.A. (2003/2004). Successive concept mapping: Assessing understanding in college science classes, *Journal of College Science Teaching*, 3(3): 12–16.

Resnick, L., and Nolan, K. (1995). Where in the world are world-class standards. *Educational Leadership*, 52 (6): 6–10 (March).

Richardson, V. (Ed.). (2001). *Handbook of research on teaching* (4th Ed.). Washington, DC: American Educational Research Association

Richland, L.E., Osnat, Z., & Holyoak, K.J. (2007). Cognitive supports for analogies in the mathematics classroom. *Science*, 316: 1128–1129 (May 25).

Ridley, D.R., & Novak, J.D. (1983). Sex-related differences in high school science and mathematics Enrollments: Do they give males a critical headstart toward science and math-related careers? *Alberta Journal of Educational Research*, 29(4): 308–318.

Ripple, R.E., & Rockcastle, V.N. (Eds.). (1964). *Piaget rediscovered*. Ithaca, NY: Department of Education, Cornell University.

Robinson, G.E., Fernald, R.D. & Clayton, D.F. (2008). Genes and social behavior. *Science*, 322: 896–900 (November 7).

Roland, D. (2009). *Contract shools*. Posted in: http://www.showmedaily.org/2009/01/contract-schools.html

Rowan, B. (1994). Comparing teachers' work with work in other occupations: Notes on the professional status of teaching. *Educational Researcher*, 23 (6): 4–21.

Rowe, M.B. (1974). Wait-time and rewards as instructional variables: Their influence on Learning, Logic and Fate Control. I. Wait-time. *Journal of Research in Science Teaching*, 11 (2): 81–94.

Ruiz-Primo, M.A. (2000). On the use of concept maps as an assessment tool in science: What have we learned so far? *Revista Electronica de Investogacion Educativa*, 2(1).

Ruiz-Primo, M.A., Schultz, S.E., Li, M., & Shavelson, R.J. (1998). *Comparison of the reliability and validity of scores from two concept mapping techniques* (No. 492). Los Angeles, CA: Center for the Study of Evaluation, Standards and Student Testing.

Ruiz-Primo, M.A., Schultz, S.E., Li, M., & Shavelson, R.J. (2001). Comparison of the reliability and validity of scores from two concept-mapping techniques. *Journal of Research in Science Teaching*, 38(2): 260–278.

Ruiz-Primo, M.A., & Shavelson, R.J. (1996). Problems and issues in the use of concept maps in science assessment. *Journal of Research in Science Teaching*, 33: 569–6.

Ryle, G. (1949). *Collected papers*, Vol. II. Critical Essays. London: Hutchinson.

Sadler, P.M. (1995). Personal communication.

Sadler, P.M. (1995). Astronomy's conceptual hierarchy. In Perry, J. (Ed.), *Astronomy education: Current developments, future coordination*. San Francisco: Astronomical Society of the Pacific, pp. 46–60.

Saha, L., & Dwarkin, G. (Eds.). (2009). *International handbook of research on teachers and teaching* (Springer International Handbooks of Education.) London: Springer.

Sarason, S.B. (1993). *The predictable failure of educational reform.* San Francisco, CA: Jossey-Bass.

Schmitt, H.H. (2006). *Return to the Moon: Exploration, enterprise, and energy in the human settlement of space.* New York: Praxis Publishing, Ltd.

Schwab, J.J. (1973). The practical 3: Translation into curriculum. *School Review,* 81(4): 501–522. [See Chapter 1, p. 1.3]

Sedlak, M.W., Wheeler, C.W., Pullin, D.C., & Cusick, P.A. (1986). *Selling students short.* New York: Teachers College Press.

Senge, P.M. (1990). *The fifth discipline: The art and practice of the learning organization.* New York: Doubleday.

Service, R.E. (2008). Eyeing oil, synthetic biologists mine microbes for black gold. *Science,* 322: 522–523 (October 24).

Service, R.E. (2009). Is silicone's reign nearing an end? *Science,* 323: 1000–1002 (February 20).

Shavelson, R.J., Lang, H., & Lewin, B. (1994). *On concept maps as potential "authentic" assessments in science.* Los Angeles: CRESST.

Shavelson, R.J., & Ruiz-Primo, M.A. (2000). On the psychometrics of assessing science understanding. In Mintzes, J., Wandersee, J., & Novak, J. (Eds.), *Assessing science understanding* (pp. 304–341). San Diego: Academic Press.

Shayer, M., & Adey, P. (1981). *Towards a science of science teaching: Curriculum development and curriculum demand.* London, UK: Heinemann Educational Books.

Shuell, T.J. (1993). Toward an integrated theory of teaching and learning. *Educational Psychologist,* 28(4): 291–311.

Shulman, L.S., & Keislar, E.R. (Eds.). (1966). *Learning by discovery.* Chicago: Rand McNally.

Silesky, O. (2008). *Concept maps and standardized tests.* PowerPoint presentation, Sept. 23, Tallinn, Estonia.

Simon, H.A. (1974). How big is a chunk? *Science,* 183(8): 482–488.

Slavin, R.E. (1982). *Cooperative learning: Student teams.* Washington, DC: NEA Professional Library.

Smith, B.E. (1992). Linking theory and practice in teaching basic nursing skills. *Journal of Nursing Education,* 31(1): 16–23.

Songer, N.B., & Linn, M.C. (1991). How do students' views of science influence knowledge integration? *Journal of Research in Science Teaching,* (28): 761–784.

Sonnert, G., and Holton, G. (1996). Career patterns of women and men in the sciences. *American Scientist,* 84: 63–71 (February).

Stansbury, M. (2008). Students to their schools: "Got Game?". *eSchool News,* 11(5): 9.

Sakal, K.L. (2005). Language acquisition and brain development. *Science,* 310: 815–819 (November).

Schon, D. (1983). *The reflective practitioner: How professionals think in action.* New York: Basic Books.

Stecklow, S. (1994). Critical thought: Acclaimed educational reform developed by Dr. Sizer are popular but unproved. *Wall Street Journal,* pp. A1, A4, (December 28).

Sternberg, R.J. (1986). *The triarchic mind*. New York: Penguin Books.

Sternberg, R.J. (1988). *The nature of creativity*. New York: Cambridge University Press.

Sternberg, R.J. (1996a). *Successful intelligence*. New York: Simon & Schuster.

Sternberg, R.J. (1996b). Myths, countermyths, and truths about intelligence. *Educational Researcher*, 25 (2): 11–16 (March).

Sternberg, R.J. (2008). *Cognitive psychology*. Belmont, CA: Wadsworth.

Suppes, P., & Ginsberg, R. (1963). A fundamental property of all-or-none models, binomial distribution of respnses prior to conditioning, with application to concept formation in children. *Psychological Review*, 70: 139–161.

Swanson, D.B., Geoffrey, R.N., & Linn, R.L. (1995). Performance-Based Assessment: Lessons from the health professions. *Educational Researcher*, 24(5): 5–11, 35 (June/July).

Sweeney, E. (2009). The school bully: Does it run in families? *Science News*, August 5. Retrieved February 18, 2009, from http://www.sciencedaily.com-/releases/2008/08/080804111636.htm

Swiss, D. (1996). *Women breaking through*. Princeton, NJ: Petersons/Pacesetter Books.

Szabo, A., and N. Hastings. (2000). Using IT in the undergraduate classroom: Should we replace the blackboard with PowerPoint? *Computers and Education*, 35: 175–87.

Talbot, David. (2008) Una Laptop por Nino. *Technology Review*. April, 2008. http://www.technologyreview.com/business/20572/?a=f

Tannen, D. (1994). *Talking from 9 to 5: How women's and men's conversational styles affect who gets heard, who gets credit, and what gets done at work*. New York, NY: William Morrow and Co., Inc.

Tapscott, D., & Williams, A.D. (2006) *Wikinomics: How mass collaboration changes everything*. New York: Penguin Group.

Taylor, D. (1991). *Learning denied*. Portsmouth, NJ: Heinemann.

Thaler, L.K., and Koval, R. (2006). *The power of nice: How to negotiate so everyone wins, Especially you!* New York: Currency Books.

The American Association for the Advancement of Science (AAAS). (1993), *Benchmarks for Science Literacy*. New York: Oxford University Press.

Thorndike, E.L. (1922). The effect of changed data upon reasoning. *Journal of Experimental Psychology*, 5: 33–38.

Toffler, A. (1971). *Future shock*. New York: A Bantam Book, Random House.

Toulmin, S. (1972). *Human understanding. volume 1: The collective use and evolution of concepts*. Princeton, NJ: Princeton University Press.

Trifone, J.D. (2005).To what extent can concept mapping motivate students to take a more meaningful approach to learning biology? *Science Education Review*, 5(4): 122–145.

Tronto, J.C. (1993). *Moral boundaries: A political argument for an ethic of care*. London: Routledge, Chapman and Hall.

Truesdale, V. (2008). Investing in healthy teachers. *Education*, 50(10): October. http://www.ascd.org/publications/newsletters/education_update/oct08/vol50/num10/Investing_in_Healthy_Teachers.aspx

Tsien, J.Z. (2007). The memory. *Scientific American*, July: http://www.sciam.com/article.cfm?id=the-memory-code

Tufte, E.R. (2003). *The Cognitive Style of PowerPoint*. Cheshire, CT: Graphics Press LLC.

Tyler, R.W. (1977). Foreword. In Novak, J.D., *A Theory of Education* (pp. 7–8). Ithaca, NY: Cornell University Press.

University of Illinois at Urbana-Champaign (2009). *Public schools outperform private schools in math instruction.* February 25.

U.S. Department of Education, National Center for Educational Statistics. (2001) *Paving the way to Postsecondary education: K-12 programs for underrepresented youth.* NCES 2001–205. Prepared by Patricia Gandura and Deborah Biai for the National Postsecondary Cooperative Access Working Group. Washington, D.C.: 2001.

US Department of Education, May 2007. *Report of the Academic Competitiveness Council.* (www.ed.gov/about/inits/ed/competitiveness/acc-mathscience/report.pdf)

Valadares, J., & Soares, M. (2008). The teaching value of concept maps. In Cañas, A., Reiska, P., Åhlberg, M., & Novak, J.D. (Eds.) (2008). *Proceedings of the Third International Conference on Concept Mapping.* (Vol. 2, pp. 634–642). Tallinn, Estonia & Helsinki, Finland, 2008.

Valerio, A., Leake, D.B., & Cañas, A.J. (2008). Automatic classification of concept maps based on a topological classifications and its application to studying human-built maps. In Cañas, A.J., Reiska, P., Åhlberg, M., & Novak, J.D. (Eds.), Concept Mapping: Connecting Educators, *Proceedings of the Third International Conference on Concept Mapping.* Tallinn, Estonia & Helsinki, Finland, Vol I, pp. 122–129.

Valitutti, G. (2006). ESPLORANDO ... SCOPRIAMO. PowerPoint presentation on studies in Urbino Italy.

Vance, M., & Deacon, D. (1995). *Think out of the box.* Franklin Lakes, NJ: Career Press.

Villarini-Jusino, A.R. (2007). Theories that are needed by educational researchers and practitioners: A Critical Reflection. A contribution to the debate What theories do we need in education? *Culture y Educacion,* 19(3): 249–255.

von Glasersfeld, E. (1984). An introduction to radical constructivism. In Watzlanick, P. (Ed.), *The Invented Reality* (pp. 17–40). New York: Norton.

Von Krogh, G., Ichijo, G., & Nonaka, I. (2000). *Enabling knowledge creation.* New York: Oxford University Press.

Vygotsky, L. S. (1962). *Thought and language.* Cambridge, MA: MIT Press (edited and translated by Eugenia Hanfmann and Gertrude Vakar).

Vygotsky, L.S. (1986). *Thought and language.* (Translation & editing by A. Kozulin). Cambridge, MA: The MIT Press.

Wainer, H. (1993). Does spending money on education help? *Educational Researcher,* 22(9): 22–24.

Waitley, D. (1995). *Empires of the mind: Lessons to lead and succeed in a knowledge-based world.* New York, NY: William Morrow and Co., Inc.

Walker, J.M.T., & King, P.H. (2003). Concept mapping as a form of student assessment in the domain of bioengineering. *Journal of Engineering Education,* 19(2): 167–179 (April).

Waterman, R.H. (1995). *What America does right.* New York Penguin, Plume.

Welch, J., with Welch, S. (2005). *Winning.* New York: HarperCollins.

White, J.B., & Suris, O. (1993). New pony: How "Skunk Works" kept Mustang alive: On a tight budget. *Wall Street Journal,* pp. A1, A12 (Sept. 21).

Whorf, B.L. (1956). *Language, Thought and Reality. Selected Writings of Benjamin Lee Whorf* (edited and with an introduction by J.B. Carroll). Cambridge, MA: The MIT Press.

Wiggins, G. (1989). Teaching to the authentic test. *Educational Leadership*, 49(7): 45 (April).

Wiggins, G., & McTighe, J. (2008). Put understanding first. *Educational Leadership*, 65(8): 36–41.

Wilshire, B. (1990). *The moral collapse of the university professionalism, purity, and alienation.* Albany: State University of New York Press.

Wilson, K.G., & Davis, B. (1994). *Redesigning education.* New York: Henry Holt & Co.

Wilson, M.L., & Peterson, P.L. (2006). *Theories of learning and teaching: What do they mean?* Atlanta, GA: NEA Professional Library.

Wittrock, M.C. (1974). Learning as a generative process. *Educational Psychologist*, 11: 87–95.

Wood, D., Bruner, J.S., & Ross, G. (1976). The role of tutoring in problem solving. *Journal of Psychology and Psychiatry.* 17.

Woodruff, R.B., & Gardial, S.F. (1996). *Know your customer: New approaches to understanding customer value and satisfaction.* Cambridge, MA: Blackwell.

Yumino, K. (1994). Personal communication.

Zahkaria, F. (2009). *The post American world.* New York: Norton (paperback).

Zaltman, G., & Higie, R.A. (1993). *Seeing the voice of the customer: The Zaltman Metaphore Elicitation Technique.* Cambridge, MA: Marketing Science Institute, Report No. 93–114.

Zehr, M.A. (2009). Supplementary reading programs found ineffective. *Education Week*, May 5: http://www.edweek.org/login.html?source=http://www.edweek.org/ew/articles/2009/05/05/31reading.h28.html&destination=http://www.edweek.org/ew/articles/2009/05/05/31reading.h28.html&levelId=2100

Zheng, A.Y., Lawhorn, J.K., Lumley, T. & Freeman, S. (2008). Application of Bloom's Taxonomy debunks the "MCAT" myth. *Science*, 319: 414–415 (January 25).

Ziliak, S.T., & McClosky, D.N. (2008). *The cult of statistical significance.* Ann Arbor: University of Michigan Press.

Name Index

Tsien, J.Z. 25, 27
Tucker, M. 241, 246, 248
Tufte, E.R. 140
Turque, B. 254
Tyler, R. 247

Valadares, J. 176
Valerio, A. 236
Valitutti, G. xiii, 269, 270
Van Helmont, J.B. 98
Vance, M. 121
Villarini-Jusino, A.R. 16
Von Glasersfeld, E. 93, 239
Von Krogh, G. 112–113
Vygotsky, L.S. 43, 44, 52, 53, 80

Wainer, H. 15, 16
Waitley, D. 77, 180
Walker, J.M.T. 231
Wandersee, J.H. 35, 251
Waterman, R.H. 188–189
Watson, J. 211
Weisberg, D.S. 141
Welch, J. 174–175
Welch, S. 174–175
Wells, H.G. 277

West, S.S. 200
Wheeler, C.W. 168
White, R.T. 155
Whorf, B.L. 43
Wiggins, G. 99, 243, 244
Williams, A.D. 2, 20, 180, 181, 261
Williams, W.M. 87
Wilshire, B. 155
Wilson, K. 145
Wilson, M.L. 131
Winters, L. 227
Wittrock, M.C. 54
Wood, D. 80
Woodruff, R.B. 114

Yacci, M. 113
Yumino, K. 257

Zakaria, F. xiv, 4, 257
Zaltman, G. 116, 276
Zambo, R. 138
Zehr, M.A. 8
Zembal, C. 242, 263
Zheng, A.Y. 234
Ziliak, S.T. 21
Zobel, R. xiii, 109, 110

Subject Index